Modern Welfare States

Modern Welfare States

*Scandinavian Politics and Policy
in the Global Age*
Second Edition

ERIC S. EINHORN AND JOHN LOGUE

Westport, Connecticut
London

Library of Congress Cataloging-in-Publication Data

Einhorn, Eric S.
  Modern welfare states : Scandinavian politics and policy in the global age / Eric S.
  Einhorn and John Logue.—2nd ed.
      p.   cm.
  Includes bibliographical references and index.
  ISBN 0–275–95044–1 (alk. paper)—ISBN 0–275–95058–1 (pbk. : alk. paper)
    1. Scandinavia—Politics and government—1945–   2. Scandinavia—Social policy.
  3. Welfare state.   I. Logue, John, 1947–   II. Title.
  JN7042.E45   2003
  361.948—dc21   2002029882

British Library Cataloguing in Publication Data is available.

Library of Congress Catalog Card Number: 2002029882
ISBN: 0–275–95044–1
      0–275–95058–1

First published in 2003

Praeger Publishers, 88 Post Road West, Westport, CT 06881
An imprint of Greenwood Publishing Group, Inc.
www.praeger.com

Printed in the United States of America

The paper used in this book complies with the
Permanent Paper Standard issued by the National
Information Standards Organization (Z39.48–1984).

10 9 8 7 6 5 4 3 2 1

Copyright Acknowledgments

The authors and publisher gratefully acknowledge permission to reprint the following:

Excerpts from "Of Maastricht, Social Democratic Dilemmas, and Linear Cucumbers," John
Logue, *Scandinavian Studies* 64(4):626–40. 1992. Reproduced with permission.

Excerpts from "Restraining the Governors: The Nordic Experience with Limiting the
Strong State," John Logue and Eric S. Einhorn, *Scandinavian Political Studies* 11(1):45–67.
1988. Reproduced with permission.

Excerpts from "The Scandinavian Democratic Model," Eric S. Einhorn and John Logue,
Scandinavian Political Studies 9(3):193–208. 1986. Reproduced with permission.

Contents

Illustrations

FIGURES

TABLES

Preface: Scandinavia in the Era of Globalization

"A week is a long time in politics" is the way British Prime Minister Harold Wilson once put it.

A decade is even longer. Reviewing our earlier edition of *Modern Welfare States*, which appeared in 1989, we were impressed by how much had changed in these few years. The collapse of the Soviet Union and the end of the Cold War fundamentally altered the balance of power in Scandinavia, permitting both Finland and Sweden to join the European Union. Immigration has increasingly turned the once homogeneous Scandinavian states into societies of racial, religious, ethnic, and linguistic diversity—and put the issue of civil rights for immigrants on the political agenda. Privatization has become fashionable, even for some of the Social Democrats who once saw the growth of the public sector as the surrogate for socialism.

The Scandinavian Social Democratic model offered capitalism with a human face: a redistributive welfare state that eliminated poverty and that was based on a privately owned, market economy. Transfer payments and social services raised the living standards of the worst off to near middle-class levels. The tax burden was high, but careful national economic management limited the costs of countercyclical public sector spending. The tools of state power were used to promote political, social, and economic egalitarianism. There were plenty of strains, but those strains were primarily internal to the individual Scandinavian state's system.

This model was premised on the assumption that the nation-state is the proper unit for making economic policy. In the increasingly globalized economy, this simply is no longer true. Every year power seeps from the

Scandinavia capitals of Copenhagen, Helsinki, Reykjavik, Oslo, and Stock-holm to the European Commission in Brussels, to the European Central Bank in Frankfurt, to the international commercial banks in London, New York, and Tokyo, and to multinational corporations in England, France, Germany, Holland, Japan, and the United States. This has profound im-plications for the future development of the Scandinavian Social Demo-cratic model.

Much in Scandinavia and in this book is still the same as it was more than a decade ago. The political history of modern Scandinavia is un-changed, although a bit longer. Political institutions are little changed, although they deal with new policy issues and have an overlay of Euro-pean Union law. Political actors—parties, interest groups—are funda-mentally the same, although they too grapple with new problems. Scandinavian trade unions have actually increased their already strong position, while trade unions elsewhere in the world have lost member-ship. The Social Democrats have been almost as dominant in govern-mental office as they were in their heyday.

Much, however, has changed. Among politicians and voters, a new gen-eration has come of political age, solidifying party fragmentation. The monolithic Social Democratic vote from working-class families has de-clined as the working class has become more affluent and as the wedge issue of immigration has undermined political class cohesion; party mem-bership has plummeted to half or less of what it was a dozen years ago. Women have come of age in politics, providing 40 or more percent of the members of parliament, a prime minister in Norway, a president in Ice-land, both president and prime minister in Finland, and the chair of the Swedish trade union federation.

The first edition of *Modern Welfare States* dealt with two major policy themes. The first was the development of the modern Scandinavian wel-fare state in the period between when Social Democrats took power in the depths of the Great Depression and the oil crisis in 1973–74. The second dealt with the internally generated strains that came to the fore in the 1970s and 1980s. The tax revolt led by Mogens Glistrup in Denmark and Anders Lange in Norway; the pernicious interplay between high marginal tax rates, high interest rates, and the tax deductibility of mortgage interest on the economy; and efforts to reform the tax system to avoid these prob-lems figured heavily. So did rising take-up rates for various welfare state services among the younger generation. Although taxes and welfare pro-gram take-up rates remain issues, tax reforms and welfare adjustments have ameliorated some of the difficulties.

We depicted a Scandinavia substantially ahead of the rest of Europe in terms of its provision of transfer payments and social services to its citi-zens, a region that was more egalitarian than the Continent or England, where democracy was a social and economic concept as well as a political one. Scandinavia remains more egalitarian and democratic, but in many ways the Continent has caught up on social security and services.

We devoted substantial attention to Social Democratic ideology and culture, which, we argued, had shaped Scandinavian politics and policy more than the Social Democrats had done elsewhere in Europe. We also noted their confusion in the face of the combination of welfare state internal strains and the international economic crisis, quoting then Danish Social Democratic parliamentary leader Ritt Bjerregaard's candid 1982 answer to an interviewer (Uhrskov 1982, p. 43) who asked her, "Do the Social Democrats have any idea of how to get Denmark out of the crisis?" "There isn't anybody who has a handle on it," Bjerregaard replied. "There isn't any simple answer that says 'Yes, that's exactly what we should do.' The others don't have the answer and neither do we."

In fact in the late 1980s and 1990s, both the Social Democrats and the parties of the center and center-right have been able to ameliorate the internal strains on the Scandinavian welfare model. Changes at the margins in welfare programs have reduced excessive costs and increased economic and social flexibility without undermining basic security or living standards. Tax reforms have broadened the tax base and reduced marginal rates. The pension system reforms of the 1990s constitute a preemptive strike against the reemergence of internal strains as the postwar baby-boom generation reaches pension age. Welfare state expansion could continue in services for children and for the elderly. Public finances are back in equilibrium.

Today policy issues are significantly different.

More than anything else, this is a product of globalization. The Scandinavian states have long been "porous states in an interdependent world," as we described them in the earlier edition. Today economic globalization has transformed the economic context in which they operate; they are much more dependent economically on what goes on outside their borders. Ownership of some of the crown jewels of Scandinavian manufacturing, including both Volvo's and Saab's automotive operations, has passed into foreign hands, while Scandinavian multinational corporations do more of their production abroad.

The Scandinavian countries are more dependent too on external ideological factors; witness the new emphasis on privatization, deregulation, and the glorification of the market. Every Scandinavian government has experimented with some form of privatization in one or another public-sector agency with some successes and some failures. Swedes, Finns, and Norwegians deregulated the banking sector with disastrous results similar to the American savings and loan crisis in the 1980s. Each nation has swung a bit toward the use of market forces. Yet in the midst of the neoliberal wave, perhaps the greatest market success of a Scandinavian product internationally, after Nokia and Ericsson mobile telephones, has been

Absolut Vodka, the product of AB Sprit, the Swedish state-owned liquor company.

Immigration and growing minority populations—another aspect of globalization—have changed the face of the cities and the language of the streets, as well as raising new issues of ethnic, religious, racial, and linguistic diversity. Immigration has become a divisive issue more than any other, splitting the otherwise cohesive Social Democratic working-class constituency.

Finally, the collapse of the Soviet Union fundamentally changed the Scandinavian world. Economically, it devastated the Finnish economy, producing in the early 1990s the worst economic crisis in that country since the Great Depression. Geopolitically, it permitted Sweden and Finland to join the European Union. Ideologically, it devalued Marxism as a political force. Scandinavian Social Democrats uniformly criticized the Soviet Union, as did many socialists to their left, but their discussions revolved around how to reform and democratize the Soviet system, not how to abolish it. They had long reveled in having the "middle way," as Marquis Childs wrote in the 1930s, between the crisis-prone capitalism of the West and the oppressive Communist regime of the Soviet Union. Now the latter had vanished. After the Soviet collapse, the political center of gravity shifted to the right.

The changing external context has also broadened the geographic scope of this volume. The first edition of *Modern Welfare States* looked only at Denmark, Norway, and Sweden. We saw Finland and Iceland as very different. Although these welfare state laggards had increasingly converged on the three core Scandinavian countries' programmatic standards, their politics remained characterized by Finland's peculiar relationship to the Soviet Union and by the division of the labor movement in both countries between more or less equally strong Communist-led labor alliances and the Social Democrats. Those political differences went by the boards in the 1990s. So although Finland and Iceland have very different political histories from Denmark, Norway, and Sweden, the commonalities have grown while the differences have lessened. Finland in particular has converged on the other Scandinavian countries in terms of Social Democratic dominance of government; 1966 through 2002 saw twenty-five years of Social Democratic prime ministers, exceeding Denmark's nineteen and Norway's twenty and almost matching Sweden's twenty-seven. Thus we have included them in this volume.

None of the Scandinavian countries have illusions of closing their economies or of reversing global economic trends through national measures. But the external strains of global economic competition—of open markets for goods and capital—are real. How do you maintain the attractive features of the Scandinavian welfare state in a global economy? Can you maintain substantially higher levels of social protection and economic justice, as the Scandinavians wish to do, and still be innovative, open, flexible economies? Can you still have government accountable to the electorate? Or is the welfare state fundamentally tied to a national manufacturing economy? In short, if the nation-state is no longer the appropriate unit for economic policy, how do you replace it?

One answer is to look to Brussels. At the time of the first edition of the book, Denmark was the only Scandinavian member of the European Community. Today the "Community" has become the European Union (EU) as it has moved toward a federal state, having broadened the scope of its policy making to include monetary policy and fiscal convergence; Finland and Sweden are also members. Even Norway, which rejected membership for a second time in 1994, and Iceland are closely linked to the EU through the European Economic Area. But joining Europe has been divisive, especially for the Social Democrats whose voters feared downward pressure on wages and benefits; the Scandinavians remain Euro-skeptics, in no small measure because of the EU's so-called democratic deficit, which has given disproportionate influence to bureaucrats and experts.

Another answer is to "act locally," to decentralize, to shape more policies in smaller communities or in functional areas. Some of this decentralization involves the intrusion of the market into the public sector, another cause for Social Democratic concern.

The external strains stemming from global population movements are equally real. Since the collapse of the Soviet Union and of Yugoslavia, Western Europe has become awash in Eastern European economic and political refugees, who have joined the flood of guest workers, asylum-seekers, and others reaching for a better life from North Africa, Turkey and the Middle East, and Southern Asia who were already arriving. Since 1990, immigration has become a major campaign issue, with a significant impact on outcomes of parliamentary elections in Denmark and Norway. Three Norwegian neo-Nazis went on trial for murdering an Afro-Norwegian teenager in suburban Oslo. And two new members of Middle Eastern background took their places in the new Danish parliament. So we must ask: Is the Scandinavian Social Democratic model dependent on religious, ethnic, linguistic, racial, and cultural homogeneity? How do you maintain a sense of national identity sufficient to underpin the welfare state in increasingly immigrant, diverse societies?

In short, the first edition of *Modern Welfare States* dealt with policy issues that were largely internally generated, epitomized by the tax revolt of 1973 in Denmark and Norway. By contrast, this edition deals with increasingly externally generated policy issues, epitomized by the global economic crises in Sweden in 1992, when interest rates spiked at 500 percent; Finland, in which employment collapsed in 1992–94; and in the rising issue of immigration that so colored the Danish and Norwegian elections of the late 1990s and first years of the twenty-first century.

All these changes led us to reconsider the earlier subtitle of *Politics and Policies in Social Democratic Scandinavia.* Can we still call Scandinavia "Social Democratic"? The Social Democrats' governmental dominance has become shaky. The issues that rank high on the political agenda today—immigration, privatization, deregulation, integration in the global economy—are not Social Democratic issues. To be sure, Scandinavia remains social democratic in a less partisan sense: Overarching concepts of social solidarity, of raising the standards of those less well-off in the market, of collective organization, of the welfare state model have become the common framework for all governments, regardless of partisan coloration. Yet the movement, driven significantly by globalization, is toward a diminution of the universal programs, national solidarity, and equality of results—all principles that characterized Scandinavian Social Democracy. The momentum instead is toward more of a social insurance principle in welfare programs and toward more differentiated results. Tomorrow's Scandinavia will be more a social market economy, under growing pressure from economic globalization, with less scope for the national solidarity that characterized Scandinavia yesterday.

Acknowledgments

When a book has been a periodic project for nearly twenty-five years, as this one has, there is a legitimate reason to fear that the list of those whom the authors are indebted will be as long as the volume itself. The roll of those to whom we owe thanks for aid, insight, comments, and hospitality over the period that we did the research that forms the basis for this book is extensive: Per Åhlström, Peter Bogason, Ole Borre, Gerd Callesen, Erik Damgaard, Lena Daun, Søren Dyssegaard, Leslie Eliason, Marna Feldt, Svava Guðjónsdóttir, Don Hancock, Christine Ingebritsen, Bjarne Jensen, Anker Jørgensen, Ulf Lundvik, Anders Mellbourn, Ken Miller, Hans Jørgen Nielsen, Klaus Nielsen, Sten Sparre Nilson, Erling Olsen, Gert Petersen, Niels Helveg Petersen, Martin Peterson, Bob Rinehart, Lonce Sandy-Bailey, Bernt Schiller, Hans Skoie, Sten-Åke Stenberg, Lars Svåsand, Tim Tilton, Anders Uhrskov, Birger Viklund, Steven Wolinetz, the anonymous reviewers for *Scandinavian Political Studies*, the staff of Arbejderbevægelsens Bibliotek og Arkiv (Copenhagen), Local 5 of the Danish Metal Workers Union, the Swedish Metal Workers locals at Götaverken, Saab-Trollhättan, SKF-Gothenburg, Volvo-Olofström and Volvo-Skövde, and the information services of Denmark, Iceland, Norway, and Sweden all deserve our thanks.

The text is the better for comments made by our colleagues on the first edition. Chapters 3, 4, and 10 draw in part on articles that we have previously published in *Scandinavian Political Studies* and *Scandinavian Review;* we appreciate permission to use this material.

Funding for the research involved in this volume was derived from a number of sources. Einhorn wishes to thank the American–Scandinavian

Foundation, the Danish Institute for International Affairs (DUPI), and the National Bank of Denmark. Logue wishes to thank the Fulbright Program, the National Bank of Denmark, the Swedish Bicentennial Fund, and Kent State University's Research Council for their support. We also thank John Grummel for assistance with the tables in this volume.

Our families contributed and tolerated much during the writing and revising of this book, and we gratefully dedicate the book to them.

As much as we would like to share the blame for infelicities of style and for errors of fact, interpretation, and analysis, those are, regrettably, our own.

Abbreviations and Acronyms

AFL-CIO: American Federation of Labor–Congress of Industrial Organizations

AMS—Arbetsmarknadsstyrelsen (S): National Labor Market Authority

ASEA—Allmänna Svenska Elektriska AB (S): Swedish General Electric Co.

ATP—Allmänna Tilläggspension (S): Supplementary pension

CAP (EU): Common Agricultural Policy

Comintern: The Communist International

COPA—Comité des Organisations Professionelles Agricoles (EU): Committee of Professional Agricultural Organizations

DA—Dansk Arbejdsgiverforening (DK): Danish Employers' Association

DsF—De samvirkende Fagforbund (DK): Trade Union Confederation

EC (EU): European Community

EEA (EU): European Economic Area

EMU (EU): Economic and Monetary Union

ERM (EU): Exchange Rate Mechanism

ESC (EU): Economic and Social Committee

ESOP: Employee Stock Ownership Plan

ETUC: European Trade Union Confederation

EU: European Union

GDP: Gross Domestic Product

ICFTU: International Confederation of Free Trade Unions

ILO: International Labor Organization

JK—Justitiekansler (S): Chancellor of Justice

JO—Justitieombudsman (S): Parliamentary Ombudsman

LKAB—Luossavara-Kiirunavaara Aktiebolaget (S): Kiruna Iron Mine Company

LO—Landsorganisationen (DK, N, S): Trade Union Federation

MBL—Medbestämmandelagen (S): Employees Co-determination Law

MNC: Multinational corporation

NAF—Norsk Arbeidsgiverforening (N): Norwegian Employers' Association

NATO: North Atlantic Treaty Organization

OECD: Organization for Economic Co-operation and Development

PR: Proportional Representation

RF—Regeringsformen (S): Instrument of Government

SACO—Sveriges Akademikers Centralorganisation (S): Swedish Confederation of Professional Associations

SAF—Svenska Arbetsgivareföreningen (S): Swedish Employers' Association

SKF—Svenska Kullagerfabrik (S): Swedish Ball Bearing Works

SPP: Socialist People's party

STD: Sexually transmitted diseases

TCO—Tjänstemannens Centralorganisationen (S): Central Organization of Salaried Employees

TFO—Tryckfrihetsförordning (S): Press Freedom Act

UN: United Nations

VAT: Value-added tax

VpK—Vänsterpartiet Kommunisterna: Left party Communists

DK = Denmark, EU = European Union, N = Norway, and S = Sweden.

PART I

Understanding Scandinavian Politics

CHAPTER 1

Still the Social Laboratory?

> The small nations that comprise the Scandinavian area constitute a social laboratory for the Western world.
> —Walter Galenson, *Labor in Norway* (1949)

No author feels obliged to justify writing on Russian, Chinese, British, Japanese, German, or American politics. The politics of major powers is of self-evident interest. The eccentricities of their leaders, peculiarities of their parties, and curiosities of their cultures have proved crucial in the past and are likely to affect our lives in the future.

But why read or write about Scandinavian politics?

Denmark, Finland, Norway, and Sweden are not great military powers, and Iceland is the only NATO member with no army whatsoever. With the defeat of Charles XII and the Swedish army at Poltava by the Russians in 1709, the Scandinavians were finally driven from center stage in European military affairs. The last voluntary military role was that of Sweden in the battle of Leipzig in 1813. Since then the descendants of the Vikings have become more adept at avoiding wars than at waging them. Located on the periphery of Europe with a total population of only 24 million, the Scandinavian nations[1] are more comparable to American states or Canadian provinces in their size than to major European states.

Nor are they key players in the international economic market, although they offer impressive stories of economic success. Within the life span of Finns, Norwegians, and Swedes now living, their countries have been transformed from terribly poor, backward, agricultural economies into advanced industrial societies that offer their citizens among the highest standards of living in the world. The rapidity of that change is truly remarkable. Although Scandinavian firms have become a force on the world market in a variety of areas, the Scandinavian countries lack the economic muscle to set energy prices, determine interest rates, or shape world trade patterns.

One cannot even point to the uniqueness of their political institutions, with the possible exception of the ombudsman, which originated in Sweden and was popularized in the 1950s by the Danes. The central institutions of Scandinavian parliamentary democracy are similar in structure to those elsewhere in Europe. It is just the results that are different.

Those results, how they have been achieved, and what the future holds for them are the subject of this book. Despite being more backward economically at the beginning of the twentieth century than Britain, France, Germany, or the United States, the Scandinavian countries have gone farther in realizing the potential of modern industrial society. They have virtually abolished poverty as a fact of life, achieving a level of broadly shared affluence and freedom from economic insecurity (and, for that matter, from crime) that has made their citizens an object for envy. Much of this has been a product of Social Democratic dominance of their political systems and the policy consequences that have flowed from it. By the 1970s Scandinavian Social Democratic governments had created the world's most successful and most expensive welfare states, with an elaborate structure of economic and labor market policies to underpin them. But in the last quarter of the twentieth century, this success showed internal strains, particularly around paying the increasing costs of the welfare state in a slow-growth environment. Today, external strains from economic and social globalization have been added.

WHAT IS SCANDINAVIA?

There are at least four dimensions to modern Scandinavia: the geographical, historical, political, and cultural. In this study we focus mainly on the historical and political, but the other aspects inevitably crop up.

Geographically, Scandinavia encompasses three constitutional monarchies (Denmark, Norway, and Sweden) and two republics (Iceland and Finland). Their vital statistics are summarized in Table 1.1. They all share a common historical heritage, as do Denmark's two self-governing North Atlantic territories of the Faeroe Islands and, to a lesser extent, Greenland. All were united under the Danish crown in the Union of Kalmar between 1397 and the Swedish revolt in 1521. Subsequently, the region was divided between Denmark-Norway and Sweden-Finland. The former was governed from Copenhagen and included Iceland; the latter, from Stockholm. These two states were regularly at war in the sixteenth and seventeenth centuries as Sweden rose to be a major European power and the dominant power in the Baltic, in part at Denmark's expense. After the battle of Pol-

Table 1.1
Scandinavia's Geography, Demography, and Economy

	Area km²	Population (2002 est.)	Population density (/km2)	Gross Domestic Product per capita (PPP)
Denmark	43,094	5,368,854	124.6	29,000
Finland	337,030	5,183,545	15.4	26,200
Iceland	103,000	279,384	2.7	27,100
Norway	324,220	4,525,116	14.1	31,800
Sweden	449,964	8,876,744	19.7	25,400

Note: GDP per capita in Purchasing Power Parities (PPP) are 2002 estimates converted from national currencies to U.S. dollars and adjusted for different purchasing power. U.S. GDP per capita was $36,300 in 2001.
Source: U.S. Central Intelligence Agency, *Factbook 2002.*

tava in 1709, the Swedish Empire contracted as Russia expanded west and Prussia consolidated its dominance in northern Germany. The final act in the Danish-Swedish rivalry was played out during the Napoleonic Wars. Sweden lost Finland to Russia in 1809; Finland continued to be governed as a grand duchy by a Russian governor-general under the joint Swedish-Finnish constitution of 1772 and 1789. Joining the allies in a timely fashion, however, the new Swedish crown prince (and former French marshal) Jean Bernadotte commanded one of the allied armies at the battle of Leipzig and in the postwar settlement acquired Norway from Denmark, which had remained inopportunely allied with France. Norway won independence from Sweden in 1905; Finland, from Russia in 1917; and Iceland, from Denmark in 1944.

In linguistic, cultural, and ethnic terms, Iceland shares common roots with Denmark, Norway, and Sweden. Finland, on the other hand, is totally distinct linguistically and ethnically despite the centuries of Swedish rule that left it almost as homogeneously Lutheran as the other four. But Finland and Iceland are set apart from the other three by modern historical developments—including the Finnish Civil War and Finland's special relationship with the Soviet Union between 1944 and 1989—that have created different party structures, governmental patterns, and policy choices. Although Finland and Iceland once deviated sharply from the core Scandinavian states, since the 1980s they have converged increasingly with Denmark, Norway, and Sweden. They, too, have become modern welfare states.

During much of the last millennium of European history, Scandinavia has been off the beaten path, although this has been less true in the last century, because the tides of World War II washed across Scandinavia as well. Norway and Sweden share a common peninsula, and Sweden faces Finland across the Gulf of Bothnia. Iceland is a stepping-stone in the North

Atlantic between Europe and America. By contrast, Denmark's Jutland peninsula and islands are anchored to the European mainland. The Baltic and North seas, as well as the North Atlantic, have long added a maritime dimension to their common history (see Figure 1.1).

The sea has always been a dominant factor in Scandinavian history. Although North Americans and the British think of the sea as isolating and protecting their countries from undesirable foreign forces, more often the sea has connected peoples and countries. A thousand years ago, Scandinavian Vikings traveled from central Russia to the fringes of North America via the sea and other waterways. To Scandinavians, the sea has meant freedom to trade, to travel, and to borrow ideas and methods invented elsewhere. Across those distances such ideas as democracy, advanced technology, and even the welfare state have traveled along with more mundane cargoes.

WHY STUDY SCANDINAVIAN POLITICS?

Two interrelated characteristics set Scandinavian politics apart and make it of interest to outsiders: (1) the political success of the Social Dem-

Figure 1.1
Map of Scandinavia

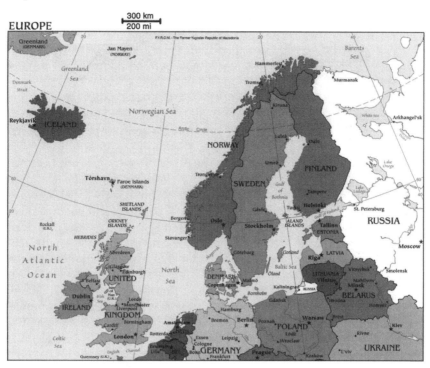

ocrats and (2) the policies pursued by Social Democratic governments since the Great Depression. In the 1930s as democracies elsewhere foundered economically or sank in the rising tide of fascism, the Danish, the Swedish, and finally the Norwegian Social Democratic parties took and consolidated power. They have held on to power through most of the succeeding decades, using it to develop what Marquis Childs, in 1936 in his classic volume on Sweden, called "the middle way"—a course between the unbridled excesses of capitalism in the United States and those of communism as it was then taking form in the Soviet Union. The Scandinavian countries became, as Walter Galenson put it in 1949 (p. 1), "a social laboratory for the Western world," a proving ground for policies only debated elsewhere.

Denmark, Norway, and Sweden have been in the forefront of developing the programs characteristic of the modern welfare state. In general, those policies have been of three sorts: (1) the provision of social services and transfer payments that make up the welfare state proper; (2) the management of capitalistic market economies to minimize unemployment and maintain optimal economic growth vital to finance welfare measures; and (3) the regulation of behavior by individuals, groups, and corporations to restrict the need for welfare and the costs of welfare programs. The aim was to guarantee a decent standard of living for those worst off in the society and to increase the degree of equality among socioeconomic groups without undercutting the dynamism of the market economy. In the process, the Scandinavian countries have developed a security net of transfer payments (unemployment, disability, and sickness insurance; old-age pensions; family allowances; rent subsidies; and special payments to those temporarily in need) and social services (medical and dental care; home assistance for the sick, disabled, and elderly; and child and after-school care) that provides a comfortable, solid floor to support the living standard of anyone forced out of the labor market. In other words, if you have to be sick, disabled, unemployed, elderly, or a single mother in an unskilled job, the place to be is Scandinavia.

These policies are hardly uncontroversial. Some foreign observers praise them for their humaneness; they are judged the noblest experiments of the twentieth century. Others remain skeptical of "creeping socialism" in its seductive Scandinavian form. Conservative periodicals focus on such social problems as suicide, alcoholism, and promiscuous sex as if their relationship to social security programs were obvious and their incidence particularly Scandinavian. Some see Scandinavian egalitarianism, with its emphasis on equality of results, as highly desirable; others see it as enforcing a deadening conformity. For Anglo-American social scientists and journalists of both left- and right-wing persuasions, Scandinavia has been a mirror for viewing what they hope or fear will be the future of their own societies.

Although the Social Democrats took most of the initiatives that built the welfare state, they had much support from other parties. This was possible primarily because the degree of ethnic, linguistic, and religious homogeneity inside the individual Scandinavian countries far exceeds that found elsewhere in Europe. Each nation's population shares a common language, a common ethnic background (although the immigration of the last few decades is eroding this), and is more than 90 percent nominally Lutheran. (Finland is something of an exception, having a significant Swedish-speaking minority and using Swedish as a second official language.) This commonality, more so than could citizenship papers, defines what it is to be a Dane, Icelander, Norwegian, or Swede. The sense of community inside each country is greater than Americans would expect. Modern media have tied the people closer together through national TV coverage. A plant closing in West Jutland makes the evening news all over Denmark, and the loss of a fishing boat in northern Norway is a national tragedy. These factors have helped to limit the focus of politics to socioeconomic issues that are susceptible to compromise. On compromise, consensus can be built.

Laboratory conditions cannot be approximated in politics, not even in Scandinavia. Still, Galenson's metaphor is well taken: The policies implemented by the Social Democrats in Scandinavia have had a greater degree of clarity, coherence, and consistency than those we are used to elsewhere, and it is easier to estimate their practical impact because Scandinavian populations are small, extraordinarily homogeneous, and the subject of excellent statistics.

The relative success Scandinavians have enjoyed in dealing with economic and redistributive issues was not foreordained. Although Denmark, where industrialization had begun in the 1850s, was reasonably prosperous by the end of the nineteenth century, the other Scandinavian countries were terribly poor. Only the safety valve of mass emigration to America prevented famine and rebellion in Norway and Sweden. At the peak of emigration in the 1880s, more than 1 percent of the total population of both countries emigrated annually. Only Ireland saw a higher proportion of its population leave for the promised land. It was particularly young adults who fled. Had they been born in Denmark, England, France, Belgium, or Germany, they would have moved to the cities of their own countries; born in Norway or Sweden, they had to move abroad. The industrial jobs simply were not there. Industrialization finally began about 1890 in Sweden and 1905 in Norway, but as late as 1930 a larger proportion of the Swedish population earned its livelihood from agriculture and forestry than from industry, mining, and construction. The degree of economic backwardness that prevailed in Norway and Sweden in the nineteenth century—and in Iceland and Finland in the first decades of the twentieth century—was comparable to that of many Third World countries today.

Political democracy is a more recent phenomenon in Scandinavia than most people realize. Norway was the first to attain parliamentary government, but that was not until 1884. Denmark followed in 1901, and Swedish conservatives did not surrender to the popular demand until after revolutions in Russia, Germany, and Austro-Hungary made the writing on the wall clear even to the most autocratically inclined. On the eve of World War I, Sweden could still be characterized as "the fortified poorhouse,"[2] in which military preparations seemed directed as much against the enemy within—the working class—as against foreign foes. Although Finland elected its first parliament in the aftermath of the Russian Revolution of 1905, it did not acquire national independence until the Bolshevik Revolution of 1917 and then fought a bitter civil war between the socialist government and the so-called White Guard. The Whites, who offered the crown of Finland to the Kaiser's brother-in-law, won with the support of a German division and threw their Red opponents and their families into concentration camps, where more died than during the civil war. Icelanders received home rule with an elected parliament in 1918.

That has changed radically. Today the Scandinavian countries epitomize the modern welfare state, but not as a result of revolution. Instead, the impressive edifice that they have constructed is a product of piecemeal reforms that shared a common direction and a constant aim.

Although the Scandinavian social laboratory has been the setting for policy experiments spanning the spectrum from alcohol to zoning, our focus in this book is on those central issues at the heart of political conflict in the development of welfare states—issues of economic distribution, redistribution, and growth. Part I discusses those questions, the degree of Scandinavian success in dealing with them, and the problems that have resulted, including the transformation of the issues of economic quantity into what we have, for want of a better generic label, termed *qualitative politics*. These latter political issues have, we argue, emerged because of the Scandinavians' success in dealing with the former group. We sketch some aspects of this argument in the next chapter.

The political context for that transformation and the major actors shaping public policy today are examined in Part II. Chapter 3 discusses the general Scandinavian democratic model; Chapter 4, political institutions; and Chapter 5, parties and interest groups. Our intent is not only to describe Scandinavian political institutions and actors but also to provide a sense of the dominant norms, values, and goals that have shaped Scandinavian policy responses to the problems of industrial society. We are persuaded that the key to understanding Scandinavian policy development is the dominant position enjoyed by the Social Democratic labor movement, but that dominance has become increasingly shaky since 1970.

However, the long-term trend since World War II of increased involvement of economic interest groups in making and implementing governmental decisions has given Scandinavian politics a corporatist character and created an alternative channel for political representation. As they have expanded their membership to encompass most citizens, economic interest groups have come to offer a functional structure of representation of growing practical importance.

The central policy areas of the Scandinavian model are the subject of Part III. To speak of a single model is to ignore clear differences between Danish, Norwegian, and Swedish policies, not to mention Iceland and Finland, where welfare state programs developed later. One could make a strong case that there is not one Scandinavian model, but five. Yet what they have in common is substantial. Regional, cultural, and historical commonalities all exist. However, they have been dwarfed since the 1950s in the core Scandinavian states of Denmark, Norway, and Sweden by the degree of commonality in policy and politics. Since 1970, Finland and Iceland have converged on that common model. We point out many differences, in part because examining the differences in policy outcomes in otherwise similar political systems provides a means for analyzing the differential impact of policies. But we do not want to lose sight of the common characteristics that make generalizations about the Scandinavian countries meaningful. Those common characteristics and the policy-making process are the subjects of Chapter 6.

Scandinavian policies and politics do not exist in a vacuum. Although geographic isolation on the periphery of Europe largely protected the Scandinavian countries for centuries against the tides of war and revolution that afflicted the rest of Europe, in the postwar period they have been integrated into the global political economy. Their economies have been internationalized, and they have struggled in foreign military, political, and economic affairs to find a balance between self-determination and internationalism. Economic globalization raises questions for some about the viability of the Scandinavian model; for others, the issue is how to adapt that model. The transnational dimension that affects domestic policy in these small, porous political systems is explored in Chapter 7.

The key to the Scandinavian model has been the radical expansion of the public sector through the creation of the highly developed system of transfer payments and social services described in Chapter 8. This system, which rests on a strong sense of social solidarity possible perhaps only in small communities, has made the abject poverty that is still found in the United States and in many other Western industrial nations a thing of the past in Scandinavia. There is evidence, however, that this sense of solidarity is being undermined by a generational change in attitudes and by the challenges of a multicultural society. We explore this theme in Chapter 11.

Perhaps the most widespread misconception about the Scandinavian countries is that they are socialistic. In fact, a smaller proportion of industry in Sweden belongs to the state than in France, in Great Britain prior to Mrs. Thatcher's privatization program, or in Italy. (The state sector is much smaller in Denmark and somewhat larger in Norway than the Western European norm.) Moreover, there has been less tampering with market mechanisms in Scandinavia than is common elsewhere. Scandinavian governments do not set minimum wages by legislation, for instance, as is done in the United States, and there is a general acceptance of a low-tariff, high-foreign-trade environment. Scandinavian welfare states are based on capitalistic market economies. We look at the problems of economic planning and policy that this entails in Chapter 9. Can these economic underpinnings of the Scandinavian welfare state be sustained in a global economy?

Chapter 10 is devoted to the labor market, where the size, strength, and centralization of unions and employers' organizations combined with the exigencies of governmental economic planning have transformed traditional patterns of industrial relations. We examine the interlock between public policy and collective bargaining; the long-term strain that that imposes; the drive for increased participation in decisions made on the shop floor, or industrial democracy; and the move to broaden the ownership of industry through collective employee funds, a move toward economic democracy. We will again examine the degree to which the Scandinavian model in this field fits into economic globalization.

It has become fashionable since 1975 to speak in funereal tones of the "crisis of the welfare state" that seems to portend its imminent demise. The term *crisis* is an exaggeration, we think. There is no question that the Scandinavian model came under strain from the economic problems that began with the oil price increases in 1973–74, but stress has never been absent, and the model has never been static. The Scandinavian welfare states proved at least as resilient to the hard times of the 1970s as less-developed welfare states elsewhere. But they have not been unaffected by external and internal strains, not least those of economic globalization in the post–Cold War world, and their future development is the subject of Part IV.

The Scandinavian model does face a variety of stresses today. In the past, consensus about the ends dampened conflict about the means. Today, in part because the ends have largely been realized, the means have become subjects of controversy, especially because the lower growth of the last quarter of the twentieth century cut sharply into the growth dividend available for distribution through the public sector. In the last thirty years, critics of the welfare state have emerged not only on the right and left but also in the center of the political spectrum. We examine their arguments in Chapter 11, as well as developing our own critique that accepts the welfare state's basic success but questions its limits and future.

Prophecy is a dangerous but irresistible temptation. In the final chapter we attempt to chart some lines of future development of Scandinavian politics and policy. First comes what we call qualitative politics, a renewed citizen concern with ideological and value-oriented issues in administrative and distributional politics. Now that basic material needs have been met, there is a return to those classical topics of political debate: democracy as a form of government designed to limit extreme forms of conflict versus democracy as citizen education; the efficiency of centralization versus the freedom of choice of decentralization; and the value of material goods versus the value of community.

Second, perhaps we are witnessing an equally basic shift in party politics and ideology. The Social Democrats have accomplished the basic mission of building the welfare state that motivated them for more than a half century. They now face the problem the Liberals did after they had won the fight in the first quarter of the twentieth century for parliamentary democracy: What do you do for an encore?

Third, the Scandinavians face a genuinely new geopolitical and geoeconomic situation. The end of the Cold War and the collapse of the Soviet Union freed Finland (as well as Austria) from treaty-imposed neutrality that kept them out of the European Union. Finland's new geopolitical freedom of maneuver in turn freed Sweden of its self-imposed constraints that had helped to guarantee Finland against Soviet demands. With Finnish and Swedish European Union membership, the separate Nordic alternative of the Cold War era is no more. Scandinavia is very much a part of Europe, whether within the European Union (Denmark, Finland, and Sweden) or outside (Iceland and Norway). And all are small states in an increasingly global economy.

To speak of a Scandinavian social laboratory is to suggest that the experiments conducted have implications beyond the laboratory walls. Since Marquis Childs (1936), that has been the ultimate justification for studying Scandinavian politics. None but the naive would argue that Scandinavian forms would thrive if transplanted elsewhere; they are too much shaped by local conditions. But the general pattern of development in industrial democracies has been foreshadowed time and time again by developments in Scandinavia. While the rest of us have struggled with separatist movements, colonial wars, and religious, ethnic, linguistic, and racial strife, Scandinavian politics has focused on the central issues of advanced industrial society: economic growth, security, and redistribution. Because they have moved to the forefront in dealing with many of the problems common to industrial democracies, there is much that is relevant to be learned from the Scandinavians' experience, both from their successes and from their failures.

That will be as true tomorrow, as they adapt to the global economy, as it was in the more insular world of yesterday.

NOTES

1. We use the term *Scandinavia* to refer to all the Nordic countries: Denmark, Finland, Iceland, Norway, and Sweden. Linguists will correctly quibble about the inclusion of Finland as Scandinavian, because Finnish belongs to an entirely different language family (with Estonian and Hungarian) than the others do; Danish, Icelandic, Norwegian, and Swedish share common roots in Old Norse. However, geographically, historically, and politically *Scandinavia* is the more commonly used term in English than *Norden,* which is the official usage encompassing Finland in what we are calling the Scandinavian countries.

2. The phrase is taken from the title of Höglund, Sköld, and Ström, *Det befästa fattighuset* (1913). For good English surveys of Scandinavian history, see Derry (1979) and Nordstrom (2000); for recent English histories of Denmark, see Jones (1986); of Finland, see Singleton (1998) and Jussila, Hentilä, and Nevakavi (1999); of Iceland, see Karlsson (2000); of Norway, see Derry (1973); and of Sweden, see Koblik (1975) and Scott (1977).

CHAPTER 2

The Perils of Success

The worker has no earth to sow and harvest, nor tree for shade. . . .
He has no cabin in which he can find comfort and security. And, if by
chance, he finds himself with a bit of land and shelter, it is seldom his,
but instead his employer's or a bank's, rendering him dependent and
insecure, vulnerable to conflicts with capital and to unemployment
when it comes.

> —Zeth Höglund, Hannes Sköld, and Fredrik Ström,
> *Det befästa fattighuset* [The fortified poorhouse] (1913)

In these times of affluence and social security, it is difficult to understand
how thin the boundary between a decent life and absolute deprivation
used to be for most people. For the unskilled worker in agriculture and
industry, the margin between having food on the table and shoes on the
kids or being put out on the street with the family's few possessions was
rarely more than a couple of weeks' wages. Sickness, injury, and layoffs
all meant disaster. Few farm families were more than a long illness or a
failed harvest away from the economic precipice. The skilled worker was
a bit better off, with higher wages when he worked and a cushion from
his trade-union benefit society and from possessions that could be pawned
when he did not. But the shadow of the workhouse, the poor farm, or
whatever the local equivalent was called, hung over them all.

The central issue in domestic politics in Western democracies in the
twentieth century was the effort to ameliorate this insecurity. The mechanisms have been many: pensions, unemployment and disability compensation, and sick pay to maintain income in the face of loss of gainful
employment; countercyclical measures to curtail unemployment; selective

labor-market policies to increase employment; distribution of some social services—most notably medical care—on the basis of need instead of ability to pay; subsidies to hold down the cost of necessities; legislation to set minimum wages and regulate hours and working conditions; child allowances to raise the incomes of families with children; housing and heating subsidies to those with low incomes; and a host of other specific programs to raise the incomes or lower the living costs of those worst off in the society. The absence in Scandinavia of the racial, religious, and ethnic conflicts that plague other industrial democracies has permitted Scandinavian politics to focus to a unique degree on those issues of economic growth, distribution, and redistribution that are at the heart of the welfare state. The consequence has been a radical growth of the state's domestic sphere of activity from the traditional role of night watchman, arbiter, and provider of roads and limited education to encompass a host of new tasks to ensure the economic security and well-being of its citizens.

The success of the state was once defined in terms of wars won, territory annexed, and colonies acquired. Today, the success of the state is better defined in terms of the economic well-being of the weakest members of society.

The combination in Scandinavia of economic expansion with an interventionist state committed to use the public sector to reduce economic inequality has, since World War II, abolished the kind of abject poverty that continues to characterize life for significant minorities in other advanced industrial democracies, including Great Britain and the United States. Although the Scandinavian countries fall short of the social paradise imagined by their less-realistic admirers, they have come closer than other nations to realizing those egalitarian aspirations that have characterized Western society since the French Revolution. They are today decent societies in the sense that the prosperity and happiness of the materially and psychologically well off are not purchased at the price of the misery of others.

Since the 1970s, Icelandic and Finnish politics and policies increasingly resembled those of Denmark, Norway, and Sweden. Previously their historical and geopolitical situations had been significantly different. Both had significant Communist parties that contested the labor movement with the Social Democrats. As a consequence, neither had the latitude for corporatist policies that the core Scandinavian states had. After the armistice of 1944 with the Soviet Union that took Finland out of her wartime alliance with Germany, some aspects of Finnish politics were shaped by proximity to her Soviet neighbor until its collapse in 1991. Icelandic party politics and governmental policy has been shaped to a considerable degree by parties based on the personality of leaders overlaid on historical cleavages between those advocating independence and those advocating union with Denmark prior to 1944.

Consequently this chapter will focus primarily on Denmark, Norway, and Sweden.

ORIGINS OF THE WELFARE STATE

The origins of the modern welfare state in Denmark, Norway, and Sweden, as elsewhere, lie in the political struggles of the late nineteenth century occasioned by industrialization and the rise of the labor movement. It was not coincidence that German Chancellor Otto von Bismarck inaugurated the world's first general pension, health, and disability insurance systems at the same time as he banned the German Social Democratic party in the 1880s. Nor is it an accident that the Scandinavian countries have both the strongest labor movements and the best-developed welfare states in the West. The success of the labor movement—and the fear of its success—and the development of the welfare state have been intimately related.

We do not have to delve far into the past even in ultramodern Stockholm to understand why the creation of the welfare state was the focus of labor's political activity. Take housing conditions as an example. On the eve of World War I, almost half the rental apartments in Stockholm consisted of one room plus, in two out of three cases, a kitchen. That one room served as bedroom for parents and babies, playroom for children, workroom for the home seamstresses who were the backbone of the garment industry, and Sunday dining room for families that generally numbered six and occasionally ten or more. The benches on either side of the kitchen table provided sleeping space for older children, one at each end of each bench when they were small, and the benches could be broadened with apple crates as they grew. Poorer families rented out their kitchen benches as sleeping space for day laborers. Primitive toilets were located downstairs in the courtyard; there were no bathing facilities other than public bathhouses. These were not the slums of Calcutta or Rio, but average working-class housing in Stockholm. The picture was similar in the working-class districts of Helsinki, Gothenburg, Copenhagen, and Oslo.

The social transformation that began in Scandinavia under the aegis of the Social Democratic governments that took power at the end of the 1920s and in the early 1930s (1929 in Denmark, 1932 in Sweden, and 1935 in Norway) presaged a more general development toward the welfare state elsewhere in the West in the postwar period. Social Democratic dominance in Scandinavia in the 1930s was less a product of the overwhelming strength of the Social Democrats (the first Social Democratic parliamentary majority did not occur until 1940 in Sweden) than of the weakness and division of their opposition. The Communists never posed a lasting threat to Social Democratic hegemony in the labor movement—in Finland and Iceland, where they did, the divisions in the labor movement pre-

vented Social Democratic dominance—and the nonsocialist parties' disagreements among themselves often exceeded their disagreement with the
Social Democrats. In the 1930s, Danish, Swedish, and Norwegian Social
Democratic government allied with the Liberal and, at crucial junctures,
Agrarian parties laid the foundations for the welfare societies of the postwar era. In the process, they accumulated the political assets that would
keep them in power for most of the next half century.

World War II reforged political attitudes; wartime sacrifice demanded
a better future. By its end a consensus had developed on both sides of the
Atlantic that society had to guarantee minimum living standards and employment opportunities not only to minimize individual hardship but also
to protect society itself from political extremism like that of the interwar
period. Those aims were solemnized as wartime goals of the allies. It is
symbolic that the Beveridge Report (1942), the blueprint for the construction of the welfare state in postwar Britain, was presented to Parliament
only a few days after the victory at El Alamein and as the Red Army's
pincers closed at Stalingrad—the turning point in World War II. In the
postwar period, most Western nations have pursued a dual strategy of
seeking economic growth through policies often loosely termed *Keynesian
economics* and of pursuing a more equitable distribution of goods and
services through public sector provision of transfer payments and social
services.

In Scandinavia, the war and the occupation of Denmark and Norway
created a new sense of national community that superseded the lines of
class division. Finnish workers also rallied to the national colors in the
Winter War with the Soviet Union (1939–40) and the Continuation War
(1941–44). Iceland accepted the benign status of "occupied neutral" by
Britain and, after July 1941, by the United States. Sweden maintained its
neutrality often precariously under a national coalition which united all
parties. After the war, the Social Democrats resumed their role as a permanent fixture of government. Alone or in coalition, the Social Democrats
governed Norway until 1965, Denmark until 1968 (with the exception of
two intervals of nonsocialist government in 1945–47 and 1950–53), and
Sweden until 1976. They used governmental power to create a network
of social services and income-security measures admired far beyond the
region's borders.

Finland and Iceland lagged behind their Scandinavian brethren. Social
Democratic dominance came later in Finland in the 1960s, and the party
divisions formed during Iceland's push for independence continue to
shape that country's party system today. However, by the 1980s, policy
convergence between the three core Scandinavian countries and two peripheral ones had become clear. The collapse of the Soviet Union, the end
of Finland's special relationship with the Soviet Union, and the reemergence of independent Baltic states as a buffer between Russia and Scan-

dinavia at the beginning of the 1990s marked the end of an era. The five Scandinavian countries are more alike today than at any other point since the Napoleonic Wars.

Until the early 1970s, the Scandinavian democracies seemed to have found a way to combine a healthy mixture of growth and welfare. Their economies expanded regularly for nearly a quarter century without obsessive pursuit of spectacular growth, although Iceland's economy followed the ebb and flow of its fisheries and Finland was significantly dependent on trade with the East. Social services and income transfer programs were developed with broad domestic political support from the parties of the center—liberals and agrarians—as well as the left. Labor unions, working simultaneously with Social Democratic governments and across the bargaining table with employers, increased their influence, promoted their members' interests, and avoided significant confrontation. The conjunction of interests between Social Democratic governments in Denmark, Norway, and Sweden and the well-organized, Social Democratic–led trade unions encouraged the gradual development of a system of consultation between government and interest groups on making economic policy, and of cooperation afterward in implementing it. This system of consultation and cooperation was subsequently extended to other policy areas. If the price of influence was the loss of interest-group autonomy, the advantage of coordination was that policy involved greater consensus and hence was more likely to be carried out without obstruction. In all three core Scandinavian countries this system of organized interest representation and policy implementation developed alongside the traditional parliamentary channels. Avoidance of sharp political conflict, the pursuit of consensus, and a pragmatism that set social peace above commitment to ideology all became hallmarks of the Scandinavian political scene. By the end of the 1950s, a basic yet comprehensive welfare state had been accepted even by the conservatives in Scandinavia.

Across the rest of the political spectrum in the 1950s and 1960s there was a remarkable degree of consensus on the development of the welfare state. Such things are relative, of course. There were always some critics on the extreme left and right flanks of national politics. Scandinavians were impressed by the degree of disagreement. But by international standards, the area of disagreement was very small. If Swedish intellectual Herbert Tingsten perhaps exaggerated the "end of ideology" in his pathbreaking 1955 essay,[1] he can be forgiven.

This book explores the policies and the limits of the Scandinavian version of the democratic welfare state. It is about the Scandinavian model of democracy, including political institutions, parties, and policy. But it is also a book about the achievements and limitations of a particular kind of solidaristic welfare state and of Social Democratic parties. In Scandinavia more than elsewhere in Europe, the Social Democrats have had the opportunity to restructure society after some version of their own vision. It is a distorted reflection of their vision, surely, but it has been distorted by the desire to avoid the consequences of extreme political conflict and by the desire to achieve, by compromise with the center and right, a consensus for policies that would be impermanent if enacted by narrow parliamentary majorities.

For the better part of the twentieth century, the achievement of economic security for the worst off in society was the central political issue in Scandinavia. More than any other, it was that vision that powered the Social Democrats in creating the welfare state. The construction of the basic structures of the welfare state was completed in the early 1970s, some forty years after the Social Democrats began the edifice, incorporating some foundation stones put into place by liberal governments just after the turn of the century; the average medieval cathedral took a century longer. The ornamentation is not finished today, but the grandeur and simplicity of the vision that inspired the architects is fading while the cost of maintenance and repairs rises.

Let us put the argument succinctly: The welfare state has fallen victim to its own success. In the last three decades, the political scene has been transformed. The old political patterns have been fragmented with the rise of new, qualitative demands, new lines of division around immigration, and increasing external pressure from economic globalization.

BEYOND QUANTITATIVE POLITICS: POLITICAL FRAGMENTATION

Since the 1970s, the Scandinavian political scene has become chaotic, at least by the previous placid standards of the region in the postwar period. The constant challenge of forging coherent government in a multiparty parliamentary environment was exacerbated when both Danish and Norwegian party systems fragmented in 1973 (as the number of parties in parliament increased from five to ten in Denmark and five to eight in Norway) and destroyed the existing and manageable five-party parliamentary constellation. In Norway and Denmark, Social Democrats in 1973 experienced their lowest level of support since 1930 and 1906, respectively. In 1976, the Swedish Social Democrats were ousted from office after forty-four years in power while support for the party fell to its lowest level since 1932. Along with party fragmentation and the declining electoral support for the Social Democrats came governmental instability: weak minority governments, shifting parliamentary alliances, and frequent governmental crises. It was the end of an era.

Although Sweden avoided party fragmentation in the 1970s, its party system fragmented at the end of the 1980s and early 1990s, as Christian Democrats, Environmentalists, and the rightist New Democrats all won seats in parliament. Across the region, Social Democrats saw their support fall, although they still remained the natural party of government. Only in Finland where the welfare state was still under construction did the Social Democrats strengthen their hold on government. Since 1966, Social Democrats have held the Finnish prime ministership for twenty-five years, and they have occupied the presidency since 1982.

What has happened to Social Democratic Scandinavia? There is no simple answer to that question. One can find a common denominator for the answers, perhaps, in terms of a fragmentation of politics. Fragmentation of the party system is clear in the rise of new parties and fission of old ones. Less obvious but equally important is the fragmentation of the political agenda: The once clear focus on economic growth, distribution, and redistribution has been fractured by the appearance of new issues—moral, cultural, and environmental—that cut across the old economic dimension. Beneath this surface fragmentation is an explosive growth in voter volatility, a rising willingness to change parties among young and old alike that reflected growing alienation from so-called normal politics. Effective government continues, but the extraordinary stability that characterized Scandinavian politics and policy in the postwar period is gone. In its place one senses uncertainty, if not malaise, and a lack of clarity and purpose. With the completion of the basic structures of the welfare state, the means used to achieve welfare goals—the high taxes, centralization and bureaucratization of administration, and corporatist tendencies—have become increasingly suspect. Achieving the ends focused attention on the means. Building the welfare state was inspiration enough for four decades; making it work, it seems, is not.

There is an element of irony in the fact that, as the capstone of the welfare state was being put in place between 1965 and 1973, the demands made on the state were being transformed from the quantitative, to what we, for want of a better term, call *qualitative*—a renewed emphasis on ideological and value-oriented issues.[2] The last part of the twentieth century witnessed a renewed consciousness of fundamental political values in Scandinavia as elsewhere, belying the earlier comfortable expectations that shared affluence would lead to an "end to ideology."

The reappearance of qualitative politics began on the left. Its earliest manifestation was the Danish "Easter Marches" against nuclear weapons in the early 1960s inspired by Britain's Campaign for Nuclear Disarmament. In their breadth of support, the Easter Marches suggested that the Cold War anticommunist mobilization was no longer sufficient to keep issues of military and foreign policy out of the political debate. The student revolt that broke out at the University of Copenhagen in March 1968 marked the watershed. Following the example of their comrades in Berkeley and Paris and with the ingratitude of youth, the largely middle-class beneficiaries of the explosive expansion of the universities under the

Social Democrats demanded rights hitherto reserved exclusively to senior professors. Within a year, every university in Scandinavia was affected. Student demands ran the gamut from ending the war in Vietnam to student control of university curricula. Welfare and security were rarely mentioned.

The torch of the qualitative revolt passed out of student hands on Tuesday, December 9, 1969, as the iron miners of Svappavaara, north of the arctic circle, laid down work in a wildcat strike. They were joined on Wednesday by their colleagues in Kiruna and, on Thursday, by those in Malmberget. As a group, the iron miners were the best-paid blue-collar workers in Sweden. The state-owned mining company that they worked for was administered by the Social Democrats. Their parents had grown up in the grinding poverty of the subsistence rural economy of northern Sweden. If there was any group that epitomized the quantitative benefits of Social Democratic Sweden, it was the miners. Their strike, directed as much against their own union and the relations of power in Social Democratic Sweden as against their immediate employer, acquired a symbolic role in the dark of that Arctic winter as they stayed out in January and into February. Inspiring other wildcat strikes, their strike set in motion the push for the transformation of authority patterns in the economy that is chronicled in Chapter 10.

The antiauthoritarianism of the students and the miners was followed in 1972 in Denmark and Norway by the bitter referenda on whether the two countries should join the European Community, today's European Union. In both countries, the business community and its parties provided unqualified support for membership; in both, the Social Democrats and the trade union federation provided more qualified support. The reason for this unusual alliance was simple: Both sides saw membership in the European Community as crucial to continued economic growth. Business perceived that as a good in itself. Labor perceived it as a means to higher living standards for the working class. Together they comprised the political establishment, and they said "yes" to the European Community.

In both Denmark and Norway, the 1972 European Community referendum campaign became the most bitter political conflict since the German occupation. It pitted advocates of economic growth against those who maintained other values, including socialism, Lutheranism, and loyalty to national particularism. In Norway, the left made common cause with the agrarian and Christian parties—both culturally conservative—to send Norwegian membership in the European Community down to defeat 54 percent to 46 percent. In Denmark, where the farmers' organizations backed the European Community, membership was ratified solidly (63% to 37%) but the issue remained.

Subsequent referenda in Denmark on further European integration in 1986, 1992, 1993, and 2000 solidified those lines of division. In fact, Danes voted narrowly in 1992 against the Maastricht Treaty and in 2000 against full integration in the common European currency, the Euro. Similarly the second Norwegian vote on joining the European Union in 1994, when the Finns and Swedes had voted to join, went narrowly against (52% to 48%), with the lines of division drawn much as they were in 1972. This issue will be discussed further in Chapters 4 and 5, and the referenda results are available in Table 4.3.

The same sort of struggle was played out in the Swedish nuclear-power referendum in 1980. Opposing nuclear power was an unlikely alliance of the agrarian Center party and the Left Communist party. Supporting it was an equally peculiar group of growth-oriented bedfellows that included the Conservatives, Social Democrats, and Liberals. The tide of public opinion was such that during the campaign the position of the Social Democrats and Liberals was reinterpreted from favoring nuclear power to favoring its gradual phase-out. The 1994 vote on Swedish European Union membership split party voters and party blocs in a similar fashion as Swedes voted narrowly in favor (52% to 47%) of joining Europe.

The common denominator of the new issues was that they cut across the existing partisan lines. The radicals of the urban left found themselves making common cause with rural traditionalists, while the Social Democrats and Conservatives, both dedicated to economic growth, formed an uncomfortable, de facto alliance. Many voters, understandably, were disoriented. Others found the new alliances refreshing. Both reactions cut into the strength of party loyalties among voters, not least because of the additional underlying trends in voter attitudes—a rising suspicion of the bureaucracy vital to provide social services and transfer payments, and a discontent with the rapid rise in taxes needed to pay for them.

None of the Scandinavian countries were immune to the new qualitative politics. Since the watershed elections of 1973 in Denmark and Norway shattered the stability of the party system that had flourished since World War I, every country has had new parties pushing new policy issues crash the doors of parliament. What has developed is a pattern of swings between destabilizing elections with high voter volatility raising new issues and periods of relative stability as government responds.

Internal Strains

Initially these new issues primarily revolved around internally generated strains of the welfare state: growing bureaucracy, high taxes, and the sense that burdens were not equally shared. Few wanted to dismantle the welfare state itself, but the dislike of its economic underpinnings and administrative structure was both widespread and intense.

Consider the appeal of Mogens Glistrup's new Progress party in the Danish election of 1973. A successful tax lawyer, Glistrup had become a

television personality overnight by proclaiming during a prime-time interview at the tax deadline in 1971 that he paid no income tax by using
presumably legal loopholes. Other reasonably intelligent Danes also used
tax law loopholes to avoid paying taxes, he said. At this, hard-taxed Danes
(production-line workers were then paying around 40% of their wages in
direct taxes and 20% or more of the remainder in indirect taxes) pricked
up their ears. Although tax lawyers are generally a reticent breed, Glistrup
quickly demonstrated a flair for self-publicity and for the catchy proposal.
Among his more memorable proposals: sell Greenland to the gullible and
imperialistic Americans; consign tax records to the Midsummer's Eve
bonfires traditionally used to rid the land of witches; and replace the Danish military with a tape recording saying, "We surrender," in Russian. He
was anything but the typical right-wing demagogue. The lilt of his Born-
holm accent and the pleasing mixture of absurdity and rationality in some
of his more radical proposals disarmed even left-wing critics. In the 1973
election, his party exerted an ecumenical appeal on the dissatisfied,
regardless of economic class or political background (Borre et al. 1974,
pp. 7–8), polled 16 percent of the vote, and emerged second only to the
Social Democrats in parliamentary seats. A breakaway right-wing Social
Democratic faction, the Center Democrats, attacked the property tax and
polled 8 percent.

The Glistrup phenomenon epitomized the political backlash against the
combination of the growing bureaucracy and high taxes necessary to run
the welfare state. But it was not unique to Denmark. In the same year,
dissatisfied voters in Norway provided fertile ground for a new tax resisters' party unblushingly named for its founder, the elderly, right-wing
editor of a dog fanciers' magazine. If "Anders Lange's Party for the Sharp
Reduction of Income Taxes, Excise Duties, and Governmental Interference" was not a name that rolled trippingly from the tongue, at least it
was a clear statement of the party's program. Voters sent Lange to
parliament.

In Finland, the Rural party, a splinter from the agrarian Center, ap-
pealed to somewhat similar sentiments. It had its best elections in the early
1970s through the early 1980s and then revived in the late 1990s to 2003
as the True Finn party. In Sweden the New Democrats, a populist rightist
party with an antibureaucratic orientation, broke into parliament in the
1991. The New Democrats lost their seats in 1994. However, Lange's party,
renamed the Progress party, and Glistrup's party, now transformed
through schisms and new leadership into the Danish People's party, have
become fixtures of the parliamentary constellation. In the last decade the
issue of immigration has breathed new wind into the sails of both.

Interestingly enough, none of these new parties of the right attacked
the core programs of the welfare state. More than one of them pushed for

improved programs, especially for pensioners. It was the mechanisms of the welfare state that they attacked.

If the new right fed on discontent with the bureaucratic and financial underpinnings of the welfare state, it was matched in the center of the political spectrum by a culturally conservative but economically centrist movement that supported the broad outline of the Social Democratic project but opposed the impact of the welfare state on families and women's roles. Norway long had a Christian party that reflected these views, and similar Christian parties broke into the Finnish parliament in 1970, the Danish parliament in 1973, and the Swedish parliament in 1985. These morally conservative parties seem to have become common and permanent features of Scandinavian politics, rather than just a Norwegian anomaly as in the 1930s through 1960s. They have taken part in government in all four countries in the 1990s. Unlike religious parties and factions in the United States, Britain, and Canada, the Scandinavian Christian Democrats were also "Christian socialists" and favored public programs to help the poor, elderly, children, and others.

In the center-left, environmental issues acquired a new prominence among the young and the growing grassroots organizations. That was particularly true in Sweden and Finland, which had added nuclear power to their energy sources. The nuclear power question juxtaposed economic growth and environmental costs, quantitative benefits versus qualitative costs. Environmentalists won parliamentary representation in Finland in 1983, in Sweden in 1988, and in Iceland in 1999.

What was happening was that the success of welfare state in spreading economic prosperity diminished the salience of welfare state issues. Economic insecurity seemed increasingly remote. Fifteen years of continual economic expansion had eroded the sense of social solidarity that had borne the welfare state.

As social services and income security were increasingly regarded as the natural order of things, incremental improvements in the system generated little increased support. They certainly did not create the same intense enthusiasm as the initial reforms. What is drawing sick pay from the first day, rather than the fourth, compared to the initiation of the sick pay system? Or what is adding dental care to the national health system compared to the creation of the national health system?

The economic crunch of the latter part of the 1970s in Denmark and Sweden (while Norway was protected by the North Sea oil boom) tended to refocus attention on economic issues and to strengthen the popular appreciation for the virtues of the welfare state. The political beneficiaries of the economic crisis were initially the Social Democrats, even in Denmark where Anker Jørgensen's minority Social Democratic governments presided from 1975 to 1982 over rising long-term unemployment with increasing helplessness. But as the figures in Appendixes A and B indicate,

Social Democratic support gradually eroded as it became clear that the Social Democrats had no miracle cure for hard times. All the countries attacked the tax problem, however. They broadened the tax base and cut marginal tax rates.

External Strains

In the 1980s and particularly the 1990s, external factors connected with economic globalization and the neoliberal agenda of privatization, deregulation, and the establishment of a single, integrated global market created new strains on the Scandinavian welfare state. In their very nature, these causes of strain cannot be addressed at the national level. Treating their symptoms, however, has become part of everyday politics.

For small, open economies like those of Scandinavia, international trade has long been a fact of life, as we will discuss in Chapter 7. What was new in the 1980s and 1990s was dismantling controls on international financial transactions, with a resulting exponential growth in various forms of speculation, and the rapid growth in genuinely multinational corporations. International currency transactions exploded from $10–20 billion daily in 1973 at the demise of the fixed exchange rates of the Bretton Woods agreement to $1.2 trillion daily twenty years later (Greider 1997, p. 243), an increase of roughly 100 times. While most of the former went to finance international trade and investment, more than 95 percent of the latter had more speculative goals. The magnitude of these financial flows dwarf the ability of national governments to manage them, as the Swedes learned to their chagrin in 1992. In their abortive effect to defend the value of the Swedish krona after exchange controls had been dismantled, the Swedish Central Bank pushed short term interest rates over 500 percent.

The Scandinavian welfare model had rested upon the assumption that the nation state was the relevant unit for making economic policy. Carefully designed national economic policies underpinned the welfare state. Without strong countercyclical measures, for instance, the cost of generous unemployment compensation at Scandinavian levels was clearly excessive; the Scandinavians could afford to be generous only if unemployment rates were kept low. Full integration into the global market meant the loss of national economic sovereignty.

It would seem, at first glance, that the question of European Union membership fits into this global context. Certainly it has been a divisive issue, as the various hard-fought referenda campaigns suggest (see Table 4.3). It has produced a great deal of political fragmentation, especially within the Social Democratic constituency. And the European Union has created a highly competitive market many times the size of Scandinavian domestic markets. However, in many ways, the European Union offers an *alternative* to globalization: It creates an economic unit roughly the size of the United States that is not wedded to a free-trade ideology and that can deal with globalization from a position of strength. In essence, it offers the opportunity to respond to the pressures of globalization with a set of European policies.

Privatization, deregulation, and marketization were also imported with economic globalization as mechanism to adapt to the global market. All have won substantial support on the right and in the center of the political spectrum in Scandinavia since the 1980s, and have received some grudging Social Democratic support as well. They have brought restricted results to date in Scandinavia, in no small measure because of the fact that, first, the Scandinavians had relatively few state enterprises; second, those that existed were driven on market principles; and, third, public provision of services tended to be high quality and generally efficient. Thus the gains were few outside telecommunications and the disruptions caused by privatization, contracting public services to private companies, and marketization were substantial. These goals, however, remain on the agenda for some center-right parties and politicians.

The minority cabinets, shifting parliamentary alliances, frequent elections, and alternating governments that have characterized Scandinavian politics since the 1970s look like political instability only in comparison to the extreme stability that was standard in the region previously. It has certainly not made the Scandinavian countries ungovernable. The continuing Scandinavian emphasis on broad majorities for major legislation has contributed significantly to policy consistency. So has the growing ability of minority governments to slalom from one coalition to another on varying policy issues. But the succession of weak and alternating governments exacerbated the problem of trying to formulate coherent policies. It has subsequently contributed to policy inertia in the face of major global changes.

THE ECONOMIC LIMITS OF THE WELFARE STATE

The Scandinavian welfare states showed their strengths and weaknesses during the international economic crisis that began with the oil price increases of 1973–74. Although Norway benefited from the energy price explosion as it brought its North Sea oil fields into production and escaped the general downturn, the recession gripped Denmark and drove the Swedes to full utilization of their range of countercyclical economic policies. That is explored in Chapter 9. The Swedish policy of countering the downturn by producing for stock, providing investment incentives, and using selective labor-market measures, all financed by borrowing abroad at depressed recession interest rates, was initially successful. Had the international recession been short and followed by rapid economic growth—the postwar pattern—we would all be studying the success of the Swedish bridging measures.

It was not. The international recession lasted longer than even pessimists had feared, and the boom that should have eliminated Swedish stockpiles never came. There are limits to how long a small country as dependent as Sweden on international commerce can use an expansionary domestic policy to counter the effects of the international economic cycle. Indeed, Swedish success in maintaining full employment worsened Sweden's competitiveness by permitting wage increases at rates substantially above those of Sweden's major trading partners. Interest rates turned up, raising the costs of the stockpile policy. The repeated devaluations of the Swedish krona since 1977 and the rapidly growing foreign debt were symptoms of the severity of the problems.

The international economic downturn not only put severe pressure on the economic policies underlying the Scandinavian welfare states, it also revealed serious structural weaknesses in their design. Although originally constructed for the hard times of the 1930s and 1940s, Scandinavian welfare programs were re-engineered in the late 1960s and early 1970s to fit the supposition that the economic problems of the cyclical market economy could be managed. Hence benefit levels could be set high because (1) that helped maintain consumption and made good countercyclical economic sense and (2) few needed the benefits for an extended period. (These themes are taken up in detail in Chapters 6–10.) Thus, for example, reforms in 1967 and 1970 raised unemployment compensation in Denmark from a level designed to keep body and soul of the unemployed together to the level of 90 percent of wages up to a ceiling fixed at the average industrial wage for up to two- and one-half years. The careful restructuring of the tax system to encourage housewives to enter the labor market,[3] and the costly subsidies to day-care and after-school facilities to lure mothers of small children to take paid employment also reflected the assumption that unemployment above the frictional level was a thing of the past.

Unfortunately the premise was erroneous. Unemployment compensation in Denmark, and retraining and emergency employment programs used in its stead in Sweden, have become major expenditures. Emergency welfare payments—equivalent to the public assistance of the past—became a significant expenditure as well. To cut these programs in the midst of economic crisis (which nonsocialist governments sought to do in both countries in the early 1980s) seemed not only heartless, because it singled out the victims of the crisis for additional burdens, but also of dubious economic value, because a sharp decline in domestic demand would worsen the crisis. Yet the failure to take remedial action earlier had already produced horrendous budget deficits—exceeding 10 percent of the Gross Domestic Product (GDP) in both Denmark and Sweden—that drained the domestic capital markets, drove up interest rates, and led to heavy foreign borrowing. The deficits were simply too large to be sustained, especially because they were being used to finance consumption. The elimination of the deficit became a central policy problem after 1982.

In short, cyclical benefits—unemployment compensation, employment programs, rent subsidies, social assistance, and the like—that go up as the economy goes down, proved themselves by sustaining relative prosperity for the individuals and families affected and by maintaining demand during the economic crisis. But like the Swedish program of producing for stock, they were better designed to bridge a sharp, temporary downturn than the lengthy slumps that have occurred since 1973, most recently in Finland and Sweden in the early 1990s. Social services originally considered adjuncts to economic policy, such as day-care programs, acquired a life of their own with the professionalization of personnel and development of their own ideologies of service that resisted cutbacks. Well designed to distribute the benefits of economic growth in an egalitarian fashion, the Scandinavian welfare states were ill prepared to be egalitarian about distributing the costs of economic decline.

Expanding the public sector was the Scandinavian Social Democrats' surrogate for socialism. If domestic and foreign political conditions preclude attacking poverty and inequality directly through workers' control of production, then one could pursue the same aims via the public sector, milking the capitalist cow as it were and, to mix metaphors, using the capitalist engine of production as the dynamo for public sector expansion. The Scandinavian welfare states rested on the Social Democratic assumption that capitalism was by nature dynamic and expansive, although anarchistic, and, if managed properly, could produce a large growth dividend for redistribution.

Some welfare state programs have clearly increased the dynamism of capitalism. Massive job retraining and heavy subsidies for those who moved to find new work increased the flexibility of the labor market. The public sector paid the cost of adding mothers of small children to the labor force. The solidaristic wage policy pushed by unions in conjunction with the Social Democrats accelerated the process of industrial renewal by pushing up wages in inefficient firms while holding them down in efficient ones. All of these probably increase the competitiveness of Scandinavian firms in the global economy. But the very size of the public sector and the problem of financing it has increasingly seemed to undermine the efficiency of the capitalist dynamo.

First, especially during recessions, the public sector shows some tendency to crowd out the private sector. This is clearest in the credit markets where public-sector deficit financing between the mid-1970s and the mid-1980s tended to crowd out industrial borrowing, at least in Denmark. Not only did it kept rates on borrowed funds above the levels prudent capitalists find attractive, it tempted them to buy high-yield state bonds, rather than plants and machinery. Possibly there are similar tendencies in the labor market: public and service employment in Denmark is now almost twice that in industry. The municipal workers' union in Sweden has surpassed the metal workers to become the country's biggest trade union.

Second, financing the public sector is an expensive proposition. Scandinavian governments tax almost everything imaginable—necessities as well as luxuries, virtues as well as vices, and, above all else, income. Taxes do affect behavior patterns. We may not be as quick as Pavlov's dogs, but the learning process is just as certain. When your marginal tax rate hits 70 percent, as it did in Denmark in 1983 at about $20,000 (about $50,000 in 2003 prices) in unsheltered taxable income, you run for the nearest tax shelter. At those rates, every loophole acquires a constituency of users that extends beyond lawyers, accountants, and the very rich to include one's neighbors: machinists, schoolteachers, carpenters, and secretaries. Far from stifling initiative, high marginal tax rates give Scandinavians every incentive to divert normal taxable income into tax-sheltered forms of savings or consumption.

One can hardly fault the tax rationality of the investor who makes his decision based on posttax income, not the pretax profitability of the investment. But this does little for the efficiency of the economy.

So use of tax loopholes cut the tax base, forced increases in marginal rates, and thereby further increased the attraction of tax loopholes. The consequence was further tax-driven economic decisions and increased pressure on governmental revenues. Thus it is not surprising that tax reforms that would broaden the tax base became a central political issue in Scandinavia in the 1980s and 1990s. Nor was it surprising that it took too long to reach political agreement on this question, making the results of broadening the tax base far more disruptive for those who had shaped their lives around minimizing their taxes—and for the economy as a whole. Both the Danes and Swedes induced predictable real estate price collapses when they finally reduced the most widely used tax avoidance technique, the deductibility of increase on mortgage debt for owner-occupied homes.[4] Real estate price deflation combined with deregulation of the banking industry helped to produce a banking crisis in Finland, Norway, and Sweden.

Economic pressures came from outside as well as inside the welfare state. Economic globalization undercut the viability of national economic policy to secure full employment and economic growth. National mechanisms that rested on the assumption that the nation-state was the appropriate level for making economic policy were far more useful in the 1960s—when the basic premise was still correct—than they were in the 1980s and they were more useful in the 1980s than they are in the first decade of the twenty-first century.

With increasing globalization came pressure to conform to more of the international average rates of welfare provision and of taxation. Specifically in the Danish, Finnish, and Swedish cases, international practices found expression in the norms of the European Union. Although overt compulsion to harmonize welfare and tax policies with those of the Continent was far less than opponents of the EU maintained, in fact expensive welfare programs financed by high employer taxes, like those in Sweden, constitute a competitive disadvantage when other things are equal—which, of course, they rarely are. But talking about the welfare state as a means to increase national economy efficiency is very different from talking about it as a means to increase social and economic justice.

POLITICS IN AN ERA OF MORAL AMBIGUITY

Basic Scandinavian welfare programs, including unemployment compensation and the national health system, had their origins in local benefit societies based on the solidarity of a small group (e.g., a union, a farmers' organization, a neighborhood). In their original form, these benefit societies owed their existence to the clear connection between obligations and rights. The right to benefits was based on the obligation to contribute; without the latter there could not have been the former.

One of the common slogans of the nineteenth-century Scandinavian labor movements phrased the concept simply: "Do your duty; demand your rights." The rights were justly yours because you performed your duties. Indeed, one of the moral homilies endlessly repeated in the nineteenth-century Social Democratic press was the moral superiority of the good trade unionist who did his duty to his fellows not only over the scab but also over the corrupt and decadent individualism that characterized the bourgeoisie, which claimed rights but dodged duties. The ultimate triumph of the labor movement thus represented not only economic justice but moral justice.

If there is any tragedy in the Scandinavian welfare states, it is that in their eagerness to see benefits generalized and minimum levels raised, the cord between rights and duties has been cut. What were once two sides of the same coin have been separated. The connection between benefits and obligations remains at a societal level, but it is far more abstract than the concrete individual obligation of the past. The sense of social solidarity that the popular movements promoted remains an engrained cultural norm that can be invoked to justify paying the heavy costs of social programs. But its force has diminished, and the limits it puts on the pursuit of individual interests are increasingly nebulous. The presence of immigrant groups that lack the norm of social solidarity with the broader community creates further strain.

If collective measures to guarantee economic security permit greater individualism, surely that is good. After all, the intention in abolishing economic insecurity was to increase individual freedom. But what if it also encourages an exclusive and narrow egotism?

Unlinking benefits and obligations encouraged the use of the former if not the avoidance of the latter. The general availability of high benefits has prompted an expansion of their use. It is your tax money that pays for them, so why not use them? Thus supplemental unemployment compensation, intended to support the incomes of those forced to work part-time by their jobs, such as longshoremen or workers in fish packing plants, has become a general program of public assistance for those who otherwise would have chosen to work part-time. Day-care programs, designed for working mothers, become places to park children while shopping. The state has found itself, often unwittingly, expanding programs that have tended to crowd out society's obligations between family and friends. The aim has been the virtuous one of stepping in to protect the weakest, to provide them what the networks of family and friendship have failed to do. But why should Grandma take care of the kids when day care is available, and why should you do the grocery shopping for old Mrs. Hansson next door when the city provides home assistance for the elderly? Your taxes pay for it anyway. So state programs have tended to crowd out those earlier relationships, atomizing society, creating need for greater state aid, and changing norms.

One notes evidence of changing public morality more in anecdote than in statistics, in the stories of the doctors who employ each other's wives as secretaries just long enough for them to qualify for unemployment compensation, or the tales of well-to-do parents buying an apartment (and writing the interest payments off against the marginal taxes) to rent it to the daughter, a university student who, with a child but no job, can draw the maximum public rent subsidy. Perhaps the most lasting problem of the economic crunch after 1973 and continued high unemployment is the generational shift in attitudes that it encouraged. For many of the young entering the labor force, the welfare net was their first resort, not their last one.

In the small group where social security is provided through reciprocal obligation, there is a natural limit on this kind of behavior—the censure of one's friends and withdrawal of benefits, if not ostracism and expulsion. The group incapable of imposing such discipline cannot persist. The freeloader is a demoralizing influence who renders the faithful performance of obligations ludicrous.

But when the connection between obligation and benefit is gone and the citizen deals with the state, not his or her workmates or neighbors, the stigma attached to using the system inappropriately is much diminished. One no longer victimizes friends and colleagues but cleverly fools some distant opponent. Glistrup's comment that the tax resisters of today are the modern equivalent of the Resistance fighters of World War II is the perfect gloss of the rip-off artist's rationalization. He has the pleasure not only from maximizing his own advantage but also the satisfaction of chalking it up as a courageous act of individual rebellion against distant oppression. The situation is analogous to eating dinner at a restaurant with a large group of friends. Once the decision is made to split the tab equally, why restrain yourself in what you order? What you pay is determined almost entirely by what the others choose, but what you eat is your own choice. As a consequence, the bill grows larger than anyone wants to pay.

NOTES

1. Tingsten, who was one of the outstanding intellectual figures of Sweden in the middle of the twentieth century, argued that generalized prosperity presaged the "end of ideology." The sources of the growing consensus, Tingsten suggested, were both political and economic. Democratic forces—left and right—had seen their ideologies perverted in the totalitarianisms of Stalinism and fascism. Support for constitutional democracy was strengthened by the experience of the 1930s and 1940s. Moreover, economic growth supported by pragmatic planning and Keynesian economic management had mitigated the struggle over economic distribution. Tingsten launched the argument in a series of articles in *Dagens Nyheter* in 1952; it was presented in English in Tingsten (1955); the definitive presentation is Tingsten (1966). His premise was picked up in American social science and was a prominent feature on the intellectual landscape between 1960 and 1968. See Lipset (1960, ch. 13) and Bell (1960).

2. Our concept of qualitative demands includes Ronald Inglehart's (1977) "postmaterialism" of the left and a comparable group of qualitative demands from the right. Inglehart found a generational division over "materialist" and "postmaterialist" values. The former values were held by the Depression–World War II–Cold War generation and emphasized security, material prosperity, and economic growth; the latter were typified by the student radicals of 1968 and emphasized equality, environmental, peace, and Third World issues. In the last decade, qualitative demands from the left have been matched by nonmaterial demands from the right, particularly on issues of family policy and maintaining national community against immigration.

3. Sweden, Norway, and Denmark in that order top industrial nations in tax incentives to encourage wives to enter the labor market rather than having husbands increase their income by a comparable amount. Ironically the tax incentives to encourage wives to seek jobs were increased sharply in all three countries between 1974 and 1978 as the recession sent the economies of Denmark and Sweden from labor shortage to labor surplus (OECD 1981, p. 29).

4. This tax subsidy for home ownership is much less disruptive in the United States, where tax breaks for the well-to-do are a dime a dozen and where marginal tax rates for the middle class and working class are low. Although the American income tax system is the object of massive complaint, the marginal rates for most Americans have always been too low to turn them into tax-calculating machines.

PART II

Scandinavian Democracy Today

CHAPTER 3

Is There a Scandinavian Democratic Model?

> Which government is the best? The one which teaches us to rule ourselves.
>
> —Johann Wolfgang von Goethe

It was not foreordained that the Scandinavian countries would become democratic models. The political history of the sixteenth and seventeenth centuries in Scandinavia was as bloody as that elsewhere in Europe. One of the more striking episodes of the period was the fashion in which Danish King Christian II celebrated his ascension to the throne of Sweden in 1520: He executed eighty-two of his noble coronation guests on the charge of heresy. The Swedish revolt, which followed, and the dissolution of the Union of Kalmar, which linked Sweden-Finland with Denmark-Norway, can be interpreted as a post hoc check on the abuse of royal power, but it was a trifle late for the unwitting nobles in Stockholm castle. Both the Danish and the new Swedish state participated with gusto in the religious wars of the seventeen century; Christian IV of Denmark and, in particular, Gustav II Adolf of Sweden did their parts in the Thirty Years' War to devastate Germany in the name of the Reformation.

Political developments in Scandinavia in the eighteenth and nineteenth centuries had more in common with those of the Central European countries, such as Germany and Austria, than with those of the Anglo-French western fringe of Europe. In 1719, after the debacle of Swedish defeat by the Russians, Sweden-Finland did replace the royal absolutism of Charles XI and Charles XII with a constitutional regime with power vested in the Estates General; Sweden thus claims the second longest constitutional history in the world after Britain. However, this parliamentary Age of Liberty ended when Gustav III recovered royal prerogatives through a coup d'état and a new constitution in 1772. Remaining parliamentary limits on the king proved of restricted practical value. Thus, for example, Gustav III dealt in 1788 with the parliamentary ban on waging offensive war on Russia by the simple stratagem of dressing Swedish troops in Cossack uniforms borrowed from the Royal Opera and staging an attack on a Swedish border post in Finland; he then led the Swedish in a "defensive" war. Even after the creation of modern parliaments in the last century (1814 in Norway, 1849 in Denmark, 1866 in Sweden), royal governments that jailed opponents for blasphemy and lese majesty continued to rule against majorities in the popularly elected lower chamber until the establishment of parliamentary supremacy.

THE EVOLUTION OF DEMOCRACY

The early constitutions (1809 in Sweden, 1814 in Norway, and 1849 in Denmark) were designed to limit the king, not to establish popular rule. Sweden's first modern constitution limiting royal powers was adopted in 1809 after Sweden lost Finland to Russia and King Gustav IV Adolf was overthrown. The Swedish Estates General was finally replaced by a modern bicameral parliament in 1866.

Norway acquired its first (and current) constitution in 1814 in the brief period after it became independent of Denmark and before it was forced to acknowledge the terms of the Treaty of Kiel, which awarded Norway to Sweden. French Marshall Jean Bernadotte, called to be crown prince of Sweden after the overthrow of Gustav IV Adolf, had the wisdom to agree to govern Norway under its terms. Full Norwegian autonomy was achieved in local affairs in 1884; full independence from Sweden, in 1905. The otherwise absolutist Russian Tsar governed Finland as its Grand Duke under Gustav III's Swedish-Finnish constitution of 1772 and Act of Union and Security of 1789, which had granted the sovereign far reaching powers with an Estates General until a Finnish general strike in the revolutionary year of 1905 forced the establishment of a modern parliament.

The king of Denmark continued to rule as an absolute monarch until 1848 when the spirit of the European liberal revolutions of that year reached Copenhagen; like several other European monarchs, he judiciously conceded a constitution that year, which took effect in 1849. Iceland's separate status under the king was recognized in 1874.

Parliamentary supremacy and democratic elections lagged behind constitutional government in Scandinavia by half a century or more. (See Table 3.1.) The supremacy of parliament over the king in selecting the cabinet was not established until 1884 in Norway, 1901 in Denmark, 1903 in Iceland, and 1917 in Sweden and Finland. The final steps in establishing

Table 3.1
Development of Political Democracy in Scandinavia

	Denmark	Finland	Iceland	Norway	Sweden
Constitutional restrictions on monarch	1849	1917*	1874	1814	1809
Establishment of modern parliament	1849	1906	1874	1814	1866
Parliamentary supremacy	1901	1917	1903	1884	1917
Universal manhood suffrage	1915	1906	1915	1898	1918
Women's suffrage	1915	1906	1915	1913	1921

*In 1917 Finland declared its independence of the Russian Empire.

democracy were extending the right to vote to the working class and to women, moves that finally made parliament truly representative of the people. Broad suffrage for men appeared first in Denmark in 1849 and was gradually extended in other Nordic countries. Finland in 1906 was the first European country to enfranchise women, and women made up 10 percent of the first parliament elected in 1907. Norway followed with women's suffrage in 1913, Denmark and Iceland in 1915, and Sweden in 1921.

Although *democracy* is an often-used term, it is not a concept that is easy to define; its meanings are numerous and disputed. Democracy is the quintessential moving target: It changes in response to citizens' demands. Even in the Scandinavian countries, where the consensus about some aspects of democracy is substantial, new studies that reinterpret and reassess the evolving Scandinavian democratic experience appear regularly.

Modern definitions of democracy, which are generally qualified by such prefixes as *representative, constitutional,* or *political,* reflect not only efforts to be precise, but also the general limitations placed on the concept. This is probably most obvious in recent American empirical democratic theory. Robert Dahl (1971, 1989) is so rigorous in his definitions that he has eschewed the term *democracy* entirely. Instead, he uses the neologism *polyarchy* and stresses its defining characteristics as free participation by citizens and free contestation by parties and other organized groups. The competitive requirement is also emphasized by G. Bingham Powell (1982, p. 3), who argues that there must be at least two parties or blocs capable of winning an election and forming a government, and by Joseph Schumpeter, who defines democracy as "that institutional arrangement for arriving at political decisions in which individuals acquire the power to decide by means of a competitive struggle for the people's vote" between parties (1950, p. 269). For both Schumpeter and Anthony Downs (1957), making governmental policy in democracies is incidental to the competitive struggle for power.

Few Scandinavian political scientists or politicians would accept so narrow a focus on contested elections as the be-all and end-all of democracy. They would be more comfortable with Arend Lijphart's insistence that democracy, in its literal and everyday meaning of "government by the people," still requires Lincoln's qualification as "government for the people." In other words, a perfectly democratic government would act "in perfect correspondence" with the desires of all citizens (Lijphart 1984, p. 1).

The competitive struggle for power through elections is crucial, but with time and success, democracy has become multidimensional. As Giovanni Sartori notes, at least in some countries, including the Scandinavian ones, "democracy denotes *more* than political machinery; it also denotes a way of living, a 'social democracy.' In particular these democracies have gone a long way toward the maximization of equality—equality of status, of opportunity, and of starting points" (1968, p. 117).

Nevertheless, the machinery of government remains the starting point for any analysis of modern democracy. Understanding the institutions of government—the subject of Chapter 4—is essential for understanding how political ideas and values are turned into political actions. Almost equally important are those structures for political participation—parties and interest groups, which are the subject of Chapter 5—that have joined the delegation of power and become essential attributes of institutional studies of modern democracy. There is no question in Scandinavia that these organizations have deepened democracy, creating new channels for political participation that provide the governed with greater control over their representatives than is the case in many other democracies.

Our survey of the Scandinavian democratic model is completed in Chapter 4 with a look at the protection of citizens' rights against an intrusive government, and how these various institutional and political structures relate to each other in making policy. We also consider challenges to democracy stemming from regional and global integration in Chapter 7.

STAGES OF DEMOCRACY

Academic discussions mirror historical experience. The Scandinavian democracies, like other Western democracies, have evolved through stages of growing inclusiveness and scope (see Lipset and Rokkan 1967, pp. 26–30, and Dahl 1989, ch. 17). Inclusiveness is representation in its broadest sense: How much of the population participates in making the rules and setting the goals of social life? Its expansion to encompass the entire adult population in Scandinavia required decades of political struggle. Similarly, the scope of democracy has broadened from a narrow constitutional and political focus first to include social issues and subsequently economic property rights. Within each of these areas, the stages of inclusiveness can be traced. Our point is that democratic goals, procedures, and values have been dynamic and expansive.

Scandinavians have come to view the growth of democracy to involve three distinct stages. The first, *political democracy*—the supremacy of a parliament elected by universal suffrage—was achieved in the first two decades of this century, and it was not fully accepted by segments of the Scandinavian right until 1945. Only since World War II has political and constitutional democracy enjoyed nearly universal support. Lowering the voting age to eighteen and modernized constitutions in Denmark (1953), Sweden (1970), and Finland (2000) completed this process.

With the foundations of political democracy in place, constructing *social democracy*, with its goals of equality and social solidarity, took center stage from the 1930s to 1960s. Bitterly contested at first, social reforms finally received strong consensus support in the postwar period. They helped to shape a better and more democratic society as well as a structure that could withstand social, political, and economic stresses. The cumulative impact of such stress, however, has forced a reappraisal of social programs during the past decade.

Finally, *economic democracy*, in which the organization of the production and distribution of goods and services become accountable to democratic principles, which originated conceptually in the rural and industrial popular movements of the nineteenth century, became the focus of reform in the 1970s. The debate on economic democracy is broader and less clearly defined than that on the political and social stages. It turns on the relative role of domestic and foreign markets and economic forces as well as political and corporatist forces. Consensus on both the content and the range of desirable outcomes in the economic-democracy debate is still quite tentative.

Political Democracy

Political democracy requires institutions that allow substantial popular participation in the governing process and procedures that ensure that citizens and groups can participate in government more directly and continuously than merely as occasional voters. In common with other Western parliamentary systems, parliamentary elections in Scandinavia determine who governs. The executive branch is responsible to parliament and can be dismissed at any time by a vote of no confidence, except in Finland where executive authority is divided between an elected president, who is not subject to a vote of no confidence, and the prime minister, who is. The basics of parliamentary democracy are simple and may help to explain greater citizen participation in elections and skepticism to inherently complex schemes such as govern the European Union.

Unlike the British Westminster model with single member constituencies, where elections usually produce clear parliamentary majorities for a single party, Scandinavia's European-style system of proportional representation guarantees the election of numerous parties. Since 1918 single-party majority governments have been the rare exception. (See Table 4.2.) Even during periods of majority government, as in Norway between 1945 and 1961, the Scandinavian states resemble Lijphart's "consensual model," which assumes limitations on majority rule through the sharing of power, the dispersal of power, a fair distribution of power, the delegation of power, and a formal limit on power (1984, p. 30).

In Scandinavia, these limitations are clear. First, most governments are minority governments, formed either by a party or a coalition of parties lacking a parliamentary majority. Legislation requires the active or passive support of one or more nongoverning parties. Majority coalitions—the next most common form—also restrict the dominant coalition partner. Single-party majorities are the rarest outcome. Second, Scandinavian parliaments disperse power to relatively strong committees, whose usually secret deliberations keep close tabs on executive policy making. Committees work out the compromises that can ensure parliamentary majorities for the legislation. Third, power is delegated geographically to local and regional governments, and functionally through reliance on corporatist participation typified by the Swedish *remiss* or consultation system. Such delegation does not approach a federal system. However, in practice and tradition, local governments have substantial autonomy, and corporatist bodies have become increasingly important channels for the representation of economic and occupational interests in the postwar era. Fourth, the distribution of power is enhanced by the proportional electoral systems of the three countries. Parties with modest voter support are assured some parliamentary representation. Finally, there are some limits on the power of parliamentary majorities, particularly in Denmark with its specific provisions for national referenda on most legislation when demanded by one-third of the members of parliament; a similar constitutional provision exists in regard to constitutional amendments in Sweden. Advisory referenda may also be held when required by specific legislation. Referenda have become more common in all the Scandinavian countries during the past two decades mainly on European Union issues.

Scandinavian democracy places particular stress on consensus-building mechanisms. The systematic use of consultative processes in drafting legislation at the national level that offers a voice to all major interest groups.

The corporatist patterns of representation on major governmental commissions clearly restrict the power of the parliamentary parties to legislate as they see fit. The general pattern in drafting major reform legislation is to turn the investigation of it over to a royal commission that includes not only representatives of the government but also of relevant interest groups. What is striking is the degree to which these commissions give representation to interest organizations likely to be critical of the government position. The Danish Low Income Commission, for instance, established by a Social Democratic government in 1982 to offer suggestions on how to make redistribution more effective, included as many representatives from business and farm organizations, which could be expected to be critical, as from sympathetic labor groups. The lengthy process of pension reform in Sweden in the 1990s was a similar process leading to major legislation. Major interest organizations, including the union federation, the employees' organizations, and the farmers' associations, are directly represented on all-important commissions involved in drafting legislation.

This consultative process in the drafting stage is complemented in Sweden by the practice of *remiss,* which entails sending legislative proposals out to relevant interest organizations for comment and suggestions for amendment. The voluminous comments—both solicited and unsolicited—not only provide expert organizational feedback, but have also enabled Social Democratic governments to integrate the organized groups supporting the bourgeois parties into the decision-making process (see Vinde and Petri 1978, pp. 24–29). While their parties may be out of power, they retain means of direct access to the decision-making process in which their influence is directly related to the expertise that they can bring to bear. The process encourages an objective debate about the real merits of the government's proposals, charting areas of consensus as well as those of disagreement.

A second practice that integrates widely divergent interests is that of enacting what are known as *framework laws.* Framework laws are essentially legal skeletons to be fleshed out through local bargaining and agreement. A classic example is the Swedish Employee Participation Act of 1976 (Medbestämmandelagen, generally referred to as the MBL), which was intended to expand radically employee rights of participation in the workplace. Although the law set certain broad standards, what those meant in practice and how they were to be implemented were left to collective bargaining. A series of MBL agreements was envisioned: a national agreement between the trade union federation (Landsorganisationen [LO]) and the employers' federation (Svensk Arbetsgiverforening [SAF]); agreements covering industrial branches between branch employers' organizations and industrial unions; and agreements between management and union locals in individual plants. The agreements were years in negotiation, and the process encouraged a great deal of flexibility and compromise by both employers and unions. While neither side abandoned its views, both sides have become quite skilled at what we can call *antagonistic cooperation;* that is, continued advocacy of antagonistic interests within the context of the common pursuit of productivity and efficiency. The dependency of the Nordic countries on foreign trade, and their sensitivity to competitive pressure from abroad, help to restrain the antagonism.

The consequences of including representatives of the major—and antagonistic—interest groups in drafting legislation and, in at least some cases, in implementation are significant. First, the process includes minorities. If, during long periods of Social Democratic tenure, the influence of business interests on legislation in parliament through business-oriented parties has been restricted, it also has often been substantial as a result of such corporatist arrangements. Second, it has permitted the Social Democrats to keep their opponents divided and to limit the vehemence of the opposition, even when the opposition seemed permanently excluded from power. Third, it has encouraged the organization of the previously unorganized by providing additional and appealing channels for influence. In short, the practice checks the majority, while making the minorities more responsible.

The essence of Scandinavian political democracy is broad participation in the political process: vertically, through strong political parties and interest organizations, and horizontally, through strong local and regional government. Evidence of such participation is clear. Voter turnout in the recent years has usually been over 80 percent in national elections in Denmark, Iceland, Norway, and Sweden; the Finnish turnout has been lower at about 65 percent. By international standards, Scandinavian parties and interest organizations have large, active memberships and are internally democratic; thus they are effective instruments for popular representation. Access to radio and television is generous and free. There are generous direct or indirect financial subsidies for parties in Scandinavia. The party press is vigorous and subsidized in Norway and Sweden.

Recent Scandinavian discussions of political democracy have transcended a narrow electoral focus to examine cultural, educational, and judicial policy questions as well as social and economic issues. These discussions have revolved around three principal dimensions that have come to define the modern Scandinavian concept of political democracy. The first is *liberty,* or those individual freedoms and rights that require enforcement and guarantees by the state. The second is *participation,* or the ability of the individual to take part in political decisions, especially on issues that have a direct impact on the participant. The third is *equality,* or the equal opportunity of citizens to participate in the country's political process. There are inherent tensions among these dimensions of political democracy. For instance, in terms of effective participation, what is the trade-off between the individual's independent expression of his or her own views and the need to become a disciplined member of an organization? Moreover, there are tensions between the dimensions. For example, maintaining relative equality may require limitations on some personal economic freedoms.

It is particularly in the area of political equality that recent Scandinavian debate has differed from debate in other pluralistic political systems (Martinussen 1977, p. 3). No modern democracy can claim that all or nearly all citizens really participate equally. All governments, democratic as well as authoritarian, require that substantial decision-making powers be delegated to public officials. All systems have created positions of privileged power. However, democratic governments must consider to what extent and on what grounds their deviations from equality of political power can be justified.

The Scandinavian discussion has moved in the postwar period from earlier legal, constitutional, and institutional issues to the current focus on social and economic factors.[1] Amid the prosperity and social programs of the late 1960s, many commentators expressed growing concern about the continuation of substantial inequalities in the distribution of political resources. "One citizen, one vote" was no longer a sufficient description of political rights. "Votes count but resources decide" is the succinct way the Norwegian political scientist Stein Rokkan (1966, p. 105) summed up the distinction between formal participation and political resources. *Political poverty*—those vast differences in access to political resources that deny significant numbers of citizens the opportunity to participate equally in the democratic process—became a major issue in the political debate. Several democracy or "power" studies since the 1970s have sought to illuminate the problems of democracy in a globalized, technocratic society.[2]

American observers will note that civil rights receive less attention than participation and equality in the Scandinavian debate. After 1945 there were no significant challenges to these rights, but immigration and increased ethnic diversity in the last twenty-five years has renewed concerns about protecting civil and minority rights. Prior to the economic boom in the 1960s, immigration to Scandinavia was very limited. The Scandinavia-wide free labor market established by the Nordic Council in 1954 allowed Nordic citizens to take up employment in any of the five countries. Except for numerous Finns who sought industrial jobs in Sweden in the 1950s and 1960s, the measure resulted in little migration. But the labor shortage of that period induced governments to open the doors to foreign workers. By 1974, one-fourth of the work force of many industrial plants in Sweden was foreign born. These workers have been guaranteed economic and social equality by both political and trade union organizations. When hard times fell upon Denmark and Sweden in the mid-1970s, entrance was restricted, but those already in residence enjoyed full protection.

Refugees from non-European countries have been more challenging to Scandinavian liberalism. The trickle of refugees in the 1970s from countries like Chile, whose political persecution was undeniable, turned in the 1980s and 1990s into a flood of desperate people from the Middle East, Asia, the Balkans, and elsewhere. Public resources were severely taxed by large numbers of people from very different cultures. Moderate critics of an open-door policy feared a backlash of resentment and inadequate services. If refugee status was accorded everyone who was economically wretched and politically dissatisfied, the numbers could be staggering. Less liberal critics feared openly for the cultural survival of their small societies and some saw conspiracies to overwhelm Scandinavia with aggressive foreign activists. The 1987 and 1988 Danish national and Norwegian local elections saw gains by fringe parties running on openly xenophobic platforms, and attacks on immigration have been a staple of the fringe right parties' campaign rhetorical since then. Unlawful administrative practices to slow immigration in Denmark resulted in a major political scandal (the "Tamil scandal") and the punishment of several ranking Justice Department officials including the impeachment and conviction of Justice Minister Erik Ninn-Hansen in 1995.

Concern for civil rights also becomes more imperative when one considers the enormous range of interaction between the citizen and the government in the welfare state. More than half the national income is channeled through the government. Citizens are taxed for these resources and then receive their tax monies back again (less administrative costs) in transfer payments and entitlements to public services. Enforcement of complex and heavy taxation can raise significant civil rights questions. Distribution of transfer payments and social services can raise equally significant questions of fairness. Assuring due process and fairness in the modern welfare state is neither easy nor automatic. Innovative institutions, such as the ombudsman, originally unique to Sweden and now generally used throughout Scandinavia, have become increasingly important.

Social Democracy

The assumption that social democracy is the inevitable result of government by Social Democratic parties is simplistic. Like political democracy, social democracy—a set of broadly held values and widely supported public policies that have reduced the class and regional differences between social groups and individuals—involves matters of degree, and comparison over time and between societies. It is closely related to distribution of material and cultural wealth, without being limited merely to economic indicators. Social democracy differs from political democracy in its focus on equality of results. It is no more subjective than current definitions of political democracy, but there is far less consensus on its content and more open dispute about its characteristics.

Although it is no longer fashionable in the West to oppose political democracy, social democracy is a highly contested goal in many Western societies. Few openly oppose "equal opportunity," but social democracy also insists on a high degree of "equality of result." In Scandinavia, however, social democracy enjoys broad support, even from conservatives, although some economists see dangers in excessive government and populist pressures (contrast Heckscher 1984 with Lindbeck 1994). This is the result of decades of political hegemony by the Social Democratic parties, for whom social democracy was as high a priority as the earlier fight for political democracy. Although vigorous domestic critics have sought to revive a theoretical debate, they generally accept the basic welfare state and focus their attack on what are considered the excesses of recent years.

Two concepts characterize Scandinavian social democracy: equality and solidarity. Both descend, of course, from the Enlightenment, and particularly from the slogan of the French Revolution: Liberty, equality, fraternity. During the nineteenth and early-twentieth centuries, equality was primarily a political issue in the struggle for universal suffrage. After the attainment of basically equal political rights, a new debate arose about economic and social rights. The principles of equality were extended into the economic and social spheres, implying equality of opportunity as well as greater equality of result (Heckscher 1984, p. 5; Myrdal 1971, pp. 14–19). The decline of economic liberalism, with its emphasis on laissez faire, and the experience of Bismarckian Germany strengthened support on the right for social policies more appropriate for an urbanizing industrial society (Kuhnle 1981a; Baldwin 1990, ch. 1).

Solidarity also became important in the struggle to guarantee industrial and rural workers and their families a minimum standard of living and security. It drew upon collectivist traditions stretching back to the guild system, as well as on the role of the church as an instrument of charity and social relief; today it is particularly enshrined as a value by the labor movement. It, too, emphasized equality of result.

The degree of equality of results is typically measured through surveys of social conditions. In response to complaints in the late 1960s that excessive reliance on raw economic statistics failed to measure the quality of life, statistical agencies in many Western countries began to compile "social accounts" and to compare those accounts between nations and among groups within nations. Current level-of-living surveys reveal that Scandinavian living standards are among the highest and poverty rates among the lowest in the world. Although inequalities among citizens in Scandinavia are less than those in most other countries, they remain substantial. As a result, there is genuine concern that prolonged high unemployment (as in Denmark and more recently Sweden and Finland) could widen the gaps and undo several decades of progress toward social equality.

Conservative critics do not deny the existence of these social differences. They suggest, however, that policies emphasizing equality of results extract increasing costs in political liberty and economic efficiency—problems unlikely to be revealed by social indicators alone. Redistributive policies enjoy greatest support when rapid economic growth makes the costs relatively less burdensome. In periods of lower growth or stagnation, however, implicitly contradictory priorities come into overt conflict (Lindbeck et al. 1994, pp. 1–21).

Economic Democracy

Economic democracy is the least clearly defined and the most vigorously contested aspect of the Scandinavian democratic model. It includes three elements: microdemocracy at the plant level (often termed *industrial democracy*), macrodemocracy in making national economic policy, and a share in the ownership of capital for employees as employees.

Early proponents of democracy, such as America's Thomas Jefferson and Denmark's N. S. F. Grundtvig, understood that economic oligarchy could not easily coexist with political democracy. Recent Western political discourse has been distorted by the compartmentalization of economic and political issues bequeathed by nineteenth-century liberalism. However, that false dichotomy is dissolving today. Charles Lindblom (1977, esp. pp. 161–69) has suggested a strong, or even absolute, connection between the existence of relatively free markets for the production and distribution of goods and services and political democracy. Carole Pateman (1970) and, more recently, Robert Dahl (1985) and Robert Lane (1985) have emphasized the importance of economic and workplace democracy in achieving the ideals of political democracy. In Scandinavia, the concern was that the concentration of economic power would undermine political democracy. The systematic Norwegian "Power Investigation" of the 1970s, for instance, devoted about a third of its final report to domestic concentrations of economic power and transnational projections of economic power into Norwegian society, primarily through multinational business enterprises (see Norway 1982).

The origins of economic democracy as a social and political issue may be traced to the early experience of self-management in the worker cooperatives, which, in the nineteenth-century labor movement, were considered to be the new society in the womb of the old. Scandinavian consumer and insurance cooperatives played an even more active role in democratizing the economy and organizing its weaker elements. The strength of the cooperative movements in Scandinavia attracted considerable outside attention in the 1930s as a "middle way" between predatory, monopolistic capitalism and authoritarian, state socialism (Childs 1936). Recent studies provide a more balanced perspective on the economic importance of cooperatives. However, their political importance in teaching democratic values and procedures at the local level and in organizing the economically weak ought not to be dismissed (Heckscher 1984, p. 111; Scott 1975, pp. 114–22).

The economic democracy debate peaked in the 1970s and 1980s as major reforms opened the firm to employee participation from the shop floor to the boardroom. The impetus came from those within the Social Democratic and Labor parties who were not content to accept the welfare state as the culmination of the democratic struggle. They rejected the radical Left's infatuation with state control through nationalization and were dissatisfied with limiting workers' participation to collective bargaining. Advocates of economic democracy reopened the question of greater equality of economic power without offering the old socialist panacea: another state agency only indirectly accountable to popular control.

Although considerable economic democratization occurred at the level of the firm and has become the accepted way of conducting business, the push for macroeconomic democracy through wage-earner funds (see Chapter 10 for details) foundered in the 1980s. The Swedish Social Democrats enacted a very modest version after they returned to power in 1982, but the next nonsocialist government promptly abolished it. The control of capital remains an interesting subject for discussion, but the contemporary economic-democracy debate today no longer focuses on issues such as direct political control of the economy or even employee ownership and influence. Reviving market forces to generate economic growth, new jobs, and regional development are seen by most as critical for the survival of the welfare state. Privatization of state enterprises (limited as they have been), strengthening competition in both the public and private economic sectors and coping with globalization frame the current debates.

In Scandinavia, both microeconomic participation and macroeconomic policy coordination focus upon corporatism. Economic issues are the domain not only of political parties and civil servants, but also of labor unions, professional associations, employer associations, and farmers' groups. Economic democracy not only encompasses the substantive interests of these large groups (nearly every Scandinavian employee or producer is likely to belong to such an organization), but also involves their internal organizational democracy. Not surprisingly, the new emphasis on markets, competition and particularly international forces challenges corporatism, but Scandinavians are not ready to abandon economic security and social democracy merely to accommodate the latest ideological fads.

The struggle between efficiency and democracy is an ongoing issue with deep historical roots.

SCANDINAVIAN DEMOCRACY IN THE GLOBAL SOCIETY

Globalization has changed the context for Scandinavian democracy. The influx of immigrants and refugees, both political and economic, has altered the domestic discussion of rights. For the first time in decades, civil rights are again a matter of discussion. Opening citizenship to the foreign born has been an issue as has granting voting rights to foreign citizens who are Scandinavian residents. The compromise has been to give other countries' citizens the right to vote in local, but not national, elections. Citizens of other Scandinavian countries have voting rights in local elections in the community in which they reside in all five countries; citizens of non-Scandinavian nations have the right to vote locally in Denmark, Finland, Norway, and Sweden (Petersson 1994, p. 18).

Democratization of the Baltic republics, in which the Scandinavian states have been directly involved, has provided an outlet for Scandinavian sociopolitical evangelism. In previous years Scandinavian economic, social, and political development aid had been focused on Africa and Southeast Asia, not very fruitful soil for democratic seed. In the Baltic republics, by contrast, the Scandinavia model has had substantial appeal. There is also support for the new democracies of Central and Eastern Europe.

In the European Union, the Danes and, in recent years, Finns and Swedes as well have pushed for greater openness and greater citizen access. They have been among the foremost critics of the EU's so-called democratic deficit. At the time of the Maastricht treaty referendum in Denmark in 1992, one disgruntled Social Democratic proponent of the European Union remarked in an unguarded moment that "the EC [European Community] administrative ideal is essentially identical to that of Louis XIV" (Logue 1992, p. 638). A sign of the difficulty in grappling with this issue is the fact that the European Union's own language for this subject is a bit convoluted. EU policy makers and civil servants espouse the principle of *subsidiarity*, which, translated into common English, sensibly calls for having decisions made at lower levels (i.e., that of the nation-state) where possible. Other EU buzzwords, like *harmonization* (of regulations) and *convergence* (of economic policies), seem doctrinaire and intrusive on national democratic prerogatives.[3]

Democracy is to Western politics what the great medieval cathedrals were to Western religion. Like those great edifices, the construction and preservation of democracy is a perpetual task. Democracy requires both great vision and attention to detail. Scandinavian democracy followed this pattern: an ambitious project requiring decades of careful construction. Despite its late advent in Scandinavia, political democracy has sunk its roots deep, and a participatory political culture has grown up alongside democratic institutions. Consequently, the democratic impulse has come to touch every social and economic issue. Thus, all collective concerns become political, and the debate on democracy renews itself. The dissatisfaction that Scandinavians habitually express toward the status quo can best be described as creative discontent.

NOTES

1. Contrast, for example, the authoritative volume *Nordisk Demokrati*, edited by Koch and Ross (1949), with *Nordic Democracy*, a survey of the same topic, edited by Allardt et al. (1981). The former volume, which was written in the Scandinavian languages primarily for a domestic audience, emphasizes the legal, ideological, and historical development and characteristics of democracy. The latter collection covers such topics only briefly, while devoting substantial attention to Scandinavian public policy. Each is indicative of its time. The 1949 volume reflects the decade's intense ideological atmosphere. Democracy required defense in the wake of the recently defeated fascist threat and the surge of communist support at the end of the war. By contrast, the 1981 study is an academic compendium. It is not a struggle for the soul; its focus is on effectiveness, not legitimacy. Another comprehensive survey is Lauwerys (1958).

2. For a thoughtful, early consideration of political poverty, see Dahl Jacobsen (1967, pp. 6–10). Such concerns also spurred ambitious interdisciplinary studies of political power and democratic values in each of the Nordic countries. The first and most extensive of these was the Norwegian Power Investigation *(Maktutredningen)* (see Norway 1982), which investigated the content and distribution of political power in Norway between 1973 and 1982. Danish studies were coordinated by the Institute for Political Science at Århus University (summarized in Damgaard et al. 1984) and by the Danish Low Income Commission (1976–81) (see Denmark 1982, pp. 113–21, and Valentin 1980). A Swedish Royal Commission was established in 1985 with the mandate to investigate the distribution of power and democracy; its final report appeared in several volume starting in 1987 (Petersson 1987 and later). A second round of studies followed in Denmark (Madsen, Nielsen, and Sjöblom 1995), Norway (Østerud 1999), and Sweden (Petersson 1998) in the 1990s. Finland's constitutional reform in the 1990s engendered similar studies and debates.

3. Prior to the 1992 Danish referendum required for acceptance of the Maastricht Treaty on European Union, the Danish government mailed hundreds of thousands of complete copies of the lengthy and complex text to households. The effort seems to have strengthened opposition. In the words of then Minister of Justice Hans Engell, "People thought they would learn by reading it, but instead they got a text that even some in Parliament had trouble understanding" (*Politiken*, June 7, 1992, cited in Logue 1992, p. 638).

CHAPTER 4

Institutions of Democracy

> Political democracy is . . . regarded as self-evident to such a degree that it is no longer debated or even analyzed.
> —Gunnar Heckscher, *The Welfare State and Beyond* (1984)

Early in the struggle for political liberty, Scandinavian reformers confronted a classical democratic dilemma: Large polities preclude inclusive citizen assemblies. How, then, should democracy be structured? Nineteenth-century Scandinavian democrats chose to channel citizen participation through representative institutions; it has only been in the twentieth century, particularly since World War II, that the idea of direct democracy through referenda has gained much support. The nineteenth-century democratic debate in Scandinavia drew on the writings of John Stuart Mill—particularly *Representative Government*—which harmonized well with the ancient Scandinavian tradition of representative government. That tradition stretches back to ancient and medieval assemblies (*thing*) (Scott 1975, p. 42–43). The new challenge was to add democratic content to these representative traditions and, in Sweden, institutions.

How well the Scandinavian countries conform to modern democratic standards in choosing, influencing, and dismissing their rulers is the subject of this and the chapter that follows. This chapter focuses on the nuts and bolts of political democracy: those political rules and institutions that form the context for democratic political competition and policy making.[1]

THE DIVISION OF POWER

In most countries there is a distinction between how power is allocated by the constitutions and how it is actually exercised. Denmark, Norway, and Sweden are not exceptions to this rule. Although national governments are formally divided into the three branches—executive, legislative, and judicial—the divisions of power between them is anything but equal. In common with most parliamentary systems, executive and legislative powers in modern Scandinavia are not clearly separated. Ministers are usually members of parliament, although this is not an absolute requirement. In Norway, cabinet ministers with parliamentary seats yield them to deputy members from their party while serving as ministers.

Courts are completely independent of electoral politics, and all judges are permanent civil servants appointed on the basis of their qualifications. Similarly, at the subnational level, elected municipal and county councils select the executive leadership, but in all but the largest cities, day-to-day administration is in the hands of professional civil servants.

By North American standards, power in Scandinavian governments is in theory extraordinarily concentrated. All are unitary rather than federal states. The national government is supreme, and subordinate governmental units have no claim to sovereign power. The boundaries and powers of subnational governmental units can be made and remade by the national government, and precisely that has happened in the past twenty years. Central government supremacy derives from the predemocratic royalist tradition. However, this constitutional norm has regularly been relaxed, as it was when autonomous status was granted to Norway (1814–1905) under Swedish rule, and Iceland (1918–44) under Danish rule, and the Swedish-speaking Åland Islands under Finnish rule after World War I. The Faeroe Islands and Greenland, which were governed as Danish counties until 1948 and 1979, respectively, enjoy similar autonomy today.

Despite the supremacy of the national government (i.e., the "state"), power is distributed vertically and horizontally to municipal and county governments as well as to special agencies that perform specific functional tasks separate from regional and local governments (transportation and public health are common examples). As the scope of government and the size of the public sector have expanded rapidly in the last quarter century, the national government has delegated increasing administrative authority to these local governments. Today they are the principal providers of most social services.

The powers shared by these several governmental levels are important means of encouraging political participation and accountability. Too much power in the hands of the national government, even in pursuit of legal equality and administrative efficiency, will inevitably be accompanied by complaints over excessive centralization and domination by a distant national government. On the other hand, too much leeway granted local political authorities in the name of home rule may engender complaints of neglect, inefficiency, and inequality. The past decade has seen increased experimentation with autonomy and innovations by local and regional governments. Danish, Swedish, and Finnish membership in the European Union has cumulatively added a fourth level of political authority with growing impact.

Just as power is concentrated in the national government, formal authority is concentrated in the legislative branch. The checks and balances Americans expect between executive, legislative, and judicial branches are absent. Once again, this may be explained by the history of democratic advance against royal prerogatives. The nineteenth-century struggle for constitutional government sought to restrain the executive by forcing a constitution on the monarch. That occurred in 1809 in Sweden, 1814 in Norway, and 1849 in Denmark. Initially, the parliaments created by or strengthened under those constitutions shared power with the royal executive.

However, as the struggle for greater democracy intensified in the second half of the nineteenth century, the issue became a struggle between parliament and king over ministerial responsibility; that is, over who hired and who fired the prime minister and cabinet ministers. Under the nineteenth-century constitutions, the king's executive power was still exercised directly through his ministers. The struggle between king and parliament focused on making the prime minister (and thus the executive cabinet) responsible to a parliamentary majority instead. Parliamentary supremacy was established in Norway in 1884, Denmark in 1901, and Sweden in 1917.

Royal power in Scandinavia had previously been checked by political realities dating back to the Magna Carta (*Håndfæstning*) forced upon the Danish King Erik Ploughpenny in 1284. Denmark's two centuries of royal absolutism (1660–1849) rested upon urban support and a civil service drawn from the petty nobility. Swedish kings never dispensed with the national parliament (*Riksdag*) after its creation in 1435, and it played a decisive role in the eighteenth century.

Under this system, courts administered the royal laws and were subordinate to—rather than a check on—the royal executive. With the establishment of more modern forms of government, an independent judiciary arose, but not judicial review. Only in Norway, where the principles of Montesquieu and the precedent of the American constitution had some influence on the charter drafted in 1814 for a newly, if temporarily, independent state, is there a lengthy tradition of judicial review. The judiciary in Scandinavia is not so much a check on the other branches as a guarantor of due process and constitutional procedures. Specific institutions, such as the ombudsmen and administrative tribunals, monitor the actual performance of executive agencies.

These historical developments have concentrated political power in parliament, which is constitutionally supreme. In practice, matters are not so simple. Legislation originates with the executive (the "government"), but is strongly influenced by the parliamentary process and the political parties, which are discussed in detail in the next chapter.

Although, in constitutional theory, the monarch in Denmark and Norway retains some residual executive power, in practice that power exists only so long as the monarch makes no effort to exercise it. The Icelandic president has limited powers as a guardian of constitutionality and as an occasional deterrent of excessive partisanship. The Finnish president has since 1919 been a genuine political actor, especially in foreign relations. Over the past decade, however, Finnish presidents have played a more limited role. Real executive power lies with the government or cabinet headed by the chief executive: the prime minister, literally in the Scandinavian languages, the Minister of State (*Statsminister*). The cabinet governs collectively; that is, decisions are made on behalf of the entire government. The power of the prime minister depends upon the parliamentary strength and political composition of the government. Even though the prime minister is the leader and symbol of the government, in Scandinavia, perhaps in large measure because of the multiparty system, the post has accumulated few of the "presidential" attributes seen in several other modern parliamentary systems (see Lijphart 1984, ch. 5). Sweden was a partial exception in that only three men (a fourth for three months in 1936) served as prime minister between 1932 and 1976. Long tenure inevitably gives officeholders additional informal powers: Experience is always a political asset. Ironically in the last quarter of the twentieth century Swedish and Norwegian prime ministers have been changed regularly, while Denmark became the country of continuity with only three prime ministers between 1975 and 2000.

Politicians in executive office rely upon the civil service to carry out policies and to provide information on how well the policies succeed. The existence of a professional civil service in Scandinavia long predates democracy, dating at least to the seventeenth century in Sweden. Its traditions are one of the major sources of Scandinavian political culture. How the bureaucracy functions, the relationship between career civil servants and cabinet ministers, and their ties to political parties and interest groups are crucial questions for a modern parliamentary democracy. We discuss these questions later in this chapter.

CONSTITUTIONS

Despite a long tradition of relying upon written law, the Scandinavian constitutions have quite different historical roots. Common to them all is a lengthy period of development and regular constitutional tinkering. Norway has the oldest written constitution in Europe currently in force. It dates from 1814 but has, of course, been significantly amended. Finland's constitution of 1919 established it as a republic, and Iceland modified its home rule constitution of 1918 to replace the Danish king with a republican form of government at independence in 1944. Sweden's current constitutional laws, which continue the tradition of dividing the constitution into several basic laws, came into force in 1975. Denmark's constitution dates from 1953, but, like Sweden's, builds upon its predecessors.[2] These documents are moderately detailed, but each leaves substantial leeway to parliamentary interpretation. As the most recently revised, Sweden's and Finland's constitutions are closest to current practice. In the other Scandinavian countries, a greater role is played by the "unwritten constitution."

The Norwegian Constitution

Born amid the turmoil of the Napoleonic Wars, the Norwegian constitution is Europe's oldest; gradually it has evolved into a modern instrument of government. Norwegians are more emotionally attached to their constitution than any other European people. Its creation marks the rebirth of the modern Norwegian nation. Eidsvoll, the town where it was written, is a Norwegian historical shrine. The date of its promulgation, May 17, 1814, is celebrated as a national holiday. Even modern amendments are carefully written in the archaic language of 1814. Although greatly amended since its adoption, it reflects the spirit of the French Revolution—quite an achievement in the year 1814. Its formal structure has changed little.

Reflecting American and French influences, the Eidsvoll constitution divides government into three branches: the executive, personified by the king; the legislative or parliament; and the judicial, where considerable detail attaches to the Constitution Court of the Realm or court of impeachment (*Riksrett*), while in more concise terms provision is made for the Supreme Court. No specific Bill of Rights was included, but in the final section, along with provisions for constitutional amendment, several basic civil rights are enumerated. A Norwegian scholar has noted ironically the lack of philosophical passion in the restrained legal text composed by sober jurists (Andenæs 1949, p. 71).

The Norwegian constitution, surely among the most liberal existing in 1814, has served in all seasons. The Eidsvoll document has survived the following events: an abortive attempt to become an independent kingdom (1814), the tensions of union with Sweden (1814–1905), the debate over establishing a republic just after independence in 1905, and, more recently, the improvisation of a government-in-exile (including the king) during

the German occupation of World War II (1940–45). The transition of the
Norwegian polity from a "civil servants' state" (*embetsmensstat*) to a parliamentary democracy occurred without significant structural changes in
the written constitution. Voting requirements found in article 50 have, of
course, been greatly changed. Initially only 7.5 percent of the adult population could vote; today the suffrage is universal. In addition, several provisions of the constitution, such as the right of the king to delay legislation
(article 79), are no longer valid following the establishment of parliamentary supremacy. The battle over this principle was decided in the dramatic
events of 1884, when the king (then the Swedish King Oscar II) peacefully
yielded his powers of veto. The constitution is silent on the actual mechanism of parliamentary party government, which has been the norm for
nearly a century.

There are two unusual provisions that survive in the Norwegian constitution. The first is the provision that each Storting, or Parliament, will
sit for a fixed period of four years (article 71). Hence, parliamentary elections occur at predictable intervals and the government of the day cannot
resort to a sudden election. Intended to protect the independence of parliament, this provision could result in prolonged political deadlock. In
practice, however, Norwegians have either found an alternative governing majority or carried on a consensual government. Norwegian politicians are thus forced to cooperate.

The other Norwegian idiosyncrasy is the modification of unicameralism
(single-chambered legislature). The Storting is elected as a whole, but does
most of its legislative business as two chambers. Three-quarters of the
members sit in the Odelsting and the remainder sit in the Lagting. On
some issues, such as budgets and votes of confidence, the parliament may
reassemble as a whole, while on others separate sessions are prescribed
(article 73). This form is the result of the historical experience of parliamentary assemblies as of 1814. Two-chambered assemblies (bicameral)
were the rule, but they were usually based either on significant class divisions (e.g., the British parliament) or geographically distinct entities
(e.g., the American senate). Lacking either of these, the Norwegian constitutional fathers designed a hybrid (Storing 1963, pp. 77–83).

The Danish Constitution

In contrast to the continuity and historical prestige of the Norwegian
constitution, behind the Danish constitution of 1953 is a history of controversy and tumult. Denmark made an enormous and sudden political leap
in 1848–49 from absolute, if unusually enlightened, royal despotism to
genuine political liberalism when the king, aware of the revolutions
sweeping Europe, accepted the principle of constitutional government.
The June 1849 constitution was complicated by the presence of the duchies

of Schleswig and Holstein in the Danish realm. Schleswig was partially and Holstein almost entirely German-speaking, and Danish liberalism could not overcome German nationalism or political machinations. Two wars with the German powers followed, and in 1864 Denmark became the first victim of the modernized Prussian army. Both duchies were lost and so was much of liberalism's political credibility. In 1866 amendments restricted suffrage to the upper chamber (Landsting) and permitted the king to appoint twelve of its sixty-six members. This turned the upper chamber into the political bastion of wealth and privilege.

The 1866 constitutional changes initiated a thirty-year struggle (1872–1901) between the king and upper chamber on one hand and the popularly elected lower chamber on the other. The struggle finally concluded with royal acceptance of parliamentary supremacy in 1901 when a government based on a majority in the lower chamber was appointed. The 1915 constitution confirmed the system change of 1901 and recognized parliamentary supremacy.

Many progressive Danes felt that the 1915 constitution left too much power with the more restrictively elected upper chamber. The reformist coalition of Social Democrats and Radical Liberals formed in 1929 found some of their legislation stymied by the Landsting. Agitation for reform continued even after the coalition won a majority in the upper house. In 1939, a proposed new constitution removing the remaining restrictions on electing the upper house failed by a very narrow margin to receive the qualified majority in the national referendum required for constitutional change. Parliamentary democracy itself was not directly an issue, but some Conservatives and especially some agrarian Liberals (whose electoral base was declining) still felt that there ought to be an effective check on the possibility of legislative excesses by popular majorities.

After World War II, these issues seemed trivial and constitutional reform recommenced. Following the exhaustive work of a multiparty constitutional commission, the current constitution was proposed by a right-of-center government. Parliamentary support was broad, and this time there was sufficient support in the referendum. Although there was opposition on the far right, the main fear prior to the referendum was apathy because, practically speaking, nonvoting constituted opposition. The government cleverly scheduled simultaneously a referendum on a change in the Law of Royal Succession. The new law would allow the crown to pass to either male or female heirs (King Frederik IX had only daughters). This change was popular and probably helped to draw out otherwise apathetic voters. Even in the democratic age, some citizens may be stirred more by a matter affecting the monarchy than by constitutional reform.

The new constitution was proclaimed in 1953 on the traditional Constitution Day, June 5. Many of its changes were to bring the constitution's text in line with the political practice of the preceding thirty years. This is evident in Part III of the constitution where ministerial responsibility and parliamentary confidence are clearly specified (sections 13 and 15). The upper chamber was abolished (Part IV), but new and extended provisions for national referenda act as a check on the unicameral parliament (Folketinget).

As discussed further below, obligatory referenda have been expanded to include not only constitutional amendments, but also changes in the voting age (section 29), and any moves to cede sovereignty to international organizations, such as the European Union (section 20). Although there is no right of initiative (i.e., legislation directly by referenda), section 42 provides for referenda on any nonfinancial bill when demanded by one-third of the members of parliament. In practice, such referenda have been rare. Frequent parliamentary elections have been Denmark's preferred way of assuring that the government enjoys public support. Ironically, the referendum is now perceived as an inherently conservative instrument, far more so than the upper chamber that it replaced; it is a check on parliamentary majorities.

Part VIII comprises a bill of rights similar in spirit to the preceding constitution, but made more explicit in the wake of the German occupation during World War II. Protection of property rights from expropriation, again by means of referendum safeguards (section 73, subsection 2), reflects a fear of state takeovers of business that was strong among the nonsocialist parties just after the war. Except in the matter of the land-use laws (1963) and petroleum concessions (1970s), this has not been a significant issue in the past forty years. The disappearance of constitutional issues (except indirectly in connection with European Community membership) from the Danish political agenda since 1953 ends Denmark's century of preoccupation with constitutional questions.

The Icelandic Constitution

Modern Iceland's constitutional history began when Danish King Christian VIII revived the Althing as a consultative assembly in 1843. Absolutism ended in Iceland as in the rest of the Danish realm when the new King Frederik VII peacefully conceded constitutional rule in the wake of several European revolutions in 1848. This assembly revived the name Althing, which had graced the annual islandwide citizens' meeting that had provided Iceland's government prior to the union with Norway in 1262 and had continued to have some legislative significance until the establishment of Danish absolutism in 1662. Tracing its origins to 930, the Althing thus has claim to the title of oldest legislative assembly in the world.

In the century that followed its reestablishment, the Althing became the focal point for the Icelandic struggle for national self-determination. The country acquired limited rights to home rule in its constitution of 1874—the thousandth anniversary of Icelandic settlement, albeit with a bicameral Althing in which the Danish king appointed the upper house, a minister for Iceland and retained the right to veto legislation. More extensive rights of self-determination were granted in 1903, after parliamentary supremacy was established in Denmark. The upper house was also made more representative, the home-rule cabinet made responsible to the Althing, and the minister for Iceland was required to reside on the island. The Danish–Icelandic Act of Union of 1918 provided virtually complete home rule except in foreign affairs under a personal union in which Iceland and Denmark shared the same king. It also permitted either party to request a revision in the treaty after 1940.

The German invasion of Denmark in April 1940 led the Althing to dissolve the personal union on an emergency basis, creating de facto independence. Complete independence followed in 1944 under the terms of the Act of Union, after a referendum in which 99 percent voted for independence. Iceland became a republic. The president, directly elected for a four year period, plays a purely symbolic role although, reflecting earlier powers of the Danish monarchy, the president retains the constitutional right to refuse to sign legislation, forcing it to a popular referendum; this power has remained unused. The country has a unicameral parliament of sixty-three, elected by proportional representation with supplemental seats every fourth year. It functions as a typical parliamentary democracy with the anomaly that prior to the 1991 constitutional revisions, like the Norwegian Storting, the unicameral Althing divided itself into two chambers to consider certain legislation (for additional details see Karlsson 2000, pp. 195–223).

The Finnish Constitution

Finland's constitutional history is peculiar by almost any standards. Although Finland was annexed to the Russian Empire in 1809, the Russians continued to govern Finland under the joint Swedish-Finnish constitution of 1772 and Act of Union and Security of 1789. Thus, ironically, the Czar as "autocrat of all Russia" ruled in Finland as a constitutional monarch, albeit on the basis of a very conservative document. It provided for an Estates General—the *Lantdag*—with four estates (peasants, clergy, middle class, and nobility), with consultative rather than legislative powers. Consultation was not prioritized: After receiving the allegiance of the Lantdag in 1809, Russian czars did not call it back into session again until 1863. The Czar ruled through a Governor General who came to be increasingly at odds with the Estates General in the latter part of the nineteenth century. A modern, unicameral legislative body, the *Eduskunta*

(*Riksdag*), was not established until after a general strike extracted legislative reform in the revolutionary year of 1905.

The post–civil war Finnish constitution of 1919 established a republic. It also created a mixed parliamentary-presidential system of government. It continued the unicameral parliament, elected by universal suffrage and through proportional representation established after 1905. The prime minister and cabinet were appointed by the president but responsible to parliament, which could vote them out of office. The president was elected by an absolute majority of an American-style electoral college for a six-year term until the electoral college was abandoned. Since 1994, Finland's president has been directly elected.

Finland's president shared substantial executive responsibility with the prime minister. The division of power was, in theory, rather like that in France in the Fifth Republic since 1958: The president had primary responsibility for foreign policy as well as, in the Finnish case, a suspensive veto on legislation. Given the exceptional importance of Finland's relations with the Soviet Union throughout the Cold War, the president's foreign policy role often was key.

Presidential powers expanded in practice during Urho Kekkonen's extraordinary presidency from 1956 to 1982. Kekkonen governed with divided parliament and a succession of twenty-one governments. Constitutional revisions under his successor Mauno Koivisto restricted this "imperial presidency." The new Finnish constitution of 2000 further strengthened the powers of parliament vis-à-vis the presidency, making Finland more clearly a parliamentary democracy, although it continues to accord the president both the suspensive veto (which can be overridden by a simple parliamentary majority) and a special role in foreign policy. It places European Union affairs firmly in the hands of parliament and the prime minister.

The new Finnish constitution, following the Swedish and Danish practice of periodically updating the constitution to codify new rights, also provides extensive citizen rights to education, training, social security, health and medical services, and employment. It also requires the government to encourage political participation, protect minority cultural and linguistic rights, to promote full employment, and to ensure a healthy environment. Even biodiversity receives constitutional recognition.

The Swedish Constitution

The Swedish constitution has evolved over a longer period than either the Danish or Norwegian constitutions, although its current version was adopted in the 1970s after years of consideration and debate. Its predecessor—and Sweden's first modern constitution—was the constitution of 1809. It was drafted after the Swedish army deposed Gustav IV, following the disastrous war against Russia that cost Sweden Finland. Those original constitutional documents were sufficiently flexible to accommodate both the early kings of the Bernadotte line, who ruled as well as reigned, and the transition to parliamentary democracy. After the establishment of parliamentary supremacy in 1917 and equal suffrage for both houses of parliament in 1918, there was a recurring desire to modernize the letter as well as the spirit of the laws. Systematic reform proposals started in earnest in the 1950s, and by the late 1960s a consensus emerged.

The current constitution, like its predecessor, consists of four basic laws. The most important is the Instrument of Government (*Regeringsformen—RF*), which defines the institutions and enumerates their powers. The new RF, which entered into force in 1975, was the most changed element. The Act of Succession (*Successionsordning*) defines the line of inheritance for the throne. In 1979, Sweden followed Denmark's example of allowing females to succeed to the throne. The Press Freedom Act (*Tryckfrihetsförordningen—TFO*) of 1949 also has constitutional status; its origin lies in the law of 1765, which was the world's oldest legal provision for a free press. Finally, there is the Parliamentary Act of 1974 (*Riksdagsordningen*), which deals mainly with the organization of parliament. Parliamentary reorganization occurred in 1967–68 when the upper chamber was abolished and the lower chamber expanded to 350 members (effective from the 1970 election). Because the terms of the chambers had been staggered and the indirectly elected upper house had had an absolute Social Democratic majority since 1945, this reform made the composition of government more sensitive to voter preferences on a single election day. No sooner had this been done than the 1973 elections produced an even division between the government and the opposition. The number of seats was subsequently reduced to 349.

Such tinkering is perhaps in part the result of a long and secure constitutional tradition. Amendment of the constitution requires action by two successive parliaments (i.e., a general election intervenes). In 1979 another safeguard was added: One-third of the members of parliament may request a national referendum on a proposed amendment. In 1994 the normal electoral period was extended to four years.

The constitution is comprehensive in its guarantees of individual liberties and due process. Chapter 1 of the RF explicitly extends those guarantees to the social and economic spheres: "The personal, economic and cultural welfare of the individual shall be fundamental aims of the activities of the community. In particular, it shall be incumbent upon the community to secure the right to work, to housing and to education, and to promote social care and security, as well as a favorable living environment." This "general welfare clause" legitimizes the Swedish social legislation of the past half century. Such language emphasizes a positive dimension to human rights as well as the protection of civil liberties expected of a liberal constitution. These provisions are strengthened in the TFO, which guarantees Sweden's policy of public access to all governmental documents except those of a personal nature or vital to national security.

Scandinavia's tradition of "rule by law" is reflected in the importance attached to constitutions. In Norway, Denmark, and Finland, the birth of the constitution is considered to be the birth of the modern state. All seek a balance between tradition and modernity, and between individual and collective rights. New challenges have appeared: Accommodating European integration (mainly in Denmark, Finland and Sweden, but also in Norway and Iceland as a consequence of its accession to the looser European Economic Area arrangements) will change political and legal procedures.

REPRESENTATION AND LEGISLATION

Proportional Representation

Scandinavians elect their representatives from among the slates offered by six or more political parties. Although the British model of single-member constituencies (one representative for each geographic district) was used during the first phase of parliamentary development, proportional representation (PR) was adopted between 1909 and 1921. Although PR had historically been one of the aims of the Left (liberals and socialists), it was in fact introduced principally to protect the representation of traditional conservatives in parliament. This concession made the conservatives more amenable to universal suffrage and parliamentary supremacy. Thus, it became part of the democratic settlement less because it was inherently democratic (although it was) than because it fit the tactical need of the moment. Once in place, however, it has ensured representation for all minorities that lacked the geographic concentration necessary to win seats in a single-member district system.

Proportional representation raises some interesting questions for democratic government. The exceptionally close geographic ties between electors and their representative found in the United States and, to a lesser extent, in France, are absent in Scandinavia. Although most parties seek regional balance on their slates, Scandinavians are mainly concerned with the representation of interests. Deputies represent different economic and social groups more than geographic and administrative districts. Under PR all significant groups are likely to be represented in parliament, but it is difficult for a single party to achieve an absolute majority. Therefore, one cannot say, as in Britain, that the electors directly choose their government. After each election a workable majority must be pieced together. In the past quarter century, government in all five countries has been through formal or informal coalition.

Each Scandinavian country has different if complex electoral rules that require some description because of their continuing political importance (see Petersson 1994, pp. 53–58). The Norwegian system has deviated most from full proportionality because it had a relatively large number of small constituencies. Until recently there were no "supplementary seats" to help small parties with modest but geographically diffuse voter support win representation; in 1989 a limited number (eight) were added to reduce the overrepresentation of large parties. Rural districts have tended to be slightly overrepresented despite periodic technical adjustments (see Carstairs 1980, pp. 95–97). The Icelandic system also overrepresents rural areas, but thirteen supplemental seats ensure proportionality among parties. Alone among the Nordic countries, Finland lacks supplemental seats, but a smaller number of larger constituencies provides substantial proportionality.

In Denmark and Sweden, the electoral outcome is much closer to mathematical proportionality because a significant number of supplementary seats are used to redress the underrepresentation of smaller parties in the constituency seats. In Denmark, 135 seats are filled in multimember constituencies and forty come from the supplementary lists. Two additional seats are reserved for each of the self-governing territories (Greenland and the Faeroe Islands). In Sweden, an analogous system elects 310 members from multimember districts and thirty-nine from the supplementary lists. To prevent very small parties from sharing the supplementary seats, both countries have established minimum barriers. In Denmark, normally a party must either win a constituency seat or 2 percent of the national vote in order to gain representation. In Sweden, the barrier is a more formidable 4 percent of the national vote. Several parties hover around these thresholds.

The effect of an electoral system on the process of representation illustrates the complexity of democratic politics, and the electoral system has a direct effect on the number and nature of political parties. The issues are both philosophical (how does one make government most representative?) and practical (how does one make representative government effective?).

One consequence of proportional representation is the rarity of single-party parliamentary majorities. In Finland, Denmark and Iceland single-party majorities are unknown. In Sweden, the last single-party majority was in 1968–70; in Norway, 1957–61. Coalition and minority governments are the norm. This does not necessarily imply fundamental political instability. Between the end of World War II in 1945 and 2000, the average life of the government was twenty-one months in Finland (including caretaker governments) and thirty-three months in Denmark and Iceland. It was forty-four months in Norway and sixty-six months in Sweden. Given this variation, as well as that of other PR countries, the electoral system

cannot be considered in isolation. Norwegian political stability is reinforced by the constitutional provision that parliament may not be dissolved before the end of its four-year life. In Sweden, dissolution is
allowed and extra elections may be called, but ordinary elections have to
be held every fourth year on schedule. Consequently, although there have
been governmental resignations, there have been no early parliamentary
elections since the new constitution commenced operation in 1970.

Despite their complexities, electoral rules in the five countries have long
ceased to be a political issue. Scandinavians accept the multiparty outcome of elections, even when extremely fragmented as in Denmark or
Norway in 1973, as reflecting the legitimate representation of all shades
of political opinion. The conventional view of the electoral history of the
interwar years—that allowing small extremist groups into parliament permitted them to subvert constitutional government as in the case of Weimar
Germany—is not accepted in Scandinavia. Subjecting protest movements
to careful public scrutiny during electoral campaigns has inoculated the
body politic against serious authoritarian infections. Better that the energies of dissident groups be directed toward electoral or even parliamentary activities than subversive or violent actions. The extraordinary
pluralism of partisan opinion in the Scandinavian parliaments is regarded
primarily as the healthy expression of political pluralism in society at
large, not as a barrier to effective government.

This is because the Scandinavian countries fit the so-called consensual
model of representative democracy, which aims at restraining majority
rule (see Logue and Einhorn 1988). Recall that in the older British, or
Westminster, tradition, voters choose between two alternative teams, each
of which claims to offer voters a clear choice. In the Westminster model,
the majority rules with relatively few restraints so long as its majority
remains secure. Even large minorities are excluded from any direct-
governing role until they become a majority by winning an election. Coalitions and compromises occur *within* parties prior to elections.

In contrast, consensual democracies disperse and constrain power. Indeed, the laws make electoral majorities rare and tentative. Under favorable conditions, consensual democracy requires that important policies
enjoy broad support across the political spectrum for enactment (Elder,
Thomas, and Arter 1982, pp. 9–16). PR assures that parliamentary majorities will normally require the participation of more than a single political
party.

The Parliaments

Parliament is the focus of Scandinavian politics. Each of the five countries today has a unicameral parliament, although, as mentioned, the 165-
member Norwegian Storting handles much of its business in two

divisions. The sixty-three-member Icelandic Althing did the same prior to a 1991 constitutional amendment that made it purely unicameral. The Danish Folketing has 179 members, four of whom are from the autonomous territories of Greenland and the Faeroe Islands. The Finnish Eduskunta has 200 members. The Swedish Riksdag is by far the largest with 349 members. Internal organization follows traditional parliamentary norms. A speaker assisted by several deputy speakers presides, and collectively this group arranges the daily proceedings. The Swedish speaker enjoys somewhat greater power, for the current constitution gives him the power to facilitate the formation of governments following elections.

In common with all modern democratic legislatures, most of the parliamentary work takes place in the standing committees. These have grown in number and importance since 1945. There is usually a committee for each functional division of governmental business; these usually correspond to a governmental ministry. The Nordic countries typically have seventeen to twenty-four ministries, while in Iceland eleven suffice. Committees perform two vital functions. They consider budgetary and other legislative matters relevant to their functional area, and they oversee departmental activities within their purview. When the government enjoys a working parliamentary majority, committees have less leeway in modifying government-sponsored bills. In most parliamentary systems they would have none, but the Scandinavian tradition is to seek as broad a political foundation for important legislation as possible. When such a majority is not present, committees loom even larger in the bargaining process. An important aspect of committee work is that the proceedings are secret, although committees have wide discretion in deciding what aspects of their work are to be made public. Formal public hearings, in the manner of United States Congressional committees, were unknown, but in Sweden and Denmark there have lately been experimental open parliamentary hearings on controversial issues. This interest stems from a desire to increase public interest in parliament and policy, and also from dissatisfaction with the sluggish pace of parliamentary and royal commissions.

Public debate remains the principal activity of plenary (general) sessions of the parliament. These are regularly scheduled as part of the legislative process. The parliamentary year usually starts in October with the prime minister reporting on the state of the nation and the government's political goals. Following this so-called Throne Speech (no longer given by the monarch in Denmark and Sweden), there ensues a general political debate. Another general debate precedes the closing of parliament, usually in early June. Debates on current issues occur periodically throughout the year, especially on budgetary matters, and often follow questions and interpellations (more formal queries) to ministers.

Bills are given three readings, and public debate is most common at the second reading. When the government enjoys a secure majority such debates may be informative, but they are not politically significant. If, however, the government's support is in doubt, as is often the case with minority governments, parliamentary debate and tactics may be critical.

Parliament's most crucial task is to choose and, on rare occasions, to dismiss the executive branch of government. The fusion of powers between the executive and legislative branches—the hallmark of parliamentary democracy—is most visible in this function (Damgaard 1997, pp. 13–16). In addition, the Scandinavian parliaments share four functions with most other modern democratic legislatures. First, they are a mechanism of deliberation, where governmental proposals are subject to public scrutiny and debate. Private legislation (bills submitted by individual members) is rare. The committees face the daunting task of questioning civil service experts, who must defend the government's position. Committees rarely have access to comparable technical expertise, although Denmark and Sweden have tried to make limited professional assistance available to committees, party groups, and individual members. The main source of independent opinion will be the parties' own contacts and outside experts willing to make their knowledge available. Nothing like the panoply of committee staff and research services available to the United States Congress can be found in Scandinavia (or elsewhere in Europe). Increased public funding for political parties has expanded their research capabilities. Nevertheless, large and complex policy investigations are usually delegated to the so-called Royal Commissions discussed below (see Arter 1984, ch. 4; Damgaard 1990, ch. 6).

A second function is that of training future political leaders. Parliaments are educational institutions, although like most schools, not all students learn equally well. Political careers in Scandinavia usually follow a predictable course; bright and ambitious members gradually work their way on to the more important committees, usually in areas of personal political interest. Within the party groups, the articulate and intelligent—provided they also are politically astute—are given greater responsibility for explaining and defending the party's positions. Party groups usually assign specific policy tasks to individual members. The policy spokesmen of the larger parties become "shadow ministers," although less formally so than in two-party parliaments like Great Britain with a recognized opposition.

A third and related task is educating the citizens. Plenary debates, questions, and interpellations focus public attention on public issues. The press has long covered parliamentary affairs, and radio and television now bring the debates quickly to the public. The Internet has made vast amounts of parliamentary material accessible. Rules on direct transmission of proceedings are liberal, but most broadcasts are excerpts in regular news programs. The staid style of Scandinavian parliamentary proceedings makes for difficult television viewing, and journalistic treatment may make politics more accessible to the public even if bias may be introduced.

Some politicians and commentators have been concerned about what is considered the boring format of Nordic parliamentary politics. In Scandinavia members are inevitably courteous and businesslike; there is none of the sharp and often entertaining repartee and aggressive heckling as in the British House of Commons. Proceedings are occasionally televised, but they have not created a new spectator sport. Periodic studies have called for shorter and more focused debates. In addition, committee meetings and proceedings that could produce detail and independent expertise of use to an attentive press and public are closed. The problem is not easily solved. The need for compromise in a multiparty PR system requires a modicum of good will and dispassionate bargaining, both of which may be strained if debate becomes too sharp or vituperative. On the other hand, the educational function can only work if people pay attention.

Parliament's fourth function is to serve as a check on executive power, to be democracy's emergency brake. Parliamentary scrutiny may at times be a hindrance to smooth government, but democracy is often well served by such obstacles. Every government knows that there are dozens of alert men and women in the opposition parties, aided by an assertive press corps watching their actions. Committees will demand discreet but detailed explanations of every significant public event. Even if the government chooses not to act, parliament is able to debate the matter and force the government to respond or make way for those who will. Matters rarely reach such a state, but parliament is to be an instrument for all seasons. Like most legislative bodies, the Scandinavian parliaments tend to react rather than act; like large beasts, they may be slow to anger, but once enraged, a discredited minister or a cabinet cannot expect to escape lightly. Parliaments cannot lead, but they can make it clear to the government when a change of course is in order. Once again, the closed committee proceedings are often the most effective instruments of parliamentary control. An unusually powerful example of such supervision of day-to-day affairs is the European Union (formerly Market) Relations Committee of the Danish parliament. No Danish minister participating in the Council of the European Union will commit Denmark on major policy questions without informing this Committee and being certain of its acquiescence. This is an extreme example of parliament exercising control of important ministerial decisions, but parliamentary committees commonly play an important oversight role. Following accession to the European Union, the Swedish parliament created a similar committee (Europautskottet) closely modeled on the Danish example.

It is difficult to assess Scandinavian parliaments as distinct institutions. Along with the expansion of governmental activity in the past thirty years has come a notable increase in the parliamentary workload. Parliamentary committees are more numerous and meet more often. Some regularly monitor policy details. Parliament itself debates, questions, and votes more frequently than before. Policy details and technical matters do not always benefit from parliamentary micromanagement. Given Scandinavia's consensual political norms and the reality of coalition government, parliament's role is to set the policy course, to monitor performance, to urge reforms, and to communicate public reactions to the government and the bureaucracy. This is done with much less deference to executive dignity and expertise than earlier.

Open Access to Information

An important supplement to formal constitutional rights is access to government documents and records. The Nordic countries differ in their individual secrecy and access traditions. Sweden has long had the greatest freedom of information in Europe, with public documents generally open to inspection unless they contain matters sensitive to national security or personal information about individuals. Given the scope of modern government, these are considerable exceptions, but numerous internal policy documents are available. Tax information about private citizens has long been a matter of public record, causing some Swedes to worry about the balance between public access and personal privacy. Nevertheless, agencies at all levels of Swedish government routinely display current papers for inquiring journalists and others. Such access allows the press and other watchdogs to supervise the process as well as the ends of public policy.

Denmark and Norway have a tradition of secrecy that has resisted recent legislation to open up the government. Public access laws in the 1970s maintained barriers to those wishing to see internal administrative papers, and many administrative agencies have interpreted access requirements very conservatively. The closed nature of most legislative committee hearings is another obstacle to public scrutiny. The tradition of coalition government may explain the desire to maintain the confidentiality of political horse trading (see Einhorn 1977).

During the Cold War national security presented the greatest obstacle to freedom of information in the Nordic countries with severe restrictions, not only on technical documents, but also on foreign and security policy discussions within parliamentary and governmental walls. Since 1990 much of this has been published and caused vigorous if rather academic debates.

Representatives and Politicians

Citizens and officeholders are linked in several ways. Organizational and party activities bring politicians into regular contact with attentive and active citizens. Given multiparty proportional representation, Scandinavian parties cannot act unilaterally. A party's proposal is a bargaining position. Nowhere have party leaders better excelled at disposing of unpopular or impractical party positions when they stand in the way of higher priorities. As Danish Prime Minister Jens Otto Krag commented in explaining one sudden change of party policy, "you have a position until you take another one." Consensus is possible only when the bargaining parties have coherent positions and are willing to pursue their goals pragmatically.

Scandinavian politicians have become full-time professionals. Today it is difficult for most members to pursue a vocation while serving in parliament; farmers and civil servants are privileged in this regard. Indeed, the career guarantees and advantages to the latter have encouraged so many public employees to run for elected office that some claim civil servants are overrepresented in the parliament. Not only may civil servants run for legislative office, but they also receive leaves of absence while serving. Thus, the civil servant M.P. who loses office faces nothing worse than a return to a public job. For those in the private sector, the economic risk of holding public office may be far greater.

There have been two notable developments in the face of Scandinavian politics in the past generation. Women have dramatically narrowed the gender gap in the corridors of political power. From typically about 10 percent of parliamentary seats in 1960, women now hold 35 to 45 percent (see Table 4.1). (Women's representation in laggard Iceland jumped from 5 percent in 1979 to 15 percent in 1983 as a result of a separate women's list that sought to dramatize women's underrepresentation in political life.) Women have held or hold the presidency in Iceland (Vigdis Finn-

Table 4.1
Increase in Women's Representation in Parliament, 1960–2000

	1960	1970	1980	1990	2000
Denmark	10% (1960)	17% (1971)	24% (1981)	34% (1990)	38% (1998)
Finland	14% (1962)	22% (1970)	26% (1979)	38% (1991)	37% (1999)
Iceland	2% (1963)	5% (1971)	5% (1979)	25% (1991)	35% (1999)
Norway	9% (1961)	9% (1969)	26% (1981)	36% (1989)	36% (1997)
Sweden	11% (1960)	14% (1970)	26% (1979)	33% (1991)	43% (1998)

Sources: Bergqvist et al. 1999, p. 298; and *Nordic Statistical Yearbook 1987*, pp. 366–69; *1997*, pp. 126–35; *2000*, pp. 122–30.

Note: The year in parentheses is the year of the election.

bogadottir) and Finland (Tarja Halonen), the prime ministership in Norway (Gro Harlem Brundtland), and a growing share of ministerial posts. In 2003, Anneli Jäätteenmäki became Finland's first female prime minister. Meanwhile, the average age of elected officials has fallen steadily with occasional ministers attaining office while still in their twenties.

THE EXECUTIVE

The Monarchy: A National Symbol

Kings and queens excite the imagination, even in a democratic age. A century ago, Walter Bagehot (1867, pp. 63–64) stressed the importance of such archaic institutions as the monarchy, calling them the "dignified parts" of government; they do not govern, but they enhance the legitimacy of those often less-exalted political elements (officeholders, parties, etc.) that in fact do govern and are sullied with the debris of political struggle. No one in modern Scandinavia associates the contemporary monarchy with the power and arbitrary rule of yore. The broad popularity of twentieth-century monarchs has all but quelled the republican sentiments that were significant during the final political struggle for constitutional democracy between 1870 and 1920. As a symbol of national unity and identity, the monarchy provides continuity in an age of bureaucratic politics.

The power of prestige and especially of example remains a final vestige of royal influence. During such national emergencies as World War II, symbolic royal leadership proved to be inspirational for a demoralized population and political leadership. Pictures of Norway's old King Haakon and Crown Prince Olav in combat dress with military staff and of Denmark's equally venerable Christian X riding his horse unguarded through German-occupied Copenhagen remain vivid memories of that period.

In Norway and Denmark, the monarch formally presides over the council of state; the only other formal role is facilitating the formation of a new government following an election or resignation. In theory, this latter power could be significant given the numerous parties and the unlikelihood of a clear parliamentary majority. The monarch will normally ask for advice from the several parties, starting with the largest. If a clear consensus emerges, the task is a brief formality. Otherwise, the monarch may be forced to call for successive rounds of political negotiation. Before World War II, a Scandinavian king could be expected to put forward his personal suggestions for resolving a stalemate, but now the monarch is expected to resist such temptations. Thus, recent Scandinavian monarchs have made little use of these residual powers. Since 1975 the Swedish king does not participate at all in the process, and in both Norway and Denmark it is considered bad form to force the monarch into an active role.

Ironically, royal prestige and influence have been increased by the electronic media. The political discretion and personal popularity of recent monarchs has been amplified by media coverage. Modern royal rituals, such as addressing the nation by television on New Year's Day, allow for discreet entreaties on behalf of the community and against selfish pursuit of particular economic interests.

The two republics accord the president in theory far greater power. However, today the Icelandic president in practice plays a symbolic role similar to that of the monarchs. By contrast, the Finnish president has shared executive power with the prime minister, primarily driven by the imperatives of foreign policy until the end of the Cold War (see Arter 1999, pp. 224–44).

Cabinet Government: A Collective Executive

The essence of parliamentary government is the overlapping of executive and legislative power. Neither monarchs nor parliaments actually run the government. Long before the democratic era, parliaments and privy councils served as advisory bodies to the sovereign. In the democratic era, parliament represents popular sovereignty, and executive power must rest upon the consent of the legislature. Effective government requires joint action by the executive and parliament. Under the modern Swedish constitution, positive parliamentary support is required for a government (the ministers) to take office, while in Denmark and Norway, the requirement is that there not be a majority opposed to the commission granted by the monarch. The essential rule is that the parliament can force a government to resign by expressing lack of confidence.

Because proportional representation makes a single-party majority very unlikely in a multiparty system, Scandinavian governments are normally coalitions. Since World War II, the only significant period of one-party majority government was in Norway between 1945 and 1961; the Swedish Social Democrats also held a brief majority between 1968 and 1970. Table 4.2 summarizes the basis of parliamentary support for the Scandinavian ministries since 1945.

The consensual model dominates modern Scandinavian politics. In Denmark and Sweden, the usual form of government is a minority cabinet that must rely on one or several support parties for parliamentary backing. Since 1961, Norway has had fewer majority coalitions and only minority governments since 1985. Finland and Iceland have predominantly had majority coalition governments, but the parties in those coalitions have shifted with regularity. An important consequence has been the continuing importance of parliamentary politics in Scandinavia in comparison to such majoritarian systems as that of Great Britain.

Table 4.2
Parliamentary Bases of Government Support as Percent of Years, June 1945–April 2003

	Denmark	Finland	Iceland	Norway	Sweden
One party majority	0	0	0	23	6
Majority coalition	13	82	96	12	15
One party minority	32	9	4	51	69
Minority coalition	55	4	0	13	10
Caretaker	0	4	0	0	0

Source: Calculated by authors from Appendix C and Petersson 1994, p. 113. Figures may not add up to 100 percent because of rounding.

Following the general election, parliament assumes its role as an electoral college for the executive. In practice, when the sitting government's position remains viable (i.e., if it is likely to be backed by a parliamentary majority), the government continues as before. When there is doubt about whether the government still has sufficient backing, a round of tactical political maneuvers ensues. The Swedish constitution is quite specific about the role of the speaker as catalyst and the necessity for a positive majority to confirm the new government. In practice, this has been interpreted as meaning that a government does not have a majority against it (Petersson 1994, pp. 96–97).

Danish and Norwegian procedures are based more on custom than constitution. Both use the monarch as the referee for successive political consultations. In Denmark, where majorities historically have been the most ephemeral, the monarch usually is guided by the advice of the outgoing prime minister in choosing the candidate prime minister for a new government. This is usually the leader of the largest party bloc; it may also be the person recommended by successive meetings with party leaders representing the largest collective bloc. Upon this advice the monarch appoints a royal investigator to try to form a government with the broadest possible backing. The resulting government is still often short of a majority. Despite the rarity of majorities, prolonged cabinet crises even in Denmark are rare. Months of caretaker government, such as in Belgium and the Netherlands are unknown except in Finland prior to 1975.

Role of the Cabinet

Each government department is headed by a minister (in Sweden and Norway the formal title is Counsellor of State, or *Statsråd*) who has three duties. First, in Denmark, Iceland, and Norway, he or she is responsible for running a specific department. In Sweden and to some extent Finland, ministers play a less-direct role in day-to-day administration as a consequence of the uniquely collegial executive form. Second, the minister represents his or her department in governmental policy making. Finally, each minister participates, although not equally, in setting overall governmental policies.

A minister's role as chief executive officer shows remarkable variation among the three countries. In Denmark, Iceland, and Norway, ministers are responsible for the daily operation of functional ministries. They execute policy directly. In Norway, ministers are usually assisted by politically appointed deputies (secretaries of state, or *statssekretere*). In Sweden, however, ministries concentrate on planning, budgeting, and setting administrative guidelines, while leaving most of the functional matters to administrative agencies headed by permanent civil servants (Vinde and Petri 1978, pp. 14–22). Finland historically was similar to the Swedish model, but has moved to a middle position with ministers having more direct administrative responsibility.

These differences have historical roots. In Denmark and Norway, nearly two hundred years of absolutism established a firmly hierarchical administrative tradition, while in Sweden and Finland, the system of advisory councils (originally advisors to the king) built a more collegial system (Petersson 1994, pp. 127–31). Both systems proved suited to the rapidly increasing military and economic goals of the state in that period. In the past fifty years, the administrative burden has once again grown rapidly, and the organizational differences have declined. Most policies require autonomous but politically accountable administrative agencies.

The distribution of ministries differs little from other Western states. There are typically twenty or so departments with some fluctuation though Iceland gets along with eleven. Especially busy ministers in Sweden and Norway may have a vice-minister in addition to the political secretary of state. Danish prime ministers have considerable freedom to adjust cabinet portfolios in part to allow important coalition leaders to serve as specialized ministers without full control of a ministry (Knudsen 1995, pp. 290–302). Scandinavian ministers are usually expected to be good managers and accessible to citizens.

The cabinet (government) makes policy and must balance three factors. First it must decide *what* is to be done and chose between ministerial preferences. Secondly, it must *balance resources* (money) with costs, a task that inevitably is shouldered by the finance ministry. Thirdly, it must *secure parliamentary support* through the dynamics of coalitions and consensual politics. Although civil servants and occasionally outside consultants assist in this process, it must remain in the hands of democratically accountable politicians: the ministers as individuals, the cabinet as a collective, and finally, the prime minister.

The Role of the Prime Minister

Despite the tradition of collective cabinet responsibility and the necessity of coalition government, the prime minister is still first among equals.
The prime minister oversees the executive government as a whole rather
than a functional ministry. From time to time special programs are placed
in the prime minister's office, and more recently it has developed mini-
ministries to oversee important policy areas such as foreign and defense,
relations with the EU, and so on. In the context of Scandinavian politics,
that usually means engineering consensus within the governing party,
among the coalition partners both inside and outside of the cabinet, and
sometimes among top governmental civil servants. Thus, even though
there are few overt constitutional restraints on the prime minister, the
political requirement of maintaining a workable majority in the coalition
cabinet or in parliament has been very restrictive.

The traditional right of the government to dissolve parliament and call
new elections varies greatly among the Scandinavian countries. In Norway, as noted, the Storting sits for fixed four-year terms and early elections
cannot be called. In Sweden, parliamentary terms were limited to three
years between 1974 and 1994, but are now four years again. As before a
premature dissolution remains a last resort, but has never occurred under
the new constitution. Denmark's four-year term has not discouraged regular use of snap elections to seek to break political deadlocks. Between
1971 and 1998, twelve parliamentary elections were held, often long before
the Folketing reached its statutory four-year limit. Finland and Iceland
permit early elections, but they have been called far more rarely than in
Denmark.

It has long been the function of the prime minister to lead the government in parliament. This is done in a variety of ways. The government's
program, which the prime minister declares at the start of the new parliamentary session, sets the parliamentary agenda. This is paralleled by
the annual budget (and often supplementary budgets), which provides
the essential resources and details. In response to these documents, there
is a general political debate during which the opposition parties also present their objections and alternatives. Regular exchanges between ministers
and members trace the course of political business. The prime minister
has increasingly had to take the government's program directly to the
public through radio and television. Communication has become part of
the prime minister's responsibility, although all ministers find this part of
their daily routine.

The prominence of the prime minister as the leader of the government
prevails over the maneuvering of coalition and minority government. Political requirements usually ensure that this public attention is shared by
other prominent party leaders. Media images and personalities have be-

come crucial, especially during electoral campaigns but also in daily politics. Long tenure in office has been especially true of Social Democratic prime ministers (Sweden's Tage Erlander served from 1946 to 1969), with Danish Prime Minister Poul Schlüter (1982–93) the notable nonsocialist case. Norway's formidable (and Scandinavia's first woman leader in modern times) prime minister, Gro Harlem Brundtland, maintained her hold (1981, 1986–89, and 1990–96) despite setbacks such as the defeat of European Union membership in 1994.

THE BUREAUCRACY AND JUDICIARY

Scandinavian democracy faces no greater challenge than the interaction of popular government and professional administration. That challenge has grown with rapid simultaneous expansion in the size of the public sector and the scope of governmental programs. Public budgets have hovered between 50 and 60 percent of GDP and public employment between 32 and 39 percent of the labor force during recent decades, except in Iceland where it has been significantly lower. At the core of democracy is the opportunity both to choose those who will make policy and to participate in that process. However, implementation of those policies is in the hands of others who are not elected. So, too, is the judicial process that ensures compliance with the law. This section examines two aspects of public administration: the civil service and its relationship with the political system and the form and role of the judicial system in the policy process.

The concept of a professional civil service originated in Scandinavia in the seventeenth century. Political centralization through growing royal power required a well-trained corps of civil servants to administer the growing mercantile, military, and colonial interests of the state. When Denmark and then Sweden were reduced to minor European powers with few overseas colonies, the military and colonial bureaucracy declined, but the tradition of professional public administration remained. Norway occupied a middle ground between the status of internal territory and overseas dominion, and was governed by loyal but increasingly native administrators. Important internal social and economic reforms were often the result of bureaucratic initiative. Long the preserve of the urban aristocracy, this early civil service was anything but democratic. Its general honesty and competence were combined with a paternalism that fit in well with the so-called enlightened despotism of the age. The Napoleonic era reinforced these values even as the ideology of the French Revolution challenged aristocratic dominance.

The Contemporary Civil Service

Today, public employees may be divided into three groups. The first is made up of the traditional public administrators. In addition to the nu merous clerks performing the routine tasks of modern administration, this group includes university-trained specialists who administer traditional activities necessary for continuing public services. Financial, managerial, and technical experts, including top civil servants and military and diplomatic personnel, comprise this group. Most of these civil servants are appointed and promoted on the basis of merit. An exception would be among those bureaucrats working closely with cabinet ministers, especially in Sweden and Norway, where proper political affiliations may be required in addition to technical competence. These are the policy makers. How such professionals are recruited, their relationships to other political institutions (especially political parties), and their attitudes toward the political process are important for Scandinavian democracy (see Mellbourn 1979).

The second group is made up of technical and professional public employees carrying out essential public services. These are public servants, such as teachers, health professionals, and technical personnel. These government employees do not make policies directly, but they interact continuously with the public, who depend upon their competence and responsibility. In Scandinavia, regional and local governments are often their employers. Some professionals like doctors and dentists may be in private practice, but they receive a significant portion of their income from public agencies.

The third group comprises service and production workers who are employed by the public sector for political or historical reasons, but whose jobs are analogous to those in the private-market economy. This group would include such traditional public enterprises as railroads and postal service and public utilities. Most of these agencies are increasingly run as commercial enterprises, and some such as telecommunications and transportation have been privatized or rely on outside contracting in recent years.

Each category poses important questions for democratic policy making. The first group, the leading civil servants, shares decision making with politicians. They comprise an elite, not only because of the positions they hold, but also because of the educational and social background often associated with top bureaucrats. In Denmark, Norway, and Sweden, the social and economic characteristics of top civil servants and leading politicians have become increasingly similar (Higley, Brofoss, and Gråsholt 1975, pp. 254–58; Damgaard 1975, pp. 277–79). Professional elites are much more politically diverse than earlier. There has also been an important increase in social mobility as higher education (an obvious requirement for top administrative posts) and full-time careers have become more accessible to excluded groups (women and those from low-income backgrounds). Although advancement in the civil service has long been based on merit, only in the past generation has recruitment become genuinely open and competitive. Only recently have women begun to appear at the upper reaches of the bureaucracy at all, and privileged social and economic background is still an enormous advantage.

Civil servants are not directly responsible for policy, but have considerable influence on its implementation. This power has several dimensions. First, civil servants have the expertise. Second, public administration is still monopolistic either by law or professional custom. Third, civil servants are represented by powerful labor unions with close ties to the labor movement in general, and Social Democratic and Labor parties in particular. These have been effective channels to power. Finally, as already noted, a substantial number of elected representatives are also public employees (Heckscher 1984, pp. 149–53). When a third of the labor force is employed by the public sector, their enjoyment of full political and civil rights inevitably creates a conflict of interest. As elected officials, civil servants sometimes are involved in deciding issues affecting the programs upon which they work. The situation is comparable to that of elected representatives who, because of their private interests (e.g., farming), rely upon substantial state subsidies and regulation; civil servants and their organizations do not differ significantly from other interest groups.

The Judiciary and Civil Rights

The judiciary is a special element in the civil service. Those who serve in the courts and justice departments are expected to be more than just technically competent. In their administration of justice they are also safeguarding the rights of the citizen, particularly in the latter's increasingly complex dealings with public officials and the state.

Justice is a core element of Scandinavian democracy and policy. It also predates popular government. "The country shall be built upon the law" (Med lov skal man landet bygge) was a principle of medieval Scandinavian government. Arbitrary and unlawful actions are scarcely absent from Scandinavian history, but the principle of due process is well established.

The organization of the judicial branch is similar in all three countries. There are local and municipal courts to which cases are initially brought. Regional appeals courts are available should the initial outcome be disputed. Both plaintiff and defendant may appeal a judicial decision. Also, there is a Supreme Court for final appeal. Special courts are available, as are administrative courts within the public administration. In addition to labor, tax, and customs courts, there are important quasi-judicial appeals boards within the social security system. All judges are appointed by the minister of justice, but as civil service appointments rather than political-patronage posts.

Civil Liberties

Civil and political liberties were not a central focus of the Scandinavian constitutions of the nineteenth century. The Norwegian constitution of 1814, which represented the greatest break with previous practice of the three, devoted little attention to individual liberties, and its provisions barring Jews and Jesuits from admission to the country reflected the general intolerance of difference in Norwegian society. (The prohibition against Jews was repealed in 1851 after considerable political agitation, but the prohibition against Jesuits stood until 1956.)

The Norwegian constitution's guarantees of basic political freedoms were also strictly circumscribed.[3] Although the Danish constitution of 1849 provided broader guarantees of freedom of the press and assembly, those did not prevent the regular jailing of opposition journalists and agitators in the nineteenth century. The Swedish constitution was most liberal in its provisions for freedom of the press; indeed, the Freedom of the Press Act (Tryckfrihetsförordning), one of the three basic laws that make up the Swedish constitution, dates in its original formulation to 1766. However, none of them comes close to providing the breadth of freedom of the American Bill of Rights. Explicitly racist speech, for example, can be a criminal offense in the Nordic countries.

The constitutional revisions of this century have expanded and codified civil liberties. This is obvious in the postwar Danish, Swedish, and Finnish constitutions. The Swedish constitution that came into force in 1975 and was amended in 1976 and 1979 is the most sweeping in this regard. Most of the freedoms enshrined in it are protected against legislative action that might limit them; they, like similar American guarantees in the Bill of Rights, can only be changed by constitutional amendment. Procedures for constitutional amendment represent significant hurdles: Constitutional changes require passage of identically worded resolutions by two sessions of parliament with an intervening general election, and any constitutional change can be sent to a binding referendum by a minority (one-third) of the members of parliament. The Danish constitution of 1953 provides a number of unusual freedoms in its article 8, including economic rights and both the right to free public education and the right not to send one's children to school, provided they receive an equivalent primary education. Those are similarly protected by amending procedures that require referenda. The Finnish constitution of 2000 provides far-reaching guarantees of political and civil rights, including rights of gender equality and even protection of foreigners against extradition when they may face torture or the death penalty. It goes on to provide rights for children ("to influence matters pertaining to themselves to a degree corresponding to their level of development"); to demonstrate and to form interest organizations without a permit from government; to equal opportunity for education; to social security, unemployment, sickness and disability compensation and to health, and medical services; and it imposes upon the government the obligation to strive for full employment and to insure housing for everyone.

The expansion of constitutional protections of civil liberties in the postwar period is paralleled by the provision for cultural and, in some cases, governmental autonomy for ethnic minority groups. The Danes have developed what is close to a surrogate for federalism by granting local autonomy to groups that are distinctly different from the national majority, the most obvious cases of which are the Faeroe Islands and Greenland, which are part of Denmark. Clearly, both are distinct entities geographically and ethnically, but until the relatively recent past (1948 in the case of the Faeroes and 1979 in the case of Greenland) they were administered as part of the unified kingdom. In both cases, local autonomy extends even to foreign economic policy. The Faeroe Islands, for example, did not join the European Community with Denmark, and although Greenland did join as a Danish county in 1972, it withdrew unilaterally after attaining autonomy. However, unlike the extension of those constitutional guarantees that reflected concern with the archaic nature of previous guarantees, the provision for ethnic autonomy is less a matter of philosophy than a political response to pressure for independence. The Faeroese actually voted narrowly for independence in a 1946 referendum, but ambiguously elected a majority in the local parliament that supported union with Denmark; the 1948 autonomy agreement was the result. Since the mid-1990s several Faeroese parties are again pursuing independence. The provision of autonomy for Greenland preempted secessionist sentiment.

A somewhat analogous situation exists as a result of international agreement on the Danish-German border. The German minority in South Jutland, although lacking any form of regional autonomy, has substantial cultural autonomy financially supported by the German government; the Danish minority in Schleswig-Holstein has a similar degree of cultural autonomy. Likewise the Sami (Lapp) populations of northern Scandinavia have been given special privileges in governing their traditional communities.

The Faeroese, Greenlanders, and Germans in the border areas have long traditions behind them. More problematic are the recent immigrants who flooded into Sweden and then Denmark and Norway first as "guest workers" and later increasingly as refugees. Nordic citizens residing in another Scandinavian country are accorded broad rights by reciprocal agreements as are to a lesser extent citizens of EU/EEA countries. Moreover all of the Scandinavian countries except Iceland have recently provided all immigrants with substantial political rights, including the rights to vote and hold office at the municipal and county levels without citizenship after three years' residence. Although the philosophical desire to include the immigrants in the political community without granting citizenship itself played a role in this expansion of the franchise, so did pragmatic party considerations. The Social Democrats reasoned that the largely working-class immigrants were their voters.

Whatever the causes, voting rights enable immigrants to defend their own interests, and a number of immigrant spokesmen have won council seats. In 2001 two Danes of non-European origin won parliamentary seats. What is perhaps most noteworthy is the fact that the extension of voting rights has led to the integration of the immigrants into the existing political parties, making them substantially less exposed to political attack. At the same time, there has been an attempt to extend to them considerable rights of cultural autonomy; the Swedes have gone farthest in protecting cultural diversity by guaranteeing the right to instruction in school in the language spoken at home.

Although the final determination of constitutionality of governmental actions rests with the parliament and, ultimately, the electorate, there has been a trend toward limited judicial review in recent years. Matters involving human rights, due process, and relations with the EU have increased judicial activity. Courts determine whether administrative or legal actions are breaches of the constitution, and these decisions no longer focus narrowly on the legislation in question but rather on constitutional principles. All five constitutions have procedures for setting up courts of impeachment against ministers who violate the law, although such proceedings have been rare. Despite this expansion of judicial review, contested political questions are rarely decided by courts. Courts may review administrative regulations and practices based on the broad provisions of enabling legislation. Political minorities must resort to parliamentary tactics and electoral contests rather than to clever lawyers. Nevertheless, access to judicial bodies for the protection and enforcement of individual civil and economic rights remains an important element of Scandinavian democracy. Increased involvement in regional organizations, such as the European Union may presage greater reliance on courts to adjudicate differences between national laws and administrative procedures on the one hand, and treaty obligations on the other. Moreover there seems to be a new assertiveness by courts to uphold the letter of the constitution; in 1998 the Danish Supreme Court invalidated a law regulating perceived malfeasance by a group of Folk Colleges (the Tvind schools).

Popular participation in the administration of justice occurs in two forms. In all three countries, lay judges, or assessors, join regular judges in trying cases and deciding appropriate awards and punishments. Only in Denmark have juries participated in criminal cases in recent years. Also in Denmark, the recent trend has been for juries to participate with judges in determining appropriate sanctions, and no longer merely to determine guilt or innocence. They too have evolved into using lay assessors. Finally, it is important to emphasize the extensive participation of laypeople in numerous special courts (e.g., labor courts) and investigatory commissions (see von Eyben 1981).

The Ombudsman

Last but certainly not least on the list of Nordic institutional protections for individuals is that Swedish innovation, the ombudsman. The origins of this institution lie in the Swedish experience with abuse of royal power. That abuse took place during the final and disastrous period of Swedish absolutism, beginning with the royal coup d'état in 1772, and culminating in the 1808 war against Russia that led to the loss of Finland—almost half the kingdom—in 1809. The constitution forced on the new king, Jean Bernadotte, established the institution of ombudsman, which was placed under parliament specifically to investigate and restrain royal government. In recent years, the ombudsman system has been elaborated in Sweden and has taken root in Denmark, Finland, and Norway as well.

The problem of protecting citizens against bureaucracy is as old as bureaucracy itself. Charles XII, who had considerable time to observe Turkish practices during his enforced stay there after his defeat at Poltava, established the post of chancellor of justice (justitiekansler, known popularly as the JK) in 1713 as a royal agent to check the abuses of civil servants; that position still exists and the overlap in duties between the chancellor of justice and the parliamentary ombudsman is generally resolved by consultation between the two. By 1809, however, parliament insisted on its need for independent control of misadministration, and the justitieombudsman, generally known today as the JO, was the result. Elected by parliament for a four-year term, the JO's duties include the supervision of public officials (including the courts) to see that they follow the law, the inspection of public agencies, and, if necessary, the prosecution of public officials. The JO cannot overturn decisions or provide redress, but he has wide-ranging powers to gather the relevant information from the administration, to criticize officials, to prosecute them for flagrant abuses, and to recommend changes in law to parliament. Although the Swedish JO responds to formal complaints—around three thousand a year in recent years—he also has the power to raise cases on his own, either on the basis of press or other reports, or as a result of his personal inspections.[4] The JO has initiated 200 to 300 cases annually in recent years, of which roughly half have ended without admonitions or other action.

The JO's practice differs notably from that of American redress procedures through the courts. First, it only infrequently involves any kind of court action: Only fifty-two cases out of some 32,000 cases filed between 1968 and 1978 led to prosecution or disciplinary action (al-Wahab 1979, pp. 164–85). There is no cost to the complainant and no lawyers are involved on either side, except in the rare case that actually goes to court. The ombudsman's sanctions are such that he is encouraged to be flexible in seeking to resolve complaints that have merit (as 10–15% are found to have), and when he finds systematic problems it is his obligation to propose legislation to alleviate them.

With the growth of bureaucracy—which Balzac characterized as "a giant machine run by dwarves"—and the extension of the scope of the JO's authority, the number of cases has exploded from fewer than 100 annually in the first part of the last century to the current rate of more than 3,000 per year. The JO's staff has expanded concomitantly, and the ombudsman institution has been extended through the creation of specialized ombudsmen, each with his own staff, to deal with competition and antitrust issues (1954); the press (1969); consumer affairs (1971); equal opportunity (1980); and avoidance of ethnic discrimination (1986). The ombudsman system has proven singularly adaptable to the problems of bureaucracy in modern society because of its flexibility and nonlitigious nature. The ombudsman institution has been borrowed by a number of other countries including Great Britain, New Zealand, and a number of local governments in the United States and Canada as well as nongovernmental organizations. (See al-Wahab 1979 and Caiden 1983.)

DIRECT DEMOCRACY AS A CHECK ON GOVERNMENTAL MAJORITIES

The provisions discussed above protect individuals against capricious acts by bureaucrats and provide basic protection for ethnic minorities. But how can the people at large be protected against an overzealous parliamentary majority of some duration and stability?

The Scandinavians have not been strong believers in direct democracy for its own sake. Recall and initiative, for example, are unknown. They have, however, made increasing use of referenda on constitutional issues, and to resolve questions so divisive that a parliamentary majority is an insufficient basis for legitimate decision. (For a general account of Scandinavian referenda and their impact, see Nilson 1978 and Petersson 1994, pp. 164–67.) These referenda have played a crucial part in the process of political decision making in all of the countries in the postwar period.

The importance of referenda as a check on majority rule is best established in Denmark. With nineteen national referenda since 1916, the Danes are second only to the Swiss in Europe in the use of this instrument. The Danish constitution requires that all constitutional changes be approved by two sessions of parliament with an election intervening and by a majority exceeding 40 percent of the eligible voters in a referendum. Furthermore, any legislation except finance and tax measures can be sent to a referendum by one-third of the members of parliament; rejection requires a majority in excess of 30 percent of the eligible voters. (This provision represented a quid pro quo to the more conservative parties of the abolition of the upper house of parliament in the 1953 constitution.) It was a sign of the times that popular referenda could be seen as a conservative counterweight to Social Democratic dominance in government. Moreover, any legislation involving a surrender of national sovereignty can be sent to a referendum by one-sixth of the members of parliament. While such Danish referenda are binding, Swedish and Norwegian referenda have been advisory, although, since 1979, the new Swedish constitution has included the possibility of binding referenda on constitutional amendments (which also go through the process of being approved by two sessions of parliament with an intervening election) when one-third of the members of parliament demand one.

Before World War II, the issues going to referenda involved one of two matters: constitutional questions and prohibition. Constitutional questions went before the voters with some regularity. Norwegians ratified independence—the vote was 368,208 for and 184 against—and the establishment of a monarchy in two separate referenda in 1905. Icelanders voted on their status in the union with Denmark in 1918 and for independence and a republic in 1944. Danes approved the sale of the Danish West Indies (Virgin Islands) to the United States in 1916, the reunification with North Schleswig in 1920, and 92 percent supported the effort at constitutional revision in 1939, although the turnout was not high enough to ratify the changes.

The thorny issue of prohibition was enacted by referenda in Iceland (1908), which was then part of Denmark, and Norway (1919) but rejected in Sweden (1922). The defeat of prohibition in Sweden, and its repeal by popular votes in Norway in 1926 (under pressure of threatened retaliation against Norwegian fish exports by the wine-producing countries), in Finland in 1931, and in Iceland in 1933 marked the end of the campaign for legally enforced abstinence at the national level, although restricting the use of alcohol has remained an important question.

In the postwar period, only the Danes have sent constitutional issues to the people. The Danes adopted a new constitution by referendum (1953) and have held five votes on lowering the suffrage age, while special referenda have been held on independence (1946) and on autonomy (1979) in the Faeroes and Greenland, respectively.

Occasionally controversial political issues are still put to referenda. Referenda can settle the most divisive issues in a way that parliamentary parties cannot. Indeed, voters have repeatedly reversed parliamentary majorities. A plurality of Swedish voters approved the Social Democrats' supplemental pension plan in 1957, although there was not at the time a majority in parliament in its favor. Danish voters in 1963 rejected a group of four laws regulating land use that parliament had approved. In 1969, at the height of the student rebellion, Danish voters used a referendum on lowering the voting age from twenty-one to eighteen to demonstrate their disapproval of the rebellious young. Despite clear parliamentary approval (103 to 65), voters rejected it overwhelmingly (79% to 21%), sending it down to defeat in every electoral district in the country (Nielsen 1970). (Eventually the voting age was lowered by referenda to twenty in 1971 and to eighteen in 1978.) In the aftermath of Three Mile Island nuclear accident in the United States in 1979, the Swedish government in 1980 sent the increasingly divisive question of the national nuclear program to a referendum. Hence only rarely since the 1930s in Denmark (once) and Sweden (thrice) have referenda been used to guide domestic policy issues. Constitutional and EU relations have been the key issues.

The most dramatic and common use of referenda in recent decades has been on the issue of membership and relations with the European Community/Union. (See Table 4.3.) Norwegian voters rejected membership in the European Community in September 1972, despite an overwhelming parliamentary majority for membership. Under similar circumstances they did so again in 1994. Danish voters approved membership in 1972, and there have been five additional referendums on Denmark's relationship to the EU since 1986. Swedish and Finnish accession to the European Union in 1994–95 also required hotly contested referendums.

Despite the theoretical difference between the binding referenda in Denmark and the nonbinding referenda in the other Nordic countries, all of the governments have generally followed the voters' advice, at least for

Table 4.3
European Community/Union Referenda in Scandinavia, 1972–2000

	Denmark						Norway		Sweden	Finland
	1972	1986	1992	1993	1998	2000	1972	1994	1994*	1994
Yes	63.3	56.2	49.3	56.7	55.1	46.9	46.5	47.8	52.3	57.0
No	36.7	43.8	50.7	43.3	44.9	53.1	53.5	52.2	46.8	43.0
Turnout	90.1	75.4	83.1	86.5	74.8	87.5	79.2	88.8	82.4	70.8

Notes: The referenda were the following: Denmark 1972: Joining the EC; 1986: EC package; 1992: Maastricht Treaty; 1993: Edinburgh agreement modifying Maastricht; 1998: Amsterdam Treaty; 2000: Common European currency. Norway 1972 and 1994: Joining the EC/EU. Sweden 1994: Joining the EU. Finland 1994: Joining the EU.

*Remaining 0.9 percent of ballots were blank.

a while. In 1955, 83 percent of Swedes voting rejected changing from driving on the left side of the road to driving on the right, despite the views of the government and common sense; after this advisory referendum, the Swedish government reaffirmed its intention to make the change anyway, but that was not done until 1967. The Swedish government also drew the lesson that offering voters only two choices might lead to awkward results; hence in both the supplemental pension question in 1957 and the nuclear-power question in 1980, voters chose among three alternatives, and in neither case did any alternative win a majority. Thus, the outcome was sufficiently ambiguous that there was room for interpretation.

The Danish system of relatively common referenda that can be called by recalcitrant parliamentary minorities clearly imposes some restraint on majorities. Most referendum issues cut across party loyalties and threaten voter defections in the election that follows. The effect is to persuade the parliamentary majority that a preemptive compromise with the obstreperous minority may be in order. Referenda on extremely divisive issues permit a determination of the real (if perhaps fleeting) opinion of the people who are, after all, the source of sovereignty. The agreement to call a referendum also enables the government to escape disruptive demonstrations and, at least on the nuclear-power issue in Sweden, to make a graceful policy adjustment. As we will discuss below in Chapter 7, the Danes and Swedes have lost policy flexibility through the de facto commitment to submit major EU policies to referenda. This has given EU opponents a constitutional unique opportunity to override parliament in a major ongoing policy area. However, unlike Switzerland (and the United States) no Nordic country allows legislation to be passed simply by popular vote (initiative).

A characteristic of the European Union and the nuclear power referenda campaigns is that, like the prohibition campaigns of the interwar period, they were the cause of mass mobilizations in what the Scandinavians call *popular movements.* Popular movements have, in Scandinavian political culture, a degree of legitimacy that rivals that of the established parties, in no small measure because the term denotes the agrarian and labor movements of the nineteenth century. While the new popular movements have much in common with the single-issue movements of other countries, they have also served as a check upon parliamentary majorities. The simplicity of the answers that they offer, which is part of their mobilizing appeal, hardly prepares them for the give and take of the political game in the long run, but it serves them well in the short run. In their ability to mobilize, they can check the parliamentary majority by demonstrating that it is out of step with a significant portion not only of all voters but also of the majority's own voters. It is the threat that such popular mobilizations pose to party loyalty that makes the referendum an effective counterweight to parliamentary majorities.[5]

LOCAL AND REGIONAL GOVERNMENT

Home rule, or decentralization, poses another challenge to modern Scandinavian democracy. Providing citizens with the public services that have increased so dramatically in the past half century requires an administrative apparatus that reaches into every nook and cranny of the country. The democratic ethos, however, demands participatory government. These dual pressures, for both local autonomy and a high standard of universal public services, have dominated thinking about local government in Scandinavia since the mid-1960s. Although national politics may dominate the consciousness of Scandinavian citizens, especially given the long history of a unitary (centralized) political system, most daily governmental services are within the purview of county and municipal authorities.

The three Scandinavian countries have roughly similar local-governmental structures. Local government is guaranteed by national constitutions and historical tradition, but deciding the extent and content of local and regional home rule is entirely a matter for the national government.

The basic unit of local government is the municipality. The municipality provides most daily governmental services: public safety, day care, primary and secondary education, leisure and recreation, building and land-use planning, sanitation, and so on. Its resources come principally from local taxation, which throughout Scandinavia is mainly a proportional personal income tax on all residents. Substantial block grants (often amounting to 40% of the local budget) are received from the national government. The grants are awarded according to complex formulas and are designed to allow all municipalities to provide a minimum of required public services. This, of course, is a point of political conflict. Giving localities the power to tax and spend is relatively easy. There are, however, significant differences in the tax base of various municipalities.

Municipal government has undergone dramatic changes in recent years. The number of municipalities has been reduced dramatically through consolidation in Denmark, Norway, and Sweden (Table 4.4) to allow thinly populated rural units to marshal the fiscal and administrative capacity required by the modern welfare state. With national subsidies, this has largely been accomplished. Current difficulties focus on the declining tax base and increasing fiscal demands for social services and infrastructure maintenance in the large urban areas. The solution has been for national governments to focus on minimum standards and allow municipalities to embellish services supported by local votes and taxes (see Bogason 1987, pp. 184–86, 190–200).

The second unit of local government is the county except in Finland, which has less formal regional structures. Counties correspond loosely to

Table 4.4
Local and County Government, 1999

	Number of municipalities*		Number of counties
Denmark	275	(1388)	14
Finland	460		--
Iceland	213		21
Norway	435	(744)	19
Sweden	288	(1037)	23

*Numbers in parentheses are prior to consolidations (1964–73). Minor adjustments are made periodically.

traditional provinces and have not been subject to as many geographic adjustments as municipalities. Still, there has been a significant expansion of their roles. Counties have specific policy responsibilities: medical and hospital care, regional transport and communications, special and advanced schools, and some recreational and cultural facilities. There is some overlap with municipal government as well as coordination by the county authorities prompting some discussion of whether the latter should be abolished (Lindbeck et al. 1994, pp. 193–98).

County councils, or legislatures, are elected every four years simultaneously with municipal councils in Denmark, Sweden, and, since 1976, in Norway; Icelandic county boards are appointed by the component municipalities. A system of proportional representation guarantees broad representation. Although there are some nonpartisan candidates, especially for municipal councils, practically all the winners are drawn from the national political parties. Local and county councilors are paid although usually not full-time positions.

Executive power at the regional and local level is determined by the constellation of parties in the councils. Specific council members are elected to administer functional departments, often assisted by professional administrators. County prefects have lost much of their executive power (especially in Denmark and Sweden) and now act mainly as inspectors for the national governments. The national ministries of the interior or local government are responsible for local and regional affairs.

Additionally, each country makes provisions for metropolitan areas. The largest cities (e.g., Copenhagen, Oslo, and Stockholm) have merged local and regional authority. Large metropolitan areas have created regional authorities to undertake specific tasks (typically transportation, waste and sewage disposal, and planning). An interesting regional cooperation in planning, environmental, and communications policies has developed during the past thirty years across the Øresund region between the Copenhagen, Denmark, and the Malmö, Sweden, metropolitan regions. The completion of a massive bridge and tunnel project across the Øresund in 2000 could have significant economic, political, and cultural implications for the region's nearly two million inhabitants.

At first glance there may appear to be as much local autonomy in centralized democracies as in nominally federal systems. In practice federal systems tend to be larger countries that permit, and even encourage, significant policy variations (and thus, also inequalities) between component governments. Scandinavian local autonomy is circumscribed by detailed national standards partly because of the sense of national political community that, if anything, has increased during expansion of the welfare state. Local and regional government deliver the services—health, education, transportation, and the like—that Scandinavian citizens use every day. New regional and metropolitan governments and organizations provide efficiencies of scale. Although the issue is politically controversial, private contractors deliver an increasing proportion of services.

STRUCTURING THE DEMOCRATIC WELFARE STATE

Democracy is an ancient ideal, but a relatively new practice. This is also true in Scandinavia. Only in Norway is democracy more than a century old, and Swedish conservatives did not concede the principles of parliamentary supremacy and universal suffrage until 1917–18. In less than fifty years, however, the three Scandinavian nations became strong democracies. Governments are chosen in free and highly competitive elections; governments are held responsible to parliament, and civil rights are zealously guarded against encroachment. The reason for such strength is not only formal democratic institutions, which are similar to those in other Western countries and to those that were tried and failed in Central and Eastern Europe during the interwar period. A common tradition of consensual and constructive negotiation has been more important in ensuring political democracy and the interaction of parties, interest groups, and other political actors, as we discuss in the next chapter.

There is a final element that must be remembered when considering the Scandinavian democratic experience. The scale of Scandinavian politics is, by German or British, or even more so, by American standards, very small. It is hard to spend much time in the countries without actually meeting members of parliament. Before the unhappy increase in political violence of the past two decades, Scandinavian monarchs rode bicycles and prime ministers took trams. Because of the close ties between interest organizations and parties, easy access to leaders pertains not only in old, upper-class business and professional circles, but also in labor and farming circles. That access, in a pinch, may be the access of the streets. Between one-quarter and one-third of the population of each of the three countries lives within an hour's journey of parliament. Each capital city is also the country's major population center, and local politics remains vibrant. If someone really feels strongly, he or she can easily demonstrate his or her discontent, and that too has become a regular channel for articulating political opinion. Even the normally staid Swedish business community has recently adopted demonstrations as a form of political expression. Jefferson and de Tocqueville would not be surprised by the strength of Scandinavian political democracy.

Even in these relatively small countries, government can still appear overwhelming to the citizen who confronts a large and multilayered bureaucracy and numerous elected and appointed councils. Parties and interest organizations often duplicate this structure. Precisely because there are so many ties between people and their government, democracy, particularly its libertarian aspects—a sense of freedom for purely individual decisions—seems incomplete and deficient. This realization has strengthened the importance of organizational connections between citizens and their government: the parties and interest organizations that are scarcely visible in the formal constitutions but vital for political democracy.

NOTES

1. For recent comparative studies of the political institutions of the Nordic countries, see Elder, Thomas, and Arter (1982, pp. 100–58); Lindblad, Wahlbäck, and Wiklund (1984); Petersson (1994, pp. 77–140); Arter (1999, pp. 200–244); and Gress (2001).

2. For the current texts of the Scandinavian constitutions consult Peaslee (1965) and Blaustein and Flanz (1971 and later).

3. Consider freedom of the press. Article 100 of the Norwegian Constitution provides, "There shall be liberty of the Press. No person must be punished for any writing, whatever its contents may be, which he has caused to be printed or published, *unless he willfully and manifestly has either himself shown or incited others to disobedience to the laws, contempt of religion or morality or the constitutional powers, or resistance to their orders. . . .*" (emphasis added).

4. One of the more spectacular cases arose from the ombudsman's inspection of a debtors' prison in 1824. The ombudsman found a prisoner who had been held for twenty-three years following his bankruptcy in 1800. The prisoner had been sentenced to two hours of public humiliation but had made the mistake of appealing the sentence. The court never ruled on his appeal, and prison officials refused to release him because there had been no judgment. When the ombudsman went to the court, he found that the file had been lost (personal communication, Ulf Lundvik, former JO).

5. In Denmark the anti-EU campaigns have generated a new type of political party: parties contesting only EU Parliamentary elections and Danish EU referenda. See Chapter 5 for a discussion of these so-called Euro-parties. In Norway, the anti-EU movement has relied both on popular movements and dissident factions, especially within the Social Democratic party.

CHAPTER 5

Political Actors: Parties, Voters, Interest Groups

All that talk about strict party discipline is nonsense. Of course a politician is welcome to hold other views—just so long as he doesn't try to do anything about them.
—K. K. Steincke, Danish Social Democratic Cabinet Member,
1924–26, 1929–39

Because direct democracy is impossible in all but the smallest communities, modern democracy has been based on the representative principle. But how are citizens to control their representatives? Although this has been a thorny problem for political theorists since Rousseau, a common system of citizen control of representatives has grown out of the practice of politics in Western democracies.

Organizations provide both channels for political participation and mechanisms for citizens' control of their representatives. They fall into two broad types: political parties that contest elections and interest organizations that articulate the common interests of their members vis-à-vis elected officials. These organizations work to do the following: structure citizen participation in politics, recruit new representatives and control the existing ones, provide a free flow of information from the leaders to the led and vice versa, control policy choices, monitor policy implementation, and coordinate national and local political efforts with those of government and private organizations. Their role in the democratic process is hard to overestimate. In fact, the existence of democracy in modern society without the structure that parties and interest organizations provide is almost inconceivable.

There was a time when the form of Scandinavian parties and interest groups seemed chiseled in granite. Their structures, coalitions, and even their voting support were constant. That stability has, however, been replaced by an increasing dynamism since 1973. Coalitions have fragmented, voters have become more mobile, and new structures of citizen participation—the so-called grassroots movements—have appeared alongside the existing interest groups.

Before we turn to discussing how political participation is structured in Scandinavia, two fundamental facts deserve comment.

The first is the unequaled strength of organizations in Scandinavia. This is clearest in the trade-union field where, in 1997, 80 percent or more of Danish, Finnish, Icelandic, and Swedish employees belong to their unions as do 55 percent of Norwegian employees; that contrasts with 30 to 35 percent in Canada, Germany, and the United Kingdom and only 14 percent in the United States. Employers, farmers, and other occupational groups are also extremely well organized. Even groups only tenuously organized elsewhere, such as renters and consumers, enjoy the protection of reasonably strong organizations in Scandinavia. Party membership percentages are high by international standards. Contributing to the strength of organizations is the attention they themselves pay to maintaining membership, the fashion in which certain transfer payments are administered (in Denmark, Finland, and Sweden, for instance, it is almost a necessity to be a member of a trade union to be eligible for unemployment compensation), and—most important—the prevalent cultural attitude that collective organization is the proper way to achieve one's interest. The historical record in Scandinavia seems to demonstrate the efficacy of strong organizations.

The second fundamental fact is the matter of scale. Scandinavian societies are very small indeed. Recall that the largest, Sweden, has about the population of a medium-sized American state. Scale is far from trivial. For the Scandinavian citizen, the chances of being able to follow and understand politics are improved; even such relatively complex matters as managing the national economy seem comprehensible to informed laypeople. (No doubt the existence of a national press plays a major role in this regard.) For leaders, the scale limits the possibilities of acquiring delusions of grandeur. These constraints are strongest on the political representatives of the labor and agrarian movements. The political elite are expected to maintain a modest lifestyle. Anker Jørgensen, Danish prime minister between 1975 and 1982, continued to live in a four-and-a-half-room walk-up flat in a Copenhagen working-class neighborhood. Thorbjörn Fälldin combined the Swedish prime ministership with running a family farm. In the early 1960s the Danish Prime Minister Jens Otto Krag entertained Soviet Premier Nikita Khrushchev at his modest home with his wife—a noted actress—preparing a home-style Danish dinner. Swedish Prime Minister Per Albin Hansson died in a tram in 1946. Olof Palme's assassination in 1986 demonstrates how accessible Scandinavian leaders remain. Palme was assassinated while walking home unguarded from a movie with his wife. Even though these leaders were far from a cross-section of the represented, the scale of Scandinavian politics and the political culture kept them from distancing themselves too much from the led.[1]

THE PARTY SYSTEM

Political parties—those organized groups that contest elections—are at the heart of modern representative democracy in Scandinavia. They serve to recruit and train the political activists of today and the political leaders of tomorrow. They are the channel through which citizens control the personnel of government on election day, and their discipline and clear enunciation of positions give voters substantial control over government policies between elections. Parties have been the principal agent in the development, first, of political democracy and, second, of the programs that make up the modern welfare state. Even today, when parties in government seem more concerned with muddling through than enacting their various visions of a better society, parties provide the principal reflection of changing citizen attitudes, even as they also try to shape attitudes. The balance between them in coalitions reflects—more than any other institution in society—the predominant beliefs and aspirations of citizens. That reflection is distorted, to be sure, because party activists and elected representatives have more consistent and coherent views than party voters, but the system still provides the closest representation of citizen attitudes yet achieved.

Commonalities

Each of the Scandinavian party systems is a world of its own. There are, however, eight commonalities in the party systems of the five countries that permit their joint analysis.[2]

First, all five countries have multiparty systems with similar parties. Although the system of proportional representation used in elections facilitates the creation of new parties and stabilizes the support of old ones, the existence of multiparty systems predates the establishment of proportional representation. It reflects instead the lines of socioeconomic and political division that existed at the end of the nineteenth century and that found expression in the establishment of liberal, conservative, and Social Democratic parties.

Scandinavian party names can be misleading. The Danish party names Venstre (Left) and Det radikale Venstre (Radical Left) reflect placement on the political spectrum as it was in the last century; today they are to the right of center and in the center, respectively. As politicians have become conscious of modern public relations techniques, they have sought labels that attract rather than distinguish. In Finland, Norway, and Sweden, Farmers have become Centrists, and the Swedish conservatives changed their name in 1969 from Högerpartiet (the Right) to Moderata Samlingsparti (Moderate Unity party). Mogens Glistrup's seizure of the term Fremskridt (Progress) in 1971 to designate his party that sought to turn the clock back in practically every area of public policy wins the sweepstakes in the misnomer category.[3]

Scandinavian parties began to develop in the latter half of the nineteenth century. During the struggle between liberals and conservatives over parliamentary supremacy in Denmark, Norway, and Sweden, the shifting alliances between factions in the parliaments began to take on fixed and permanent character. It is possible to speak of a clear party distinction in Denmark, for example, from the election of 1872. Modern party organizations began to develop in the same period outside parliament, as the *Liberals* and the new *Social Democrats* sought to mobilize potential supporters, to register them to vote, and to get them to the polls on election day. Given the high property qualifications required for voting, this was no easy task. The *Conservatives*, who were dominant in government in the period, turned to organizing outside the halls of parliament only when it became apparent that this was an effective tool for their opponents.

By the mid-1920s in each of the three countries, two more parties joined the original three. The radical wing of the Social Democrats organized *Communist* parties in Scandinavia as elsewhere between 1918 and 1923. The agrarian groups within the Liberal parties organized separate *Agrarian* parties as well. That basic five-party system (which expanded to six in Norway in 1933 when a Christian People's party, reflecting fundamentalist religious values, was added to the party spectrum) proved very stable until the 1973 elections when, in the aftermath of the highly divisive national referenda on membership in the EU, the number of parties represented in parliament jumped from five to eight in Norway and five to ten in Denmark.

In Finland and Iceland, this basic pattern existed as well, although with some modifications. In both countries the struggle for national independence influenced party formation; otherwise conservative nationalists (who were at the heart of the political establishment in predemocratic Denmark, Norway, and Sweden) sought a very different political regime than that provided by the Russians and the Danes in Finland and Iceland, respectively. Finland quickly developed a party to represent its Swedish minority, so that it had a six-party system in the 1920s. Iceland lacked a separate liberal party, and had united labor party until the Communists split off in the 1930s, turning a three-party system (Conservatives, Agrarians, and Social Democrats) into a four-party system.

The second commonality of the party systems of the three countries is that not only did all share the same basic party system from the 1920s through 1973 (with due allowance for the Christian People's party in Norway, the Georgists in Denmark, and the Swedish People's party in Finland), but also the major parties can be arranged along the familiar Left-Right scale on economic policy. The only real exception to this unidimensionality is the urban-rural distinction that divides the center of the political spectrum. The convention in political science and popular discussion has also been to divide the major parties between the nonsocialist, or bourgeois, camp (Conservative, Liberal, and Agrarian parties), and the socialist bloc of the Social Democratic (or Labor) and Communist (or radical socialist) parties (see Berglund and Lindström 1978, pp. 16 ff). This division of the party spectrum is meaningful in historical and ideological terms, but has less effect on coalition formation. Despite the dramatic changes of the 1970s, the new parties can be placed in the same blocs and along the same continuum, although the traditional five-party model no longer can accommodate the new parties of the Center and Right. The explosion in the number of parties stimulated the development of a variety of new analytical models (see Borre and Andersen 1997; Petersson 1994, ch. 3; and Einhorn and Logue 1988). Those changes are reflected in the model of the party system presented in Table 5.1.

The most basic division in the party system is between the socialist (or labor) parties and the nonsocialist (or bourgeois) parties. The former includes the Social Democratic and radical socialist parties that espouse the interests of labor and have an increasingly distant Marxist ideological heritage. The latter includes the liberal, agrarian, Christian, and conservative parties of the center and right, which represent the interests of the self-employed, farmers, managerial employees, and the business community; their ideological heritage includes nineteenth-century liberalism, social liberalism, conservatism, and agrarian populism. Take the term *bloc* with a bit of salt. Disagreements within each bloc are often as great as disagreements between them.

As can be seen in Appendixes A and B, votes and seats have been evenly divided between the socialist and nonsocialist blocs for the last half century in every country except Iceland, where the socialist parties have polled only 35 to 40 percent of the vote. The Social Democrats have typically won 80 to 90 percent of the socialist bloc vote in Denmark, Norway, and Sweden, but the bourgeois vote has been more evenly divided among three or four parties whose relative strength has varied over time. Social Democratic dominance in government (see Appendix C) has stemmed from the consistency with which the party has dominated the socialist

Table 5.1
Scandinavian Party Systems: Major Parties Contesting the 1998–2003 Elections by Ideological Placement

	DENMARK	FINLAND	ICELAND	NORWAY	SWEDEN
Radical socialist	Socialist People's Party Unity List	Left Alliance	People's Alliance	Socialist Left Party	Left Party
Social Democratic	Social Democrats	Social Democrats	Social Democrats	Labor Party	Social Democratic Workers Party
Center parties "Post-materialist"		Greens	Greens Women's List		Environmental Party
Urban Liberal Personalist	Radical Liberals Center Democrats			Liberals	Liberals
Rural Agrarians Christian Ethnic	agrarian Liberals Christian People's Party	Center Party Christian League Swedish Peoples Party	Progressive Party	Center Party Christian People's Party	Center Party Christian Democrats
Conservative	Conservative People's Party	National Coalition	Independence Party	Conservatives	Moderate Unity Party
Right Protest	Progress Party Danish People's Party	True Finns		Progress Party	

Note: Includes only parties that won seats in one of the elections of this period.

bloc, the fragmentation of bourgeois bloc, and the possibility for coalition across bloc lines that the division of the bourgeois vote encourages.

In Finland and Iceland, however, the socialist vote was split down the middle between Social Democrats and Communists. Given the constant distrust and frequent animosity between the two labor parties, the division in the labor movement prevented the Social Democrats from obtaining the same dominance in government that they achieved in Denmark, Norway, and Sweden in the 1930s. In Finland the Agrarians, Conservatives, and Liberals dominated the government in shifting coalitions until the mid-1960s; in Iceland, the conservative Independence party and agrarian Progressive party alternated in power. In both cases Communists and Social Democrats were more likely to participate in coalitions with other parties than they were with each other. This changed in Finland in the end of the 1960s, leading to a level of Social Democratic dominance comparable to that in Denmark, Norway, and Sweden. In Iceland, however, the labor parties together rarely polled more than 40 percent of the vote, the nonsocialist vote was usually split between only two parties, and Social Democratic–led governments remain a rarity.

Third, with election systems that precluded winning parliamentary majorities without near majorities among voters, multiparty systems in Scandinavia forced the creation of formal or informal party coalitions. These have often cut across the lines of division between socialist and nonsocialist blocs. This is particularly true for Denmark, where the Social Democrats have nearly always relied upon one or more nonsocialist parties for parliamentary support and in Sweden where Social Democrats have often reached across to centrist parties. In Norway, cooperation between the Labor and nonsocialist parties on domestic issues has been less common, largely because Labor had its own majority from 1945 to 1961. Finnish and Icelandic parties have demonstrated a remarkable flexibility in their coalitions.

A fourth commonality is that Scandinavian parties are national in scope, although some have regional bastions, especially where strong local economic interests, such as farming or heavy industry, reinforce geographic identities. Specifically regional parties have had no success, except in Greenland and the Faeroes, which really have separate party systems from the Danish norm, formerly among the German minority in south Jutland, and the Swedish People's party in Finland. The national parties' organizations dominate local elections, although nonpartisan lists and local parties win some council seats in smaller towns. For that reason, municipal and county elections in Denmark and Norway play the same role that off-year congressional elections or by-elections play in the United States and Great Britain, respectively.

A fifth common characteristic is organization. Scandinavian parties have an elaborate organizational structure with regular local meetings, dues-paying members, and a plethora of subsidiary organizations including party youth organizations and a party press. The older parties all have close ties to economic interest groups: farm, labor, and business. Each party recruits its next generation of leaders from those who are active in the organization, and these, of course, absorb the party's values as they rise through the ranks. The shared values among party elite and members—plus the party members' control of nominations—ensures party cohesion and discipline in the party group in parliament; that makes stable coalition governments possible. Several of the new parties of the 1970s, however, lack this cohesiveness between their elected officials and their voters.

A sixth commonality, since 1973, has been a rise in new parties, particularly on the right and in the center. Five or six party systems have become seven or eight party systems as Christian parties have entered parliament in Denmark, Finland, and Sweden as well as Norway; Green parties have joined parliaments in Finland, Iceland, and Sweden; and new rightist parties have outflanked the traditional conservatives in Denmark and Norway.

A seventh common factor has been a significant decline in party loyalties among voters. Today's voters are more likely to be loyal to a bloc—socialist or nonsocialist—than to a party. This is particularly true on the bourgeois side of the spectrum where voters move easily between Conservatives, Liberals, Christians, and Agrarian, responding to attractive party leaders. There has been a more moderate tendency of the same sort on the labor side, especially since the EU question shook the loyalty of Social Democratic voters in the 1970s in Denmark and Norway and in the 1990s in Sweden.

The final constant that sets Scandinavian politics apart from politics in the rest of Europe has been the hegemony enjoyed by the Social Democratic party since it came to power at the depths of the Depression. The great capitalist crisis of the 1930s, long predicted by Social Democratic theoreticians, brought the socialist parties into government elsewhere in Europe. But they quickly lost power to the conservative Right, as in Great Britain and France, or to the fascists, as in Germany and Spain. Only in Scandinavia did the Social Democrats both take and hold power. Since then they have achieved an unparalleled record of success in free, contested elections: The Danish Social Democrats held power for fifty-one years since coming to power in 1929; the Swedish Social Democrats sixty-two years since 1932; the Norwegian Labor party forty-five years since it took power in 1935; and the Finnish Social Democrats twenty-five years since 1966. (The German occupation accounted for five of the years the Social Democrats were out of power in Norway and two in Denmark.) In power, they used the government to transform society. Even out of power, their ideas have been dominant. Nonsocialist governments have served primarily as caretakers of Social Democratic accomplishments.

The Scandinavian Social Democratic Labor Movement

The extraordinary success of the Scandinavian Social Democratic parties is worth a book in itself.[4] Each is a substantial organization with a century of history behind it. Each has its pantheon of heroes, and its history of ideological debate, factional struggles, and political practice. And each has moved from orthodox Marxism when in the opposition, to pragmatic reformism when in power. (That their common story is not as well known as that of the German Social Democrats or French Socialists is not a function of lack of innate interest. The major cause, beyond language, is that Scandinavian Social Democrats have had the opportunity to practice politics, not just to write about it. Winning elections turns socialist writers into policy makers.) All Scandinavian Social Democratic parties are massive organizations with tens of thousands of dues-paying members, hundreds of local branches that hold regular meetings, and thousands of elected representatives on city and county councils. Some local Social Democratic organizations have monopolized city offices for six or seven decades and have taken on some of the characteristics often ascribed to American urban political machines, although rarely their corruption. Apparently, Social Democratic internal democracy and party culture convey some immunity against the temptations of power.

Organization is a necessary but far from sufficient condition for Social Democratic political success. The reasons go beyond mere numbers to understanding the development of the party's appeal and its internal values. Organizing in a virtual political vacuum in the final decades of the last century, Social Democratic orators, agitators, and journalists articulated inchoate popular feelings and beliefs; they evoked the evangelical fervor of a secular religion. Their socialist gospel took the material discontents of everyday life, elevated them into abstractions like justice, dignity, equality, and solidarity, and then offered a concrete program to achieve them. It was a heady mixture, not least because the growing labor movement offered an opportunity for individual advancement within the movement, while serving to advance the collective interest of its members' class.

Above all else, the Scandinavian Social Democrats owe their political success to propagating that belief in unified collective action. It starts with unity within the labor movement. Social Democrats began organizing in a vacuum in the 1870s in Denmark, in the 1880s in Norway and Sweden, in the 1890s in Finland, and in the first decade of the new century in Iceland. They were able to create a united class movement without the religious divisions of Germany or the clerical-anticlerical split that existed in France and Italy. Swedish and Danish Social Democrats opted early for revisionism; they sought pragmatic alliances and reforms rather than revolutionary conspiracies and fantasies.[5] The schism between moderates and radicals in the wake of the Bolshevik Revolution produced small, healthy, Communist parties in Norway[6] and Sweden, but they were decimated through Bolshevization—the imposition of the Soviet model—in the 1920s. Even though the Communists' revival during the Resistance and World War II briefly made them a rival to the Social Democrats in some areas after the war, their decline was nearly as precipitous as their rise in the wake of postwar Stalinism and, after 1948, the Cold War. Thus, the relatively even division between communists and socialists in France, Weimar Germany, Italy, Portugal, and Spain at varying points in time had no equivalent in Scandinavia. There was a single trade-union center—called Landsorganisationen, or LO—in Denmark, Norway, and Sweden; the contrast to the multiple union federations of France and Italy is clear.

Finland and Iceland developed differently. They looked more like the situation in France or Italy after World War II. In both countries the labor vote was split down the middle between Social Democrats and Communist-dominated political alliances: the People's Democrats in Finland and the People's Alliance in Iceland to the left. As noted above, this division gave labor much less political power than otherwise would have been the case. Further, it was a significant source of labor conflict around collective bargaining, as we will discuss in Chapter 10. Reflecting the severity of the party conflict in Finland, the labor federation even split in the late 1950s and early 1960s into two federations, one Communist and one Social Democratic. Not until the end of the 1960s in Finland and the beginning of the 1990s in Iceland did this division decline in importance; today they look more like the other Scandinavian countries. The Social Democrats and People's Alliance even fielded a common slate in Iceland's 1999 election.

The ties between party and the unions are strong. Historically, they were seen as two legs of the same movement, and walking on two legs is definitely superior to hopping on one. The institutional ties between them remain strong today.

The labor movement organizes an exceptionally large portion of its potential members. Even before World War I, Danish unions were said to have organized half the urban blue-collar labor force. Today, trade unions organize four-fifths of all employees. The Social Democratic parties are mass organizations themselves, enrolling as dues-paying members between 5 and 10 percent of party voters. Party membership has declined dramatically over the past two decades but was still about 50,000 in Denmark, 71,000 in Norway, and over 177,000 in Sweden in 2000. Thus, most Social Democratic voters are current or retired members of a labor union, or party members, or have household members who are.

Beyond these two central organizations, there were a number of subsidiary political organizations. By 1920, the good Social Democrat not only belonged to his party and trade union, he also read the local Social Democratic newspaper, rented his apartment from the workers' housing cooperative, got his exercise by playing soccer for the Workers' Ball Club "Forward," vacationed at his union's vacation settlement, and drank beer brewed by the workers' co-op. His wife bought the family's food from the co-op grocery, belonged to the Social Democratic women's organization and the trade-union ladies' auxiliary, and used the oversized Sunday edition of the Social Democratic newspaper for a table cloth for the rest of the week. His children belonged to the Social Democratic scouts, and there were presents for them at the union's Christmas party. When he was unemployed, his union provided unemployment compensation and ran the employment service. When he was too sick for work, the union's sickness and health benefit fund paid the doctor and kept the family from being evicted. And when he died, the union's funeral benefits covered the cost of burial through the Workers Mortuary Society, and the union banner followed his body to the cemetery while mourners listened to the funereal strains of the trade union's brass band. The labor movement was not just a matter of economic and political organization; it was a way of life.

This helped to create and maintain a peculiar culture inside the labor movement that was characterized by the principle of solidarity. "You rise with your class," as the Swedish phrase has it, "not out of it." The sense of solidarity—of the need for collective action and collective responsibility—was deeply rooted in the practice of trade union locals. But it was also a product of the very rapid conversion of traditional societies into modern ones that carried forward the cohesion of the traditional peasant community into a modern group identification. This process was most pronounced in Sweden and Norway, which were, on the eve of World War I, still profoundly rural societies and where industrialization took place in small, isolated towns, rather than in the cities. The new industrial workers moved easily from the solidarity of the village to that of working-class organizations.

The close ties between unions and party, the mass blue-collar base of both, and the pattern of recruitment of party leaders from the ranks of the movement distinguished the Scandinavian parties from many of their counterparts elsewhere in Europe until the current generation. The Danish Social Democratic party holds the world record for putting blue-collar workers in the prime ministership: Social Democratic prime ministers include a cigar sorter (Stauning), a typographer (Hansen), a lithographer (Hedtoft), and a laborer (Jørgensen) as well as three university-trained economists (Krag, Kampmann, and Nyrup Rasmussen). The Scandinavian labor movement, in the words of the "Internationale" (the socialist anthem), sought "no condescending saviors, to rule us from their judgment halls"; it trained its own leaders in its youth movement and in trade-union night schools. Those who came from middle-class backgrounds also served apprenticeships in the ranks. (The career pattern of someone like Olof Palme, who was born into an upper-class family but entered his party career as Prime Minister Tage Erlander's personal secretary, is absolutely atypical.) Their recruitment patterns and their close ties with the unions gave Scandinavian Social Democrats a distinctly pragmatic outlook that ultimately led them down a reformist path, not because of a rejection of Marxist analysis but because of an intense realism: How can we actually put our principles into practice? The making of policy was coupled with ideological discussion, but that discussion focused on the concrete problems of achieving socialism in Scandinavia, rather than on abstract theory (see Tilton 1990, on the evolution of Swedish Social Democratic thought about socialization).

The unity and solidarity of the labor movement stood in stark contrast to the bitter historical division of its opposition. The nonsocialists were divided historically into three camps: the Conservatives, who had opposed parliamentary democracy, particularly in Denmark and Sweden; the Liberals, who had been the Conservatives' bitter opponents in the nineteenth century; and the Agrarian parties, which represented the farmers' movement. The Social Democrats were able to exploit this disunity to take power briefly with minority governments in the 1920s (1920, 1921–23, and 1924–26 in Sweden; 1924–26 in Denmark; and two weeks in 1928 in Norway). During the dark days of the Depression, neither the Liberals nor the Agrarians trusted the Conservatives; at key junctures in the 1930s through 1950s, they cooperated with the Social Democrats in preference to the Conservatives.

Together the parties of the Center—the Liberals and Agrarians—and the pragmatic Social Democrats undertook an implicit but fundamental compromise in the 1930s. With an eye to what was happening to the south, Scandinavian Social Democrats put socializing the means of production on the back burner, while the center parties accepted a state role in managing the economy and the use of the public sector for redistributive purposes. Here was the basis for the welfare state consensus that, with economic growth, has transformed the Scandinavian countries from poor, backward societies—"the fortified poorhouse" (Höglund, Sköld, and Ström 1913)—into rich and egalitarian societies within two generations. As the Swedish Social Democratic economist Gunnar Adler-Karlsson put it in presenting his theory of "functional socialism,"

in Sweden all the parties of the economic process have realized that the most important economic task is to make the national cake grow bigger and bigger, because then everyone can satisfy his demanding stomach with a greater piece. We have maintained the *goals* of socialism, but have chosen the means to realize them in a more sophisticated way than by socializing the means of production. (1967, p. 18)

Instead, the Social Democrats socialized some of the functions of ownership (putting them in the hands of the national or municipal governments or making them subjects for collective bargaining) without socializing ownership itself or undercutting the market mechanism.

Although the party has retained its electoral preeminence during the last two decades, it has lost the moral certainty of the superiority of its vision of what society should be. Its voters have become middle class: They also own cars and summer houses and are concerned about high taxes and other bourgeois party issues. Sniped at by the Left and facing a far more unified opposition on the right, the charmed lease on governmental power that the Social Democrats held for a half century in Scandinavia has expired.

Meanwhile, on the Left Flank

Since 1960, Denmark, Norway, and Sweden have witnessed the rise of a radical socialist party different from the dogmatic, pro-Moscow Communists who had, by the end of the 1950s, ceased to be more than a minor irritant on the Social Democrats' left flank. Between 1958 and 1964, the traditional Communist parties in all three countries either lost their position to homegrown radical socialist groups independent of Moscow, or were taken over by similar factions. After 1990 the remaining Communists essentially evaporated into other radical socialist parties.

The People's Democrats in Finland and People's Alliance in Iceland, which were both broader, Communist-dominated electoral alliances that had been far more successful than the Danish, Swedish, and Norwegian Communist parties, also moved toward more independence of the Soviet Communist party in the 1960s. By the end of that decade, they too fit the radical-socialist rubric more than they did the Communist one.

This process started in Denmark, where the Danish Communist party (CP) expelled Aksel Larsen, who had chaired the party for twenty-six years, for his purported "Titoist revisionism" after the party's 1958 convention. The Socialist People's party (SPP), founded in February 1959 by Larsen's faction, proved to have substantially greater popular appeal than the old CP. In the 1960 elections, it polled twice the vote that the CP had in 1957, and the SPP replaced the CP in parliament. Its electoral success had prompt repercussions to the north. A left-wing faction of the Norwegian Labor party organized a similarly named Socialist People's party in time for the 1961 elections, where it repeated the Danish SPP's success by replacing the CP in parliament. Its electoral alliance with the anti– European Community faction of the Labor party and with the Norwegian

CP brought its reorganization as the broader Socialist Left party after the 1973 election. Confronted by the likely formation of a Swedish equivalent, the old leadership of the Swedish Communist party relinquished the chairmanship of the party to what we would subsequently call its Eurocommunist wing under economist C. H. Hermansson in 1964. This change, of course, was reflected symbolically by changing the party name to Vänsterpartiet Kommunisterna (Left party Communists—VpK) in 1967 and to Vänsterpartiet (Left party) in 1990.

The development of this independent socialist left eventually drove the Moscow loyalists into the wilderness and added new voters from the feminist and environmentalist movements to the blue collar core. The new breed of Scandinavian radical socialists had more in common in the 1970s and 1980s with Eurocommunism as exemplified by the Italian CP than with any other movement. The Danish SPP was, in fact, made up of "premature Eurocommunists," but excommunication from the international Communist movement freed it of the ballast of dogma and dogmatists to develop an independent stance that ultimately enabled it to incorporate students, feminists, and Greens into a working-class party (Logue 1982 and 1984). The strain of doing so split the party in 1967, leading to the creation of the Left Socialists (Venstresocialisterne) and other radical fragments to the SPP's left. The Norwegian SPP and its Socialist Left successor and the struggled with this same problem (Logue 1982, pp. 249–90). The Swedish VpK, the Finnish People's Democrats, and the Icelandic People's Alliance also sought to encompass the new grassroots movements, although with less success. Finland and Sweden saw the rise of successful Green parties in the 1980s and 1990s and an explicitly feminist party won seats in the Icelandic parliament in the same period. Icelanders sent a Green party to parliament in the 1999 election.

The Gorbachev reforms and revelations that began in 1985 and that were followed by the fall of Communism in Eastern Europe in 1989 and the collapse of the Soviet Union in 1991 had a clear impact on all Scandinavian radical socialist parties. Although the Gorbachev reforms seemed to point the way forward for the Communist bloc, its subsequent collapse meant that "really existing socialism" ceased to exist and reform Communism was found to have shockingly little voter support in the immediate post-Communist elections in Eastern Europe and the former Soviet Union. Those radical socialist parties that were closer to their Communist roots, particularly the Finnish People's Democrats and Swedish VpK, found themselves in a crisis of confidence; both the People's Democrats and the VpK changed their names, to Left Alliance and Left party (Vänsterpartiet), respectively. But Scandinavian radical socialism survived the collapse of the Marxist model to the east. In fact, the Swedish and Norwegian radical socialist parties had their best elections ever in 1998 and 2001, respectively.

What happened?

Although the radical socialist parties all began with a far more socialist perspective on social reform than the Social Democrats (i.e., the welfare state was an attempt to stabilize capitalism and an inadequate replacement for "real socialism"), and even more of a trade union/blue collar male profile than the Social Democrats, over time they have become perhaps the most stalwart defenders of welfare state measures, particularly those that benefit women and children.

The Social Democratic push to join the European Union—which poses the threat of a "harmonization down" to the social welfare standards of the Continent—offered the radical socialists the opportunity to wrap themselves in the national flag to defend Social Democratic accomplishments at home while opposing international (or at least European) capitalism. They did so with alacrity and succeeded in cutting into in the core Social Democratic labor constituency. In Norway and Denmark, where this process had begun with the 1972 European Community referenda, an entire generation has grown to political maturity in an atmosphere in which the Social Democrats were no longer seen as the natural home for all but sectarian leftists. Moreover, because of their identification with the existing public sector, the Social Democrats were unable to capture the direct democratic wave of the last quarter century. For them, centralization and bureaucratization were acceptable means to an admirable end, not grounds for protest. Issues relating to European Union membership placed discontent with distant and bureaucratic government on the ballot, and the referenda campaigns transformed a vague ill ease into concrete political protest. In part, what was underway was a generational shift. For the older generation, which had grown up under the old dispensation of poverty and periodic unemployment, the benefits of the welfare state were worth almost any cost in bureaucratization. But for the younger generation that had grown up with full employment and relative affluence, the mechanisms that made the welfare state work had become the target for protest. Their radicalism was directed against the established order, which happened to be the system the Social Democrats had created. They supported the aims of the welfare state, including its collective aspects, but the means that they proposed stressed participation, decentralization, direct action, and community control, instead of effective, bureaucratic administration. Hence, the socialist vote splits along generational lines, with the left getting a higher proportion of younger voters while older voters going far more heavily Social Democratic. Thus, for example, the Left party polled 15 percent of the vote among those under thirty and 7 percent of the vote of those over sixty in the 1998 Swedish election while the Social Democrats won 30 percent of the vote of the younger group and 41 percent of the older group in the 1998 Swedish election (Holmberg 2000, p. 79).

In parliamentary terms, the creation of an independent Left receiving between a quarter (Denmark and Sweden) and a third (Norway) of the socialist vote in the last election (Appendix A) has been a mixed blessing for the Social Democrats. The erosion of their vote from the left was obviously a negative. So was having to deal with a left-wing alternative that could not be ostracized as a foreign body in the national political system. On the other hand, in practical parliamentary terms what the radical socialists advocated was usually in the Social Democratic party program anyway. Consequently, their votes tended to be reliable support on most domestic policies, and Social Democratic minority government in Denmark and Norway could usually depend on the parties to their right to support military, foreign, or European policies opposed by the left. Since the 1960s, Social Democratic governments have regularly used radical socialist parliamentary seats in assembling majorities.

The Bourgeois Bloc: From Disunity to Alternative Government

The principal protagonists of nineteenth-century party politics were the Liberals and the Conservatives; until the turn of the century, the Social Democrats were little more than minor Liberal allies in Norway and Sweden. Even in Denmark, where industrialization and urbanization were more advanced, their strength was limited to Copenhagen and a handful of other industrial towns.

The chief issues of the period were parliamentary supremacy and the extension of suffrage. Both were promoted by the Liberals and opposed by the Conservatives. The dispute was a bitter one, exacerbated by the Conservatives' use of their control of the machinery of government to jail their opponents, and it left the Conservatives and Liberals hereditary enemies.

The lines of political division came to follow socioeconomic patterns. Conservatives drew most of their strength from the aristocracy (except in Norway), large landowners, and urban professionals. Liberals were strongest in rural areas and, in urban areas, among shopkeepers, craftsmen, and intellectuals.

Nineteenth-century Conservatives and Liberals alike lacked a coherent ideology comparable to the Social Democrats' advocacy of Marxism. The Conservatives' ideological stance was truly conservative: preserve the established, predemocratic patterns of political power (including the king's power to appoint his ministers regardless of the majority in parliament), the authority of the state church, the special role of the army, and the prevailing pattern of property distribution and economic relationships. Along with that went the preservation of existing responsibilities of those born to property and authority, including their responsibilities to their tenants. Liberals were far more heterogeneous in their views, except in their unified assault on the existing structure of political power, which they sought to replace with parliamentary supremacy and a more democratic suffrage. Radical intellectuals, bohemian cultural figures, Christian fundamentalists, farm laborers, comfortable farm owners, modern capitalists, and traditional artisans marched shoulder to shoulder in the Liberal assault on the established political order.

The Fragmentation of Liberalism

The achievement of parliamentary supremacy between 1884 and 1917, and the extension of suffrage to practically all adults between 1898 and 1921, transformed the political scene. Broadening the suffrage strengthened the Social Democrats, and the achievement of political democracy removed that issue from the political agenda for all but extremist parties of the Left and Right. Its place was taken by cultural, regional, and above all else, economic issues.

The struggle for political democracy had been the magnet that attracted to the Liberal label the otherwise divergent interests of farmers, the urban middle class, intellectuals, artisans, antimilitarists, and the free-church congregations (which were at odds with the established, Lutheran state church in Norway and Sweden). With victory, liberalism began to crumble into its component parts. The Danish Liberal party split in 1905, as its antimilitarist wing parted company with the mother party to form the Radical Liberals (Det radikale Venstre). The Radical Liberals took the support of smallholders, artisans, and intellectuals, while the old Liberal party retained the support of the more prosperous farmers and gradually became predominantly an agrarian party. Independent agrarian parties developed to defend the economic interests of the vulnerable farm population before World War I in Finland and Iceland and in the early 1920s in Sweden and Norway. Swedish Liberals further split in the 1920s between prohibition and antiprohibition factions; Denmark got a third liberal party in 1919 with the establishment of the Justice party (Danmarks Retsforbund), which espoused the economic philosophy of the American reformer Henry George; and a Christian People's party developed after 1933 in Norway to promote the religious and cultural values strongly held in southwestern Norway.

The division of the Liberals, previously the dominant political grouping among voters, opened the way for shifting parliamentary constellations and a succession of minority governments in the 1920s. Ultimately, however, the division encouraged the creation of the alliance between the Social Democrats and Liberals or Agrarians in the 1930s in Denmark, Norway and Sweden in which the Social Democrats were the dominant partner. That alliance held into the 1960s and it formed part of much of the basis for long-term Social Democratic dominance of government.

By contrast in the same period in Iceland and Finland, where the labor vote was split relatively evenly between Social Democrats and Communists, the political fulcrum balanced further to the right with the Agrarian Center dominating the government in Finland in the 1950s and 1960s and control shifting between the conservative Independence party and agrarian Progressive party in Iceland.

A Credible Bourgeois Alternative

Three primary themes have characterized the bourgeois parties since the 1960s:

1. Successful movement toward offering a unified alternative government to the Social Democrats;
2. increasing fragmentation of the bourgeois bloc with the rise in Finland, Sweden, and Denmark of Christian parties patterned on the Norwegian example, and the explosive appearance of right-wing protest parties in Denmark and Norway in the 1973 elections; and
3. decline of partisan allegiance to individual nonsocialist parties and the growth of a pool of mobile voters who shift regularly between parties in that bloc.

In the postwar period, the bourgeois parties in Denmark, Norway, and Sweden moved from being either junior coalition partners of the Social Democrats, or parties of "permanent opposition" (1945–65), to being parties of alternative government (1965–present). The long road to a credible bourgeois alternative government really began when Conservatives established their credibility as democrats during the Resistance. In the context of the mobilization of a national community in all three countries during World War II, the historical antipathies among bourgeois parties suddenly paled. The early postwar attempts to put together nonsocialist majorities, however, foundered on the pragmatic loyalty of the Swedish Agrarians and Danish Radical Liberals to their Social Democratic alliance; that persisted until 1957 in Sweden, and until 1964 in Denmark. Only in Norway, where Labor had a parliamentary majority that permitted it to govern alone, was the path to nonsocialist unity reasonably straightforward. A clearly unified bourgeois alternative first developed in the early 1960s in Norway, late 1960s in Denmark, and in the 1970s in Sweden.

A unified bourgeois alternative required a blurring of the distinctions among the bourgeois parties. It was easy enough in name. The Swedish and Norwegian agrarian parties adopted the Center party label, and the Swedish Conservative party changed its name from Right to Moderate Unity. Policies were more problematic. The individual bourgeois parties had to compromise on precisely those issues that had distinguished one from the other. Eventually they managed to fashion an alternative, and more individualistic, vision of the welfare state that rested on the belief that social policy is limited by resources, and that redistribution was becoming increasingly difficult.

Bourgeois success in putting together coalition governments meant shouldering the responsibility that went with office. Although various nonsocialist parties—particularly the Conservatives—had regularly promised to reverse major Social Democratic policies (most popular was the promise to cut taxes), once in power the nonsocialist coalitions proved able caretakers of the Social Democratic edifice.

Dissatisfaction blossomed among disgruntled bourgeois voters in both Norway and Denmark where all-party bourgeois coalitions from 1965 to 1971 and 1968 to 1971, respectively, had presided over social reforms, liberalization of laws on pornography and abortion, and rising taxes. The highly divisive referenda on membership in the European Community in 1972 further weakened partisan loyalties in Norway and Denmark. This combination set the stage in both countries for the electoral earthquakes of 1973 that shattered the existing balance and relations among the bourgeois parties.

The Election Earthquake of 1973

The September 1973 elections in Norway devastated the Liberals, who had split into pro- and anti–European Community factions; between them, the two factions of Norway's oldest party elected only three members of parliament. The Liberals have not recovered from their debacle; the 1973 election eliminated the party as a political force. More surprising was the success of a right-wing protest group, which seemed only a joke up to election night, in winning parliamentary representation. Its name, Anders Lange's Party for the Sharp Reduction of Income Taxes, Excise Taxes, and Government Intervention, summed up its leadership and program of opposition to the other bourgeois parties' commitment to the welfare state. This party, renamed the Progress party after Lange's death in 1975, has remained a fixture in Norwegian politics ever since, particularly as a thorn in the side of the Conservatives.

In Denmark, the sudden election in December 1973 produced an even more astonishing realignment. One voter in three cast a ballot for a party not represented in the outgoing parliament, and brought four additional bourgeois parties into parliament: the Georgists, for the first time since 1960; the Christian People's party, for the first time ever; and two brand-new antitax parties, dissident Social Democrat Erhard Jacobsen's Center Democrats (founded as the election campaign began) and Mogens Glistrup's Progress party (founded in 1972). The last two were the big winners.

Together they polled one-fourth of the vote, and Glistrup's outrageous proposals (see Chapter 2) vaulted his Progress party over the other bourgeois parties to become the next largest party in parliament after the Social Democrats. Although Glistrup's party lost half of its seats over the next decade, and the Georgists lost all their seats in 1981, a realignment had, in fact, occurred. The number of bourgeois parties doubled from three to six, and the Christian People's party and Center Democrats were accepted into the Conservative minority coalition cabinet established in 1982.

Sweden's party system changed less dramatically, but in 1976 a sharp swing away from the Social Democrats brought to power the first non-socialist coalition in forty years. Initially the Center party, with its explicitly antinuclear and "green" program captured the new wave, and governed with the Moderates and Liberals. Although the Social Democrats returned to power in 1982 under Olof Palme and his sharply New Left tone, the era of Social Democratic hegemony was broken. In 1991 a Swedish rightist populist party—the New Democrats (Ny Demokratien)—briefly burst onto the scene, but that decade saw the growth of the Christian Democrats at the expense of the Center and Liberal parties.

The Development of the New Right

To the astonishment of many observers, both Norwegian and Danish Progress parties survived, respectively, the death and criminal conviction[7] of their founders. The Danish party, afflicted by almost constant internal squabbles between hardliners who wanted to maintain the party's purity and a more flexible faction that sought direct legislative influence, declined from almost 16 percent of the vote in 1973 to about 6 percent in 1994. It then split with Pia Kjærsgaard leading a strongly anti-immigrant faction and adopting the name Danish People's party (Dansk Folkeparti) for its nationalist (anti–European Union, anti-immigrant) program. Kjærsgaard's group surged to 7 percent of the vote in 1998, leaving the rump Progress party with just over 2 percent. In 2001, the Danish People's party polled 12 percent and the remaining Progress group lost its remaining seats. The Norwegian Progress party vote has fluctuated wildly, but party has remained unified. Its vote jumped to 15 percent in the 1997 (see Madeley 1998) and 2001 elections. In Sweden the somewhat similar rightist New Democrats jumped into parliament with 7 percent in the 1991 election only to vanish in the next election.

In Finland the contemporary "populist right" stretches back to the Small Farmers' party—later renamed the Rural party—which was led from the 1960s to the 1980s by the colorful Veikko Vennamo. During periods of economic or political tension, its support grew, but invariably soon fell back. It continues under new leadership as the True Finns party. Although it advanced slightly from one to three parliamentary seats in 2003, it currently remains a very minor fringe party.

Curiously, the new right parties that originated as antitax, antigovernment movements have, in their turn, also become supporters of the welfare state. To be sure, their generosity stops with Danes and Norwegians and certainly excludes immigrants. But they, too, now fall within the broad welfare state party consensus.

Initially, bourgeois party governments sought to avoid dependence on Progress party votes in parliament. As time has passed, however, and the new right has become part of the parliamentary everyday, it too has been encompassed in parliamentary calculations. Both Fogh Rasmussen's Danish government and Bondevik's second Norwegian government rested upon the support of new rightist MPs.

Declining Partisan Allegiance

The explosive success of the new bourgeois parties in the post-1973 period reflected the growing instability in partisan allegiance in the non-socialist bloc. Nearly all bourgeois voters in the 1950s and 1960s had a clear party preference. The agrarian parties recruited nearly all their support from the still-significant rural population. The liberals enjoyed the support not only of a historical constituency, but also of smallholders in Denmark and free church groups in Sweden. The conservatives continued to draw the votes of the business community, the old upper class, and what hereditary military caste exists in Scandinavia, and contested the vote of a growing white-collar strata with the liberals. But demographic, occupational, and generational changes undercut this comfortable pattern in the late 1960s and 1970s.

With the continued decline in farming, the agrarian parties sought to broaden their appeal, modifying their programs to attract urban voters. The Finnish Agrarian Center has maintained a permanent lock on a fifth of the voters over the past fifty years despite the decline in the farming population, and the Icelandic agrarian Progressive party likewise continues to hold a fifth of the vote. The Center party in Sweden enjoyed substantial success under Thorbjörn Fälldin in the early and mid-1970s by focusing on environmental issues, especially opposition to Sweden's ambitious nuclear power program, although in recent years it has lost heavily to the Christian Democrats who cut into the agrarian constituency. The Danish agrarian Liberals, who downplayed their agrarianism and emphasized an individualistic liberalism and economic deregulation, similarly enjoyed a spectacular election in 1975 and steady growth in the 1990s culminating in their passing the Social Democrats to become Denmark's largest party in the 2001 election.

The Liberals, whose programmatic raison d'etre—political democracy and economic freedom—had long ago become the common heritage of all major parties, were most threatened by the trends. The generation that owed them unquestioning allegiance was passing from the scene, and smallholders virtually disappeared in Denmark. The Liberals, too, turned to the pursuit of the so-called floating voters of the center-right, with some success under Hilmar Baunsgaard in Denmark in the late 1960s, and under Bengt Westerberg in Sweden in the mid-1980s. Their success underlined the continued appeal of *social liberalism*—nonsocialist social reformism—in mature welfare states. They saw increasing competition from the Christian Democrats and, among younger voters, from the Greens. Christian Democratic parties entered the Danish parliament in 1973, the Finnish parliament in 1970, and the Swedish parliament in 1991. As noted above, Green parties won seats in Finland (1983), Sweden (1988), and Iceland (1999). The Christian parties' success came at the expense of the Liberals and the Agrarian Center; the Greens won votes among the young that the Liberals might have otherwise contested. The Norwegian Liberals, split by the issue of European Community membership, lost their parliamentary representation entirely between 1985 and 1993; they reentered parliament as a shadow of their former selves. The Finnish Liberals lost their last seat in 1995 after a long, secular decline (see Appendix B) and have disappeared entirely as an electoral force. In none of the Scandinavian countries does the Liberal party, which had been key to the development of modern democracy, play a significant role except as a swing party between forming Social Democratic or bourgeois governments.

The Conservatives, contesting the same ground, managed to collar most of the floating bourgeois vote in Denmark and Norway in the early 1980s under Prime Ministers Poul Schlüter and Kåre Willoch, respectively. Distancing themselves from the Reagan-Thatcher belief that government should shrink (especially in the social welfare area), Scandinavian conservatives made only marginal adjustments to social welfare programs. Instead, they sought to create room for greater individual choice and initiative within the existing welfare state. A severe economic crisis propelled the Swedish Conservatives under Carl Bildt into power in 1991, and together with the Liberals and Center parties, they instituted some drastic reforms. There was, however, no fundamental attack on the principles and basis of the welfare state, nor were the reforms significantly reversed when Social Democrats returned to power in all three countries in the 1990s.

The cause of increased voter mobility seems to be that the natural constituencies of the individual nonsocialist parties have declined in size, without any party becoming the clear choice of the new nonsocialist white-collar employees. A portion of this group seems to see itself as broadly nonsocialist, but without particular party identification; ballots are cast on the basis of personality and immediate campaign issues. The growth of this pool of floating voters has added to the volatility of elections and complicated the problems of maintaining nonsocialist coalition governments, but it has also created more of a basis for a common bourgeois ideology. Such an ideology emphasizes the rights and responsibilities of the individual vis-à-vis the state. Without the rhetoric of "social Darwinism" found in Anglo-Saxon conservatism, Scandinavian "compassionate conservatism" is built on strong pro-nation–state ideology including restrained but comprehensive social policy.

Party Organization

The growth in voter mobility has been compounded by the general atrophy in bourgeois party organizations. Only the Agrarians, who organized all aspects of rural life as thoroughly as the Social Democrats organized that of the urban working class before World War I, have been able to maintain a powerful organization among their core constituency. With growing diversity in the labor movement (the rise of white-collar and professional unions) and appearance of the affluent worker (whose lifestyle of private home, car, foreign vacations, etc. is essentially middle class) that connection has been weakened. The new bourgeois parties in Denmark and Norway lack any tradition of party organization and, with the exception of the Danish Christian People's party, lack the ties to other organized groups that can serve as a surrogate for the existence of a party organization. The decline of party organizations has not only increased voter mobility, it has diminished the tie between voters and their representatives and made the patterns of recruitment within these parties increasingly subject to self-selection and co-optation of interest group representatives and prominent persons, rather than selection from the ranks. Even voting now encourages personalities over party lists.[8]

When Seymour Martin Lipset and Stein Rokkan postulated in 1967 the existence of a frozen party structure that reflected past historical experience, their thesis was entirely appropriate for the Scandinavia of that time. It was, however, the twilight of a historical period. Especially among the bourgeois parties, the ensuing decade would see more partisan realignment than the previous half century. The major nonsocialist parties experienced a renaissance as they turned from divided and permanent opposition to offering a unified alternative government to that of the Social Democrats. For the first time since the 1920s, alternating governments came to be the rule, not the exception. It was not a new era of bourgeois hegemony so much as the end of Social Democratic hegemony. In each case, it commenced with the socialists losing power more than the nonsocialists winning power. No matter—the bourgeois parties got their opportunity. In the tactical battles of parliamentary politics, that counts for a lot.

SCANDINAVIAN COALITION PATTERNS

> A coalition is like a marriage in which jealousy is greater than love.
> —Amintore Fanfani, former Premier of Italy

Political scientists generally expect multiparty systems to produce cabinet instability. Certainly France under the Fourth Republic (1946–58) and Italy throughout much of the postwar period are disturbing examples of the instability that revolving-door cabinets produce. Cabinet instability made implementing coherent policies almost impossible. Yet throughout most of the last half century, the Scandinavian countries, except Finland,[9] have been examples of exceptional stability in government and consistency of policy. The reasons basically are four:

1. Social Democratic dominance of a divided opposition;
2. the unique focus of Scandinavian politics on issues where compromise is possible;
3. an unusual practice of seeking broad coalitions, rather than narrow majorities, to pass major reforms; and
4. the nature of internal organization and norms in Scandinavian parties.

Social Democratic Dominance

Social Democratic electoral dominance has been a fact of political life in Denmark, Norway, and Sweden since the 1920s. In terms of election support, the Social Democrats became the largest party in Sweden in 1917, Denmark in 1924, and Norway in 1927. (In Finland, they became the largest party in the country's first election in 1907, but had their dominance shattered by the civil war.) They have held power alone or in coalition for two-thirds or more of the years since 1929 in Denmark, 1932 in Sweden, 1935 in Norway, and 1966 in Finland. Iceland is the only country in which the Social Democrats have never played the predominant role. (See Appendixes A, B, and C for party votes, seats, and governmental coalitions, respectively.)

In both Denmark and Sweden, the nonsocialist parties were divided by the bitterness left by the struggle between Liberals and Conservatives over establishing political democracy. The legacy of hostility that remained between them made a united nonsocialist coalition government an impossibility between the wars. A similar animosity between Social Democrats and Communists kept the latter out of coalition participation through the end of the 1950s in Denmark, Norway, and Sweden; the only exception was the summer of 1945 when the Communists were involved in the Liberation cabinets of Denmark and Norway as a consequence of their role in the Resistance. In contrast, both Finland and Iceland had considerable Communist participation in government, especially after the mid 1960s.

In the interwar period, formal government participation, or informal agreements to support the Social Democratic minority governments, seemed to both Liberals and Agrarians preferable to collaboration with the Conservatives. At crucial junctures in all three countries in the 1930s, Social Democratic-Agrarian and/or -Liberal agreements provided broad support for important reforms; the same was also true in Iceland in this period but it was under the agrarian Progressive party's leadership. The Social Democratic-Agrarian alliance was a feature of life in Sweden from 1936 to 1957 and led to Agrarian participation in Social Democratic governments in 1936–39 and 1951–57 as well as in the wartime national unity coalition (1939–45). In Denmark, the Radical Liberals played the same role, participating regularly in coalition governments with the Social Democrats between 1929 and 1964, despite serious foreign and security policy differences between the parties after Denmark joined NATO in 1949 (see Einhorn 1975, pp. 61–79). Social Democratic governments in Finland from the mid-1960s through the mid-1980s rested on coalitions with the Agrarian Center and the Liberals. Such coalition cabinets were less vital in Norway until the 1970s because the election system generally produced majorities for the Labor party in parliament. But a similar pattern of compromise was maintained.

Patterns of Compromise

The pattern of party coalitions proved so durable, we suspect, because the principal issues of political dispute were social and economic ones—not the racial, religious, ethnic, and cultural conflicts that are so intractable in other countries. A good portion of the consensus and compromise that characterize Scandinavian politics stems from the fact that socioeconomic issues are susceptible to compromise. It is easier to compromise on the size of old-age pensions than on racial integration. Opponents and supporters of public-sector jobs can discuss whether there should be more or less of them; opponents and supporters of abortion have less common ground. The consequence is that parties composing Scandinavian coalitions generally can reach agreement on the issues dividing them, or, as the Radical Liberals and Social Democrats did in Denmark between 1957 and 1964, agree to ignore them. Truly nonnegotiable issues are rare, although the supplemental-pension question had that status and broke up the long-standing Social Democratic-Agrarian coalition in Sweden in 1957.

Nonnegotiable issues became more common in the 1970s: Per Borten's nonsocialist majority coalition in Norway collapsed in 1971 over Norwegian membership in the European Community, and Thorbjörn Fälldin's first cabinet—the first nonsocialist government in Sweden since 1936—

collapsed in 1978 after two years in office over commissioning new atomic power plants. Foreign policy issues have traditionally limited coalition possibilities between Social Democrats and various radical socialist parties. The end of the Cold War in 1990 removed a major barrier to Social Democratic—radical socialist collaboration, but the disagreements on the EU remain sharp.

In short, we can generally conceive of the major Scandinavian parties distributed from left to right along this socioeconomic dimension; the only lasting exception to this unidimensionality lies in the urban-rural distinction that affected particularly the more urban Liberals and the rural Agrarian and Christian parties. The coalition pattern across the center of the political spectrum diagramed in Figure 5.1 persisted from the 1930s through the end of the 1950s in Sweden and through the mid-1960s in Denmark.

Since then this pattern has broken down. On the right, the residue of bitterness between Conservatives, on the one hand, and the Liberals and

Figure 5.1
Scandinavian Party Coalitions, 1930s–1950s

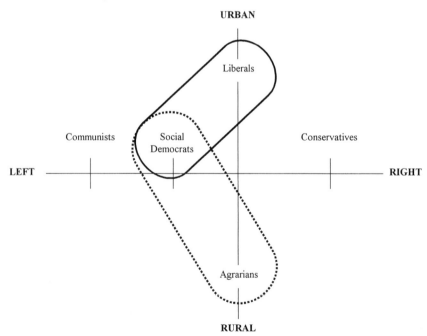

Source: From *Modern Welfare States: Politics and Policies in Social Democratic Scandinavia,* Eric S. Einhorn and John Logue. 1989. Praeger Publishers (Westport, CT). Reprinted with permission.

Agrarians on the other, disappeared. The increased acceptability of the Conservatives as coalition partners for the nonsocialists of the center after World War II gradually made the idea of a nonsocialist majority coalition a politically viable alternative. There had, after all, been nonsocialist majorities in the Danish parliament throughout the entire period of Social Democratic government, and nonsocialist majorities in Sweden had been common as well in the 1930s and 1950s.

The consequence was that in the 1960s and 1970s, to an increasing degree, a two-bloc model emerged as the alternative to the Social Democratic-Agrarian or -Liberal coalitions of the previous period (see Fig. 5.2). In both Norway and Sweden, Social Democratic minority cabinets began to depend regularly on the parliamentary backing of the SPP (later the Socialist Left party) and the Communists, without making formal agreements. In Denmark in 1966–67, again in 1973, and sporadically in late 1990s, Social Democratic minority cabinets made formal agreements on common policies with the Socialist People's party, without the SPP taking cabinet posts. Formal socialist coalitions remained elusive, however, except in Finland and Iceland where they always included at least one other party in addition to the Social Democrats and People's Democrats (now Left Alliance) or People's Alliance, respectively.

Figure 5.2
Scandinavian Party Coalitions, 1960s–1980s

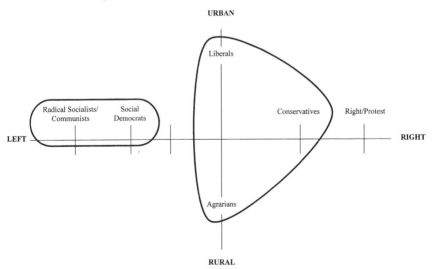

Source: From *Modern Welfare States: Politics and Policies in Social Democratic Scandinavia*, Eric S. Einhorn and John Logue. 1989. Praeger Publishers (Westport, CT). Reprinted with permission.

Meanwhile, the Social Democrats' former coalition partners, the Radical Liberals in Denmark and agrarian Center in Sweden, had moved toward collaboration with the other nonsocialist parties. As lines of division within this bloc faded, the nonsocialists recognized that their only route to power was through increased cooperation. In Norway, the four bourgeois parties in 1963 took advantage of the SPP's ouster of the Labor government to form a short-lived coalition; in 1965 the electorate gave them the opportunity to renew the experiment with a majority-coalition government under agrarian Center party leader Per Borten. This coalition foundered on the divisive issue of Norwegian membership in the European Community in 1971. It was replaced by a minority Labor government—elections in Norway cannot be called early—led by Trygve Bratteli, which staked its survival on a "Yes" vote in the 1972 European Community referendum. Norwegians narrowly voted "No" (54% to 46%), and Bratteli resigned. The replacement was another weak minority government, this time composed of the nonsocialist parties that had opposed European Community membership: the agrarian Center, Christian People's party, and the anti–European Community faction of the Liberals. The subsequent election in 1973 devastated the divided Liberals and led to eight years of minority Labor government, occasionally dependent on the votes of the Socialist Left. Despite the best economic record in Europe for that period, Labor lost the 1981 election to the Conservatives, who took the reins of government, first with the informal support of the agrarian Center and the Christian People's parties, and then with their full participation. The dominant position of the Norwegian Conservatives stems in no small measure from the disappearance of a viable Liberal alternative. But in the 1990s under the formidable leadership of Gro Harlem Brundtland Labor came back and survived another defeat over European Union membership in 1994. They gave up power to a weak centrist coalition (Christian People's, Center, and Liberal) following the 1997 elections primarily because of a tactical miscalculation by the new Labor leader Thorbjørn Jagland. The nonsocialist coalition Kjell Magne Bondevik (Chr. P.P.) collapsed in 1999 to be replaced by Labor minority government under Jens Stoltenberg, which lost the 2001 election to Bondevik's coalition; both Bondevik governments required the tacit support of the Progress party to its right.

In Denmark, the bourgeois opportunity came in 1968 when the Radical Liberals joined with the agrarian Liberals and Conservatives in a coalition that narrowly lost power to the Social Democrats and Socialist People's party in 1971. Following the 1973 election shock, the agrarians formed a minority government alone, with the narrowest parliamentary basis (22 of 179 seats) since the establishment of parliamentary democracy in Denmark. It lasted only a year before again yielding to a Social Democratic minority cabinet. In 1982 the nonsocialists under Conservative leader Poul

Schlüter welded a complex minority-coalition government from the Conservative, agrarian Liberal, Center Democratic, and Christian People's parties, with the Radicals informally adding the necessary votes. This coalition provided the longest period of nonsocialist rule since World War I, but collapsed in scandal in 1993. The Social Democrats then revived their coalition with the Radicals and held power through two elections. The agrarian Liberals under Anders Fogh Rasmussen took power in a minority coalition with the Conservatives in 2001; similar to the situation in Norway, the new government depended on the tacit support of the Danish People's party to its right.

Power eluded the Swedish bourgeois parties until 1976. Nonsocialist government was a political sensation in a country that had seen more than forty years of Social Democratic rule, but the achievements of the bourgeois parties in government between 1976 and 1982 were modest. They failed to agree on many basic policies (nuclear power was the most spectacular disagreement, but not the only one), and seemed as willing to fight among themselves as to demonstrate what their alternative to the Social Democrats should be. The bourgeois majority ultimately gave Sweden four governments in six years and the Social Democrats recovered power in 1982. A severe economic recession hit Sweden in 1990, and in 1991 the Conservatives led the nonsocialists back into government. They coped bravely with Sweden's worst recession in two generations, but lost the 1994 and 1998 elections to minority Social Democrats government under Ingvar Carlsson and Göran Persson; both Social Democratic governments depended on the support of the Greens and Left party.

The more flexible coalition patterns of the 1990s and beginning of the new century are reflected in Figure 5.3. The hard lines of bloc politics have softened. Governments increasingly seem to take votes where they can find them.

Both Finland and Iceland have tended toward broader, majority coalitions (cf Table 4.2). The Social Democrats have led most Finnish coalition governments since the mid 1960s. Generally those have included both the Agrarian Center and the People's Democrats/Left Alliance as well as the Swedish People's party. However, Social Democrat Paavo Lipponen's government (1995–2003) has included both the Left Alliance—the former Communists—and the conservative National Coalition as well as the Swedish People's and Green parties. Iceland's shifting coalitions have included all four major parties in varying alliances that, as can be seen in Appendix Table C.3, permit every imaginable permutation.

What was thought to be permanent Social Democratic government, the pattern of the 1930s to the 1960s in Denmark, Norway, and Sweden, is clearly a thing of the past. Today there is clearly an alternation of alternation of governments between Social Democratic–led governments of the left or left and center, on the one hand, varying bourgeois coalitions, on

Figure 5.3
Scandinavian Party Coalitions, 1990s to present

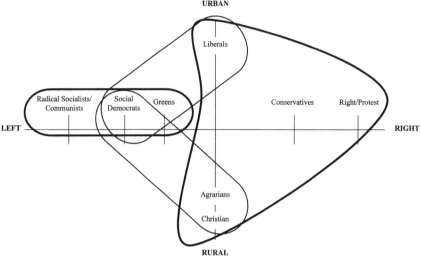

the other. Social Democratic hegemony seems strongest in Sweden and Finland but has also continued, to a lesser extent, in Denmark and Norway during the last three turbulent decades of the twentieth century.

Broad Coalitions

The third factor affecting coalition stability has been the practice of seeking broader coalitions than the minimum necessary to pass legislation. Frequently, even majority coalitions seek the support of one or more opposition parties for major legislative initiatives, choosing to weaken the proposals to get broader support. This attitude is reflected in former Danish Prime Minister Anker Jørgensen's comment that passing "major reforms by narrow majorities is a cause for misgivings." Outside Scandinavia it would be considered a cause for triumph. The obvious consequence of the practice is that reforms, once in place with broader support, are not likely to be repealed should the opposition come to power. A less-obvious result is to reduce the interbloc animosities, disorganizing the opposition by giving one or more opponents some influence, and lessening the vigor of the other side's attack on governmental policy. Note, for example, that crucial tax-reform measures in Sweden in 1981 and 1990 and in Denmark in 1985 were the outcome of agreement between nonsocialist governments and the Social Democrats in opposition. A similar consensus supported economic and social policy reforms during recent crises. By contrast, Swedish Social Democrats' efforts in the

1980s to introduce collective wage-earner funds faced implacable opposition from the nonsocialist parties. When the latter gained power in 1991, they expedited its repeal.

Internal Party Organization

The final cause of the stability of Scandinavian party coalitions lies in the internal structure of Scandinavian parties. Almost all Scandinavian parties contain considerable divergence of views, but historically the concept of party discipline has been strong and their degree of unity around their leadership is impressive, particularly in comparison to that in other countries. This characteristic has weakened notably as party memberships have declined and intraparty democracy has strengthened. Still, it is extraordinarily rare for a Scandinavian government to fall because of internal division within one of its parties.

A New Realignment?

The developments of the last thirty years in Scandinavian party politics suggest the possibility of another realignment of coalition patterns. Voters remain divided roughly evenly between the socialist and the bourgeois blocs, but the two-bloc pattern, with the presentation of coherent alternative governmental possibilities that it entails, is in disarray. The most obvious cause is the demonstrated instability of nonsocialist majority coalitions.

In both Denmark and Norway, the nonsocialist majority coalitions of the late 1960s could not be reconstructed immediately after the defeat of the Social Democrats in the early 1980s or in Sweden in 1990s. In none of the countries is an all-party nonsocialist coalition politically plausible today. In Denmark and Norway strong new rightist parties have only recently become acceptable to the moderate nonsocialist minority governments as part of their parliamentary base of support. Socialist governments over the past two decades have usually found one or more supporter in the nonsocialist bloc, but they have also regularly counted on votes to their left. Only in Finland, however, has the Left Alliance and its predecessor People's Democrats been a regular participant in Social Democratic–led coalition governments.

A second factor, related to the first, is the lack of a clear nonsocialist leading party after the temporary emergence of the Conservative party in each of the countries as the principal nonsocialist party in the 1980s. In the confusion and disunity of nonsocialist ranks, the relatively hard ideological line of the Conservatives offered a clear profile that nonsocialist voters have found attractive, not least because of the political competence of Schlüter and Willoch in Denmark and Norway, respectively, and of Carl Bildt, at the helm of the conservative Moderate Unity party in Sweden.

Bildt maintained his popularity while prime minister (1991–94), but his coalition partners were punished in the next election; Schlüter and Willoch are retired.

It is easy to overestimate the importance of swings among nonsocialist parties. In the early 1970s there were convincing swings to the Agrarians in Sweden and Denmark while the agrarian Center party in Norway tripled its seats in 1993 after leading the fight against EU membership only to fall back in 1997 as the EU issue faded. In the past decade the Danish agrarian Liberals (who have successfully thrown off their agrarian image and captured much of the urban conservative vote) emerged as the clear nonsocialist alternative under the leadership of Uffe Ellemann-Jensen and Anders Fogh Rasmussen. Nor was the American and British hard conservatism of the 1980s and 1990s successful for the traditional Scandinavian conservative parties. To push a welfare state rollback combined with privatization of state services is to risk shattering what bourgeois unity exists. Even the otherwise rightist Progress parties in Denmark and Norway and the successor Danish People's party today are centrists on welfare state issues. In Sweden the Conservatives' frontal attack on the Social Democratic "Swedish model" in the 1985 election failed and in 1991 economic recovery and moderate reform was dictated by the sharp recession underway.

The growing pool of floating bourgeois voters causes a particular problem in holding nonsocialist coalitions together. Floating voters are clearly attracted to parties with high profiles. If the coalition parties are loyal to one another, the dominant partner in the coalition invariably reaps electoral gains at the expense of its allies. To prevent those losses, the subordinate partners have to raise their public profiles, and that is most easily accomplished by open dissent from the coalition or outside it; that is precisely the tack taken by the Swedish Conservatives in 1981 as well as by the Norwegian Conservatives at the end of the 1990s. Coalition unity simply does not reward the loyal smaller parties in votes on election day.

Last, but probably most important, is the decline of Social Democratic hegemony. From the 1930s through the early 1970s, the Social Democrats appeared to be the natural party of government in Denmark, Norway, and Sweden. Flush with confidence, they proceeded to transform society, constructing what are probably the best-developed welfare states in the world. The late 1960s and early 1970s saw the final stages of that construction. To a significant extent, subsequent Social Democratic governments in Denmark and (to a lesser extent) Norway, weakened by defections to the Left over foreign policy and European Union membership, have served more as caretakers of the edifice their predecessors erected than as architects. Only in Sweden have the Social Democrats managed to push major reforms through and to project their vision of the Sweden of the future, and these have either enjoyed broad support (tax reform in the

1980s and pension reform in the 1990s) or been short-lived (wage earner funds). In Norway, the Labor party's most significant contribution was creating an Oil Fund to bank the volatile revenues of a depleting resource. This prudent measure was adapted from such unlikely hotbeds of socialism as the state of Alaska and the province of Alberta.

If this analysis is correct and (1) the demonstrated lack of bourgeois party cohesion makes stable, long-term nonsocialist coalitions improbable; (2) the current ascendance of the Swedish Conservatives and Danish agrarian Liberals proves to be as transitory as the earlier pattern in Norway and Denmark and no single nonsocialist party establishes a permanent dominance of their side of the political spectrum comparable to that which the Social Democrats have enjoyed; and (3) Social Democratic programmatic, although not organizational, hegemony is a thing of the past, then what does the future hold?

The most likely prospect is a situation similar to that of the 1920s, with an alternation between parties in government principally—between Social Democratic minority cabinets and those led by a nonsocialist party whose charismatic leader can attract temporarily a notable share of the bloc's voters—and a resulting loss of coherence in policy. Our crystal ball suggests no dramatic departures in policy and quite possibly drift while problems accumulate. However, the resurgence of reform and compromise in the 1990s promises a more positive outcome. The return of the politics of compromise will frustrate Scandinavian specialists, who seem to prefer a more orderly and purposeful pattern in politics.

PARTIES BETWEEN CITIZENS AND
GOVERNMENT: IS VOTER CONTROL A MYTH?

Parties structure the competition for office in elections in Western democracies. But in what fashion does this competition among political elites permit citizen control of government? Implicit in the "responsible party government" theory is that citizen control is indirect: Parties submit alternative policies to voters at periodic elections, and the winner, once in office, carries out the promised policies. Setting the agenda is in the hands of the party elite. In this model, voters' voices are heard periodically through elections, but their role in between is muted. Turnout is important, and here the Scandinavian countries excel: In the last twenty-five years, 65 to 75 percent of Finnish voters, 75 to 85 percent of Norwegian voters, and 85 to 90 percent of Danish, Icelandic, and Swedish voters participated.[10] In 1990s the numbers have fallen modestly for parliamentary elections. For local and European Parliamentary elections the participation rate has been much lower.

Explicit in the ideologies of the Scandinavian popular movements, however, is the thesis that citizen control ought to be direct: The party is the direct representative of its voters' interests, and the party in government is directly responsible on a continuing basis to a mass membership that should be as large a portion of the party's voters as possible. Although relatively few movement parties actually subordinate incumbent elected officials directly to the party organization, there is a widespread sense that an organic connection ought to exist between elected officials and party members and voters, and that it is the obligation of elected officials to maintain those ties through regular contact. Leaders feel that as well as shown in the following interview with former Danish prime minister and union leader Anker Jørgensen.

Anker Jørgensen. Born 1922. Son of teamster Johannes Albert Jørgensen and maid Karen Marie Jørgensen. Parents died when he was a child. Raised by aunt. Left school at fourteen. Errand boy. Short-term factory job at fifteen. Errand boy again. Unemployed. Warehouse worker for the Danish Cooperative League. Joined Social Democratic party in 1942. Active in the Resistance. Shop Steward 1946. Vice president, Copenhagen Warehouse Workers Local Union, 1950; president, 1956. National business agent for transport division within the Danish Transport and General Workers Union, 1962. Social Democratic member of parliament 1964. National president, Transport and General Workers Union, 1968. Prime Minister 1972–73, 1975–82.

The following are excerpts from an interview on August 20, 1985.

Q: As prime minister, whom did you represent?

A: In theory, of course, I was the prime minister for the whole country and for every citizen, but it's clear that I gave priority to particular groups: to those who needed someone to deal with their problems. Those are very large groups in the Danish population, even if all the members of these groups did not vote for me. It's not really a class viewpoint, but it's certainly not trying to float above the fray. . . . You can't cut yourself free—and you shouldn't cut yourself free—of where you come from. And I come from working-class circles. I was a warehouse worker.

Q: That was a long time ago. . . .

A: I've kept in touch because I meet principally with those I represent. As prime minister, I went to one or two local party or union meetings every week. It will be three or four meetings per week when Parliament reconvenes. There's almost no spot in this country where I haven't been to a meeting. Of course, that's easier to do in Denmark than the United States. . . . I still go to my old union local. I take part in the meetings, not as the speaker but as regular member.

Q: What's it like to sit in the audience?

A: You can't say too much in the discussion, or at least I feel I shouldn't. It's worthwhile just sitting there and listening to the views presented. I don't know if they'd say the same things if I wasn't there. . . . That's where I started. As a shop steward for fifty warehouse workers. Then I was chief shop steward, then local vice president . . . . I can't forget the shop meetings that I took part in all over Copenhagen.

When I drive in here [to parliament] from my home on Borgbjergvej, I drive past six or seven different businesses where I used to go to shop meetings in the 1950s. I don't think about them every day, but I do think about them often. I can still see the plant, see the lunchroom where we held meetings. . . . Ole Olsen was shop steward at one of them, an arch communist but a good guy. I remember how they all complained about our raising dues twenty-five øre.

I used to try to slip a broader perspective into our shop discussions. For a while I tried to talk about Nordic labor cooperation. They wanted to talk about their own problems: excessive overtime, the bonus system for heavy lifting, for dangerous work, not about Nordic labor cooperation. And I think that's understandable. That's what workplace problems are.

Q: You've been prime minister. You've been national president of your union. But Hans Lyngby Jepsen quotes you as saying that your best years were working in the local union. Is that true?

A: Does he? Yes, I've said that. Actually, my happiest years were the six years I spent as local vice president under Kai Petersen. He was fantastically good when he was local president. . . . The local was a mess when we came in. . . . We got it going again, got a good reputation, got many members active, ran study circles. . . . We ran study circles on art, on labor history, on the international labor movement. We even covered Australia and New Zealand in that one. It's not so easy to get warehouse workers to sit in a study circle and discuss the state of the labor movement in Australia and New Zealand. . . . I still have the mimeographed reports from one circle where we covered "workers and socialism." It's almost impossible to get people to write up the discussions after they've worked all day. Sometimes we succeeded. What we succeeded in doing was to broaden the basis for democracy.

This presupposes three crucial things. First, it presupposes that the ties among voters, members, and parties are relatively durable. It is realistic to expect the maintenance of close ties only to the extent that party voting and membership have a permanence comparable to that of the leadership. Second, it assumes a commonality of interest among party members and voters sufficient that leaders to not receive conflicting signals. The greater the similarity in views among members, the more difficult it is for party politicians to write off the views of their constituents. Finally, it presumes the existence of mass-based parties with active memberships that provide a channel of recruitment for leaders who share the values of the led. Scandinavian parties hold annual meetings and periodic congresses to update programs and to rally activists. Nevertheless, all of these are more questionable today than they were two or three decades ago. Voter mobility is up, party loyalty down, party membership is eroding, and party voters are increasingly diverse.

By international standards, Scandinavian parties were—and continue to be—distinguished by an unusual degree of social homogeneity.[11] Each party has traditionally drawn its support predominantly from one major economic group. Most blue-collar workers voted Social Democratic, most farmers voted for the Agrarian party, and so on. The extent of the class and occupational voting that exists is suggested in Table 5.2, which draws on the 1998 Swedish election survey. The pattern in Denmark and Norway is similar, although class polarization is less prominent there. In all three countries, major parties' core constituencies can be identified with occupational groups. The obvious link between party and occupational group has encouraged a degree of concreteness in party ideology, clarify in policy, and the maintenance of ties between leaders and led.

Detailed survey data establish that although the bourgeois and socialist blocs remain polarized along economic lines, class voting has declined significantly during the postwar period. Workers have drifted away from the socialist parties. This trend was least in Sweden, where the Social Democrats focused their campaign on mobilizing the labor movement. There, the labor parties' share of the blue-collar households' vote declined from about 83 percent in 1946 to about 68 percent in 1998 and the Social Democrats' share declined from 71 percent to 53 percent.

The drift of working-class voters away from the Social Democrats was far greater in Norway and Denmark, particularly in the 1970s when the European Community issue shook traditional party allegiances. Fully one-half the Labor party's 1969 voters who voted against Norwegian membership in the European Community in 1972 (which the party supported), abandoned it for another party in 1973. Although the Labor party

Table 5.2
Swedish Party Vote (Percent) by Occupation of Voters, 1998

Parties	Left	Social Dem.	Green	Chr. Dem.	Center	Lib.	Cons.	Others
Industrial Workers	17	58	3	8	3	2	7	3
Other Blue Collar	14	49	4	10	4	2	13	4
Sales & Clerical	11	39	4	14	1	2	23	6
Middle White Collar	11	35	6	13	5	7	23	0
Upper White Collar	6	26	4	12	5	7	39	1
Self-employed	5	21	5	11	5	5	45	3
Farmers	5	2	5	37	35	0	16	0
Students	22	24	6	14	25	4	4	1

Source: Holmberg (2000, p. 68).

subsequently recovered much of its loss, the labor bloc's proportion of the blue-collar vote declined from 75 percent in 1969 to 59 percent in 1985 to about 50 percent in 1997. Not surprisingly this trend is paralleled by declining class identification; the proportion of Norwegians described as consciously working class fell from 39 percent in 1965 to 23 percent in 1985.

In Denmark, the labor parties' share of the vote from blue-collar households declined from 89 percent in 1961–62 to 55 percent in 1998; the Social Democrats' share of the Danish working-class vote plummeted from 80 percent in 1961–62 to 42 percent in 1998, while the radical socialist vote rose from 9 percent to 13 percent in 1998. Much of the movement of blue-collar voters toward the right seems to have been toward tax and immigration protest parties—the Progress parties of Denmark and Norway. These parties had more success appealing to the Social Democratic constituency than traditional bourgeois parties had had. At least as long as they were perceived principally as protest movements, they attracted substantial support from young male workers.

In Denmark, and especially in Sweden, significant numbers of middle-class voters abandoned the bourgeois parties for the socialist parties during the same period, perhaps in part because of the postmaterialist values suggested by Inglehart (1977). Most of the class depolarization that Holmberg (1984, p. 92) found in Sweden between 1956 and 1982, for instance, stems from growing socialist voting among the white-collar strata. The most extreme case, surely, is Denmark, where the radical socialists have attracted sharply increasing support among younger, well-educated white collar employees. Among Danish voters with thirteen or more years of schooling in 1963–64, 80 percent supported the bourgeois parties and 20 percent supported the socialist parties; by 1987 the socialist support in this group had nearly tripled, and all of the gains went to the parties to the left of the Social Democrats. By 1994, however, younger well-educated voters had shifted away from the radical socialists and toward the center-right with over all socialist support stable at about 40 percent of their votes. Among the youngest (aged eighteen to twenty-nine) well-educated voters, 30 percent voted for socialist parties, about half the proportion between 1975 and 1987 (Logue 1984, p. 208; Borre and Andersen 1997, pp. 174–78).

A substantial portion of this white-collar swing to the Left reflects the salience of such issues as membership in the European Community/Union, nuclear power, feminism, and environmental questions for voters who have come of political age since 1968. These issues seem particularly important among employees in the growing social-service sector. Recent Danish surveys have found a clear difference in voting behavior between white-collar employees in the public and in the private sector. In 1998, the former were more likely to vote for socialist parties than were private sector workers (59% and 55% socialist, respectively). Fully 23 percent of the public sector white-collar vote went to parties to the left of the Social Democrats, while the Social Democrats got only 36 percent. Danish voter studies still show a socialist bias among those born between 1946 and 1960 (baby boomers) especially toward the leftist parties, but this distortion has declined over the past decade. At the same time there has been a noteworthy swing toward the socialist parties by those born in the 1940s, perhaps because of concern about retirement and pensions (Andersen et al. 1999, pp. 71, 87).

The principal change in voting patterns is not movement between the socialist and nonsocialist blocs but the increased circulation of voters inside the two blocs, as parties' distinguishing characteristics and voter loyalties pale. The personalities of party leaders, the prominence of the party in the months before the election, and the performance of party representatives in the television programs that have become a crucial part of the actual campaign play a far greater role. Where the traditional party campaign with mass meetings and party rallies simply confirmed party loyalties and mobilized supporters, the modern media campaign gives all parties roughly equal access to television and radio audiences. This may not encourage voters to move across the dividing line between the socialist and nonsocialist blocs, but it makes it easier to move between parties that are otherwise similar. The movement of voters among the bourgeois parties between elections has more than doubled in Sweden from the beginning of the 1960s to the beginning of the 1980s (Holmberg 1984, p. 26), and the rate is even higher in Denmark, where the choice among parties is greater and the flux in bourgeois party support has become a fact of life (Borre and Andersen 1997, pp. 160 ff). Voter volatility in Norway has also become significant (Norway 2002).

Class-based parties reflected class-based attitudes. Attitudes on land redistribution, socialization of industries, and the protection of property rights once divided party voters as clearly as did party identification. Most of these issues have disappeared from the partisan agendas over the past thirty years. However, blocs and parties continue to disagree over policy priorities and the size of the public sector and hence tax levels. Issues of privatization, deregulation, and the rest of the neoliberal agenda have become new lines of division.

In the postwar period, some foreign-policy issues have become equally divisive, including NATO and European security issues. In the most recent past, the questions of membership in the European Union and the EU's development have sparked controversies in all of the Scandinavian countries as reflected by the referenda of the 1990s. Sweden had its emotional nuclear power debate after 1975, but that issue has now been subsumed into more general environment issues. Even a cursory appraisal of polling results suggests far deeper divisions of attitudes on key political issues in Scandinavia than exist in the United States. Still, although such divisions are deep, they do not preclude compromise.

The decline in class cohesion in voting among manual workers and among the well-educated new middle class yielded offsetting flows of voters between the labor and bourgeois blocs. This meant little in tallying the votes or seats in parliament, but it was significant in judging the nature of parties, and the likelihood that members and voters could control their elected representatives. Declining class cohesion had few negative consequences for bourgeois parties given their deemphasis on organization and their avowed antipathy to class as a principle of political organization. But the movement of manual labor to the right has allowed the bourgeois parties to claim to represent all the people—a claim that they could not have made earlier.

The consequences for the Social Democrats were more far reaching. Affluence, education and growing social diversity (immigration, etc.) have eroded the once-homogeneous class culture that supported the party. This transformation can best be sensed in the physical movement of a good portion of the blue-collar working class from the densely populated, working-class city districts, with their equally dense network of bars, small shops, and close social contacts, to suburban homes in districts sanitized of bars, where social contact increasingly seems to consist of watching the same television program, itself made difficult by the appearance of dozens of cable channels instead of the one or two public channels.

What has happened is that the working class—now usually called *employees*—has increasingly been reduced to an economic concept, not a cultural one. This has profound consequences in the decline of party organizational life. For one, party membership has declined. This is most notable in Denmark, which lacks the pattern of collective affiliation of trade-union locals to the Social Democratic party common to Sweden and Norway until 1990; Danish Social Democratic party membership has fallen from the peak of 300,000 in 1947 to about 120,000 in the end of the 1980s and about 50,000 in 2000, or from more than 40 percent of its voters to about 4 percent of its voters. Norwegian Labor party membership has declined from 200,000 at its peak in 1949 to about 160,000 at the end of the 1980s to 71,000 in 2000, or from about 30 percent to 10 percent of its voters. Swedish Social Democratic membership grew from about 550,000 in 1946 to more than 1,000,000 in 1990, or from 38 percent of its voters to 42 percent, but the growth was primarily a consequence of increased collective affiliation; when collective affiliation was abolished, membership fell to 259,000 in 1992 and was 177,000—or about 9 percent of its voters—in 1999.

Membership figures say little about parties' internal life. Although there are no reliable comparative statistics on meeting attendance, the general perception is that the numbers of party members attending meetings have declined both absolutely and relatively. Many subsidiary Social Democratic organizations—clubs, newspapers, cooperatives, and the like—have folded; others, such as sports clubs, in surviving have lost their political tie. To be precise, what has been lost is not the party as a political organization; as societies for political debate and activity, Scandinavian parties are probably as active today as they ever were. It is, rather, the party as a social organization. The problem is particularly apparent in urban areas and, of the movement parties, the Social Democrats have been most affected. By contrast, farmers' parties have maintained their virtual monopoly on organized social activity in rural areas and have been able to maintain surprisingly large, active organizations, despite the sharp decline in the farming population. If this has made parties more political, it may also have made them less representative.

In this context, the well-organized, mass-based party with a large number of activists—the kind of party most likely to provide direct citizen control of leaders—seems an anomaly reserved for bad times. There is probably some truth to that pessimistic view. Today's suburban proletarian, who spends his/her evening watching TV, surfing the web, or catching up on household chores is a far less active democrat than the grandfather, who divided his evenings between playing pool in the back room at the party local and playing poker at his union hall. Party and union have become less of a social club, and the adult education programs are far less partisan. The grandchildren still vote in every election, often performing their civic duty as political consumers choosing from the smörgåsbord of parties. Their grandfather voted too, but he was, on a daily basis, part of the reference group for his leaders. They listened to him because he and they were part of the same movement: They shared a common background, a common culture, common ideals, a common identity. That community, maintained by daily contact, meant democratic control.

INTEREST REPRESENTATION: FROM PLURALISM TO CORPORATISM

The principal political channel beside parties for representation of citizens has been interest groups. Organized primarily to promote the common interests of economic groups through collective action in the private sphere, interest groups in Scandinavia have come to provide functional representation of interests in the political process. As suggested earlier, Scandinavian interest groups—trade unions, farmers' organizations, business groups, professional organizations, tenants' unions, and the like—are distinguished in international comparison by their extraordinary strength. A number have organized in their ranks practically all potential members. As parties have broadened their social bases, interest groups have come to play an increased role as functional representatives in a formal sense: They have been incorporated in making and implementing policy. This integration of interest groups in the decision-making process has generally been termed *corporatism*.[12]

The term corporatism may be unfortunate, for, historically, corporatism has been associated with oppressive state control through compulsory organizations. Fascist and other authoritarian forms of state corporatism appeared in southern Europe, South America, and Nazi Germany in the 1920s and 1930s. Philippe Schmitter's classical modern definition (1974) emphasized the compulsory, noncompetitive, state-dominated organizations of corporatism. Although state domination is rare in the Scandinavian forms of corporatism, interest groups are powerful and central to the policy process. Organizational pluralism, internal democracy, and parliamentary supremacy suggest that "democratic corporatism" is an appropriate Western European variation and an authentic form of democratic politics. Individuals join such groups to promote their economic, political, and social interests. In turn, the organizations are accountable to their memberships.

The major Scandinavian economic groups, such as shopkeepers, artisans, farmers, employers, and workers, are all highly organized relative to the same groups in other countries. Of these, the labor organizations and employers organizations have special status in that they engage reciprocally in collective bargaining in addition to the other functions of interest representation that they share with the other groups. (The Scandinavian patterns of labor relations are described in detail in Chapter 10.) Unlike the situation in France and Italy, where two or three organizations of differing political or religious colorations compete to organize the same shopkeepers, farmers, or workers, in Scandinavia there typically is only one organization for each economic interest. Where two or more interest organizations represent portions of the same economic bloc, generally the line of demarcation between them in Scandinavia is clear enough. For example, family farms and large-scale agriculture are typically represented by two different organizations. But each group, whether family farmers or large-scale farmers, usually has only one organization to represent it. Thus, Scandinavian interest groups have the stature and the degree of organization to speak authoritatively for their constituencies in the public debate and in relation to government.

Pluralism

Close relationships between parties and interest groups have characterized Scandinavian politics since the predemocratic period. Danish trade unions originated in their modern form as affiliates of the Danish section of the International Workingmen's Association in 1871, and the integral tie between unions and Social Democratic parties was preserved through collective affiliation of local unions to party locals at the municipal levels in Norway and Sweden through 1990. Farmers' organizations have historically been split politically between large, commercial farmers' organizations, which have supported the agrarian parties, and smallholders' organizations, which supported the Radical Agrarian Liberals in Denmark and Labor in Norway; this distinction has faded as the farm sector declined and became increasingly dependent on public subsidies. Although business organizations have been a bit more reluctant to establish such formal arrangements, their association with the conservative parties is similarly of nineteenth-century origin and has proven its durability. Fishermen, shopkeepers, artisans, professional organizations—in short, economic interest groups of every sort—have cultivated their party ties. Although some groups formally support several parties, those parties are invariably in the same area of the political spectrum. Interest organizations cannot always deliver the vote; they can—and do—deliver the resources.

Most interest-group lobbying in Scandinavia consists of maintaining open channels to the appropriate governmental ministries. To the extent that interest groups perceive their role as including lobbying elected officials in the American sense, it is lobbying directed toward officeholders who share their ideological convictions. This attitude is a product of the connection between party and interest groups in the popular movements. The labor and agrarian movements alike organized all aspects of life; the association of party and interest group was natural because both organized the same class and defended the same interests. The only difference between them was the arena of their activity.

This pattern did not obviate interest group conflict. Quite the contrary, it automatically gave a political dimension to conflicts between economic interests, and it threatened to spread political struggles into the economic sphere. In the labor movement, very little difference was seen between the two. Frequently, the choice between trade-union action or political action by the party was simply the choice of which was more likely to be effective in a given situation, but since 1980 these ties have become looser. As party membership has declined and voters became more passive, unions and other interest organizations may have closer ties to ordinary voters. As Swedish LO chief Wanja Lundby-Wedin put it in 2000, "the difference is that we have members. The political parties do not. We need to go to the members for discussion about what we want with our party and the ideology we have. If you only go to the voters, it is very superficial" (Barnes 2000).

The close ties between parties and interest organizations offered the possibility to achieve political settlements through direct interest-group bargaining. The fundamental document of Danish labor law, the "Basic

Agreement," for instance, was hammered out between the unions and the employers' federation to settle the 1899 lockout. It contains the same recognition of bargaining rights and regulation of the use and procedures for strike and lockouts provided in the National Labor Relations Act (1935) in the United States; the signal difference is that the Danish solution is a private agreement, with the status of law, negotiated between two interest organizations. The same is true in Norway, Sweden, and Finland. Minimum wages, maximum hours, holidays, vacations, and equal pay for women have typically fallen into the sphere of collective bargaining, not legislation.

Corporatism

Even as the close ties between interest organizations and parties provide opportunities, they also impose responsibilities. This was clear even in the 1930s when unions, which were less strong than they would subsequently become, were expected to be loyal to Social Democratic governments. They were expected to show restraint and not to impose political costs on the Social Democrats through "irresponsible" (i.e., narrowly self-interested) activities. They were, after all, two wings of the same movement. As the Social Democrats solidified their power, expectations for the integration of union demands and party policy in government intensified. That attitude was reinforced during the postwar reconstruction.

In the 1950s, the relative permanence of Social Democratic government began to affect the behavior of interest groups long opposed to the labor movement. This was most notable in the labor market, where the centralization of collective bargaining had proceeded to the point that the national union federation and employers' association sat down to bargain a single, national private-sector settlement that set the pattern for the public sector as well. Likewise, farm organizations' interests were deeply affected by national agricultural policy. Increasingly, Social Democratic governments found themselves involved in negotiating labor contracts as the third party in tripartite bargaining, because the national contract, generally negotiated every second year, was the most important domestic economic variable. This pattern reached its early apogee in 1959 in the Harpsund meetings at the Swedish prime minister's weekend home between the Social Democratic Government, the unions, and the employers. During those meetings, economic policy was hammered out before being presented to parliament. This procedure was cause for substantial complaint from the nonsocialist parties, who accused the Social Democrats of making government policy through bargaining with private groups. Nevertheless, the move constituted an affirmation of the crucial role played by organized economic interests.

In the 1960s and 1970s, the incorporation of other interests in making and implementing government policy grew apace, as did the representation of labor-market organizations on boards increasingly distant from their direct interests. This participation had long been significant and it has grown over time. In Denmark, for example, interest organizations in 1946 were represented on 187 of 413 public commissions; in 1975 they were represented on 353 of 668 (Denmark 1982, p. 117). Sweden has introduced a system in which lay boards drawn from relevant interest organizations oversee the activities of some public institutions. The argument supporting the creation of these lay boards is simple: Interest organizations have become so inclusive, and the groups represented so important, that the service of interest group representatives on lay boards was as legitimate as that of elected politicians. Indeed, the inclusive and encompassing nature of Scandinavian interest representation is sometimes cited as an explanation for the superior performance of the Scandinavian economies during most of the postwar period (Olson 1995). Although corporatism has declined after 1980 (cf. Lewin 1994), the Scandinavian countries remain strikingly corporatist to Anglo-American observers.

But even though the traditional interest groups represent the common interests of their members, there is no guarantee that they are internally democratic. Some are; many are not. To the extent that there is any guarantee, it lies in the cultural expectation that interest groups do in fact represent the collective interests of their members. However, to represent the common interest is not necessarily the same as representing the sum of the interests of the individual members. The consequence is that, as interest organizations have grown to include divergent groups, their internal cohesion has declined. This is most obvious in terms of the expanding white-collar unions' relationship to the Social Democrats: While members of long standing and the leadership firmly consider themselves part of the Social Democratic labor movement, a substantial portion of the more recent members does not.

Although the major economic interest organizations are hierarchical in their structure, those with mass memberships have almost too many positions for their activists. As a result, their recruitment to fill empty slots often smacks of impressment. The fact that considerable training and some political sophistication are necessary to fill these positions adequately has turned the trade unions, in particular, into schools for democratic citizenship. It was estimated, following the various labor market reforms of the mid-1970s, that the Swedish unions needed to train some 50,000 members a year to fill offices to which they had been newly elected or appointed (Viklund 1977). The number of elected representatives in the trade-union movement far exceeds that in other economic and political organizations; indeed, it may well exceed the total number of elected representatives anywhere else in society. Although top union officials tend to be co-opted, shop stewards and local union officials are elected for short terms and frequently are subject to recall. Danish studies indicate that about three-fifths of union members attend shop floor club meetings and about two-fifths attend local meetings on an annual basis. The relatively rapid turnover in local union, shop steward, and safety steward positions creates a large pool of those with considerable training and skill beside those currently holding the positions. There are channels for participation inside interest groups that dwarf the scope of participation in local government.

The line of demarcation between parties and interest groups, once so clear, has blurred. Consider the disappearance of the boundary between the political and economic legs of the labor movement. That division was once crystal clear: The party dealt with politics, the unions with wages, hours, and working conditions. But today the Social Democratic party has become increasingly involved in setting wages and resolving other matters traditionally in the trade-union sphere (often enacting settlements when collective bargaining breaks down). In addition, the unions have moved into politics in the last decade, taking political stands independent of the party. It was the unions that forced the Danish Social Democratic government into opposition in 1982. And in Sweden, it was the unions that imposed the short-lived wage-earner fund proposal on a reluctant party in the 1970s and forced the Social Democratic party to drop its emergency economic legislation in 1990.

The employers' federations have shown similar independence in recent years. Most notable is the Swedish case, where the Swedish Employers' Association (Svenska Arbetsgivareföreningen [SAF]) took a much more militant line than the bourgeois government in 1980. The principal cause of the general strike of that year was that the SAF sought to impose an economic policy (through private labor-market bargaining) that it could not persuade the bourgeois government to pursue. This militance has continued to affect the SAF and other Swedish business organizations. Some of these organizations took the uncharacteristic step of organizing street demonstrations against the wage-earner funds in the 1980s, without giving up the influence derived through corporatist positions.

Grassroots Organizations

Since 1960 an increasing number of new interest groups, generally known as grassroots organizations, have appeared alongside the traditional economic interest groups. Generally, these have been single-issue groups, focused on questions not clearly the province of existing groups. The first notable grassroots organization was the Campaign for Nuclear Disarmament in the early 1960s, but it was rapidly followed by a variety of anti–Vietnam War groups, feminist groups, antinuclear power groups, and mass organizations opposing membership in the EU. These national organizations have generally been based on local committees, and they are joined at the municipal level by a plethora of local organizations pushing such varied causes as rent reductions, bicycle paths, preservation of buildings, and stopping construction of parking garages. Although all of these groups emphasize their nonpartisan status, most of their leaders are drawn directly from party or interest-group activists or are, in time, recruited to those roles. Although their activities take place outside the parties, and they mobilize a broader spectrum of support than parties could on such issues, they have become a supplement to the party system, not a replacement for it. In fact, one can argue that in some ways they have served to strengthen the existing parties or broaden the party system as illustrated by the rise of Green or Environmental parties in Finland, Iceland, and Sweden.

This is most obvious because a number of grassroots organizations are closely tied to individual parties. For example, the Norwegian Folkebevegelsen mot EF (Popular Movement against the European Community) was closely associated with both farm organizations and what later became the Socialist Left party. The antinuclear groups and antiwar groups have their political ties with the Left, although the Center party managed to co-opt a good many of the antinuclear power activists in Sweden. What is less obvious is that grassroots organizations have stabilized the party system by raising explosive issues without splitting divided parties or creating new ones. Far from threatening the established party structure, they have, in effect, served as lightning rods, organizing the dissatisfied. Consider the highly emotional nuclear-power question. The antinuclear groups in Denmark, for example, are probably predominantly Unity List and Socialist People's in terms of partisan coloration, although they include many from other political backgrounds. But by raising the issue in a fashion not too closely tied to either of those parties, the Organisationen til Oplysning om Atomkraft (Organization for Information on Atomic Power) has reduced partisan confrontation on the question and enabled the Social Democrats to back out of their pro–nuclear power position with a minimal loss of face. Grassroots organizations are more effective in pushing their issues because they do not represent a partisan threat. Indeed, had Glistrup organized his Danish tax resisters as a grassroots group rather than as a party in the 1970s, his success would have been greater because other parties could have co-opted his issue. But he chose the party route, turning the tax issue into a political hot potato that could not be touched until the Progress party declined a decade later.

There are two notable exceptions to this rule. The first is the Danish Folkebevægelsen mod EF (People's Movement against the EC). Originally formed to oppose Danish membership in the 1972 referendum campaign, the People's Movement was dominated by party activists from the cohesively anti–European Community parties (Socialist People's, Communist, and Justice), but also drew many recruits from the Social Democratic and Radical Liberal parties, which were divided on the issue. Its organizational structure was maintained after Denmark joined the European Community to provide a continuing rallying point for opposition. With the advent of direct elections to the European Community parliament in 1979, the People's Movement took on a new role: It entered its own slate of candidates and captured four of the sixteen Danish seats. In the 1990s the movement split with the so-called June Movement (Junibevægelse) representing a more pragmatic Euro-skeptic force. Both groups survive, ironically, as EU parties by maintaining strict neutrality in Danish domestic affairs; any other course would cause further divisions. However, as EU issues intrude more deeply into internal affairs, they have been forced to rely on referendums and other Euro-skeptical parties (primarily the radical socialists). Anti-EU parties have typically done better in European Parliament elections than they do in the national elections, largely at the expense of the Social Democrats. European Parliament election results can be found in Appendix D.

The second, and more recent, exception are the environmentalist parties, which won parliamentary representation in Finland in 1983, Sweden in 1988, and Iceland in 1999. Their effectiveness in pursuing their environmentalist goals has depended on balancing between the two blocs and recently, in Sweden and Finland, in supporting Social Democratic governments.

Moreover, like traditional interest organizations, grassroots organizations have provided schooling in democratic participation. Typically, they have been less hierarchical in their organization than traditional parties, and many espouse (and a few practice) direct democracy. As mass organizations of principally the white-collar strata, they have organized those who proved most difficult to organize within the traditional parties, with their basis in clear economic interests. They have been quick to exploit the internet. In essence they have supplemented parties, not replaced them.

A MORE PARTICIPATORY DEMOCRACY?

The sharp changes of the 1970s, brought about by the sudden appearance of new parties and the rise of grassroots organizations, altered the cast of political actors on the Scandinavian stage. The obvious consequences included growing cabinet instability and turnover of governments. Three Norwegian governments succumbed to the mobilization of sentiment against joining the EC/EU, a Swedish prime minister resigned over nuclear power, and governments in both Denmark and Norway fell when the new parties of the right made common cause with the established parties of the Left to bring governments of the Center-Right down. The decline in partisan allegiance has increased election-day volatility and the likelihood of change of government. The last quarter century has seen more party realignment and more ferment among interest groups than has been true at any time since 1920 when the party system took its modern form.

The Scandinavian party model has always assumed a close association among party voters, members, and elected representatives that stemmed from the commonality of interest that defined the class-based parties. In parliament, the Scandinavian model was one of responsible party government, within the limits imposed by the high probability of coalition government. When voters cast their ballots on election day, they know what they are voting for. In most cases, party policies are sufficiently well articulated that voters are in little doubt; the only real exceptions have been parties that have not faced governmental responsibility for so long that their campaign platforms have become unrealistic. That has become less true in the last two decades as parties have broadened their social bases and blurred their distinguishing features. One may bemoan the loss of definition, but the modern economy has undermined the clear lines of class and economic interest that once distinguished Social Democrats, Liberals, Agrarians, and Conservatives.

The tremendous flux in the party system reflects those forces and, of course, the low threshold for entry into party competition. One may quarrel with Glistrup's and other protest movements' and parties' politics, but there can be no doubt that they articulate widely held sentiments that were not being adequately expressed by the established parties. Thus, the ease of entry by the new parties and the wider fluctuations in electoral outcomes ought to be interpreted as a sign of the vigor of Scandinavian democracy, not as some threatening phenomenon. To the extent that the old occupational groups that provided the basis for the Scandinavian parties are breaking down, more scope is created for divergent interests that seek representation; there is more of a basis for party fragmentation. The extent to which the old parties are able to articulate these sentiments varies with their flexibility and the ease with which new groups can penetrate them. The stronger their organization and discipline, the less likely they are to accommodate new groups' interests. Compare the relative difficulty that the Social Democrats have had in integrating the grassroots movements into the party to the relative success of more loosely organized parties like the radical socialists and leftists (perhaps because of the collapse of pure Marxist parties) in all of the Scandinavian countries. Similarly, rightist protest parties have channeled new and often unpleasant issues into electoral and parliamentary institutions.

The participatory demands of the 1960s, Olof Ruin (1974) wryly notes, were the cause of increased corporatism in the 1970s. Two decades later his colleague Leif Lewin (1994) noted the decline of corporatism in Sweden and more general in Scandinavia, in significant measure because of the same demands for participation. What has changed most dramatically is the institutions of formal collaboration between interest organizations. No longer can major public policy issues be solved by cozy meetings at a resort hotel or the prime minister's residence. Neither can Royal Commissions of academic, bureaucratic and interest group experts hammer out complex definitive policy agreements, although such reports continue to expedite parliamentary action.

Yet interest organizations encourage participation internally, and they serve as channels of representation as fully legitimate as other forms of political representation. In fact, the semiofficial status granted corporatist organizations, their inclusiveness in organizing such a large part of their potential members, and the scrutiny they are subjected to may impose higher demands for democratic practices. If the corporatist system is open to penetration by new organizations (as the Scandinavian ones are), it may offer the advantages that pluralism is supposed to provide in serving as a channel of participation. Take the extreme case of government imposition of a labor contract after union rejection: It is not in parliament that one has real debate of the measure at all; the government either has the majority or it does not. The debate, opposition, and participation are through the corporatist bodies: the unions. It is a form of participation that prime ministers may have cause to regret, but it is fully as legitimate and substantially more active than participation on election day.

Given their oppositional character, the grassroots movements have been startlingly successful. Sweden is slowly phasing out nuclear power and Denmark will probably never get it. Norwegian voters have twice followed the recommendation of the People's Movement to reject the idea of European Union membership, despite the fact that it had been endorsed by an overwhelming parliamentary majority. Although Denmark remains in the EU, two referendums (1992 and 2000) have created firm opt-outs in EU membership. Despite their reduced visibility today, the grassroots movements' success cannot be measured purely in goals achieved. They have also activated and empowered their members. There are fewer marching feet but many Web sites and electronic connections. Building on the political culture of the popular movements, they have spruced up the ideal model of the democratic citizen: one who is informed, active on days besides election day, and not only willing but enthusiastic about joining in the public debate.

NOTES

1. Contemporary security concerns have unfortunately reduced the access and informality of Scandinavian politics. Ministers can still be seen bicycling, but they

are likely to have a police partner along. The Nordic "Jante Laws," formulated by Danish author Aksel Sandemose (Jante's ten commandments include "never believe that you are worth anything" and "never believe you are better, wiser, or know more than others"), cut the pompous and the ambitious down to size. Much of the Scandinavian distaste for European Union officials comes from their perceived exclusive lifestyle.

2. Those interested in further reading on Scandinavian parties may find it useful to start with the works by Borre (1984); Pedersen (1987); Einhorn and Logue (1988); Petersson (1994, pp. 39–76); and Arter (1999, pp. 50–142).

3. We use the term *Social Democratic* to include the Social Democrats of Denmark, Finland, Iceland, and Sweden and the Norwegian Labor party; *Liberal* to include Det radikale Venstre in Denmark, the Liberal People's party (Liberaalinen Kansanpuolue) and its predecessors in Finland, Venstre in Norway, and Folkpartiet in Sweden; *Conservative* to include Det konservative Folkeparti in Denmark, National Coalition (Kansallinen Kokoomus) in Finland, the Independence party (Sjalfstaedisflokkur) in Iceland, Høyre in Norway, and Moderata Samlingspartiet in Sweden; *Agrarian* to include Venstre in Denmark, Center (Suomen Keskusta) in Finland, Progressive party (Framsoknarflokkur) in Iceland, Senterpartiet in Norway, and Centerpartiet in Sweden; *radical socialists* to refer to Socialistisk Folkeparti and other leftist parties in Denmark, Left Alliance (Vasemmistoliitto) in Finland, Popular Alliance (Althyudubandalag) in Iceland, Sosialistisk Venstreparti in Norway, and Vänsterpartiet in Sweden; and *new right* to describe Fremskridtspartiet and Dansk Folkeparti in Denmark and the True Finns and Fremskrittspartiet in Norway.

4. In fact, it is the subject of a number of articles and books. Among the most interesting are Adler-Karlsson (1967), Castles (1978), Esping-Andersen (1985), Korpi (1978), Milner (1989), Olsen (1984), Pontusson (1992), Rothstein (1996), and Tilton (1990). For good historical accounts on Sweden, see Tingsten (1941) and Lindhagen (1972), and on Norway, see Lorenz (1972, 1974) and Kuhnle and Solheim (1994).

5. Revisionism posited a peaceful road to democratic socialism as opposed to the revolutionary program of Marx and Engels and later Lenin. The Swedish case in contrasted with the German Social Democratic strategy by Sheri Berman (1998).

6. The Norwegian Labor party, strongly syndicalist in its orientation at the time, joined the Communist International in 1919, but withdrew in 1923.

7. Glistrup was found guilty of income tax evasion in 1978 and, after exhausting appeals in the longest court case in Danish history, ultimately served a prison term.

8. Parties have encouraged voters to select particular candidates rather than merely vote for a party list in which the party organization determines the order in which candidates are elected. Dynamic or well-known candidates can jump over less prominent candidates.

9. Finland had thirty changes in government between 1944 and 1982. Since then it has become fully Scandinavian in its political stability with only four changes through 2002.

10. Voting is voluntary but convenient. Registration is automatic and derived from the national census registry. Elections are held on Sundays in Norway and Sweden, and absentee voting has been simplified, especially in Sweden. Casting

one's ballot has the status of a civic duty. The right of nonresident (i.e., untaxed) Danes to vote by absentee ballot is severely restricted, but the 2001 nonsocialist government has promised reconsideration of the policy of "no representation without taxation."

11. Since the 1970s, political scientists in Denmark, Finland, Norway, and Sweden have done regular, systematic voting studies modeled on American and British studies; Iceland has followed more recently. Recent electoral studies include Andersen et al. (1999) on Denmark, Aardal et al. (1999) on Norway, and Holmberg (2000) on Sweden. Good articles summarizing the most recent electoral studies appear in *Scandinavian Political Studies* and *Western European Politics.*

12. For detailed discussions of Scandinavian corporatism and interest groups, see Blom-Hansen (2000), Christensen and Rommetvedt (1999), Ingebritsen (1998), Eliasen (1981), Olson (1982, 1995); on Norway, Kvavik (1976), Olsen (1983) and Olsen and March (1995); and on Sweden, Pontusson (1991), Lewin (1994), Lindbeck et al. (1994, 1997), and Rothstein (1996). The classic surveys of corporatism remains Lembruch and Schmitter, eds. (1982) and Wilson (1983).

PART III

Scandinavian Welfare States

CHAPTER 6

The Politics of Solidarity

> Democracy requires a balance between community and division, between cooperation and conflict. The central problem in democracy is to maintain community despite conflict.
>
> —Herbert Tingsten

Although the term *welfare state* is only about sixty years old (the Oxford English Dictionary credits Bishop William Temple with first using the expression in 1941), its goals and policies are much older. Protecting the physical welfare of the citizen from internal and external threats has always been a fundamental responsibility of the state. The modern welfare state's contribution to this concept is its ambitious extension of personal security beyond mere physical survival to encompass economic security and a decent standard of living. Indeed, the very concept of democracy in Scandinavia today contains social and economic, as well as political egalitarianism. In this and in the four chapters that follow, we look at how the Scandinavian countries pursue the goals of social and economic democracy.

DEVELOPMENT OF SOCIAL INSURANCE

Although there were sporadic efforts to protect people from exploitation and occupational hazards early in the industrial age, the modern welfare state's more positive goals date from the reformism of late nineteenth-century social policies and social insurance. German Chancellor Otto von Bismarck established the first comprehensive social insurance programs in the 1880s as part of his campaign to contain the spread of socialism among industrial workers. Not strictly insurance, various pensions and benefits guaranteed a meager minimum living standard in case of loss of income for urban workers and their families. Bismarck's program paralleled social reforms in Scandinavia, but the latter had rather different political origins (Kuhnle 1981a, pp. 126–36; Baldwin 1990, pp. 55–94).

The modern welfare state arose in response to urbanization, industrialization, and demographic changes. Each country, including the Scandinavian ones, followed its own road in accommodating these forces. They have, however, followed certain patterns (see the analytical schemes devised by Furniss and Tilton 1977, p. 2, and by Esping-Andersen 1999, pp. 73–94).

The first stage in Scandinavia as elsewhere was social regulation to protect society and private property from unrest caused by economic suffering (see Piven and Cloward 1971, pp. 8–42). Building upon the traditional role of the church, guilds, and charitable organizations, such policies were effective in containing social distress and maintaining the status quo. With the spread of liberal ideas in the nineteenth century, social control undertook positive as well as strictly disciplinary measures. Poor laws became less oppressive, but, most dramatically, the spread of compulsory primary education began the transformation of the rural peasantry into literate and active citizens. The great nineteenth-century political, social, and economic changes in Scandinavia were accompanied by the spread of literacy and access to a variety of cultural and educational resources.[1]

Reform measures after 1880 sought to guarantee minimal economic security for the growing middle and working classes. The ideas arose out of British utopianism and utilitarianism, which quickly took root in Scandinavia. Reformers saw the social environment as a fundamental determinant of behavior. There were no evil people, only evil environments. Such thinking was shared by socialists and nonsocialists alike. Both called for collective action: People should band together for their mutual economic security and advancement.

Following British examples, Scandinavian reformers established "friendly" (mutual-assistance) societies to protect against financial and personal hazards. The principle (and the second stage in Furniss and Tilton's developmental model) was that of social insurance. Traditional urban craft guilds, stretching back to the Middle Ages, anticipated such a mutual insurance system. Retail and banking cooperatives encouraged thrift and economy. Cooperative farming, the engine of Danish agrarian reform, allowed small farmers to take advantage of technical and scientific advances. When the state became active in social insurance measures by the end of the century, it adopted ideas already implemented on a small scale.

The financial risks of losing income because of unemployment, illness, or old age could be anticipated by savings, but such savings were beyond the means of small farmers and unskilled industrial workers earning little more than a subsistence wage. Employers were reluctant to pay more than an absolute minimum. However, labor unions were successful in Germany and Scandinavia (before Great Britain and the United States) in getting employers to pay part of the insurance fees. At an early date, the state stepped in to subsidize, regulate, and extend such social insurance. The goal was "social security" defined in minimal financial terms. Premiums were brought within reach of the urban worker, and their families received meager but genuine pensions in case of lost income. The state could guarantee social security at minimum expense to the taxpayer. Table 6.1 summarizes the origins of comprehensive social insurance mandated by legislation and often publicly subsidized. The attractions of militant unionism (Germany) and emigration (Scandinavia) were contained by these first social welfare measures.

By the time the Depression struck with full force in 1932, the Scandinavian states had a safety net of basic social insurance, albeit with major gaps in coverage and very minimal benefits. These social insurance programs reduced the stigma and civil penalties inflicted on those requiring public assistance, and they guaranteed physical survival. But they could not in themselves restore economic stability. In Denmark, Norway, and Sweden, the Depression forged sufficient political consensus to fight unemployment by means of public expenditure. The Social Democrats to-

Table 6.1
The Origins of Social Insurance: Date of Passage of First Comprehensive Social Legislation, by Type of Legislation

Type of Insurance	Denmark	Finland	Iceland	Norway	Sweden
Workers' compensation	1898	1895	1903	1894	1901
Sickness insurance	1892	1963	1948	1909	1891
Old Age	1891	1937	1909	1936	1913
Unemployment insur.	1907	1917	1956	1906	1934
Family allowances	1952	1948	1946	1946	1947

Source: U.S. Social Security Administration 1999.

gether with their political allies—usually agrarian parties—put in place the second pillar of the welfare state: fiscal stimulus to restore demand to keep farms and factories producing. These were the first steps away from the fiscal orthodoxy that public budgets must be balanced annually and, for the nonsocialist parties, that the state should undertake only minimal economic activities.

Public expenditure did not engender a rapid restoration of prosperity or lavish social spending. Unemployment and agrarian distress continued throughout the 1930s, particularly in Norway and Denmark. Rather, the immediate benefits were political. The Social Democrats committed the industrial working class to a constitutional, reformist program of pragmatic economic and social change. The principle of private enterprise—capitalism—was accepted. In turn, the nonsocialist parties accepted the necessity of state intervention at times of economic emergency, public spending to revive a stagnant economy and to relieve social suffering, and the legitimacy of orderly collective bargaining to decide how the wealth produced by industrial production would be distributed.

It could have been otherwise. In Germany and Great Britain, Social Democratic governments clung to the old economic orthodoxies and cut public spending just as the world crisis deepened. In Germany, the bewildered Social Democrats lost more than prosperity; the Weimar Republic went down with the economy into the depths of Nazism. In Great Britain, the Labour government likewise trimmed public spending and provoked a disastrous schism in the Labour party that assured a decade of conservative rule. France tried social and economic reform under the Popular Front (socialist-communist coalition) of Leon Blum in 1936, but government's mandate was based too narrowly on the left, and neither the government nor most of its reforms lasted.

Scandinavia also had its extremists, but political compromise helped keep radicalism at bay. Significantly on January 30, 1933, the same day Adolf Hitler became Chancellor the German Reich, Danish political leaders concluded a broad emergence policy package to fight the Depression.[2] These economic compromises in time added a third pillar of the welfare state: public economic policies seeking to maintain production and employment in the private sector. Initial public employment spending was directed at public works and housing. In the latter case, cooperative non-profit housing schemes dating back to the middle of the nineteenth century (some of the first public housing measures were motivated by health concerns) guided and joined public programs. A modicum of respect and cooperation between employers and unions, reinforced in part by social homogeneity, encouraged political and economic cooperation. By the 1960s, the state's economic role would expand to include managing a capitalist market economy to ensure full employment.

FROM WELFARE TO SOCIAL AND ECONOMIC DEMOCRACY

Social and economic democracy have dominated Scandinavian domestic politics since the 1960s. At issue is whether to move beyond the extensive and increasingly generous social security system to a society in which the concept of democracy and citizenship extends beyond the political and constitutional sphere to most dimensions of social and economic life. The debate focuses on whether such changes would undermine the historic welfare state compromise, or even the economic and political system upon which it was built.

The convergence of social and economic issues has been encouraged by a broader understanding that the two areas are fundamentally interdependent. Investment in human and physical capital, both public and private, accelerates economic growth and improves social life. There are trade-offs: leisure versus production, subsidizing vital if stagnant sectors versus encouraging new industries, and the like. These issues have ideological dimensions, but are susceptible to compromise. The Scandinavian countries opted for a collectivist solution: funding massive social programs through heavy and comprehensive taxation. Each country, however, followed its own path to the welfare state.

The Danes moved toward a dualistic pattern of liberal (free-market) production and trade, while redistributing the growth through a large public sector financed by steeply progressive income taxes and regressive consumption taxes. Norwegian Social Democrats mobilized public support through the postwar reconstruction and greatly expanded the public sector, mainly in areas of traditional public infrastructure: communications, power, and education. Sweden sought to combine social policy with economic modernization. Here the emphasis was on active tripartite (state-business-labor) cooperation for full employment, vocational education and training, and investment. Iceland zealously protected its vital fishing resources by extending its economic zone, and also by modernizing its seafood industry to gain foreign markets. Finland turned an exploitative economic reparations to the Soviet Union into a prosperous trading relationship until 1990. It moved from postwar reconstruction to economic modernization, and recurring center-left coalitions raised social programs to Nordic standards. Social policy began to overlap economic and political issues. The concept of citizenship expanded beyond narrow political bounds. The welfare state became an integral part of Scandinavian democracy, but it also became vulnerable to social and economic changes.

FORMULATING SOCIAL AND ECONOMIC POLICY

The construction of the welfare state has been the main domestic political issue in Scandinavia for more than seventy years. Besides political vision and popular mobilizations, it has involved hundreds of laws, thousands of regulations, the creation of public agencies employing tens of thousands, and the annual deployment of billions of kroner in scores of programs. Few Scandinavians could describe the process, but practically all could understand the results. This illustrates the commonplace but important observation that most citizens are more interested in the consequences of political decisions than in the process of making them. Yet understanding the process is vital to understanding the results. Institutions and constitutional procedures constitute the framework for making decisions about social and economic policy. Parties and interest groups act within that framework and within the other constraints detailed in the preceding chapter. Public policy—"how, why, and to what effect different governments pursue particular courses of action and inaction" (Heidenheimer, Heclo, and Adams 1990, pp. 3–4)—is the concrete outcome. It is inseparable from politics. Political action is primarily intended to affect policy and thus the lives of fellow citizens.

For constitutional democracies, public policy poses a dual challenge. First, because most public policies involve the governmental apparatus, they are inherently compulsory. Even if a particular public service benefits only a small number, its costs and restrictions may affect many. Every public policy has an economic and political price; state action must be paid for in taxes and liberty. Second, the expansion of the scope of public policy was the mechanism by which democracy was transformed from being a narrow constitutional concept into a broad social and economic one. The rights to organize, to be represented, and to vote were won in arduous and protracted struggle. They were not only goals in themselves, but means to other ends. Political democracy in Scandinavia did not lead only to political liberty. The role of the state changed from defender of the prerogatives and property of the few into an instrument for democratizing society and the economy. The state neither remained the night watchman that nineteenth-century liberals desired nor withered away as Marx predicted. Instead, it expanded its role in the center of public life. Control of the state and of public policy are the ultimate goal of the democratic political struggle.

SHAPING THE POLICY AGENDA

Demands for alterations in social and economic policy arise from changes in the perceived needs of citizens. The change in family structure, with the rapid growth in single-parent households, creates a need for day-care institutions. Workers realize that exposure to toxic chemicals in the workplace is responsible for a variety of diseases and demand regulation of the use of these chemicals. Farmers are dissatisfied with market prices for their products and seek direct or indirect subsidies. The world price of such vital raw materials as oil may suddenly rise, sending economic shock waves through the national economy and requiring economic readjustment. Those affected want an effective response, which may range from a minor administrative adjustment to major political change.

In Scandinavia, there are three main channels for such social and economic demands: interest organizations, political movements and parties, and the media. Normally, all three play a role in articulating policy demands. The comprehensive range of interest organizations, the multiparty political system, and a centralized national media ensure that even quiet voices can receive a hearing if they are persistent.

From an international perspective, Scandinavian policy making is remarkable, principally because of the role accorded the powerful and capable organizations that dominate the process of articulating and mobilizing interests in all major policy areas. The policy process often harnesses these organizations to inform the public debate and provide alternative or specialized expertise. Organizational resources can be put at the public's disposal by encouraging communication among interest organizations and between them and state bureaucracies. At some point, therefore, interest organizations as well as parties cease to be mere policy advocates but also become policy planners and administrators. Governments may delegate power to private groups to do what is deemed to be in the common interest. Economic interest organizations in particular have a powerful effect on individual welfare and liberty in Scandinavia, where they often share directly in making public policy either inside or outside of government. For example, despite the world's strongest free labor movement, the Scandinavian countries have less legislation about wages and working conditions than the United States. The reason is that the comprehensive organization of labor and industry allows such questions to be settled by collective bargaining.

The existence of comprehensive organizations in Scandinavia has, on the whole, encouraged a more enlightened policy competition. They speak for large groups and must recognize the close connection between their particular interests and society's general interest. With the growth of the European Union and other international organizations, policy advocacy no longer can remain national. Although scarcely without selfish motives, the comprehensive, technocratic, and structured nature of Scandinavian interest-group politics may be less constricting on policy response and change. These organized interests may be less restrained than earlier (Olson 1982, 1995). Because competing and countervailing interests are organized, there may also be a balance of power in the policy process corresponding to the American Federalists' view of the necessity for separating governmental powers. Interest may truly check interest and produce accommodation.

EXPERTISE AND POLICY MAKING

Policy making is an intricate and often partially invisible process. Each country has its own procedures and rituals, but the Scandinavian countries share certain common traits. Their formal policy-making processes are similar. Ministries, boards, and special commissions usually first undertake *fact finding:* determining the accuracy of policy information and its implications. This takes place within similar policy-making cultures. There is a strong rationalist, even scientific element in Scandinavian policy making; large amounts of data are collected, perhaps in the belief that facts speak for themselves. This applies even to passionate advocates of significant social and economic reforms. It was typical that, in laying the groundwork for the major social reforms of the interwar period, the Danish socialist-activist K. K. Steincke poured through statistical, legal, and sociological materials anticipating by twenty years the research advocacy later demonstrated in Great Britain's Beveridge Report (Steincke 1920; Beveridge 1942). Policy advocates are still expected to do their homework: Sweden's comprehensive pension reform of 1998 resulted from years of study, consultations, debate, and negotiations.

Combining democratic, participatory policy making, and professional administration is often complex. Although legislative standing committees specialize in policy areas and question ministers and civil servants behind closed doors, the policy-making process is quite open. Only the final phase of working out parliamentary compromises, usually necessary under conditions of coalition government, is relatively closed. Prior to that point, there will have been extensive discussion, public debate, and information gathering.

Initially, the government, parliament, and interest organizations react to proposed policy changes. The demand may be for innovation, modification, or deletion of a program. Most proposals are formulated within the ministries and through the cabinet as part of a government program, whether the ideas were originally articulated by parties, organized interest groups, or within the bureaucracy.

Policy research and development procedures vary depending on the issue. A common process is to request views and information from all parties concerned by the policy. We have already mentioned the Swedish process of broad consultation known as *remiss.* Sometimes, this may be nothing more than the collation of outside commentary. At other times it may be a full fledged fact-finding investigation by an official governmental commission comprised mainly of civil servants, but with outside experts and members of parliament usually added. Interest organizations' experts are often included, although they are expected to act autonomously from their groups. These official commissions are similar to Royal or Crown commissions in the British and Commonwealth systems and more distantly related to the ad hoc presidential commissions in the United States. Interest groups will normally be asked to provide information and advice to such commissions. A third form of the remiss process is in reaction to government reports with specific legislative or administrative proposals. Written and detailed responses are expected, and most interest organizations maintain a skilled research staff for that purpose (Arter 1984, pp. 54–56; Heclo and Madsen 1987, pp. 11–15).

Until recently, the Scandinavian governments stressed various forms of social and economic policy planning. Today, this is a consequence less of an ideological commitment to planning than of the need for a comprehensive understanding of how governmental policies and their consequences hang together. In the past, however, in Norway and Sweden, planning was at times a highly political question and was described, especially by its opponents, as a path to socialism. In practice, most planning (other than physical or land-use planning) is analogous to the traditional inquiry and policy analysis. Planning was a practice even before it became a theory of policy making. Depression and war made planning a necessity, especially in Norway, which suffered severe damage during World War II. The role of Ragnar Frisch, an eminent Norwegian economist, in developing the theory and techniques of public budgeting and economic planning, encouraged the process (Scott 1975, pp. 176–94). Planning took on an aura of "scientific policy making," in which the process would automatically yield wise solutions. Comprehensive financial and resource planning, effective in the first postwar years, was gradually replaced by more specialized sectoral plans and analyses. Planning is now either a program for meeting budgetary and policy commitments or proposals to improve governmental performance. Occasionally the opponents may draft their own report with different assumptions and alternatives. Discussion and analysis by the media assures a wide public debate.

POPULAR PARTICIPATION IN POLICY MAKING

Popular participation in making social and economic policy is channeled principally through parties and interest organizations. There are usually two opportunities for groups to protect and promote their concerns. Both in the policy-drafting stage and the legislative phase, organized interests, especially those with close ties to political parties, are likely to make their views known. The Scandinavian expectation is that arguments will be made on the basis of reasonably objective data. "Factualness" (*saklighet*), rather than subjective opinion, carries the most weight in the informational stage. The Scandinavian policy process is democratic insofar as there are several opportunities for one group of so-called experts to be challenged by other experts. Organizational strength will in part determine their power, and financial and political resources count. Large size is not, however, the only guarantee of credible expertise. In theory, there is room for independent input based on expertise. Nevertheless, the ordinary citizen's interest must normally be advanced or defended by collective action.

The co-optation of organized interest groups into the policy process—democratic corporatism—occurred early (see Chapter 5). Such interest representation is not merely accepted; Scandinavians cannot imagine rational policy making without it (see Kvavik 1974, pp. 27–89). Related to it is institutionalized deliberation. The Scandinavian policy process requires an inclusive and detailed assessment of needs, resources, and alternatives. This reinforces, of course, the premium on professional administrative leaders in interest organizations. Spontaneity, whether on the parliament floor or the town hall, is discouraged. It is not purely a matter of technocratic control, although that is often an issue. Rather, it is the Scandinavian belief that sensible people with a sufficiently long-term perspective will support policies that are both in the general interest and in their particular interest. Some new actors on the policy scene—immigrant groups, for example—have followed this organizational pattern. It is an encouraging sign of political integration.

Over the last twenty years, there have been two important changes in common among the Scandinavian countries. First, as in most other Western democracies, there has been a decline of deference to professional expertise as experts themselves have gone public with their disagreements. The policy process has become more democratic; participants have become more numerous, more active, and more varied. There have been similar pressures within large interest organizations (Ruin 1982, pp. 153–61).

Second, although consensus on past achievements of the welfare state remains strong, there is genuine disagreement about its future course. Today, the economic issues that dominated Scandinavian party politics from 1920 to 1970 have a rival: the old *urban-rural,* or center-periphery, division has reappeared in a new form. The urban-rural division involved not only economics (industry versus agriculture), but also cultural issues. In the countryside, the dominant economic activity was embedded in a way of life that was qualitatively different from that of the cities. One need not be a bucolic romantic to recognize the appeal of the agrarian movement's glorification of the family farmer as independent yet cooperative, producing what we really need, living and raising children in harmony with the cycle of nature. The new version of the urban-rural cleavage combines the cultural values of the agrarian movement with the a postmodern "techno-skeptical" counterculture reflected in the rise of Green or environmental parties and organizations in all of the Nordic countries. The rise of the antinuclear and alternative energy movement in the 1970s was the most visible form. The Scandinavian Green viewpoint has emphasized the qualitative values of community and ecology against what was seen as the crass materialism of globalized capitalism with its ideology of consumption and planned obsolescence. These issues have sometimes been difficult to include in the institutionalized process of socioeconomic policy making.

Thirty years ago, Tom Anton characterized Swedish policy making as deliberative, rationalistic, open, and consensual (1969, p. 94). Subsequently Olsen, Roness, and Sætren described Norwegian policy as involving "problem-solving, bargaining, and self-governance" (1982, p. 47). Are these accurate descriptions of how the Scandinavian welfare state was shaped? There have, of course, been exceptions and national variations. The initial creation of social welfare programs in the 1930s was controversial. The "politics of compromise" was gradually extended from political and constitutional issues to economic and social issues, but it was a long and twisted path (Rustow 1955, pp. 229–34). More recently, there have been prolonged, bitter public debates in Sweden about nuclear power in the 1970s and early 1980s and wage-earner funds into the 1990s. The question of participation in the European Community and later the European Union and European Economic Area has repeatedly been controversial in all of the Nordic countries. But on the whole, the minority and coalition governments that have prevailed throughout Scandinavia during the past twenty-five years have required substantial consensus about the policy-making process, about a rationalist policy-making culture, and about such fundamental policy questions as the welfare state and the managed economy.

ON MOTIVATIONS FOR WELFARE POLICIES

Support for welfare programs in Western democracies rests on three basic motivations. The first is *altruism,* an unselfish desire to help others. Political scientists generally denigrate the importance of altruism in human affairs, but in the real world, most people have a gut-level revulsion against letting their fellows starve to death while the grain elevators are full. The paternalistic altruism of the well-to-do played an important role in very modest welfare measures of the nineteenth century. Organized religion historically played a major role in social policy as faith supplemented altruism. After the Reformation in Scandinavia, the state inherited this vital role.

Altruism, both in its modern and nineteenth-century forms, is strong enough to keep the bodies and souls of the poor together in affluent countries, but it is hard to base a more far-reaching welfare program than the soup kitchen or the Christmas toy drive on this principle. The bulk of modern welfare state programs rest on a second principle, that of *self-insurance.* We all are willing to insure ourselves against economic risks we cannot afford whether it be the loss of our house in a fire, the death of the family's breadwinner, or catastrophic medical expenses. The entire private-insurance industry is a testimony to the strength of that human characteristic.

Social insurance programs sometimes lack the actuarial soundness of private-sector programs. They are based, however, on the same principle: the payment of regular fees (and taxes) to provide against risks that would otherwise be catastrophic—disability, unemployment, old age, and, in most societies outside the United States, sickness. We agree to the collective provision of social insurance throughout the society on premises of efficiency and the need to protect those who are worst off; our support is motivated, in no small measure, by the assumption that we ourselves face the same risks and, if we live long enough, will benefit as well.

Although the insurance principle is clearly a broader and stronger basis for welfare state programs than altruism, it too has its limitations. It is limited to risks that we all face—unemployment, disability, sickness, and old age—and to guaranteeing that the advent of those conditions does not destroy us economically. It is an inherently conservative concept in that it protects against impoverishment those who derive their livelihoods from their labor. Moreover, our aversion to risk has its own bounds. Some risks are tolerable, and the level at which one self-insures involves trade-offs between current consumption and individual savings on the one hand, and future potential consumption in the event of catastrophe on the other. Most discount the latter heavily, and opt primarily for the former. Collective social-insurance programs in democracies that are genuinely based on the insurance principle have a natural limitation not much above certain social minimum levels: We will agree to insure ourselves collectively so that there is a floor through which we cannot fall under our living standards, but that floor will not be very high. Comprehensive and compulsory coverage spreads the risks over a much larger population.

Although both altruism and social insurance have played roles in the historical development of the Scandinavian welfare states, in the last half century they have been supplemented by a third principle: *solidarity.*

Solidarity is one of those terms, like *love* or *community*, that only the brave or foolish attempt to define. It is a gut-level response as basic as that felt by an older sibling who sees a bully beating up a younger brother or sister on the playground. It involves a sense of belonging to and identifying with others. In large part, it is a willingness to tie one's fate to that of others, to share a sense of group identity—with friends, neighbors, workmates—that overrides individual interest. But it also implies an expectation of reciprocity, that others feel the same obligations. As one turn-of-the-century Danish trade-union tract, written by a craft unionist steeped in craft identity and guild traditions, put it, solidarity "means common responsibility or reciprocal obligation" (Anonymous [C. M. Olsen] 1911, p. 74).

The concept of solidarity as reciprocal obligation is closely associated with the nineteenth-century agrarian and, particularly, labor movements. That these two "popular movements" achieved greater intellectual and normative hegemony in Scandinavia than elsewhere is the most obvious explanation both for Scandinavian welfare policies and the consensus behind them. They drew their strength from the cohesion of small groups of neighbors and workmates. That cohesion permitted collective action that advanced their common interests. Social Democratic ideology expanded the boundaries of solidarity from the work-group and craft-union local to the proletariat as a class. The Social Democrats genuinely believed in what K. K. Steincke, who, as social welfare minister, subsequently laid the foundations for the modern Danish welfare state in the Social Reform Act of 1933, described as "the special ethics" of the working class. Those ethics included "a feeling of solidarity, a willingness to sacrifice, a subordination to common economical political goals" that promised a higher social order based on "cooperation and reciprocal aid" (Steincke 1920, pp. 5, 9).

When they captured power in the 1930s, the Social Democrats generalized the concept of solidarity from the small group and the working class to society at large. Where it had previously characterized the small group and excluded others, it was now extended to become an inclusive national concept; the homogeneity of Scandinavian societies eased this transition. The political slogans of the time sum it up well. Implicit in Per Albin Hansson's *Folkhemmet Sverige* (Sweden as a home for all the people) was the expansion to the whole society of the reciprocity of obligation that existed inside the family, the only institution of bourgeois society that transcended the self-interested individualism that liberal economic theorists had glorified and Social Democratic theorists had condemned.

That individualism had never been as dominant in the bourgeoisie as liberals had hoped and socialists had feared. World War II narrowed class and regional differences in all of the Nordic countries. Despite some collaboration with the Nazi occupation of Denmark and Norway, the broadly supported and often heroic Resistance elevated voluntary self-sacrifice for the common good to a new ethical standard. In Finland patriotism in the face of Soviet aggression and widespread hardship ameliorated class antagonisms and memories of the civil war. When the call came, sacrifice and solidarity were not limited to any class or social stratum. The Resistance and postwar reconstruction reshaped social ethics, giving solidarity a primacy of place. At least for a generation, national solidarity was real.

There are no natural limits on what we may reciprocally obligate ourselves to do comparable to the natural limits on altruism and social insurance. To construct a welfare state on the principle of solidarity permits higher standards of benefits. Sharing common values and common beliefs, we may agree reciprocally to support each other when sick, disabled, unemployed, or elderly at a level far above what any one of us would back in self-insurance. We may agree to provide high standards of child care, of home assistance to the elderly, and of financial aid to single mothers with low incomes unassociated with the concept of self-insurance. The limits of programs based on solidarity lie in the limits of this agreement, not in individual calculations of self-interest.

More than anything else, the principle of solidarity led to a blossoming of the welfare state in Scandinavia that went beyond comparable programs elsewhere both in level of benefits and in egalitarian aspirations. But memories of former hardships fade and new challenges—globalization and multiculturalism from immigration—test the mettle of solidarity.

THE CHANGING SCANDINAVIAN WELFARE STATE MODEL

The Nordic countries are small states that are dependent on an international economic and political system not of their making. They are never free of external constraints but, as is discussed in Chapter 7, they have sought to manage them in order to pursue policies distinct from those of many of their larger neighbors. The result today is a Scandinavian welfare state model that is a combination of four disparate elements, only the first two of which lie within the scope of what Americans consider to be the welfare state.

The first is a network of transfer payments from those currently employed to those who are not. Today, transfer-payment levels are set to provide close to full replacement of earned income for those temporarily excluded from gainful employment by sickness, temporary disability, and unemployment. Transfer payments to those permanently outside the labor market because of old age or permanent disability are lower. Although transfer payments generally tend to even out income throughout life rather than between classes, some specific transfer payments, such as child allowances, tend to raise the family incomes of unskilled or female-headed households with several children relatively more than they affect the economic status of those better off.

The second element is the provision of certain social services based on need rather than on ability to pay. Americans are most impressed by the provision in Scandinavia of hospital, medical, and dental care, almost entirely without fee. Formal education, including higher education, is provided without fees. So are a wide range of social services for the elderly. Other social services, including day care, adult education, and housing for low-income families and the elderly are provided with heavy subsidies; generally, the amount of the subsidies varies with income. As a consequence of long-standing Social Democratic efforts to remove the stigma from transfer payments and social services, both are generally accorded without means tests; that is, they are universally available to any person—regardless of income—in the appropriate category. Still, as detailed in Chapter 8 the consequences both of transfer payments and social services are to raise markedly the material welfare of the poor. You can measure the moral stature of a society, Scandinavians will tell you, by how it treats those who are worst off.

The cost of transfer payments and social services is high—between one-fourth and one-third of the GDP. Moreover, the cost is closely correlated to the general health of the economy. For example, when unemployment rises, so do welfare costs. In the mid-1990s unemployment was a problem in Sweden (8%), Denmark (6.5%), and especially Finland (15%). Unemployment benefits ran from about 3.5 to 4.5 percent of the GDP. In the United States unemployment was lower (5.5%) but comparable benefits amounted to a mere three-tenths of 1 percent of the GDP (Nordic Council, *Nordic Statistical Yearbook 2000,* p. 80; U.S. Census Bureau 2001, p. 380). Costs of other programs, such as rent subsidies and child care, also rise when the economy turns bad. The consequence of such high costs is the need to manage the economy—the subject of Chapter 9—by minimizing cyclical and structural unemployment. This is the third element of the Scandinavian welfare state.

The final key component in the Scandinavian model is a serious effort to adjust the market economy at the micro level of wage formation to curtail its tendency to generate inequality. (It is, after all, market incomes that form the foundation upon which transfers and social services are subsequently added.) This process was most pronounced in Sweden, where the "solidaristic wage policy," which became common to all the Scandinavian countries, reduced wage differentials through collective bargaining and was coupled with an active labor-market policy that sought to minimize prolonged unemployment. The consequence was higher rates of labor-force participation and lower rates of unemployment until the 1990s. The partial breakdown of both, stemming from both domestic and global factors, has been a major challenge of the past decade. Domestic solutions like the push for economic democracy and wage-earner funds, discussed in the context of industrial relations in Chapter 10, were an effort to go one step further and reduce the degree of economic inequality while increasing employee satisfaction with working life. In the past decade policies have encouraged (through collective bargaining and tax breaks) market collectivism as illustrated by the rapid growth of supplemental pensions funded and managed by the private sector. These policies will increasingly benefit those with long work careers.

In short, the Scandinavian welfare state model is far broader in its scope than the transfer payments and social services that make up narrowly defined welfare programs. To a large extent, the latter programs are remedial; they are designed to protect against total loss of market income. As the level of ambition in these programs has risen, so has the need to contain their costs by reducing the creation of inequality in the market. But how far can that aim be achieved without sapping the dynamism of the market economy that has, heretofore, generated the surplus for redistribution through the state-transfer and social-service programs?

NOTES

1. Denmark's Education Act of 1814 called for the equivalent of seven years of primary education, either at home or in schools. It was Europe's first compulsory education law. Similar measures were adopted in Norway in 1827, in Sweden in 1842, and in Finland in 1866. Basic literacy began to spread after the Protestant Reformation; Norway's first primary education law dates from 1739. For a summary of the development of Scandinavian education systems, see Sysiharju (1981).

2. The Danish "Kanslergade compromise" between the governing Social Democrats and Radical Liberals, on the one hand, and the opposition Agrarian Liberals, on the other, (1) extended the existing labor agreement without wage reductions (which the employers were demanding at the depths of the Depression), (2) provided a massive public works program to put the unemployed back to work, (3) devalued the currency to stimulate farm exports and provided agricultural price supports to stabilize farm income, and (4) pledged to restructure the patchwork of Danish poor law and social welfare provisions into a comprehensive program. In short, it contained practically all the major building blocks of what would become the Scandinavian welfare state: an interventionist state regulating the economic cycle and income formation, and regularizing social services and transfer payments. Similar compromises were reached in Sweden, Norway, and Finland. For more information, see Einhorn and Logue (1999, pp. 199–200).

CHAPTER 7

Policy in an Interdependent World

"The logic of globalization" has no more eliminated the . . . differences between welfare states than did the "logic of industrialism" decades before.

—Mark Kleinman, *A European Welfare State?* (2002)

For the Nordic countries globalization is not a distant abstraction. Just take one example. By the late summer of 1992 the Swedish economy had hit rock bottom and started to dig. The combination of domestic inflation, bank collapses, and a global recession ended the economic expansion of the 1980s. Although opportunistic devaluations of the national currency had restored global competitiveness twice during the decade (as it had done in the early 1930s), now the krona was under severe international pressure. The Exchange Rate Mechanism of the European Union had lost credibility with the international financiers, some of whom ruthlessly speculated against those currency they suspected of overvaluation. The Swedish krona was on their hit list. The Swedish *Riksbank* (central bank) and the Ministry of Finance in their elegant Stockholm headquarters prepared to defend their currency, in part by hiking overnight interest rates to an amazing 500 percent, but they could not resist the international tidal wave. The global economy had come to Sweden.

The Swedish currency (among several in Europe) was devalued, clever speculators made a quick killing, and the ideal of independent national monetary policy was knocked down several pegs. Even the less shaky currencies of Norway and Denmark swayed for a few days, reportedly in part because distant manipulators failed to distinguish between the several Scandinavian crowns. Within weeks of this international currency turmoil, Sweden would join Norway and Finland and apply to join the expanding EU.

Although public policies in the modern welfare state are usually assumed to be domestic matters, external factors have increasingly intruded. This is especially true for small countries. Although the United States, Germany, France, and Great Britain have substantial latitude for independent policy experiments, the success or failure of the Scandinavian countries' policies frequently depend on the vicissitudes of international politics and, especially, the international market.

In the past, foreign relations turned largely on defense and security issues. Although defense policies and capabilities remain important and much-studied features of Scandinavian relationships with the external environment, international influences have seeped into practically every aspect of domestic policy. This is particularly true of the policy areas that we examine in the three chapters that follow: social welfare measures, managing the economy, and labor market policies.

This chapter examines the external dimensions that shape Scandinavian domestic policies and explores how the process of forming policies within the context of external constraints takes place. Thus, our principal aim is not to discuss the Scandinavian countries' security or foreign policies—national responses to international pressures—but rather to underscore that "interdependence" and "international integration" characterize practically every aspect of Scandinavian policy. Indeed, the integration of Scandinavia into the global political economy has become so complete that almost every aspect of domestic policy has become porous: that is, substantially affected by regional and global events.

The small Scandinavian states are less actors than the acted upon in international politics. They must respond to political and economic changes around them, regardless of their preferences. Denmark has consistently acknowledged its dependence on larger neighbors, whether requiring stoic adjustment (as with Nazi Germany in 1939–40) or optimistic regionalism (as in the decision to join the European Community in 1972). Sweden has emphasized the advantages of flexible nonalignment and neutrality, but has also been soberly realistic in its foreign relations when vital interests are at stake. Norway's relatively shorter foreign policy experience since independence in 1905 has been a middle case, but has tended toward active alignment and diplomacy since World War II. Finland survived—minus several provinces—seven decades of not always peaceful coexistence with the Soviet Union.

During the interwar period, the Scandinavian countries became acutely aware of their international economic dependence for the first time. Consider the case of Norwegian prohibition. Like the United States, Norway tried the "noble experiment." From 1919 to 1926, Norway prohibited the sale of fortified wines and hard liquor. Norwegian prohibition was cut short by the vigorous protest from wine-producing countries that were also markets for Norwegian fish. The Norwegian government came quickly to terms with France to avoid trade retaliation by agreeing to buy 400,000 liters of cognac annually, despite the fact that the sale of cognac in Norway was prohibited; it was to be used exclusively for medicinal purposes if prescribed by a doctor. (This produced exactly the problem in medical ethics that could have been anticipated.) Not receiving such favorable treatment, Spain and Portugal responded by raising tariffs on Norwegian fish. The threat of idling the fishing fleet forced the Norwegian government to negotiate deals with Spain (1922) and Portugal (1923) comparable to that with France: In return for tariff reductions, Norway agreed to purchase 1.35 million liters of Spanish and Portuguese fortified wines annually that it could not sell. This direct drain on the treasury was enough to drive any self-respecting politician to his doctor for a prescription for medicinal spirits, and the government collapsed over this absurdity in 1923; its successor repealed the prohibition on sales of fortified wines to dispose of the Spanish and Portuguese purchases. Voters ultimately repealed the prohibition on the sale of hard liquor in a 1926 referendum in which fishing communities supported repeal. Note the contrast to the United States: The American experiment with prohibition could play itself out without concern for complaints from wine and liquor exporting countries.

Since 1945 larger industrial societies than the Scandinavian ones have discovered that it is no longer possible to distinguish easily between domestic and foreign affairs. This is clearest in areas of economic policy, but it extends into the nooks and crannies of most other policies as well. Obviously, trade, finance, disease, pollution and myriad other policy issues do not recognize national borders or sovereignty. Even such seemingly domestic matters as social and educational policies are partially shaped in response to international developments. For example, whether a nation's export enterprises can compete in world markets depends in large part on their production and marketing costs. Extensive social programs are a major cost to the global firm, but effective education and training can mitigate the competitive disadvantages. Smooth industrial relations can avoid costly strikes, and flexible tax systems can encourage investment and entrepreneurship. This understanding is widespread today in Scandinavia, and it is a continual consideration in debates about what policies should be pursued.

Less obvious are the policy consequences of the increasing integration of the industrial democracies into a global institutional framework for making and executing public policy. There is no neat pattern to such interdependence. The pattern of each Scandinavian state's transnational relations has its own historical, geographical, and political sources. In the

1990s Sweden and Finland joined the European Union and Iceland and Norway adhered to the looser European Economic Area (EEA) which for industrial trading purposes is the same as the EU.[1] No longer is the Nordic region economically distinct.

Sensitivity to international developments is a fundamental axiom of Scandinavian public policy. Except in the agricultural sector, the Nordic countries have rarely been protectionist during the past century. Indeed, access to markets in times of war and economic depression were major challenges. Finland turned a forced economic dependence on the Soviet Union after World War II into a lucrative market until the Eastern European economies collapsed after 1990.[2] Political parties and interest groups must recognize the external factor, but there is considerable dispute as to what the consequences of and the reactions to such dependency ought to be. The link between domestic and foreign policy has been raised in several ways. The impact of a state's domestic politics on its foreign policy (and thus on world politics) is widely accepted (see Waltz 1959, especially chapters 1, 3). More recently, the reverse—the influence of international politics on domestic politics and particularly on economic policy—has been discussed (see Sassen 1996; Gourevitch 1978, 1989). The Scandinavian experience illustrates the concept of *complex interdependence*, defined by Keohane and Nye as "reciprocal effects among countries or among actors in different countries" (2001, pp. 7–8). Given Scandinavia's history of external policy sensitivity (the speed and impact of a change in one country upon another) and vulnerability (the extent to which the affected country can adjust and counteract externally imposed constraints), it may be useful to assess the overall impact of external restraints on the democratic policy process (Keohane and Nye 2001, pp. 9–11).

THE EXTERNAL CONSTRAINTS ON SCANDINAVIAN POLICY

Three dimensions are useful in evaluating the external constraints on Scandinavian public policy. The first is geopolitical: Which geographic and international political patterns and groups describe the contemporary ties of the Scandinavian countries? With whom do they deal and how important are specific countries, international organizations, or blocs? The second is functional or geo-economic: What policy issues depend upon the actions of foreign states and entities? The third ties external relations to domestic politics: What impact do external forces have on domestic politics?

The Geopolitical Dimension

Since 1945, Scandinavian politicians and analysts have regularly cited four geographic and political perspectives as describing their foreign relations: Nordic, European, Western, and global. During the Cold War, it was useful to distinguish between Western European and "Atlantic" (NATO) dimensions as well as the Soviet Bloc. Since 1990 those distinctions are less clear, but the European Union represents an intense policy community. These dimensions reflect more than a difference in geographic scope. They reflect a difference in capacity to achieve results, in institutional avenues that can be used, and even in values. Of the four, however, only the Nordic region—which includes Iceland and Finland in addition to Denmark, Norway, and Sweden—is clearly defined.

Beginning before World War I, when the three countries sought pragmatic collaboration in a handful of policy areas, Nordic cooperation has grown to encompass a broader range of policy issues and the new states of Finland and Iceland. Like much international cooperation, functional and often minor matters have more easily been accommodated than those of real substance. Despite its origins in the romantic pan-Scandinavianism of mid-nineteenth-century intellectuals, Scandinavian cooperation has always had a large private and commercial dimension. Formal governmental functional cooperation in the modern era can be traced to the Scandinavian Monetary Union of 1875, which comprised a common currency reform in the three kingdoms (the *crown* was the new monetary unit) and a loose commitment to maintain convertibility at par between them that lasted nearly fifty years.

From the limited but increasingly regular meetings of political leaders that were introduced during World War I to the establishment of the Nordic Council in 1952, Nordic cooperation has drawn on the reservoir of good will between the countries' political elites. It has reflected, imperfectly to be sure, the policy style of the Scandinavian countries: to include all of the parties with a stake in an issue as early as possible; to emphasize concrete and technical rather than symbolic issues; and, finally, not to pursue policies where consensus is unlikely. Although Nordic cooperation has been considered a worthy goal in itself, national interests have remained primary. As a consequence, efforts to establish a nonaligned Scandinavian Defense Community and a Nordic Common Market proved abortive. Broader multilateral solutions promised more credible service to national interests.

With the establishment of the Nordic Council—an assembly composed of eighty-seven delegates from the eight Nordic parliaments and governments—proponents of regional cooperation developed an institutional forum for Nordic collaboration. In addition to the five sovereign states, there are three Nordic autonomous regions: Greenland, the Faeroe Islands, and the Åland Islands that have separate representation in the parliamentary meetings. All delegates are chosen by the eight parliaments or assemblies. Pragmatism and energy have produced concrete results through some forty institutions, particularly in the cultural, scientific, and social realms (see Wendt 1981, pp. 653–76 and Nordic Council 1997). While Nordic cooperation has led to no dramatic breakthroughs, it has spun a web of ties among Danes, Finns, Icelanders, Norwegians, and Swedes that (1) permit 250,000 of them to live and work freely in other Nordic countries with rights and benefits comparable to those of citizens; (2) encouraged thousands of collaborative publications, conferences, television programs, theater productions, and the like; and (3) created, through functional cooperation, a far stronger degree of community among the countries than has been true at any point since the Viking era.

The European region has been less clearly defined for the Scandinavian countries. Although on the region's periphery, the Scandinavian countries have learned that major European developments inevitably have a direct impact on them. Since 1945 there have been two main perspectives on Europe. One sees Scandinavia as very much a part of the Western European cultural and political sphere, and emphasizes close ties to the European Union. The other view emphasizes Scandinavia's potential as a bridge, formerly between East and West and now between Europe and the developing countries (the so-called North-South dimension).

Since 1990, Nordic-European economic relations have increasingly focused on the European Union (including for Norway and Iceland the wider European Economic Area [EEA]), but that is not the whole picture. The Maastricht Treaty of 1992 added security policy formally to the EU agenda but not at the exclusion of other international treaties (e.g., NATO, the Organization of Security and Cooperation in Europe, and the United Nations). None of the Nordic EU members have embraced the security policy aspects of the EU with much enthusiasm, and Sweden and Finland have not been tempted into NATO. In practice all have engaged themselves in political, economic, and security projects in Eastern Europe.

A third and overlapping dimension is Scandinavia's role as part of the West, not in a narrow geographical sense, but as part of the formal and informal community of advanced industrial states sharing democratic constitutional political institutions, capitalistic economic systems, and a mutually binding *regime*, or rules of interaction. This is presumably where Scandinavia belongs. In the past, this Western perspective has been as controversial as elements of European policy, especially in its earlier Atlantic formulation. Today, no Scandinavian policy maker can ignore ties with the United States, Japan, or indeed the whole structure circumscribed by the Organisation for Economic Cooperation and Development (OECD).

What is referred to as the global perspective encompasses everything else including the United Nations and its specialized agencies, especially the World Trade Organization. Scandinavians have been consistent supporters of the UN, and of measures aimed at building a sense of global community and mutual responsibility. This is not only idealism. Free of the taint of imperialism or military ambition, the Scandinavian countries have adapted their diplomatic bridge-building energies to North-South relations, particularly in economic and technical areas, to peaceful conflict resolution, and to support for various liberation movements in the Third World. As small countries aware of the dangers of great power intervention, Scandinavia directs its global policies toward strengthening principles of political equality, nonintervention, and cooperation. Since 1960, the Scandinavian countries have consistently been among the top countries in foreign aid contributions relative to the size of their economies. Scandinavian experts and political figures have served prominently in international organizations including the first two UN Secretaries General (Trygve Lie and Dag Hammarskjöld), or undertaken conciliatory diplomatic missions such as the role of the late Norwegian Foreign Minister Johan Jørgen Holst and his associates in hammering out the Palestinian-Israeli Oslo Accords in 1993.[3] Similarly in 2002 Norwegian diplomats undertook to facilitate a truce in the ethnic and political violence that has plagued Sri Lanka for decades.

The Functional or Geo-economic Dimension

It is impossible to put public policies into neat geographical or institutional compartments. For example, financial and monetary policies involve domestic institutions (e.g., finance ministries and central banks); regional organizations (e.g., the European Union's Economic and Monetary Union); and private entities (e.g., nongovernmental international capital markets); and global organizations (e.g., the International Monetary Fund). Each has its role, interest, and policy procedures. Thus, national policies are affected simultaneously through direct bilateral and multilateral interactions with other states or organizations and with private commercial organizations, as well as indirectly by global developments (such as a change in the price of a significant commodity, like petroleum). It is therefore necessary to evaluate external policy constraints by function. This is an enormous task because essentially every social activity has become part of the public policy agenda. Many aspects of environmental policy, public health, and even veterinary medicine in Scandinavia are transnational in scope; consider acid rain, AIDS, and the outbreaks of animal diseases that have periodically threatened Danish meat exports. Three important functional areas are illustrative: security policy, trade policy, and financial policy.

Security Policy

Security policy—preserving the independence, safety, and viability of a state—enjoys a historical primacy of place. A sense of security is a prerequisite for the greater political focus on other policy areas. Security and foreign policy are intricately related and indirectly tied to every other policy area. Although security policy and defense capacity lie beyond the scope of our focus on Scandinavian democracy and the domestic policies essential to the modern welfare state, security forms the context within which domestic policies have developed.[4]

The failures and successes of security policy leave lasting marks on national politics. The extreme case, of course, is that of World War II. Although Denmark, Norway, and Sweden all sought to remain neutral, only Sweden succeeded. Both Denmark and Norway were engulfed in the conflagration when the Germans invaded on April 9, 1940. Iceland was occupied peacefully by British forces shortly after the German invasion of Norway and Denmark. Icelanders accepted this as a lesser evil and were relieved when U.S. forces—still nominally neutral—replaced the British in July 1941. Allied forces made good use of Icelandic bases during the war while respecting Icelandic independence in nonwar matters. Finland was attacked by the Soviet Union in November 1939 and, through valiant resistance, prevented occupation and perhaps the fate of the small Baltic republics. Finland fought a renewed war with the USSR between 1941 and 1944 as an ally (militarily, not ideologically) of Nazi Germany, but then had to fight German troops in 1944–45 after its armistice with Soviet Russia. The Soviet-Finnish Peace Treaty of 1947 and the Treaty of Friendship, Cooperation, and Mutual Assistance placed limitations on Finnish sovereignty, but these became less onerous after 1953. The German occupations seared the political consciousness of those who experienced it, and the reverberations of that experience continued to shape Danish and, especially, Norwegian politics for nearly fifty years. Skepticism toward European integration and Germany in particular was a legacy that has only recently faded.

Security policy is not only crucial to national security, it has also been crucial to domestic politics. Even before World War II, advocates of active social policies proposed the concept of *social defense.* They claimed that a society ridden by social conflicts was vulnerable to internal violence, subversion, and external attack. After the war the same claims were made in resisting excessive military buildups. When the Cold War threatened in 1948, Denmark, Sweden, and Norway sought a collective defense arrangement that would increase their military potential but not be provocative toward the Soviet Union. After nearly a year of negotiations, plans for a Scandinavian Defense Union collapsed in January 1949. Norway and more reluctantly Denmark and Iceland turned to the Atlantic Pact and became founding NATO members. Conflict over security policy was a constant factor in election campaigns, especially in Denmark and Norway, where defense spending and NATO membership were regularly denounced by parties to the left of the Social Democrats and, in Denmark, by the Radical Liberals in the center as well. In both countries, it has stymied otherwise plausible domestic coalitions. Differences in this regard among the Scandinavian countries have been significant.

Sweden and Finland enjoyed the broadest consensus on security policy largely because of their nonalignment policies. Sweden's policy had kept the country out of war since 1815. Finland's toughness in World War II and its carefully accommodating diplomacy with the Soviet Union became sanctified in the post–1945 era. Both the public and the political leadership remain reluctant to tamper with success even a decade after the end of the Cold War.

Norway commenced an independent foreign and security policy in 1905, convinced that the world would grant it at least as much good will and respect as it did its eastern neighbor, Sweden. Norwegian maritime interests did not escape World War I unscathed, and the country's strategic position made it a German target in 1940. Unarmed neutrality was discredited, and postwar Norwegian governments have placed a strong priority on membership in the Western defense alliance (see Ørvik 1953). It was the Norwegian insistence in 1949 that any Nordic defense pact be linked to NATO, which was then being formed, that led to the collapse of negotiations about a nonaligned Nordic security system.

Denmark and Iceland found themselves increasingly important strategically at least until the end of the Cold War. Denmark's territory of Greenland became vital to North American defense in the age of air and missile power. Iceland was crucial for Atlantic naval and air operations and thus of great value to NATO despite its lack of military forces. Nearly all of the forces stationed on Iceland (at the base in Keflavik, thirty miles from the capital) were American, and they numbered more than 3,000 at their peak. Domestic opposition to their presence—especially by the radical socialist People's Alliance—was a perennial issue in Icelandic politics. Despite their differences in security policy, all of the Scandinavian countries have sought systematically, both in Nordic and global contexts, to reduce tensions. Norwegian and Danish policies of rejecting the stationing of either nuclear weapons or foreign troops on their territories in peacetime, combined with the Swedish and Finnish nonalignment and Sweden's substantial defense capacity, contributed to creating and maintaining the Nordic balance, with its low tension and relatively low force levels. After 1990 the region's geopolitical situation has become exceptionally favorable, and all are reluctant to undertake major policy changes, especially through the European Union. The United States has become a much less dubious partner, particularly because of its distance from Northern Europe.

Trade Policy

Especially for small states, the import and export of goods and services are the foundation and most crucial aspect of a state's foreign economic policy. Its central political role was apparent to the founders of the modern state, who sought to harness trade for state power. Scandinavia followed the European fashion of adopting mercantilism in the seventeenth century, liberalism (free trade) in the nineteenth century, and so-called managed trade in the twentieth century. The trend since 1945 has been toward freer trade on the basis of various multilateral trade agreements. After an abortive effort to establish a Nordic Common Market, Denmark, Norway, and Sweden joined the European Free Trade Association (EFTA) when it was established in 1960; Finland and Iceland joined subsequently. A similar failed Nordic effort preceded Danish membership in the European Community in 1972, and the rest of Scandinavia had trade agreements with the European Community/Union until Sweden and Finland joined the EU in 1995. As discussed above, Norway and Iceland have many of the trade advantages through the looser EEA.

International trade looms large for all of the Scandinavian countries. In 1997, exports were approximately 40 percent of the gross domestic product (the value of goods and services produced in a country in a year) in each of the Scandinavian countries. The size of the international trade sector, while impressive, alone does not tell the full story. The firms on the leading edge of the Scandinavian economies are totally dependent on the international market. The extreme case is Sweden, which, with a population not much larger than that of New Jersey, maintains two auto manufacturers (both largely owned by U.S. automobile companies). The reason is not that every Swede buys a new car every third month. It is that Saab and Volvo export two-thirds and three-fourths of their production, respectively. Each exports nine-tenths of the heavy trucks it builds. Other major Scandinavian companies—such as Nokia, Novo-Nordisk, Lego, Norsk Hydro, Electrolux, Ericsson, SKF—are just as export dependent.

The Scandinavian countries are archetypal examples of what economists call "small, open economies." They must react quickly to global economic and political developments. Scandinavian dependence on international trade has increased by more than 50 percent in the past forty years, which is in line with most Western countries. Like all market decisions, trade decisions are made by myriad buyers and sellers, but governments still must decide whether to accept the market passively, or whether to shape trade in line with political preferences. Scandinavian governments have encouraged the dismantling of domestic industries that cannot compete in the global economy, such as textiles and shipbuilding.[5] The Norwegians have continued to protect their farm sectors, while the Danes, Finns, and Swedes participate in the EU's protectionist Common Agricultural Program.

Exchange Rate Policy

Like trade policy, exchange rate policy is a major component of foreign economic policy. In fact, it cannot not always be easily distinguished from trade issues. With the gradual but steady relaxation of currency exchange controls after 1950, Western states have found that successful fiscal and especially monetary policies require cooperation not only with foreign governments and international organizations, but also with external business and financial institutions. The restored and robust international capital market gave the Nordic countries access to credit for both consumption and investment.

Various economic problems of the past twenty-five years have left all of the Nordic countries, save Norway, with substantial foreign debts. Foreign debt, especially for small countries, comes at a political cost. The dramatic currency crisis of 1992, which especially affected Sweden, was a sharp example of such dependency. Even a modest reduction of a country's credit rating by an international rating agency (e.g., Standard and Poor or Moody) can cost millions in increased interest payments.

Sovereign states have regularly used changes in currency values to adjust trade imbalances since the gold standard was abandoned during the Depression. Sweden in particular has made use of devaluations as mechanisms to stimulate exports. Entrance even into the outer orbit of the European Union's EMU (through adherence to the Exchange Rate Mechanism, or ERM—the so-called snake that restricts currency fluctuations) would restrict that option, but to date Norway, Iceland, and Sweden use a basket of currencies (roughly in proportion to their trade relations) as the basis for their currency values. By contrast, Danish participation in the ERM after 1982 prevented Denmark from using unilateral currency devaluations as tools of economic policy. The Danish krone has generally risen through its link to the German mark, and since 1999 fluctuated vis-à-vis the dollar and pound through its link to the Euro. Finland has opted for full EMU participation and has converted to the Euro as its national currency.

The Domestic Political Dimension

The impact of external factors on national public policies is influenced by the extent of domestic political consensus. External economic or security issues may be so important that a state cannot ignore the consequences. If, however, there is bitter partisan dispute within that state about the nature of the challenge or the desirability of a particular response, the impact of the external pressures will be even greater. Recall the nuclear power issue in Sweden as an example. Although nuclear power became politically controversial in Sweden in the mid-1970s, its transformation into political dynamite came as a result of foreign developments. The 1979 Three Mile Island plant accident made a discreet policy compromise among Swedish leaders politically unacceptable. In 1986, the Chernobyl disaster in the Soviet Union brought the issue's external dimensions into even sharper focus. The domestic political détente on the nuclear power issue (following the ambiguous long-term phase out decision chosen in the 1980 nuclear power referendum) was eroded by renewed public anxiety over foreign accidents that had nothing directly to do with the design or operation of Swedish nuclear plants. The same sources of anxiety renewed demands by Danish nuclear critics that the Swedish nuclear plant at Barsebäck, only a dozen miles from Copenhagen, be shut down quickly. Hence, internal and external constraints work both ways. Domestic policy disputes have external consequences, and foreign controversies invade the domestic policy agenda.

Immigration and the Globalized Welfare State

Fifty years ago the Nordic countries were exceptionally homogeneous societies. There were some religious and ethnic minorities: German-speaking Danes in South Jutland; Samis (Lapps) in northern Finland, Sweden, and Norway; Finns in northern Sweden; and a significant number of Balts in Sweden who had fled their countries during and immediately after World War II. Greenlanders moving to continental Denmark, Samis moving south, and even Finnish migrants to Sweden after 1950 faced prejudices and occasionally outright discrimination. Attitudes toward political refugees, typically from the communist states of Eastern Europe or from military dictatorships like General Pinochet's Chile, were generous especially in the wake of the failure to help many earlier refugees from Nazi Germany. Except for occasional openings in the iron curtain—the Hungarian revolt (1956), and suppression in Czechoslovakia (1968) and Poland (1968 and 1981), the open door was rarely entered.

The Nordic labor migration agreement of 1954 and the labor shortages of the 1960s brought a growing stream of guest workers to Sweden and to a lesser degree Denmark and Norway. Finns were the main beneficiaries of the Nordic agreements, and tens of thousands moved the relatively short geographic and cultural distance to Sweden. Guest workers—non-Nordic immigrants recruited to fill labor shortages with temporary permits—came initially from southern Europe and the Balkans, but subsequently came increasingly from the Middle East (mainly Turkey) and North Africa. After the sharp economic slowdown in 1974, this program was largely suspended. Foreign workers were occasionally subsidized to return home, but there were no mass expulsions. Moreover liberal provisions for renewal of permits and even for allowing family members to come to Scandinavia were largely maintained.

Given the economic and political advantages of life in Scandinavia compared to most of the developing world, menial jobs or even unemployment compensation and social welfare supported a standard of living that was dramatically better than in distant homelands. As political criteria for refugees eased and even repressive regimes allowed mass emigration, the Nordic countries, along with many other Western countries found themselves coping with a growing, even exploding, stream of asylum applicants. International conventions place greater pressure on receiving countries while tightening the criteria for repatriation. So was born a social and political issue that had scarcely been visible before the 1980s.

The so-called immigration problem has in the past decade become a prominent, divisive, and even demagogic political issue, especially in Denmark and Norway. Foreigners are, of course, a highly diverse group: Few even mention the majority of immigrants who are of Scandinavian or West European background. There is now free labor mobility among the fifteen EU and three EEA countries, with plans to include the "new" EU members later. Although guest workers are no longer recruited (except among highly skilled technical, scientific, and business personnel), those who came decades ago and their descendants make up the bulk of non–West European immigrants. As many have become citizens of their new country or have been born into Scandinavian citizenship, there is no precise census on "new Scandinavians." Finally the surge in political refugees over the past fifteen years has added the most controversial group of immigrants. International and European conventions (as well as domestic laws) have greatly liberalized the definition of refugee status and improved refugees' rights. All of the Nordic countries are parties to such agreements, and their terms can be sweeping. Moreover, earlier liberal, or loose, interpretations, typical in Scandinavian law enforcement and administration, have stretched the definition of *refugee* quite broadly. Especially controversial have been rules allowing family reunification, which can allow a single refugee eventually to bring in a very extended, large family. The local phrase is "an immigrant in time brings nine!"

The surge in political refugees both genuine and less so has fueled xenophobic reactions unlike any seen since the 1930s. Sweden has the longest history of significant immigration and ironically has had the least overt reactions. No established political party has made xenophobia a major part of its program, but the new right in Norway and especially Denmark has done so. Not surprisingly, negative reactions stem from the relative pace of immigration and refugee resettlement and not purely from absolute numbers. Table 7.1 summarizes some quantitative data. Note that the number of nonnationals in Sweden has been relatively steady over the past decade, while the other Nordic countries have experienced a significant rate of growth.

The most difficult issues are not quantitative but qualitative. Sweden

Table 7.1
Immigration and Refugees in Scandinavia, 1990–2000

	Denmark	Finland	Iceland	Norway	Sweden
Non-national citizens as % of population, 2000	4.87	1.70	2.61	3.99	5.50
Percent increase in non-nationals, 2000 over 1990	66%	395%	39%	21%	2%
Net annual immigration of Non-nationals (annual average 1997-99)	28,037	8,865	1,113	4,742	37,081
Annual asylum requests† (annual average 1997-99)	5754	1788	18	4141*	11245

*Norwegian average 1996–98.
†In addition to asylum requests, the Nordic countries accept an annual quota of UN refugees for resettlement.
Source: Nordic Council (2000).

had two generations to prepare the way for what are considered the more exotic immigrants of recent years. For the others it has been much more sudden. Moreover, immigrants naturally cluster in urban and suburban settings—especially given the always tight housing markets in Scandinavia. This makes their presence in urban schools and neighborhoods quite visible. Although it might be an exaggeration to talk of foreign ghettos in Scandinavia, some alarmists certainly do. Hysteria, media exploitation, and outright racism and bigotry have reared their ugly heads with increasing frequency. The attitudes of some immigrants toward marriage (often by family arrangement), toward women's roles (very traditional), and toward the native population (hostility mainly among radical Islamists) have been a source of debate. Problems of organized crime—not restricted to immigrants—heighten tensions. What does *multiculturalism* mean in formerly homogeneous welfare societies?

Globalization is not just multinational corporations, fast-food chains, and youth culture. It has a human face. Immigrants and especially refugees often have been traumatized before they arrive. It is not surprising that crime and social pathologies flourish even in "luxury" refugee camps or housing projects. Ideally immigration issues should have been discussed and weighed before large numbers of immigrants and refugees arrived in Scandinavia. They were not. In practice what can these countries do to relieve the political and social turmoil without violating broadly supported international agreements?

The Swedish experience as the first and largest immigrant host country suggests some policy alternatives. With her long-standing "active labor market" policies, Sweden has had better success in integrating immigrants into the job market. Work, training, and the social aspects of being productive helps to remove some of the stigma of being foreign. Second comes education, especially language instruction. Obviously immigrant children, including second generation children who often hold Scandinavian citizenship, should be fully integrated in order to prosper. However Denmark's tradition of state-supported private schools, which allows support of Islamic schools as well, may make this more difficult than in the other Nordic countries. Whatever religious or cultural education families wish to provide, their children must learn their new language, culture and the academic skills necessary to survive in a postindustrial society. Third, better enforcement of antidiscrimination and equal opportunity policies helps both the new and the traditional national communities to interact and understand one another. There are too many skilled immigrants and refugees who have had difficulty pursuing their profession in the face of discrimination; excluded immigrants are understandably resentful. The other side of legal protection for immigrants is efficient law enforcement against international crime that exploits the immigrant and refugee community. Here European and international cooperation is essential.

COPING WITH INTERDEPENDENCE

The many facets of interdependence cannot be easily traced. This is especially true for the porous Scandinavian states, which are deeply enmeshed in many aspects of contemporary international relations. Foreign states, organizations, and enterprises all affect the Scandinavian countries' domestic policy process. It is not, however, a passive or dependent status, but rather a complex, mutual dependency. To paraphrase Harvard's Don Price, for nations, as for people, "where one stands depends upon where one sits."

States seek to cope with international constraints in three ways. First, they shape their domestic institutions to deploy their political and administrative resources effectively. Rarely are public policy goals singular. In the pluralist Scandinavian societies, each ministry, firm, organization, or other public policy actor will have its own pattern and goals in responding to external constraints. For EU members (Denmark, Finland,

and Sweden) every ministry participates in the work of the EU Council of Ministers. There are similar domestic effects from international cooperation in security, trade, social, and health issues. In addition to national goals, there are public and private organizational goals and procedures. In particular, are the democratic corporatist policy procedures developed over three generations for domestic policy making suitable for and effective in the new milieu of international interdependence?

Second, states must persuade external actors of the legitimacy and mutual interest of their national policy goals. This is economic and policy diplomacy through bargaining, persuasion, or even force and intimidation. Even small states need carrots and sticks.

Third, states collaborate in regional and international organizations, alliances, or communities to promote common policy goals. Alliances usually have a diplomatic or military focus. Since World War II, Western nations have built a web of political and economic arrangements that some, like Keohane and Nye, have dubbed "regimes," or "sets of governing arrangements" with rules, norms, and procedures accepted by a group of states (2001, pp. 17–19). Some of these arrangements, such as the European Union, have demanded the formal surrender of sovereignty in specific and often substantial policy areas.[6]

Policy is made at various governmental levels. Local governments, "sovereign" national governments, and various transnational regional and even global bodies shape Scandinavian public policy. Thus, policy analysis can no longer stay at home. Issues of overlapping jurisdictions and the definition of political community extend beyond traditional policy frontiers. International and regional policy processes may focus on agreement in functional areas (such as collaborative economic relationships), political areas (such as the Nordic Council) or may require legal surrender of sovereignty (as is often the case in the EU). They extend from loosely defined regimes of probable reciprocal interaction (ecological agreements concerning the Baltic Sea region, for example, or improved warning procedures for nuclear accidents) to highly bureaucratic and structured political processes.

Because our focus is on domestic policy-making arrangements in the Scandinavian countries, our attention is on those requiring a surrender of sovereignty. Let us look now at how the makers of policy in Scandinavia accommodate external constraints. Each participant has a specific as well as a national perspective. We have grouped these participants into three broad and overlapping categories: state, partisan, and corporatist or organizational.

The State Perspective

Governments differ in structure and procedures, but they all share an inherent tension between their constitutional singularity (governmental regulations) and their policy pluralism (the several governmental and nongovernmental organizations required to implement a policy). Governmental policies have too often been seen as monolithic when, in fact, democratic policy tends toward the pluralistic if not the chaotic. The structure of Scandinavian government and policy making has already been described. Three centers of state policy making are concerned with external policy pressures. The government or cabinet in power must exercise authority and responsibility for policy decisions. The bureaucracy is the most common conduit for international relations; civil servants report and assess developments, interact with foreign decision makers, and follow up on national decisions. Finally, parliament, usually through its standing committees, enters into the policy making process. Its role is usually passive, but when major international commitments are undertaken, authority must be shared beyond the usual foreign and security policy ministries, and parliament's role may increase.

Foreign and regional policy are primarily executive matters. The prime minister and the cabinet (or a group of ministers) decide how to respond to foreign developments that have domestic policy consequences. Decisions are ultimately accountable to parliament, which, in a coalition government, is a genuine restraint. Nearly all ministries have an international affairs section. When issues are especially important or have broad ramifications across several ministries, interagency working groups try to coordinate national responses and share expertise and perspectives. This is usually where sovereignty resides and where the national interest is defined. The policy process has become so globalized and intertwined with domestic affairs that some Norwegians scholars—reporting on the future of the Ministry of Foreign Affairs—have suggested that it be abolished and its functions placed in strengthened international departments of functional ministries. Hence foreign economic relations would be relegated to the Ministries of Finance, Trade, and other portfolios (see Moses and Knudsen 2001).

Membership in international organizations, especially those where substantial policy making power is ceded by treaty, complicates executive government. Ministers may serve on intergovernmental councils both as representatives of a government and as organizational policy makers. In Nordic cooperation, ministers meet formally (the Nordic Council of Ministers) several times a year to implement Nordic agreements and to evaluate new proposals (from national governments usually via the Nordic Council, which assembles Nordic parliamentarians for broader collective goals). This is a typical intergovernmental organization; it is also more illustrative of the past than the future of globalized policy making.

The European Union is a far more entangling organization. Its Council of Ministers brings cabinet ministers to Brussels the prepare and implement important policies. When prime ministers assemble as the Council of the European Union, fundamental decisions and treaties may result. Since the Maastricht Treaty of 1992, a growing number of policy areas are on the EU agenda and some no longer require unanimous approval by the member states. For Denmark, Finland, and Sweden, union politics is coequal or even superior to national policy making. As nonmembers, Iceland and Norway are not similarly constrained, except in the numerous policy areas encompassed by the European Economic Area agreements. Here their influence is less than EU members'.

Civil servants are, of course, closely tied to their domestic colleagues and ministers. As they move up the career ladder, they become acutely sensitive to foreign constraints on national policy. Those in key international ministries become both intermediaries and specialists in advocating and accommodating national preferences to regional and global realities. Formal international economic conferences, like the ongoing work of the European Union Council of Ministers or the annual Western economic summit conferences, change the priorities of national bureaucracies. Domestic perspectives must now be assessed and justified in terms of multilateral interests (Artis and Ostry 1986, pp. 70–73).

Because a term of international service is usually a plus for a Scandinavian bureaucratic career, many civil servants will have policy experience in transnational organizations. For a few, it is the pinnacle of their careers. As mentioned above, the first two United Nations secretaries general, Norwegian Trygve Lie and Swede Dag Hammarskjöld, were paragons of international civil servants, and Scandinavians continue to serve the UN and many international organizations. The long tradition of a professional civil service, the quality of Scandinavian education and training for such positions, especially in foreign languages, and the objective political role of their countries help account for the overrepresentation of competent Scandinavians in international organizations. Some end their careers there, but most return to domestic posts. One can imagine the probable advantages such experiences give these officials in terms of contacts within key international and regional organizations. This is likely to have a growing impact on national policy making in the future.

Political and bureaucratic policy makers alike face an additional pressure from the internationalization of policy making: The policy process and substance within and between ministries is blurred. This is especially clear for members of the European Union. Originally the European Community governed significant but restricted policy areas, including agriculture, fisheries, and trade. Since the signing of the Maastricht Treaty of 1992 and its successors, the EU is become a significant factor in a growing number of other areas, including environmental, police and justice, economic and monetary affairs, and external relations.[7]

Parliamentary participation is comprehensive in scope, but limited in effect. On most foreign policy issues, the Scandinavian parliaments have access to information and details. They may even lead public debates. But decisive power remains with the executive. The occasional exception is notable. Between 1982 and 1988, for instance, a parliamentary majority in Denmark opposed aspects of the government's security policy. The government was forced on many occasions to append reservations (so-called footnotes) to NATO resolutions, stating the opposition of the Danish parliament. After five years, the disagreement finally caused a snap election in May 1988. The outcome did not settle the issue, in part because of the complex nature of popular and parliamentary views on security policy. The issue became moot with the ending of the Cold War in Europe in 1989–91. As the EU has struggled to forge a common security and foreign policy, Danish opinion has swung strongly in favor of NATO, including parties that had spent the previous four decades in opposition.

Normally, the institutional role of parliament is to provide a forum for partisan debate and to ratify policy decisions. It guides the general direction of foreign policy. Essentially, all of the standing committees of the Scandinavian parliaments have areas of responsibility with substantial and often decisive international import. As noted, Scandinavian parliamentary committees, although strong by European standards, are generally dependent upon other public agencies for information and technical expertise. Ministries and public commissions provide the information for parliamentary action. Parliament's role depends upon whether international policy arrangements merely advocate a certain response, which is typical of Nordic Council agreements, or whether external agreements obligate a country to do something, best illustrated by EU membership.

Nordic cooperation reveals a relatively even balance between the role of ministers and bureaucrats, on the one hand, and parliamentarians on the other. The Nordic Council was itself established through an initiative by members of several national parliaments, who felt that the failure to conclude regional agreements on defense and trade ought not to preclude pragmatic cooperation on a host of matters likely to affect many individual Scandinavians. Hence, the Nordic countries moved quite rapidly in establishing a common labor market and standardizing social benefits that allow Scandinavians to work in any of the Nordic countries (although there are some limitations with Iceland). It has functioned far more smoothly than similar European efforts. The similar cultural and educational background especially of highly trained labor has been the critical difference. Most of the Nordic Council's work is based on interparliamentary commissions reviewing and proposing specific policy measures (Haskel 1976, pp. 131–64; see also Anderson 1967). Complementing this effort are Nordic civil servants' commissions, under the Nordic Council of Ministers, that investigate common policy concerns. Bureaucrats from each of the countries concerned apply the common Scandinavian technique of "investigation" to find areas of agreement. Although the EU and EEA are more visible venues for policy collaboration, Nordic cooperation remains fundamentally pragmatic, with public policy considerations far outweighing ideology or sentiment.

The Danish parliament's European Relations Committee, created prior to Denmark's adherence to the EU in 1973, was a major innovation for parliamentary participation in policy making in a regional context. Although technically this committee merely reviews and periodically assesses Denmark's position in the European Union, its power is amplified by the country's normally thin parliamentary balance. Governments have often had to make major economic policy decisions by arranging packages that can gain broad political support. European policies have become part of such a bargain. The Committee supervises the external aspect. As the scope of European Union has broadened in the past decade, parliamentary participation has spread to additional committees and intruded into nearly every major domestic policy area in Denmark. The pressures for policy harmonization have moved well beyond trade issues.

In the past decade Sweden and Finland joined the European Union, and Norway and Iceland became part of the European Economic Area. They have all sought to emulate the Danish example of parliamentary committee oversight of EU issues in varying degrees. Sweden and Finland, as full members, have largely succeeded. The EEA arrangements are more formally intergovernmental and mainly the responsibility of the Norwegian and Icelandic governments (Damgaard 2000, pp. 156–60).

Partisanship Across Borders

The major Scandinavian political parties are all national in organization and activity. Their immediate goal is winning elections and creating viable coalitions in order to govern. Although conservative and liberal parties owe little in their origins to foreign models, the labor and socialist parties share a strong internationalist heritage. In the nineteenth century, international and regional meetings played a major role in the development of Scandinavian Social Democracy, but, since 1914, these ties have become more ceremonial; it is hard to cite any matter of importance in recent years in which internationalism has overridden a Scandinavian Social Democratic party's national interest. Only the orthodox Communists have permitted that, and that is one of the causes of the Communists' demise as an effective political force.

Although parties differed historically, today nearly all Scandinavian parties can find ideologically comparable parties in other democracies, and close ties with fraternal parties are regularly cultivated. Within the region, there is clear evidence that a successful party in one country stimulates the creation of a similar party in the others. On the left, the formation of the Socialist People's party in Denmark in 1959, for example, contributed to the formation of a similar party in Norway in 1961, and to a substantial reorientation of the Swedish Communist party in 1964. On the right, the obvious appeal of Glistrup and his Progress party's tax revolt encouraged Anders Lange to organize a comparable party in Norway in 1972–73. Those cases, however, reflect as much the similarity of issues as they do international ties.

While all major Scandinavian parties today are primarily national in their orientation, their ideologies and programs are not exclusively national in terms of goals, means, or activities. Parties have been strongly affected by foreign and regional issues. Scandinavian parties take their programs' foreign policy sections seriously. External policy influences and goals affect Scandinavian parties and policy makers in several ways.

First, they draw on foreign examples, usually those of other advanced industrial countries. A *demonstration effect* seems especially strong among the Scandinavian countries. This occurs at both a practical level (i.e., Danes asking what the Swedes are doing about a common problem or vice versa) and at a theoretical level. Ideas, perspectives, and practical measures on political issues disseminate rapidly among the democracies. The news media are quite attentive to events abroad, and Scandinavian journalists regularly read and interpret English and German media for domestic audiences. The revival of the British Labour party under Tony Blair in the 1990s was keenly followed in Scandinavia. His "third way" is highly reminiscent of the traditional Scandinavian metaphor: the middle way.

Explicit international cooperation to analyze common policy problems occurs with some regularity. Joint inquiries at the Nordic, European, Western (e.g., through the OECD), or global levels (through the United Nations system) mainly involve civil servants, but their findings are often the source of public debate. Although this process is not new, the past decade has seen renewed emphasis on benchmarking policy impact and comparing performance. Such influences cannot be weighed precisely, but clearly shape domestic debates on education, health care, and other policy issues.

Although the clear distinction between domestic and foreign affairs has broken down, elections are often fought on such matters, and foreign policy questions can make or break party political alliances. Some foreign policy issues have united parties across ideological lines (e.g., Norwegian withdrawal from the dual monarchy with Sweden in 1905, the successful maintenance of Scandinavian neutrality during World War I, Swedish neutrality for more than one hundred fifty years). In other cases, foreign issues have been highly divisive, such as Denmark's relationship with Germany after 1864, the post–1945 collective defense alternatives, and especially since the 1970s membership in the EU.

Moreover, European parties and increasingly interest organizations communicate and work systematically across national lines. The long internationalist tradition of the Left has been noted. Regional cooperation (the Nordic Council and the European Parliament [for Denmark, Finland, and Sweden]) has stimulated regional partisan collaboration in the center and on the right as well. The European Parliament and the Nordic Council are divided into party groups, but both assemblies' scope and powers are limited. Unlike other European Union institutions, the European Parliament has been directly elected since 1979. That first election was a cause of some excitement: All over Europe, voters went to the polls on a single day to elect a trans-European body. Election night, all Europe could watch the returns coming in. Direct elections have strengthened the European Parliament's legitimacy and perhaps its power. They have, however, done less to encourage the growth of transnational parties than many expected. Cross national campaigning has been relatively rare. European Parliament elections sometimes seem to be more an interim expression of sentiment on national governments' performance at home than on European policies.

The results of the most recent Scandinavian elections to the European Parliament can be seen in Appendix D. Voter turnout has been low relative to national elections, and it has been trending down. In the 1999 European election, 50 percent of Danish voters went to the polls (versus 88% in the 1998 national election), 39 percent of Swedes voted (versus 81% in the 1998 national election), and only 30 percent of Finns went to the polls (versus 65% in the 1999 national election). Between a quarter and a third of voters cast their ballots for anti-EU parties or movements, far higher than the vote the anti-EU groups generally get in domestic elections. Most of these votes come at the expense of the Social Democrats, whose share of the EU parliament vote is much lower than their national vote.

The prolonged Danish debate on EU issues has transformed some of the anti-EU activist organizations into Danish Euro–parliamentary parties. They contest elections to the EU parliament, along with the regular domestic parties, and have consistently won representation. They have used the elections in part to agitate, but they are active at the European Parliament to protect state sovereignty and to challenge EU initiatives. Although there are ample Euro-skeptics among the regular parties in Sweden and Finland, parties dedicated to the EU issues alone have not yet formed.

EU and other international policies that integrate and harmonize national policies are especially vivid examples of a growing threat to and opportunity for national institutions and political parties. Collective decision making within an integrated policy community reduces national parties in part to the status of regional parties. On the other hand, if they can link with allied parties in other participating states, their power can be maintained or even amplified. Bargaining within such communities requires not only coalitions among governments, but alliances between political parties. Such community partisanship would be promoted by a strengthening of the European parliament, which is dominated by party blocs across national boundaries. Few predict a significant strengthening of the European parliament in the near future, but directly elected parliaments have historically expanded their prerogatives.

Finally, parties may use their formal and informal contacts in regional organizations to pursue policy goals. Again, the European Union provides the best example, although similar episodes are to be found in Nordic cooperation, Western cooperation (NATO and the OECD), and global organizations (the United Nations and its agencies). High-ranking international civil servants frequently have partisan connections. Their policy role is usually central to regional and international organizations. The pattern of international lobbying has been set by interest and commercial organizations whose perspective is usually narrower than political parties, but whose tactics may be adaptable. It is to these transnational actors that we now turn.

Corporatism and External Constraints

Given the importance of interest organizations to Scandinavian democracy and policy making and the importance of foreign trade and investment to the Scandinavian economies, it is not surprising to find such organizations active beyond their national borders. Scandinavian corporatist organizations in business, labor, and agriculture primarily reflect each country's economic structure. Where foreign markets are vital, Scandinavian organizations are international in outlook and transnational in action. For those organizations still focusing closely on national issues, foreign constraints threaten to overturn traditional democratic corporatist politics.

In the Nordic sphere, significant regional agreements in security and economic policy have proven elusive. As noted above an effort to establish a Scandinavian Defense Pact in 1948–49 foundered on differences in national views. Serious efforts to build a Nordic Common Market were stymied in 1959 and again at the end of the 1960s in large part by the objections of national interest organizations. Norwegian industrialists initially feared Swedish dominance, and both Swedish and Norwegian farmers' organizations opposed including agriculture in the Nordic Common Market. Without the inclusion of agriculture, however, there was little reason for Denmark to join; the European Community offered a bigger market for the highly competitive Danish agricultural products. In economic and security issues, the region was seen as either too small or national interests too competitive. Larger and more attractive regional arrangements attracted one or more of the countries.

In areas of successful Nordic cooperation, however, credit must go to informal ties between Nordic organizations, particularly the trade union movements (and the related Social Democratic parties) and to cultural and educational organizations, such as the national Nordic Associations (*Forening Norden*). Thus, Nordic policy cooperation has been concentrated in the cultural, labor, and social spheres. Two important Nordic conventions, the common labor market and social security agreements, have real economic consequences, especially in protecting individuals; they do not, however, benefit particularly one national interest group or another.

Scandinavian interest organizations have also been visible on the European, Western, and global levels. The Scandinavian labor unions, which have a tradition of international activity dating to their origins, offer the most outstanding example. Danish unions provided significant support in the organization of Swedish and Norwegian unions in the 1880s and 1890s; strike support across national boundaries was common; and pan-Scandinavian workers' congresses made key decisions on how to structure the national labor movements in the same period. While German unions generally took the lead in establishing the international trades secretariats that linked national craft unions, it was the Danish trade union federation that took the initiative that led to the formation in 1901 of the forerunner of the International Federation of Trade Unions (Federspiel 1978) and today's International Confederation of Free Trade Unions (ICFTU).

In the years following World War II, international union attention has been increasingly focused on intergovernmental organizations: the International Labor Organization (ILO) of the United Nations; the Council of Europe's labor conventions, which set regional standards and safeguards; and, in the case of Denmark, Finland, and Sweden the EU's tripartite (labor-government-business) Economic and Social Committee (ESC). Scandinavian unions continue to have close contact with their counterparts in the other Scandinavian countries, and many continue to provide for reciprocal strike support; a few, like the metal workers, support a formal Nordic secretariat that provides some coordination. The national union federations are members of the European Trade Union Confederation (ETUC) and of the ICFTU; individual national unions are members of the International Trade Secretariats. The OECD and other international organizations (such as the ILO) provide additional forums for transnational interest group advocacy because much of their investigatory work is undertaken by specialists borrowed from national organizations and bureaucracies.

A growing number of Nordic nongovernmental organizations are finding that their interests require effective representation in the European Union, as mentioned above. Although the least powerful EU institution, the Economic and Social Committee explicitly recognizes the role of economic and social interest organizations in the policy process. It seeks direct representation of farm, employer, and labor organizations. The minimal role of the ESC and the restricted role of the European parliament in the European policy process have focused interest group activity on lobbying the European Commission—the source of nearly all policy initiatives (Buksti and Marten 1984, pp. 63–70). This development follows the precedent set by perhaps the most influential European Community interest organization, the Confederation of Professional Agricultural Organizations (known by its French acronym COPA), which has had remarkable success in channeling the European financial resources into agricultural subsidies.

In the European Community, Danish, Finnish, and Swedish interest organizations have been exceptionally strong because of the Scandinavian tradition of professional interest group administration. Scandinavian skills in foreign languages and international organization have further assisted interest group internationalism; Scandinavians have been prominent in key administrative positions.

Important over the past decade have been efforts by the Scandinavians and other EU members to address the democratic deficit (the perception that too many decisions are not ratified by the citizens and parties in the member states). These may presage interest group politics at the international and regional level. As a confederal intergovernmental organization, the EU mainly responds to the wishes of its individual sovereign members. Given the scope of the massive "acquis communautaire" (EU legal and regulatory corpus) and the EU treaties' goal of "an ever closer union" (Treaty of Rome, 1957), its decisions increasingly impinge on the democratic prerogatives of national parliaments, administrations, and courts. Thus there have been growing demands that the operation of the EU institutions themselves show greater accountability. Of course to make the directly elected European Parliament dominant would require a genuine federal union. Meanwhile the EU democracy movement has stressed procedural safeguards. Under pressure from the three Nordic members and others, the EU's administrative structure has begun to reflect some Nordic values, most notably an openness and transparency that was previously absent. The European Parliament dismissed the European Commission after a scandal in 1998. Although the new Commission was appointed by the European Council, which represents the sovereign constituent states, the new Commission cannot ignore accountability.

International interest organizations try to defend common group interests. They are alert to changes that threaten desirable aspects of the status quo. Repeated efforts, for example, to modify the European Community agricultural policies (the expensive price subsidies, in particular) have been intercepted by COPA and battled at the national level by COPA's constituent farmer organizations through mobilizing public opinion and political pressure. International interest groups coordinate the responses of national organizations, mobilizing support for a common response and assisting the national constituent organizations in responding to new policies. Organizational effectiveness depends upon simultaneous action at several points.

Democratic deficits also arise from ongoing economic globalization. For more than thirty years, multinational corporations (MNCs) have attracted both praise and criticism as a special but important variety of international actor. While Norwegian and Swedish studies of the concentration of political power have reiterated the obvious fact of economic interdependence, multinational firms have not been seen as significant constraints on national policy making (cf Norway 1982, pp. 187–215; Olsen 1983, pp. 13–38). Still, the future need for joint regional or international action to regulate MNCs has been a recurring political theme as the Nordic states have opened their economies and societies to global commercial activities. In general foreign firms may now establish and operate in the Nordic states on a par with domestic firms. The growth of cable and satellite media have ended the traditional monopolies of state broadcasting agencies. This has often been controversial. There were many calls for restrictions on foreign media during the 1980s, but technology (first satellites and then the Internet) has largely made the debate moot. Foreign firms operating with the Nordic countries, however, have had to adjust their procedures and attitudes to local customs. Unions have been successful in organizing workers in most newly established foreign firms, and labor and occupational regulations have been enforced. Moreover, the EU has placed employment and working issues prominently on its policy agenda with the support of the Nordic states.

TRANSNATIONAL IMPACT ON DOMESTIC POLICY

In the past decade world political changes have broken the mold for Nordic foreign policies. The end of the Cold War and the renewed dynamism of European integration have blurred the distinction between domestic and foreign policy. What has emerged is an overlapping web of policies and policy makers. The reality is not the neat blocks of organizational charts, but dynamic interaction between national and international, private and public bureaucracies, interests, and transactions. Clear divisions are no longer realistic, even though parties and politicians continue to argue for particular national interests. National sovereignty does imply some final and decisive authority, but only at a cost (for an optimistic survey of the positive effects of deregulation, privatization, and globalization, see Yergin and Stanislaw 1998).

Foreign policy demands differ from domestic issues, but similar consensual pressures appear to have served the policy interests of Scandinavia well. Pragmatism is not a precise concept, but it implies a willingness to recognize reality. It is also a concept that aptly characterizes

Scandinavians' dealings with international interdependence as much as with domestic issues. Scandinavian policy institutions are well equipped for global corporatism and bargaining, even if many issues remain politically contested. The future of the EU remains an emotional and divisive issue in Scandinavia, but everyone recognizes that *Europapolitik* (policies toward the EU and other European projects) now is at the head of the policy agenda. Some fiercely emotional and divisive issues such as the Vietnam War during the 1960s and 1970s and NATO and Cold War issues are gone, but pressures toward pragmatism remain strong. Globalization requires continuous and dynamic engagement by all elements of the political system. Rigidity and dogmatism are costly for all countries, but especially for the small.

NOTES

1. The European Economic Area gave access in 1993 to the EU's Single Market (free-trade zone) to former European Free Trade Association members that chose not to join the EU. Finland and Sweden joined the EU in 1995, while Norwegian membership was blocked by the 1994 referendum. Iceland never formally applied to the EU, but became an EEA member along with tiny Liechtenstein. EEA states have full access to the EU market for labor, goods, and services, but not for agricultural or fisheries products. Switzerland is the sole EFTA country that has joined neither the EU nor the EEA after a referendum rejected the latter. The Swiss government has negotiated a package of ad hoc trade agreements with her neighbors. EEA states have little influence over developing EU policy in trade areas; they must basically accept what the EU offers.

2. Finland was forced to pay a heavy reparations debt to the USSR at the end of World War II, and the payments had to be in industrial goods as well as raw materials. This burden forced modernization on Finnish industry, which improved the country's international competitive position. Trade with the communist economies later became highly profitable but left Finland vulnerable to the sudden loss of that market after 1990. For a good summary of Finnish-Soviet relations after 1945, see Jakobson (1998).

3. The role of Nordic statesmen as international crisis managers and civil servants dates back at least eighty years, when Norwegian explorer Fridtjof Nansen helped organize civilian and refugee relief after World War I. In addition to Holst, the past decade has seen other Nordic leaders involved in peace efforts, including former Swedish Prime Minister Carl Bildt in the Balkans, then–Finnish President Martii Ahtisaari in the North Irish truce, and former Danish Defense Minister Hans Hækkerup in Kosovo. Other Nordic statesmen work in Palestine.

4. Scandinavian security policy is the subject of a large and rich literature. A brief account is Einhorn and Logue (1999, pp. 226–32). See also Haskel (1976); Lundestad (1980); Sundelius (1992); Snidal and Brundtland (1993); Dörfer (1997); and Jakobson (1998). Nordic security issues also receive regular attention in the journal *Cooperation and Conflict*.

5. High-cost economies like the Nordic countries cannot compete with low-cost Third World producers for most consumer or labor-intensive goods. Their com-

petitive advantage is in new technologies (e.g., electronics, pharmaceuticals) or high-quality innovative consumer goods. World-famous Scandinavian Design is still very competitive in home furnishings, fashion, and even automotive products.

6. The literature on the European Union is enormous. For recent detailed studies of its impact on policy see Wallace and Wallace (2001).

7. Denmark negotiated significant reservations to the Maastricht Treaty but in practice has felt the growing importance of the EU. The new Nordic members, Sweden and Finland, have fewer reservations. See Ingebritsen (1998).

CHAPTER 8

The Social Welfare State

Others got more ore so silver and red
    From mountain and plunder and spoil.
In Denmark, however, there is daily bread
    Even on the tables of those who toil.
When it comes to real riches, we have gone far
    When few have too much and fewer too little.
                 —N. F. S. Grundtvig (1820)

The economic and social changes that swept across Western Europe during the second half of the nineteenth century gave rise to what was then called "the social question": the rapid growth of a class of propertyless urban industrial workers, who were herded into the hastily constructed slums of the cities and who seemed to grow poorer as society grew richer.

Responses differed with political attitudes. Conservatives, while resisting demands for political democracy, were also concerned about the consequences of industrialization, urbanization, and other seemingly inexorable trends. Liberals held that constitutional government should simultaneously protect life, liberty, and property from autocratic tyranny and mass anarchy, but social and economic issues should not overly concern the state. Radicals wanted political democracy to be an instrument for far-reaching social and economic reform.

The removal of ancient restrictions on the economic and social liberties of ordinary people paralleled progress in political liberties and civil rights detailed in the previous chapters. Only in Denmark was there a substantial feudal tradition, and, in 1788, the Danish form of serfdom was abolished. By the middle of the nineteenth century, trade and commerce were gradually liberated from state control, as liberalism and laissez faire replaced mercantilism. Guild monopolies were abolished in 1846 in Sweden, 1862 in Denmark, 1868 in Finland, and 1869 in Norway; the compulsory craft associations that had replaced the guilds in Sweden were dissolved in 1864. Free and compulsory public elementary education, which was established in 1814 in Denmark, 1827 in Norway, 1842 in Sweden, and 1866 in Finland, spread literacy, surely a prerequisite for the exercise of individual freedom in the modern age.

Still, these formal rights of socioeconomic equality were belied by the reality of growing inequality. Despite relatively rapid economic growth, the poor seemed to be becoming poorer and more numerous. In Sweden, for example, the number of paupers tripled in absolute numbers between 1810 and 1910 and increased by one-fourth relative to the population. The official 1907 income statistics showed the top 1 percent earned more income than the bottom 50 percent. An official study of wealth distribution in 1908 found that the top 1 percent owned nine times the wealth owned by the bottom 60 percent; in fact, the top 1.5 percent owned as much as the entire rest of the population put together (as cited in Höglund, Sköld, and Ström 1913, pp. 59–63). Lack of statistics make accurate comparison to inequality at the beginning of the nineteenth century impossible, but there is no question that in the public perception, inequality had grown in size and scope. Many believed that only the emigrants' flight to America kept the problem from growing to revolutionary proportions.

THE DEVELOPMENT OF SOCIAL WELFARE

The recognition that individual liberty and technological progress offered no automatic escape from the poverty that accompanied industrialization prompted a movement at the end of the nineteenth century for relief for the victims of urban industrial life.[1]

Scandinavian liberals and radicals had been allied in the struggle for parliamentary democracy, but with its achievement, they now differed as to how the new constitutional order should be used. For radical democrats, the goal was social change and democracy. That included both equality of opportunity and, at least to some considerable extent, equality of result. Each person should not only have the opportunity to develop his or her full potential, but should also be assured that inequalities of endowment and achievement would not have severe consequences for the physical and cultural needs of the individual, and his or her family. Hard work and genius would still be rewarded, but all would inhabit the same social and economic world. In the Danish reformer and theologian N. F. S. Grundtvig's words, the goal would be a society where "few have too much and fewer too little."

The process of creating that kind of society in Scandinavia went through four stages. The first step saw the gradual conversion of existing inconsistent, spotty, and often private programs of social assistance and social insurance into national programs. This stage started in the 1890s and continued until the Social Democrats consolidated their power in the 1930s. The second stage was characterized by the Social Democrats' efforts to establish a basic safety net of welfare programs to guarantee an adequate, although modest standard of living for all—the aged, the sick, the disabled, the unemployed, low-income families with children—without the stigma of the old poor law. This stage began in the 1930s and concluded in the 1960s. The third stage, also dominated by the Social Democrats, raised the income-replacement ratios for average employees temporarily forced out of gainful employment to 80 or more percent of market income and generalized social services, previously only available in large urban areas, to small towns and rural areas through massive municipal consolidation. This stage began in the prosperous 1960s and was largely completed in time for the oil crisis of 1973–74. The fourth stage commenced in the 1970s with the expansion of expensive new services that had largely previously been provided within the family, especially childcare programs (pre- and after-school care) and home care for the disabled and elderly. Simultaneously, cost constraints in other social programs, globalization pressures (e.g., immigration and economic integration) have forced administrative and programmatic reforms. Some of these are controversial.

The Private Origins of Public Welfare, 1890–1930

The roots of the social policies that began to emerge in the 1880s stretch back through the ideas of the Enlightenment, when politics turned from dynastic and religious struggles to become an instrument of economic and social action, to the religious ideals of the medieval church concerning charity and Christian equality. Although the church concentrated upon saving the soul, it did not neglect the body. Many modern social programs and institutions can be traced back to the activities of religious organizations in their care for orphans, the poor, the sick, and the elderly. Charity is a universal religious principle.

The Reformation and the growth of the state, however, divided charity between secular and religious authorities. Moreover, it was increasingly an instrument of policy. Paupers were not just a blight on the conscience; they were a threat to the health and security of the community. "Poor laws" sought to protect public health and security in the growing towns and cities of the late–Middle Ages. They balanced mercy with economic and public policy. By the nineteenth century, the Scandinavian states, as all other European states, had a coherent, if not necessarily humane, social policy to take care of the totally impoverished. The work houses demeaned their beneficiaries, who were generally stripped of civil and political rights, and were plagued by scandal. They were the target of continual outrage from Scandinavian social reformers and revolutionaries alike, but they were no worse than their European equivalents.

A second source of the modern welfare state was the guilds, which kept their grip on Scandinavian manufacturing until the middle of the nineteenth century. Their primary interest was the economic security of their members. In part, this was promoted by mutual insurance against economic loss caused by accident, unemployment, illness, or death. When the guilds were dissolved, their political and economic functions passed easily to the rising labor movement and other economic interest organizations. Access to health, unemployment, life, and burial insurance recruited many members for the new unions, particularly in the skilled trades. Modern Scandinavian social policy dates from the decision at the end of the nineteenth century to use state funds to subsidize these insurance programs. It was a decision that permitted the extension of such benefits as unemployment compensation to the unskilled. For example, in Denmark the sickness insurance funds received about one-fourth of their revenue from the state after 1892. Half of the unemployment insurance premiums in 1907 were contributed by the public sector. Old-age insurance after 1891 was entirely funded by the state and local governments, while nearly compulsory workers' compensation ("nearly compulsory" in that although employers did not have to insure their workers, they were legally liable for job injuries) was entirely paid by the employers (Kuhnle 1981a, p. 140).

A third source of the Scandinavian welfare state was the experience of other, more advanced industrial societies. German Chancellor Otto von Bismarck sponsored several comprehensive social-insurance laws in the 1880s, in part to lessen the attraction of socialism and militant labor unions. These acts included sickness insurance (1883), workers' compensation (1884), and old-age pensions (1889). Although the political reasons that motivated Bismarck were not as compelling in Scandinavia, the political, social, and economic attraction of the German innovations clearly reinforced early Scandinavian reforms and encouraged a broader base of political support. British social and economic reforms, particularly after the Liberal electoral victory in 1906, also contributed to the growing Scandinavian consensus (Kuhnle 1996, pp. 233–63).

A final contributing factor to the establishment of the welfare state was emigration. Seventy-five years of emigration that started in the 1840s (on a massive scale from Sweden and Norway, more modestly from Denmark) contributed to social policy in two ways. First, emigration was an enormous safety valve. It reduced overpopulation in rural districts without crowding the slums of industrial towns; remittances from family members in North America helped other Scandinavians to emigrate, and provided resources for some of those who remained behind. Second, emigration alerted leaders that conditions were unsatisfactory for many social groups. This encouraged reform proposals, including a growing number of parliamentary and Royal investigatory commissions, and social legislation.

In sum then, the first stage of social reform coincided with the push for parliamentary democracy. Its sources were humanitarianism, reformism, and enlightened self-interest; its institutional forms, however, mixed the medieval with the modern. By the end of World War I, a comprehensive, albeit exceedingly meager, social welfare system protected Scandinavians from many of life's perils. Conservatives saw that it protected the weak, discouraged acts of desperation, and left undisturbed the fundamental order of society. Liberals accepted the policies for similar reasons, but also for the element of self-help and educational prospects for the growing industrial working class. Liberals could appreciate the large private contributions by employers and employees that made for only modest demands on public funds. Social Democrats deplored the system's stinginess, but public subsidies helped make social benefits provided by labor unions financially viable. Moreover, it was a base upon which they could build. Because of these different motives, such social programs enjoyed broad political support.

Missing from the Scandinavian debate were the extreme laissez-faire views of such political ideologues as Englishman Herbert Spencer, whose works enjoyed wide currency in the United States. Later, American philosopher Graham Sumner coined the term *social Darwinist* to describe policies that urged nonintervention by government in social affairs. That way the fit would survive, while the weak perished. Given the racial and ethnic heterogeneity of the United States, social Darwinism could justify callous neglect of outsiders. In homogeneous Scandinavia, such views conflicted with most political and religious opinion and made little headway.[2]

Building the Basic Security Programs, 1930–60

The second stage in building the Scandinavian welfare state began when the Social Democrats consolidated their hold on power in the 1930s. One might well date the birthday of the Scandinavian model from the historic compromise hammered out after exhaustive negotiations at the Kanslergade ("Chancellor's Street") home of Danish Prime Minister Thorvald Stauning in Copenhagen on January 30, 1933, between his Social Democratic/Radical Liberal government and the Agrarian opposition, which promised relief for industry, farming, and ordinary citizens devastated by the Great Depression. Similar compromises emerged in Sweden and Norway for an active response to the crisis and for expansion of the rudimentary welfare state. What makes the date of Denmark's Kanslergade Compromise ironic is that at the same time Adolf Hitler took over the German government in Berlin with a very different Nazi solution to the global crisis (for details see Einhorn and Logue 1999, pp. 199–200).

These reforms, interrupted but encouraged by World War II, accomplished four things. First, the existing patchwork of social legislation was rationalized, modernized, and made comprehensive. Second, transfer payments and social services were expanded so as to provide an adequate minimum, particularly for urban families. Third, the punitive measures designed to discourage welfare use were stripped from the law, and, when possible, programs were made universal to eliminate the stigma attached to receiving assistance. Fourth, social programs were increasingly integrated with economic policy. Spending on social security, housing, education, and other ambitious programs would be used to stimulate stagnant economies during the Depression years. As is discussed in the next chapter, several Scandinavian economists anticipated Keynes's economic theory, postulating that spending on worthy public projects would stimulate overall economic activity. This would raise incomes, reduce unemployment, and lead to material progress.

Mass poverty was conquered in Scandinavia primarily through economic modernization and growth, not social welfare programs. Agricultural reforms and development, as well as international trade, lowered the price of food, ended recurring crop failures, and consigned famine to a grim chapter in history books. Organizational, political, and technical changes at the end of the nineteenth century transformed the Scandinavian countries from a poor European outpost into comfortable, if not yet affluent, societies. Social programs protected those who could not or did not participate directly in the economic expansion. The most severe test came with the economic collapse of the 1930s. The Depression affected both industry and agriculture and threw one-fourth of the labor force out of work. Economic insecurity spread to many others. This common predicament allowed imaginative politicians to forge the formidable alliance between industrial workers and farmers noted above (called in Scandinavia the "Red-Green coalition") that made possible both comprehensive social welfare programs and renewed governmental activism in managing the economy.

Unlike most other European democracies, the internal challenge to constitutional government in Scandinavia in the 1930s was relatively mild. (Finland is a partial exception as the Depression came only a decade after the short but bloody civil war.) The weakness of such domestic foes was a result of early successes in social policy, and of the social reforms of the 1930s. Those social reforms replaced the demeaning poor laws and an inconsistent patchwork of social welfare measures with a coherent program to provide a modest but adequate standard of living for all forced out of gainful employment. Special measures, especially child allowances, raised the living standards of the families of unskilled and agricultural laborers, whose market income was insufficient to provide an adequate living for large families.

In addition, the promise of reform defused some of the social tensions. Severe economic problems remained, but, as British social historian R. H. Tawney (1920) once noted, it matters less what a society has already achieved than the direction in which its face is set. This is analogous to the concept of *social defense,* advocated by many Scandinavian reformers since the 1930s. Popular loyalty to democracy could not be won solely through intellectual and moral arguments, however. It was also sustained through practical programs that assured each citizen a just and secure place in society. The progress toward social reconciliation proved its value in the patriotic resistance movements in occupied Denmark and Norway during World War II, and the commitment to armed neutrality in Sweden. The war created broader national democratic alliances in Scandinavia against foreign threats and demonstrated that domestic solidarity was a requirement for effective national defense.

Tightening the Social Security Net, 1960–75

The third stage of social policy commenced in the late 1950s and 1960s and went beyond marginal improvements in basic benefits. The Social Democrats, first in Sweden, but then throughout the region, launched an ambitious and comprehensive expansion of social security programs. More was at stake than the elimination of poverty, squalor, and misery. The new goal was to secure a lifelong, middle-class standard of living for all, and to increase economic equality in society. The portion of lost market income replaced by social insurance against sickness, disability, and un-employment was raised from roughly 30 to 40 percent to 60 to 90 percent of average worker wages. Principles of pragmatism, choice, and insurance gave way to state activism, universal national programs, and ideological debate. However, administration of welfare programs was decentralized to local governments, which acquired the capacity to handle the new tasks of providing social services to the elderly and children through consoli-dation and new tax revenues in the 1960s and 1970s. The welfare state once again became an ideological issue and a mechanism for promoting political and social change.

Toward a European Social Market Model, 1975–present

The economic crisis of the last half of the 1970s and early 1980s pro-duced severe economic pressures on existing welfare state programs as well as demands for new programs. Costs for major programs—such as health care and old-age pensions—soared as the population aged. For the first time in decades, Scandinavian program benefits were trimmed and eligibility criteria tightened. Nevertheless there were expensive program expansions, especially in child care and home care for the elderly where rapid growth in utilization of high quality public programs enabled women to combine paid employment with raising a family. In effect many of women's functions of caring for children and for parents were socialized; by the end of the century, the Scandinavian housewife was an endangered species in philosophy as well as in practice. Meanwhile non-European immigration accelerated and introduced clients with quite different cultural expectations. While the Scandinavian welfare state model demonstrated its viability, it also had to adjust.

European and global economic integration introduced additional pressures. By the mid-1990s all five Scandinavian countries were either full EU members or closely tied to Europe through the EEA agreement. EU economic and social conventions have pushed restructuring Scandinavian policies. Active labor market policies as well as expanding educational opportunities have assisted this transition. Many of the new programs—from childcare to supplementary pensions—are especially valuable to the employed. Costs have been partially met by reducing passive income support. Those outside the labor market will not face hardship, but can no longer expect fully equal treatment. In practice, if not in political rhetoric, the Scandinavians increasingly resemble their West European neighbors. These new and changed programs and their consequences are explored in the remainder of this chapter.

SOCIAL SECURITY

Social security and social welfare are, in common usage, somewhat ambiguous terms. We use both terms to mean a range of programs that protect the entire population from material poverty as a result of sickness, old age, or other involuntary loss of income. Implicit in this definition is access to such vital services as education and health care. Programs can focus on treating objective problems, such as inadequate housing or poor nutrition, or they may pursue less-tangible goals, such as greater social equality. Progressive social reformers, whose work commenced in earnest just over a century ago, initially targeted tangible poverty. They were progressive in that they were mainly motivated by humanitarian concerns rather than by a desire to control the poor and to maintain social order. Moreover, their policies sought to reduce poverty by treating causes as well as victims.

On the eve of World War II, the Scandinavian countries protected their citizens with a relatively comprehensive, largely compulsory system of social insurance. There were some remaining gaps in coverage, and benefits were still meager. The war affected the evolution of the welfare state in two ways. Although destruction and losses temporarily reduced resources for social programs, wartime patriotism, solidarity, and common hardships broadened support for social security. The general leftward shift in politics maintained this support after the war. Postwar recovery took priority over social programs, but marginal improvements appeared throughout the 1950s. By 1960, few gaps remained in the Scandinavian social security systems. Although citizens in need could avail themselves of benefits "from the cradle to the grave," to use the British term, those benefits still provided only a minimum living standard. Access to medical facilities assured patients a high standard of care, subject to available resources. Patients suffering from nonacute illnesses could still expect to spend considerable time waiting for treatment. Decent housing was increasingly regarded as a right, but that did not prevent severe shortages. Finally, by 1960, all of the Scandinavian countries recognized that their high-quality but class-based educational systems would not serve the needs or numbers of postwar children.[3] Education too became a means of promoting both social welfare and social democracy.

The early 1960s were a transition period for social policy. The social security system was complete, if short of resources. Politically, there were two courses. The nonsocialist parties declared that enough was enough and promised to maintain the comprehensive basic program, while a proportional share of additional resources would gradually overcome shortages. The socialists called for an ambitious expansion of social programs, seeking not only to provide a higher service level but also to use social policy as a means of promoting greater social equality and democracy. Social Democratic parties increasingly saw the expansion and, especially, the redistribution of economic and social welfare as the means toward democratic socialism. This was in lieu of comprehensive economic planning and state ownership, which appeared obsolete in the age of Keynesian economic management.

Symptomatic of the new agenda and the resulting political struggle were the complex maneuvers that dominated Swedish domestic politics in the late 1950s over the Supplementary Pension issue (known in Swedish as Allmänna Tilläggspension and by the acronym ATP). ATP would symbolize a change in social-policy goals from providing a universal safety net, to guaranteeing that the living standard attained by employees during their working years would be maintained following their retirement. It sought greater equality as well as a higher standard in social security. The Social Democratic proposal, which was adopted in 1959 after a referendum and a vigorous parliamentary and electoral struggle, promised every wage earner with the equivalent of the generous pensions previously available only to civil servants and top managers: Upon retirement after thirty years of work, a typical employee receives annually 60 percent of his or her yearly salary, based on the fifteen best-paid years. The new supplementary pensions were designed to be fully funded (by employers and employees) and actuarially sound. An autonomous trust fund was established, which quickly became enormous. This new economic power, initially feared by the nonsocialists as a new mechanism for state control of the economy, was prudently invested in municipal and housing bonds. This too had social consequences. The heavy investment strengthened the local infrastructure and ended Sweden's chronic housing shortage. Since 1974, limited ATP investment in corporate stock has been permitted.

By the 1990s demographic and economic changes made the original system unacceptably costly. Reforms in 1998 have made pensions dependent in part on economic and demographic trends and allow younger employees to direct some of the funding toward various alternative, privately managed individual retirement accounts. This comprehensive pension system will be increasingly based on "defined contributions" rather than political promises that underlay the German, Italian, and even the U.S. old-age pension systems. Over time, its holdings will include substantial foreign investments as well as a significant portion of Swedish securities.[4]

Although Sweden was first to guarantee substantial pensions to all retired employees, the other Nordic countries have also expanded their comprehensive programs. Since the 1980s more comprehensive schemes have been encouraged by legislation and by collective bargaining agreements. Voluntary tax-subsidized programs have grown, but they tend to be regressive, in that wealthier taxpayers benefit most. Together these programs make old age income security more feasible and may reduce the direct role of the state, as private and employee pensions raise the elderlys' income in lieu of public support.

The extent of the social expenditure explosion during the past forty years is indicated in Table 8.1. Note how the Scandinavian countries leapfrogged the European norm in the 1960s and into the mid-1970s. During this period, economic growth was high, so the expansion in absolute and real terms for individual beneficiaries was especially dramatic. Note also while Finland clearly lagged behind the rest of Scandinavia in the 1960s, it had matched or exceeded the others by the end of the 1990s. The effect on public finances has also been enormous. Public social expenditures have continued to grow as rapidly since the 1960s as they did from 1930 to 1960, when the basic social programs were enacted. When one recalls that an impressive basic social security system was already in place at the time this expansion started, the effects become even more remarkable. Note that growth rates have slowed significantly since the early 1990s as the economy has improved.

Until 1970 welfare programs were assumed to be self-limiting. They were designed to deal with the failure of the market economy to satisfy all citizens' basic needs. It was logical that full employment and better management of the economy would reduce the demand for transfer payments.

Table 8.1
Public Social Expenditure Transfers, as a Percentage of GDP, 1960–99 (average for period)

	1960-73	1974-79	1980-89	1990-99
Denmark	9.5	14.0	17.1	19.1
Finland	6.6	11.2	13.9	20.3
Iceland	8.1	4.9	4.9	6.6*
Norway	10.3	12.9	12.7	15.9
Sweden	10.0	15.9	18.3	20.9
EU (15) average	11.4	12.3	16.5	17.3
United States	6.4	10.2	11.0	12.6*

*Average 1990–96. Icelandic figures reflect lower cash transfer payments and different demographic basis (i.e., fewer elderly).
Source: OECD (1999b, 2000).

Trends in the economy and society, however, undermined these assumptions. The speedup of production in manufacturing and the spread of cost-efficient managerial practices in Scandinavia shoved the old, ill, and weak out of employment faster than had been the case in the past, increasing demand for transfer payments. While improved techniques for managing their economies made Scandinavian countries relatively immune to domestically generated cyclical downturns by the 1960s, their increasing integration in the international market made them more sensitive to global economic factors. The impact of the international cycle was demonstrated with a vengeance after 1974, creating radically higher demand for transfer payments to the unemployed, and for job training and emergency employment programs. The decline of the extended family and—in the 1970s and 1980s—of the nuclear family increased the need for services for the elderly and for children. Rising life expectancy added to demands. The consequence was an increase in the number of those needing basic transfer payments at the same time as the general level of transfer payments was raised in the 1960s and 1970s.

Under the impact of these changes, two roughly defined groups emerged in the Scandinavian discussion of social policy in the last two decades. Social conservatives favored a basic welfare state to prevent tangible social misery and threats to public health and order. They believed that once a social safety net is in place, social policy should aim at increased administrative efficiency and self-reliance. Social radicals, on the other hand, saw social policy as a means to greater social equality and democracy. They were less interested in social insurance than in social change. The disagreement between them resulted in a protracted political struggle, but by the late 1990s a compromise emerged. Universal social insurance and benefits remained in place, but increasingly individuals were encouraged to save and invest. Privatization of some public utilities and competition in provision of health and other public services allowed greater choice and promised market efficiencies. Whether the latter will materialize remains to be seen.

Trends in Scandinavian social policies since 1945, and especially since 1960, reflect a sustained and broadly supported push toward social democracy defined in terms of equality of opportunity and equality of result. Still, many of the earlier themes in social security policy remain evident. Although the comprehensive social security program is no longer based primarily on actuarial (risk-calculation) principles, it has kept many of the characteristics of social insurance. In some areas, citizens have choices as to providers (of housing, primary medical and dental care, education) and there are some coinsurance charges (deductibles paid by the beneficiary). The comprehensive range of current programs is illustrated in Table 8.2.

SOCIAL PROGRAMS IN OPERATION

Scope of the Programs

In Scandinavia everyone is "on welfare." Although the young and the old receive most of the benefits of the welfare state, all citizens continuously receive comprehensive social services and support. A popular phrase is "the richest 90 percent support the poorest 90 percent." It is both a right to receive such benefits and an obligation to pay for their heavy costs. At some time in their lives, everyone uses one program or another, whether it is medical care, family benefits, or income security for those whose normal sources of income are removed by illness, unemployment, disability, or old age. In addition, special allowances are available to those whose normal income is insufficient to pay for such necessities as adequate housing, child care, or family expenses. Indirectly, education is a social program that seeks to make the individual more self-reliant. While some benefits are means tested (i.e., only people whose income and wealth are below specified levels receive the assistance), most benefits are universal; if a Scandinavian fits into a specific age or need category, services or money are forthcoming. As a consequence, there is no more stigma attached to receiving social welfare benefits in Scandinavia than there is to receiving Social Security benefits in the United States.

Scandinavian social benefits resemble those available in most advanced industrial societies (cf Adema 1998, pp. 20–23, and Hansen 1999). In some cases more generous benefits are available elsewhere. What sets the Scandinavian programs apart, however, is the comprehensive nature of the

Table 8.2
Scandinavian Social Welfare Programs

I.   Old Age Cash Benefits:
    1. universal benefits based on residence
    2. supplementary Retirement Benefits (based on employment earnings)
    3. employer/employee public and private pensions (tax subsidized)
    4. early retirement pensions
II.   Disability cash benefits and pensions (earnings based for employees)
III.   Occupational injury and disease (public and private)
IV.   Sickness benefit (earnings based)
V.   Services for elderly and disabled people
    1. Residential care
    2. home-help services
    3. day care and rehabilitation services
    4. other benefits in kind
VI.   Survivors (dependents)
VII.   Family cash benefits
    1. family allowances for children
    2. family support benefits
    3. benefits for other dependents
    4. single parent cash benefits
    5. maternity and parental leave
VIII.   Family services (day care and other household and personal services)
IX.   Active labor market programs (e.g. training, education, mobility)
X.   Unemployment (earnings based)
XI.   Public expenditure on health (hospital, medical services, rehabilitation, etc.)
XII.   Housing (income based and tax expenditures)
XIII.   Other contingencies (natural disasters, veterans, war injuries, refugees etc.)

Source: OECD (1998). *Social Expenditure Database, 1980–96.* Paris: OECD.

overall package of social benefits and the relatively generous level of benefits provided. Table 8.3 summarizes the range of services and the relative
level of spending in the five countries.

A perusal of Table 8.3 indicates, first, that one-fourth to one-third of the
gross domestic product is distributed through the government for various
welfare purposes. To put this in perspective, in 1998, spending on social
welfare alone in Denmark, Finland, Norway, and Sweden was as large in
proportion to the national economy as the total spending of all U.S. levels
of government—federal, state, and local—for all purposes, including social security, debt service, and national defense. Second, general transfer
payments (which are not means tested) to provide income security against
illness, short-term disability, unemployment, and old age account for
about one-half of all social spending (these are included in items 1, 2,

Table 8.3

Social Security Expenditures by Purpose in the Nordic Countries, 1998

	Denmark	Finland	Iceland	Norway	Sweden
Social Security expenditure PPP/Euro per capita	6978	5240	4160	5652	6557
Public social security expenditure as percent of GDP	30.0	27.3	18.3	30.0	33.3
Thereof (% GDP):					
1. Health and dental care, including sick pay	5.6	6.0	6.8	8.9	7.5
2. Unemployment benefits and Training and employment costs	3.4	3.2	0.5	0.8	3.1
3. Family, maternity, and child benefits and services	3.8	3.4	2.3	3.6	3.7
4. Old age, disability, home-care, etc.	14.5	11.9	9.4	12.8	16.0
5. Other (housing, survivors, etc.)	1.8	2.1	1.0	1.3	2.5

*PPP = purchasing power parity to adjust for currency fluctuations. Euro = new European currency unit worth approximately U.S.$1.17 on January 1, 1999. The nominal Euro exchange rate fell below $1.00 after January 2000.
Source: Nordic Council, *Nordic Statistical Yearbook, 2000,* tables SOEX01.

and 4). Essentially these are the programs that grew out of the mutual-insurance societies of the nineteenth century. Payments specifically targeted to raise the incomes of those in particular need (item 5) amount to only about one-tenth of the income security payments; some of these programs can be traced back to the old poor relief. Provision of social services (education is not included in these figures), on the other hand, is more specifically targeted to the aged and to families with children. Medical care, which is provided to all without regard to ability to pay, is the principal component of item 1; that, too, has its origin in the mutual insurance societies. The social services listed in items 3 and 4, which are specifically targeted to the children and the elderly, are, by and large, a creation of the 1960s and 1970s, when the welfare state increased provision of services previously provided by housewives. The provision of infant, preschool and after-school child care has been the largest social program expansion in the past thirty years.

What do these numbers mean for recipients of specific benefits? The range and scope of social welfare programs are increasingly complex and exact comparisons are difficult. (For comparative current information, see the U.S. Social Security Administration's biennial *Social Security Programs throughout the World.*) The principal goal of social policy during the past forty years has been to protect the living standard of the average family from loss of income due to age, illness, child care, or unemployment. Income replacement levels for low and median families are high. Paid maternity and child-care leaves, sick pay, and unemployment compensation replace, on the average, 70 to 90 percent of net income. Old age, early retirement, and disability pensions replace—depending on the circumstances—between 42 and 96 percent of previous income. These levels are high by U.S. standards. In the United States there is no general national system of paid maternity, child care, or sick leave. Unemployment compensation in the United States varies between 40 and 60 percent of the average industrial wage for twenty-six weeks (although that is sometimes extended by another thirteen weeks) and, as a consequence of the time limit, is paid to only about two-fifths of the unemployed during peak times of unemployment. Danish unemployment compensation, by contrast, averages around 80 percent of previously earned income for average workers and for low-income employees with children the replacement rate (i.e., all social benefits less taxes) approaches 100 percent of after-tax income (OECD 1996, pp. 57–60; Martin 1998, p. 25). Swedish provisions run for up to 60 weeks and are complemented by a host of training, educational, and temporary work schemes. Finnish and Norwegian unemployment compensation can last up to 100 and 156 weeks, respectively. (see Table 9.4.) Danish provisions run for up to two years with conditional extensions for an additional three-year period.[5]

Combined with high and progressive income tax rates, the income-security system means that disposable personal income (real take-home pay, including social benefits) varies little for many Scandinavian families regardless of illness, unemployment, or whether he or she is a parent staying home with an infant. This approach evens out income over a lifetime. Heavy taxes during the years when one is gainfully employed cover the cost of transfer payments that provide income when one is out of work. Social services have much the same effect. The result is that the Scandinavian welfare states redistribute more income between the healthy and the sick, the economically active and the elderly, the childless and the fertile within economic classes than between classes. Despite the rhetoric of using the public sector to promote economic equality between classes, the bulk of redistribution is between generations, not between class or income groups. This fact unquestionably contributes to the welfare states' broad political support despite the high taxes required to finance them.

Typical Families: The Hansens

Aggregate figures tell us little about how such programs affect the daily lives and of ordinary people. To measure the effects of this comprehensive social security system, let us look at a typical Danish family, the Hansens at the start of the new century. In addition to their employment salaries, the Hansens receive a social income that includes both transfer payments and social benefits. That social income is quite substantial and tends, over a lifetime, to even out some of the inequality in the distribution of market income.

The examples below are based on a Danish statistics (Ministry of Taxation, 2001), but would not differ significantly from Finnish, Swedish, or Norwegian examples. In 2001, the Danish krone was worth about twelve U.S. cents with roughly comparable buying power.

Svend and Ingrid Hansen: Skilled Worker's Family

Svend and Ingrid Hansen live with their two children, ages five and ten, in a modest row house just outside Copenhagen. Svend works as an assembler for a small electronics firm and earns the equivalent of $30,360 annually. Ingrid works part-time in an office and earns $23,530. Their incomes are about the national family average. In addition, they receive annually about $2,025 in child allowances; their home is worth about $120,000 and heavily mortgaged. Fortunately they bought it about eight years earlier, and house prices have continued to outpace both inflation and average wages. The Hansens are taxed separately and pay just under 36 percent of their adjusted income in national and local income taxes; nearly all transfer payments are taxable. Mr. Hansen's employer pays some insurance charges and contributes toward his private pension (which supplements public pensions and now cover more than 80% of the labor force). In Denmark these charges are modest; in Sweden they approach 40 percent of the base wage. The family pays a 25 percent value-added tax (VAT) on all consumer goods and services including food. (The VAT is a universal and significant source of tax revenue in all European countries.) Scandinavia's notorious excise taxes cover all forms of energy and automobiles as well as so-called luxuries (alcohol, tobacco, soda, etc.).[6] Hence the Hansens take good care of their twelve-year-old Volvo (bought five years ago) and make regular use of their bicycles and public transport. Nevertheless, their home is filled with modern gadgets and they have a modest beach house several hours south of their home. This they finance in part by renting it out most of the summer. They each enjoy nearly six weeks of paid vacation, and love to spend the Easter holidays at a warm resort. Critical too is child care for their young daughter, for which they pay only about 25 percent of the actual cost. The municipality pays the rest. Even their older son uses municipal "free-time" care after school. All of their medical care is covered by the national health program, and their children's dental care is free. Mr. Hansen broke a tooth last year and his out-of-pocket expenses for a new crown would have considerable had he not been prudent enough to buy supplemental insurance.

In December 2000 the Danish Tax Ministry calculated that a typical blue collar family like Svend and Ingrid Hansen pay the equivalent of about $28,000 a year in income, sales, and excise taxes. Schooling and after-school care for their two children cost about $21,176, so less than $7,000 of their taxes remain for all other public services. Last year Ingrid spent two days in the hospital for a minor procedure. A Danish hospital bed averages $650 a day (Denmark, Ministry of Taxation 2000).

This is an average living standard in contemporary Scandinavia, but it is perhaps three times higher than fifty years ago. Their living standard depends on two incomes, which was much less common in the 1950s. The Hansens still have access to their union and municipal leisure and educational activities as well as good and safe public transport. Thus they manage with a single car and make good use of their bicycles on the many bicycle paths.

Per and Eva Andersen: A Professional Family

Svend's older sister, Eva, went to business school and works as a managing director for an American-affiliated company. Her husband, Per, is a public school teacher, working part-time. Their children, aged fourteen and nineteen, no longer require child-care services, but Per has gotten used to working about 60 percent time and carrying the main housekeeping burden. Per earns about $24,000 and Eva about $98,000, which is a very good salary in Denmark (although modest in comparison to her colleagues in the United States). Together they pay just under 50 percent of their income in income taxes (60% more than their American friends) and pay the VAT and excise taxes on their consumption as well. They live in a home valued at $300,000. Eva's company located in Denmark in part because of the country's skilled workforce, but also because it doesn't have to pay for expensive fringe benefits (medical insurance in particular) that is the norm in the United States. Eva and Per have been tempted to accept an assignment in the United States to make the larger and more lightly taxed American salary, but they wanted their children to finish school in Denmark. As an affluent family they have received fewer subsidies, although they received the standard child allowance until their son turned eighteen and paid only 30 percent of the child-care center costs. Now their son is beginning medical school, and there is no tuition to pay. Every Danish student receives a monthly stipend of about $450, which if supplemented by some summer or part-time work, is sufficient to support a comfortable student lifestyle. Loans are also available.

Lotte Hansen: Unskilled Worker, Single Mother

The third Hansen is Lotte, who is divorced and has an eight-year-old daughter. With her daughter in school, Lotte took a job as an orderly at the local old-age home with a salary of $20,000 per year. She receives an $1,800 annual rent subsidy and the standard $1,000 child allowance. As a single mother, she is entitled to at least $4,000 in child support from her ex-husband, but since he emigrated to Australia and stopped making payments, the state also provides that $4,000 as a child-maintenance advance. Her income taxes are 35 percent of her total income and of course she pays the same VAT and excise taxes as her siblings. At family gatherings, it seems as if Lotte has more money for luxuries (last year it was a week in Thailand) than her brother Svend in part because she lives in public housing. The consequence is that Lotte, despite her much lower market income, is able to provide a standard of living for her child equivalent to those of her brother and sister.

Anne Hansen: Pensioner

The last Hansen is Mrs. Anne Hansen, a seventy-eight-year-old widow and pensioner. Anne's old-age pension is not lavish ($12,000 annually), but it is supplemented by another $1,500 from her late husband's supplementary and company pension, and she receives $1,500 in rent subsidies. Her apartment is old, but in town, and quite convenient by her standards. Anne, too, must pay income taxes, which amount to about 28 percent of her income. With expenses for home maintenance and medical care met by the government, Mrs. Hansen can indulge herself. She recently acquired a new color television set, after much urging by her children. Her only other extravagance is six or seven women's magazine subscriptions. She takes great pleasure in being able to mark her grandchildren's birthdays with the substantial gifts that she and her husband Otto, a machinist, had been unable to provide their own children in the tight years after the war and in the 1950s. When she reflects on the threadbare poverty of her grandmother's last years, she invariably concludes that she has been blessed. When her eight-year-old granddaughter pressed her last Sunday to tell her about life in the good old days, Anne answered, "These are the good old days." Her response had been spontaneous, but the more Anne thought about it, the more convinced she was that she had spoken the truth.

The Hansens are ordinary people. To upper-middle-class Americans their salaries may seem low, in part because exchange rates do not easily translate living standards, but also because a substantial part of personal income is provided through subsidies, benefits, and public services. Moreover, a significant part of the obviously high material standard of living in Scandinavia stems from a culture of permanence. It is a culture in which there is more intergenerational accumulation and transfer of goods than Americans expect, and in which consumer durables, such as Svend Hansen's Volvo, are made and maintained to last a generation. The narrow income range in the Hansen family is typical of Scandinavia. The crucial difference between being comfortable as opposed to just scraping by is the availability of a second income. Women have entered the paid-labor force for more than economic reasons, and there are personal costs as well as gains, but the economic incentive is compelling.

Although taxes in the Nordic countries have remained at or over 50 percent of GDP, high marginal rates of income taxation have been reduced. Currently maximum rates range from about 42 percent in Norway to just under 60 percent in Denmark, Sweden, and Finland. This is a reduction of about 15 percentage points; average tax rates have also been reduced. Individual income taxation (there is no marriage penalty or bonus) has encouraged two income families.

All of the Nordic countries have egalitarian wages even before the tax and social benefit systems come into play. After taxes and benefits are taken into account, a professor earns little more than a metal worker over a lifetime. The demands and rewards of each profession are sufficiently different to curtail judgements as to comparable worth. The narrowing of income differentials among blue-collar workers is largely a consequence of the solidaristic wage policy in collective bargaining, which is discussed in Chapter 10; although they have not reached parity with men, women have narrowed the wage gap significantly. That many women with small children tend to work part time does affect the statistics. The prestige of professions requiring university training slipped in the past generation. This may in part be the result of narrowing economic differences and increased educational opportunities. But it is a trend that is not without costs. During the 1990s the Nordic countries faced growing shortages of highly skilled scientific, medical, and technical personnel as well as the steady loss of top managers. Globalization has created a small but growing world market for such people. The reduction of top income-tax rates as well as a rise in private sector salaries are noticeable responses, but there has been no abandonment of a strong commitment to economic equality.

Table 8.4 compares recent income distribution data as well as poverty rates. The income figures are before progressive income taxes and social benefits are taken into account. Note the significantly greater degree of equality in income distribution in Scandinavia relative to the United States or Great Britain before taxes and transfer payments. But while the Scandinavian numbers reflect the relative equality of incomes, there still are notable income differentials. Social science research confirms that income equalization stopped in the 1980s and differentials have grown modestly in the past ten to fifteen years.

Table 8.4
Income Distribution and Poverty

	Percentage Share of Income (pre-tax/pre-benefit) by relative share of income units			Gini Index	Relative Poverty Rates (Percent) ca. 1991	
	Lowest 20%	highest 20%	highest 10%		Pretax/ Pretransfer	Post tax/ Post Transfer
Denmark	9.6	34.5	20.5	24.7	23.9	3.5
Finland	10.0	35.8	21.6	25.6	9.8	2.3
Norway	9.7	35.8	21.8	25.8	9.3	1.7
Sweden	9.6	34.5	20.1	25.0	20.6	3.8
Canada	7.5	39.3	23.8	31.5	21.6	5.6
Great Britain	6.6	43.0	27.3	36.1	25.7	5.3
U.S.A.	5.2	46.4	30.5	40.8	21.0	11.7

Notes: Income distribution data approximately 1991–93. The Gini Index measures departure from "perfect equality"; higher number means greater income inequality. Poverty data: percentage of people below the "relative poverty line" (40% of median income). E.g., 3.5 = 3.5 percent of population below poverty line.
Sources: World Bank, *World Development Indicators, 2001*; and Kenilworthy (1999, p. 1130).

The table also illustrates perhaps the greatest achievement of the welfare state: the radical reduction of people living in economic poverty. Although pretax, pretransfer poverty rates in Denmark and Sweden are similar to those in the United States, Britain, and Canada, the effects of Scandinavian social and tax policy measures are dramatic: 80 to 90 percent reductions in rates of poverty. Note that such measures are also effective in all of the cases, but the United States still has a considerably more sizeable poor population (Kenilworthy 1999). Such numbers are problematic because it can be difficult to weigh benefits in kind, as opposed to benefits in cash. Moreover, equal access to social benefits does not mean equal use. People in poor health obviously benefit more from access to collectively paid medical care than the healthy. But all rest more secure with the knowledge that should illness strike, their personal finances will survive largely intact.

The Scandinavian social security systems no longer differ greatly from the programs found in most advanced industrial societies (see Table 8.1), but when direct services like child and home care are added, they are more comprehensive, more generous, and, inevitably, more expensive. Table 8.5 compares recent social expenditures by advanced industrial societies. Although the Nordic countries have the highest gross public social expenditures, their taxes on transfer payments and other countries' man-

Table 8.5
Gross and Net Social Expenditures as a Percentage of GDP at Factor Prices, 1997

	Gross public social expenditure	net publicly mandated social expenditure*	net total social expenditure#
Denmark	35.9	26.9	27.5
Finland	33.3	24.8	25.6
Norway	30.2	25.1	25.1
Sweden	35.7	28.5	30.6
Germany	29.2	27.2	28.8
Netherlands	27.1	20.8	24.0
U.K.	23.8	21.9	24.6
U.S.	15.8	16.8	23.4

*Includes effects of differences in mandatory private social programs, tax treatment of benefits, and tax expenditures for social purposes.
#Includes the effect of voluntary private expenditure.
Source: Adema (2001, pp. 27–28).

datory and voluntary fringe benefits and direct expenditures narrow the gap significantly. Most transfer payments in the Nordic countries are directly taxed, which claws back some of the universal benefits going to the wealthy. The ten percentage point gap between Scandinavia and the United Kingdom disappears when such adjustments are made. Even the United States approaches a similar overall social expenditure rate when voluntary social expenditures, such as company-provided health insurance, are included. Of course, such voluntary social expenditures do not cover the entire population. Nearly one in six Americans has no health-care insurance, and many more are inadequately insured.

The current Scandinavian political debate centers not on means or ends, which are generally accepted, but on whether the system is efficient, sufficient, and affordable. No one doubts that it provides a remarkable degree of individual security and prosperity, which was the goal of those who labored for half a century to create the welfare state. Its significance for Scandinavian democracy turns on whether social security of itself is sufficient for social democracy.

SOCIAL DEMOCRACY

Political democracy and social policy evolved from different roots. The former originated in an earlier respect for written law and constitutional due process and became the means of social change. Modern social policy originated in a collective concern for all elements of society and a larger sense of citizenship. During the past century, however, political and social democracy have converged. In describing a rather similar pattern, the English social theorist T. H. Marshall (1965, p. 86) summarized the British experience as a struggle for civil rights through the eighteenth century, for political democracy in the nineteenth century, and for social rights and democracy in the twentieth century. Scandinavia fits this pattern well.

Scandinavia lagged behind Great Britain and the United States by about fifty years in the first two of Marshall's stages, but it has caught up in the struggle for social citizenship and democracy. In the past forty years, Scandinavian social policy has sought to do more than provide a "decent minimum." Social policy has become an integral part of democratic life. The welfare state simultaneously reinforces and challenges political democracy. Its ultimate goal is to confer upon its citizens social rights, the adoption of which have been no less controversial than civil and political rights were in their time.

What are the results of a century of Scandinavian social policy? Recall that the welfare state has always had two goals that allowed it to attract broad political backing. The first was to protect society from the consequences of industrialization and urbanization. Here the precedent was the poor laws of late medieval times, when the landless and jobless became a potential threat to public order and private property. It was a matter of charity and enlightened self-interest. Scandinavian poor laws provided relief, but they did little to reduce the sources of poverty. The first real steps toward social democracy were the abolition of serfdom, the introduction of basic civil rights (including the right to emigrate), and the introduction of free, compulsory primary education in the last quarter of the eighteenth and first half of the nineteenth centuries. Scandinavia did not have revolutions, but it benefited from others' revolutions.

The second goal of social policy was to cement an increasingly mobile and class-conscious population to the state. The "fortified poorhouse" of the pre–World War I era was transformed within a generation to the "people's home," to use two expressions from the Swedish context. Although politics is the source of social policy, Scandinavia's evolutionary history reminds us that one generation's social policy can affect the next generation's politics.

By the time the drive for political democracy arose in earnest in Denmark and Sweden in the middle of the last century, a majority of the population was literate. It is hard to overestimate the importance of education and literacy in shaping modern Scandinavia. Mass literacy preceded industrialization and mass politics. Education and the folk high-school movement transformed Scandinavian peasants into modern farmers. It seems probable that a literate working class was able to resist ruthless exploitation better, and to defend its interests more effectively than an illiterate proletariat. Mass literacy is the reason why the agrarian and labor movements' press was a decisive weapon in the fight for democracy and economic justice.

Education beyond basic literacy became a salient element in Scandinavian social democracy with the introduction in 1844 by Christen Kold and N. F. S. Grundtvig of the "folk high school" (folkehøjskole) in Denmark. Spreading soon to Norway and Sweden, and then beyond, and serving primarily young rural people with a mixture of religious, cultural, and practical subjects, it also provided important organizational and political skills. Rural youths' horizons were stretched in these egalitarian and democratic institutions. Later the labor movement continued the tradition in numerous workers' education programs.

After World War II, democratic trends reached the formal state educational institutions with a massive expansion of secondary and higher education. The change was not only in numbers enrolled; the Social Democratic governments insisted on more egalitarian and less-authoritarian schools and universities. What politicians started, the rambunctious student movement of the late 1960s finished as governance became the principal university issue. In the past twenty years expanded access again became a policy priority as the information economy demanded new technical skills. Currently 20 to 25 percent of the adult population in Scandinavia has completed a postsecondary education. Many other adults engage continuously in continuing education programs that are widely available and heavily subsidized.

Scandinavia is not utopia, but it is an important experiment in the effort to create social democracy. Scandinavian social democracy is not primarily an economic program or system. It is compatible with a variety of ownership forms, although probably unimaginable under laissez faire capitalism or state socialism. It is primarily a social order that emphasizes citizenship. It extends inalienable rights and undeniable obligations beyond those normally associated with political citizenship into the economic and social realms. As T. H. Marshall wrote, "citizenship requires a bond of a different kind, a direct sense of community membership based on loyalty to a civilization which is a common possession" (1965, p. 101). A national community requires detailed social legislation and administration, which often fall short of expectations and demands. It is the commitment to such a national community—despite debate over its details, problems, and varying priorities—that characterizes contemporary Scandinavian social democracy. Not surprisingly when the European Union emphasized a common social policy in the late 1990s, Scandinavia and the Netherlands were the models (EU 1999).

EVALUATING THE WELFARE STATE

Despite myriad social statistics, there are no entirely objective criteria for judging the success or failure of social policy and democracy in Scandinavia or elsewhere. Social indicators give us a more complete picture of social conditions and changes during recent years. Historians and others can trace social change over longer periods than statisticians can assess. However, the criteria for judgment remain subjective. First, should the earlier or the current generation's standards apply? Second, should the achievements be compared with similar programs in other countries, or should they be viewed according to a narrow national perspective?

By the criteria of the founding generation of the welfare state, the current social standard is an extraordinary success story. Medical, nutritional, educational, and housing standards far exceed what would have seemed realistic targets a generation ago. Part of this is the result of social policy. People, as a matter of right, are provided with funds or services that allow them to attain a material standard of living that resembles the national norm. The abject poverty of previous generations has been consigned to the history books, and similarly the psychological insecurity fostered by the economic catastrophe of illness or unemployment is a thing of the past. Some obviously disadvantaged groups, such as single mothers and their children as well as the elderly, have been the target of specific programs designed to improve their economic position, as the accounts above suggest. Recent immigrants and refugees remain economically and socially disadvantaged, but social programs to help them to overcome cultural barriers.[7] To the extent that severe material deprivation still exists, it is associated with mental illness and with alcohol and drug abuse.

Although drug addiction is a new problem, abuse of alcohol has been a subject of sporadic policy initiatives in Scandinavia for three centuries. It has proven an intractable social problem. In the decades immediately prior to World War I, prohibition inspired a mass movement in Norway and Sweden; it had strong support in the Social Democratic ranks. In the interwar period, Norway experimented briefly with national prohibition; Sweden voted narrowly against prohibition, but undertook systematic policies to make drinking difficult, including the use of ration books. Neither route was markedly successful. In recent years, more moderate policies of discouraging consumption of alcohol have been pursued to comparably little effect. Swedish policy, for example, calls for keeping liquor store hours short and inconvenient—especially prior to holidays. The result, seemingly, has been to encourage advance planning, rather than to discourage drinking. Denmark's liberal policies are reflected in higher alcohol consumption statistics, but official statistics may be misleading. Impressionist evidence suggests that alcohol abuse is a more serious problem in Sweden, and the strict regulations in Norway and

Sweden apparently encourage significant illegal distilling. Affluence has changed both drinking habits and the problems of alcohol. Tipsy people riding home on a streetcar are less of a social problem than those who drive home in their own cars. Alcohol consumption is apparently lower than it was a century ago, and alcoholism is better treated as a medical disease than as a moral disorder. But, despite the welfare state, the problem remains. Ultimately, European Union harmonization of national rules may end Nordic "prohibitionism" (see Kurzer 2000).

Comparisons of the results of Scandinavian programs with those in other countries are now more easily obtained. As we have seen, the Scandinavian difference has become less significant relative to many other EU countries. Still, Scandinavian countries rank high on those social indicators closely associated with welfare programs. Scandinavian infant and maternal mortality rates are among the lowest in the world, and length of life expectancy among the highest; the effects of free health care, special prenatal and child health programs, and the general effort to raise the living standards (especially housing standards) of low-income families with children presumably all play a role. Most dramatically, as we have seen above, material poverty is substantially reduced.

Even though Scandinavian success in reducing economic inequality is comparatively impressive, it should be remembered that the Scandinavian public sector absorbs 50 to 60 percent of the GDP.[8] In that context, Scandinavian achievements in income redistribution would seem less impressive if one assumed that interclass redistribution was a priority of the Scandinavian welfare states. In fact, however, it is not and has never been. From their origins in the mutual-insurance societies of the guilds and other occupational groups, the income-security programs of today that absorb the bulk of welfare state spending have been designed to protect average citizens against involuntary loss of income from employment. These programs primarily redistribute income within income classes, not between them. In doing so, they provide a degree of economic (and psychological) security to the working and middle classes previously reserved for the rich. This provides an important source of equality in life experience as well.

The enormous commitment of resources to the welfare state means that these funds are not available for other public and private uses. When typically 50 percent of family incomes are collected in direct and indirect taxes, as in Scandinavia, there is inevitably less individual choice. Even if, over a lifetime, these resources are likely to benefit nearly everyone, the wait can be long. Moreover, every good social program competes with every other good social program for resources, often leaving dissatisfied clients. The increased generosity of social programs has been accompanied by a growing uniformity and administrative complexity. Such equality may be just, but not always efficient. Citizens whose lifestyle differs notably from the norm may be penalized. Never has there been greater individual freedom to choose a lifestyle, but never has the state placed sharper economic restrictions on specific forms of consumption. One may smoke, drink, and drive to excess in Scandinavia, but it will be expensive. Still, many do, to the chagrin of social planners and the discreet delight of social anarchists.

As we discuss in Chapter 9, social policy is expensive. It is hard politically, economically, and socially to choose between one attractive program and another. People want as much of all of them as is possible. Nor are they as happy about paying taxes as consuming social benefits. Swedish economist Henrik Åkerman has coined the "Christmas tree theorem": "If a Swede must choose between improved hospital standards and a trip to Mallorca, he will take both" (Andersen 1984b, p. 135).

Social policy does not produce sudden and dramatic changes in social values. The welfare state still exists mainly in the context of an advanced capitalist economy, although it is probably the materialistic and industrial values that offend many social critics—Left and Right—rather than private ownership. Detailed social surveys suggest that progress in social policy is slow, particularly in recent years of slow economic growth. Scandinavians, like others, judge achievements mainly against expectations, not against earlier conditions (see Erikson 1985). Top-notch health care today differs dramatically from the standards of 1960 or even 1980. As affluence increases, larger relative gains are necessary to yield perceptible social advances.

Social democracy has not produced uniform, restrictive, or inefficient societies, even though uniformity, limitations, and inefficiencies remain. Many of the idealistic hopes of domestic and foreign advocates have not been fulfilled. Conservative critics find elements of envy and mediocrity in the egalitarian zeal of recent decades. No one could deny that such elements exist, but they were also part of the homogeneous Scandinavian cultures of the prewelfare age. Excellence in the arts, sciences, humanities, and business are surely far more prevalent today than a century ago, when thousands of Scandinavians emigrated to find greater opportunity and liberty. Now the reverse is the case: Refugees and economic immigrants from nearly every corner of the world strain Scandinavian hospitality and resources. If one assesses social conditions in comparative terms, Scandinavian achievements are impressive.

NOTES

1. For a discussion of the development of Scandinavian social welfare measures in general see Kuhnle (1996) and Ploug and Kvist (1995); for Norway, see Kuhnle (1981a) and Kuhnle and Solheim (1985, pp. 41–109); in Denmark, see Greve (2000) and Knudsen, ed. (1993); and in Sweden, see Elmåer (1969). Current programs in

Nordic and other Western European countries are described in some detail in Hansen (1999) and U.S. Social Security Administration (1999).

2. Herbert Spencer coined the term *survival of the fittest* and used it in the social context. His harsh philosophy found resonance in the Calvinist strains of American social thought. As a mature man, Spencer's own humanitarian sensibilities were shocked when he observed urban misery (in England and America), and he began to doubt the wisdom of total laissez-faire social policies. While similar "social Darwinist" thinking was to be found in most industrial societies, in Scandinavia no democratic political party has ever made it part of their social program.

3. Until the 1960s, the Scandinavian secondary education system followed the European model of dividing, or tracking, pupils into academic and nonacademic courses based on their performance in primary school. Hence, a child's educational and, thereby, economic future was largely set at age eleven or twelve. To a significant extent, the child's social background influenced the educational track on which the child was placed. Comprehensive high schools became universal in Sweden in the 1970s, while Norwegian and Danish secondary schools (gymnasia) expanded their academic offerings and increased their intake significantly.

4. Ironically Swedish socialists have introduced individual retirement choices that were first initiated (with many problems) in Britain during the conservative Thatcher era (1979–90) and that are a priority for conservative Republicans in the United States. However, the individual element in Sweden involves 2.5 percent of an 18.5 percent pension tax (split evenly between employers and employees) and tops up a comprehensive and universal pension and benefit system.

5. Chronic high unemployment in Denmark led to significant tightening of unemployment provisions in the 1990s. Especially younger unemployed workers must now accept "activation" programs including education, training, and temporary publicly supported employment. Early retirement schemes have eliminated many unemployed older workers from the labor force, but their popularity with employed workers led to restrictions in 1999. Higher unemployment in Finland since 1990 has also caused a rapid growth in employment policies.

6. In Denmark sales and excise taxes on cars exceed 120 percent, and they are not much lower in the other Nordic countries. Gasoline in 2001 was about $1.00 a liter (U.S.$3.75 a gallon). The OECD estimated in 1996 that Danes and Norwegians pay consumption taxes amounting to about 33 percent of their purchases. The rate for Finns was 27 percent and Swedes 23 percent (OECD 1996, p. 48).

7. Linguistic, cultural, and educational challenges are large, especially as the cost of unskilled labor in Scandinavia is high. Of course, most of the immigrants and refugees are by definition much better off than prior to their arrival, but this is small comfort as the years pass and the second generation tries to enter the labor market.

8. OECD statistics reflect "current receipt of government as percentage of GDP," but nearly half of this sum is returned to citizens as social security cash benefits. Nordic countries use fewer tax expenditures (i.e., targeted tax deductions) than other OECD countries, especially since the tax reforms of the 1980s and 1990s. See Strand (1999).

CHAPTER 9

Managing the Market Economy

It will never happen . . . that there will be more to distribute than what is produced.
— Arne Geijer, Chair, Swedish Federation of Labor (1971)

The cost of welfare programs discussed in the preceding chapter and the ability of society to support them depends upon how the economy performs. Since the Social Democrats came to power in the 1930s, full employment and sustained economic growth have been pillars of the welfare state and broadly supported policy goals.

The Scandinavian welfare state developed in response to the economic insecurities of industrial society. If the economy could be effectively managed, there would be three desirable results. First, economic hardships, including unemployment, poverty, and other material causes of social distress, would be reduced. Second, economic growth would produce the resources for better social services and individual living standards. Third, a dynamic economy could be directed toward narrowing the large differences in wealth, income, and economic power that accompanied industrialization.

From the mid-1950s to the early 1970s, a Keynesian consensus on how to manage economic policy developed in all Western industrial democracies. It called for the government to use fiscal policy (taxing and spending) not only to meet its obligations, but also to keep the economy running at full capacity. Whenever the economy threatened to overheat (leading to inflation) or to stall (leading to recession), the government would apply timely correctives. The state's economic role expanded as a result of the increase in governmental regulation, the growth of the government itself, and its new, activist role of manipulating the market economy to achieve desirable ends: low rates of unemployment and inflation, high levels of income and wealth, and high rates of investment and growth. Despite recent actions of most advanced industrial countries to reduce the role of government in economic matters, no society is likely to return to the laissez-faire principles of the nineteenth century.

Despite important national variations, Scandinavian economic policies rested on a common Keynesian commitment to maintain macroeconomic balance, while allowing the private market to determine fundamental microeconomic choices. This is scarcely unique among democratic capitalist political economies. But the Scandinavian countries' small size and inclusive policy process allows policies to work faster and more effectively than in most other Western countries. Moreover, the Scandinavian governments have developed precision-guided economic instruments that focus on specific policy targets rather than on the entire economy.

Whether it was because of the new economic wisdom or in spite of it, Scandinavia shared in Western Europe's unprecedented postwar boom. Table 9.1 illustrates that since 1960, Nordic economic growth has been close to the European average. The outstanding Norwegian performance between 1975 and 1985 and since 1999 is largely a consequence of offshore petroleum production.

Behind these statistics is a dramatic change in economic lifestyles and expectations during the golden years of 1957–74. In the mid-1950s, Scandinavians enjoyed decent but austere living standards. Automobiles, private homes in urban areas, and foreign vacations were luxuries reserved for the well-to-do. Twenty years later, the Scandinavians expected and enjoyed the fruits of affluence. Cars, private homes well stocked with appliances, gourmet food and drink, and foreign vacations were mass consumer items. Regular increases in real wages and improved social benefits and services had become a way of life.[1] Then, in 1974, the first oil crisis triggered a global recession and a reconsideration of our theories of economic management.

In retrospect, the warnings of economic difficulties had been numerous. Inflation, which had typically hovered around 4 or 5 percent in the early 1960s, began to accelerate in the late 1960s to 8 to 10 percent. A comprehensive system of cost-of-living indexing shielded most wage earners from its immediate impact. Inflation seemed tolerable, and many discovered how to exploit it by heavy borrowing; interest payments were tax deductible, and the value of the principal eroded with inflation. Incomes policies (political limitations on wage increases) were discussed and applied periodically. In the 1970s, however, inflation accelerated as oil-price increases worked their way through the Scandinavian economies. Cost-of-living escalators and tax calculations institutionalized the inflationary

Table 9.1
Real GDP Growth per Capita and Inflation, Average Annual Rates, 1960–2002

	1960-73	1973-79	1979-89	1989-99	2000-02#
Denmark					
GDP growth	3.6	1.2	1.4	1.7	1.9
inflation	7.0	10.6	6.7	2.3	2.7
Finland					
GDP growth	4.5	1.9	3.2	1.2	3.0
inflation	6.8	12.4	7.5	2.2	2.3
Iceland					
GDP growth	4.0	4.2	2.0	1.3	3.1
inflation	14.3	38.6	36.5	4.9	6.2
Norway					
GDP growth	3.5	4.3	2.3	2.7	1.6
inflation	5.3	8.0	7.1	2.4	5.9
Sweden					
GDP growth	3.4	1.5	1.8	1.1	2.2
inflation	4.9	10.6	8.0	3.0	1.7
European Union					
GDP growth	4.0	2.1	2.0	1.6	1.9*
inflation	4.7	9.1	4.8	3.2	2.0*
United States					
GDP growth	2.7	2.0	2.0	2.0	2.2
inflation	3.6	7.6	5.2	2.4	1.9

*Euro 11
#Real GDP (not per capita) and preliminary estimate.
Sources: OECD (2000); Den Danske Bank (2002); OECD (2001c).

process. As a consequence, the Scandinavian countries' competitiveness declined and they lost a portion of their share of international trade. Public spending soared, and tax protest limited the ability to raise revenues. Government borrowing to finance the resulting deficits increased to disturbing levels. For a decade after 1974, the international economy remained in what journalists termed *stagflation*: an unpleasant combination of stagnation and inflation. Both stagnation—or mild recession—and inflation were familiar economic problems. But the heretofore unknown simultaneous appearance of the two puzzled economists and politicians. Stagflation challenged the economic-policy consensus. International economic conditions slashed economic growth, strained public finances, and pushed unemployment up.

Three common assumptions continue to characterize Scandinavian economic policy. First, economic growth, modernization, and global competitiveness are judged to be vital to providing the resources for an affluent and technologically advanced society. Second, increased economic equality between individuals and families (including a democratization of ownership of productive resources) is desirable, if only to make markets function better. Third, the management of the economy should be responsible to democratic decisions and representative organizations including labor, farmers, business, and others (i.e., democratic corporatism).

Of these concepts, all but the concept of economic growth raise new questions. Is large scale redistribution of income compatible with a market economy? Are policies promoting income equality compatible with sustained economic growth? How can public policies be held accountable to the principles of democratic government, private property, and individual liberty? Does the inclusion of economic interest groups in almost all aspects of policy making threaten the common interest?

These questions are, of course, not unique to Scandinavia. But they are more prominent there than elsewhere in the West because the Scandinavian governments have gone farther than most in seeking to manage the market economy. This chapter assesses the historical legacy of economic issues and the role of the state in economic affairs. It also examines the institutional framework for making and executing national economic policy as well as the various goals of economic policy. Finally, it analyzes the content of and prospects for Scandinavian political economy.

THE STATE AND ECONOMIC DEVELOPMENT IN SCANDINAVIA

Scandinavia's managed economies conform to the ideological precepts of neither liberalism nor socialism. Rather, they have borrowed generously from both. The Scandinavian countries have been set apart by their insistence that economic issues are inexorably linked to the discussions of democracy and social justice. In Scandinavia, a vigorous debate continues on how much economic democracy and justice are compatible with viable national economies in the international market.

Modern Scandinavian political economy, in common with most of Western Europe, has historical roots in the struggle between two alternative economic ideologies: feudalism and mercantilism. Feudalism was most pervasive in Denmark, incomplete in Sweden and Finland, and essentially absent in Norway and Iceland. The stagnant and decentralized collectivism of feudal economic relations was broken in large part by the desire of the central government to increase its political power and economic resources (Olsen 1962, pp. 24–43). The growth of international trade, already important in Scandinavia by the seventeenth century, was encouraged by economic specialization and governmental activity.

Mercantilism, a policy of state economic controls for political ends, flourished briefly in Denmark and Sweden. Swedish overseas colonization (and related trading) was short-lived, and, with Sweden's general decline as a European power in the eighteenth century, even European territories were ceded to Russia and Prussia. Denmark (including Norway until 1814) remained more prominent as a small mercantile nation, benefiting significantly from the slave and sugar trade, and, later, from its role as a neutral conduit for trade during various European wars.

Administrative reforms in both countries during the seventeenth and eighteenth centuries greatly increased the economic resources of the central state. But much of this wealth was squandered on overambitious and unsuccessful foreign policies.

During the nineteenth century, the role of the state in the economy declined as industrialization and the modernization of agriculture began. The speed and timing of economic modernization varied in the three countries. Industrialization started in Denmark around 1855, in Sweden a few years later. After 1890 industrialization took hold in Norway and Finland as well. Icelandic industrialization consisted initially of modernizing and servicing its fishing fleet and fish processing industry, which started in the early twentieth century, and did not culminate until after World War II. Industry in the form of aluminum smelting appeared in first in the 1960s. The pace of industrialization was fastest in Sweden and Norway. Ownership of industry was highly concentrated in Sweden; to a lesser extent, in Norway; and broadly dispersed in Denmark. All became firmly capitalistic. However, the development of producer and consumer cooperatives (an idea from Britain) had a significant impact in agriculture and later in consumer and housing sectors.

Liberal economic ideas made faster progress in Scandinavia than did liberal political ideals. The abolition of the guilds in the 1860s marked the definitive transition to a liberal market economy, although some residual restrictions on labor mobility would survive for another two decades. The achievement of parliamentary democracy in Scandinavia between 1884 and 1918 coincided with the apogee of liberal ideas in economics. Although the basic principles of parliamentary democracy reflected economic liberal influences, the idea of laissez-faire never achieved the same predominance in Scandinavia as it did in England or, especially, the United States. The state remained active in economic and social policies, particularly in areas of agrarian reform and amelioration of poverty in both rural and urban settings. Such traditional and natural monopolies as railroads and communications remained under public control or were closely regulated.

The resurgence of active state participation in economic matters resulted from a series of emergencies that demanded collective action, regardless of political ideologies. Twentieth-century world wars and global depressions reduced the credibility of the market as a guide for significant social and economic matters. Also important were more gradual socioeconomic changes, such as the steady movement of workers from agricultural settings to employment in urban industries and services. Scandinavian economic policy was defined by the demands these changes created. Changing economic theories were not without their influence, but policy innovations were shaped principally by political or economic necessities.

Despite their common neutrality,[2] World War I was the first shock to the largely preindustrial economic policy structures of the Scandinavian countries. Sweden in particular faced severe resource and food shortages as naval warfare affected supplies to the neutrals. By the last years of the war, food supplies had grown so short that hunger was widespread in the larger cities. Norway, too, suffered significant material shortages, but initially this was offset by the rising earnings of its merchant navy. As submarine warfare escalated, however, Norway suffered severe material losses. Denmark suffered less wartime disruption because it enjoyed greater agricultural self-sufficiency. Indeed, sectors of the Danish economy prospered from increased exports to Germany. In each country, emergency legislation increased the state's role in economic management to a level not seen for a century. After the armistice, these common emergency economic measures—a form of "wartime socialism"—did not remain in place long (Derry 1979, pp. 301–6).

In peacetime, economic management proved to be nearly as troublesome as during wartime. Despite industrial growth in the 1920s, unemployment remained high. Labor unions continued to expand. But they were unable to reduce the hardships brought about by unemployment. Brief Social Democratic minority governments had little effect; indeed, their economic policies were exceedingly orthodox. In Denmark, restoration of the gold standard by the Social Democrats in 1924–25 stimulated the most severe unemployment heretofore seen in the country. The Swedish Social Democrats studied more radical measures, but adopted an incremental approach to economic change because direct state ownership of major industry (nationalization) appeared politically and economically unattractive (Tilton 1987, pp. 146–52). Unlike America's Roaring Twenties, the postwar decade saw most European economies stagnate, stimulating work by several young Swedish economists in Stockholm, including liberals like Bertil Ohlin, Knut Wiksell, and future Social Democratic ministers Ernst Wigforss and Gunnar Myrdal. They argued that idle resources, especially labor, were the core of the industrial problem. Increased government spending (especially on public works, but also on social programs) would be a partial solution. By increasing spending and, thus, the demand for goods and services, income would be channeled to under-employed sectors of the economy and, secondarily, throughout the economy. If such intervention was justified by war, why not by the disaster of mass unemployment?[3]

The global depression that started in 1929 destroyed confidence in the status quo, while the spread of authoritarianism strengthened the case for reform and compromise. Leadership and support from beyond the working class created Scandinavia's historic compromise. Between 1929 and 1935 Social Democratic governments came to power in Denmark, Norway, and Sweden with sufficient political strength (usually in alliance with the Liberals or Agrarians) to act. In Iceland in 1934 and in Finland in 1937 they joined Liberal or Agrarian governments as junior partners. On the very day that hysterical Berliners cheered Hitler's appointment as chancellor, leaders of the Danish Social Democrats, the Radical Liberals, and the agrarian Liberals concluded the so-called Kanslergade Compromise at the apartment of the patriarchal Social Democratic prime minister, Thorvald Stauning. Following a pattern initiated by the new Social Democratic government in Sweden in June 1932, the Kanslergade compromise called for government intervention to stabilize farm income, to provide emergency employment, and to extend existing labor contracts to avert a lockout threatened by employers to force down wages; this consensus set a pattern for governmental activism in managing the economy that would hold sway throughout Scandinavia for the rest of the century. The Social Democratic governments sought new policy tools that would stimulate economic growth, reduce unemployment, and improve national economic security. Then, as later, political ideology provided the inspiration, but few practical formulas.

Much of the Scandinavian response to the Depression was by trial and error, rather than applied theory. For example, Sweden's improving economy after 1933 was in large part stimulated by exports that were in turn encouraged by an undervalued currency and the forced abandonment of the gold standard. Spending on public works and social programs adhered to the Social Democratic agenda, but their positive effects on the economy were at the time quite limited (Lindbeck 1974, pp. 22–23; Gourevitch 1989, pp. 87–106). Still, Scandinavian Social Democrats, especially in Sweden, introduced the economic policies that became the norm after World War II in all Western industrial countries. Those policies are generally associated with the reformist British economist John Maynard Keynes, whose theories explained why governmental management of the economy was both necessary and practical. His precepts called for governmental spending, preferably on useful programs, during times of economic recession, and governmental restraint during periods of excess activity and inflation. Swedish policies, which were the most innovative in part because of the influence of the Stockholm school, were set apart from the nascent Keynesian policies of other Western democracies in the early 1930s principally by their coherent effort to reinflate domestic demand. Employees on emergency public works, for instance, were paid regular scale instead of subsistence wages. In the later 1930s, the Swedes began to experiment with managing the business-investment cycle through the use of tax-advantaged investment funds accumulated by business in boom years and released for investment in plant and equipment during downturns. This countercyclical investment policy was developed further after the war, particularly in the 1960s, but was deemed ineffective in the 1980s, in part because of financial globalization.

Governmental passivity and the insistence on an annual balanced budget—principles dogmatically held during peacetime by most economists and by liberal and conservative politicians for generations—were discarded completely in Scandinavia (Samuelsson 1968, pp. 234–35). With the exception of the United States under Roosevelt, the balanced-budget principle was widely and rigidly applied outside of Scandinavia during the Depression with unpleasant consequences. Efforts to cut public spending as revenues fell simply worsened the crisis, and, when applied ruthlessly in Weimar Germany in 1930, helped to pave the way to power for Adolf Hitler (see James 1989, pp. 231–62).

The stimulative measures of the 1930s were enacted by the new Social Democratic and Labor governments in coalition with parties representing the distressed agricultural sector. This Red-Green coalition set two precedents that have continued to characterize Scandinavian economic policy. First, the state undertook a commitment to ameliorate economic hardships by public action. Unemployment and economic depression were no longer accepted as inevitable, natural hardships to be passively endured. Second, important economic legislation was based on broad political coalitions across the divide of economic ideology. The new pattern meant that the major economic measures would be based on the broadest possible political support. Large interest organizations and their associated political parties framed sweeping package deals. The role of parliament was reduced to ratifying these compromises (see Söderpalm 1975, pp. 258–78).

World War II accelerated the growth of the economic role of the state. In Sweden, the government undertook substantial economic planning, while enemy occupation forced strict controls on Norway and Denmark. Following the liberation in 1945, Norway and Denmark commenced reconstruction programs relying heavily on state direction. This was especially the case in Norway, which suffered severe war damage in its northern regions. Finland's war damage was most severe in the north, where German troops laid waste to many towns after Finland left the war in 1944 and was required by the armistice agreement to expel German forces. Finland lost most of the province of Karelia and the key city of

Viipuri (Viborg). Most burdensome were the heavy reparation payments (mainly in the form of industrial goods) demanded by the Soviet Union. All required additional governmental initiatives. Sweden and Iceland suffered no direct war damage (several ships were sunk), and demand for their products during the war actually strengthen the Swedish and Icelandic economies. Henceforth, governmental management became an accepted and normal part of economic policy, although politicians would argue over questions of degree and technique.

Postwar Economic Policies

The pattern of postwar Scandinavian economic policy is similar to other smaller industrial countries and responds to general Western economic trends. To get an overview, it is useful to define four periods. The first was a period of recovery from the dislocations of World War II. The second, a remarkable period of sustained economic expansion from the mid-1950s until the oil crisis of 1973. The third, a subsequent period of crisis and adjustment that called into question many of the political and economic formulas of the postwar era. The fourth period, which continues today, is one of adapting to the realities of economic globalization and the new neoliberal theory of the world economy without abandoning core goals of Scandinavian economic policy.

Recovery (1945–55)

The severity of the problems of reconstruction varied enormously, from Norway and Finland with substantial war damage to Sweden with none. In the postwar period, economic management of one type or another became a common feature of Scandinavian politics. Denmark adhered to a relatively pragmatic and liberal policy once the immediate postwar emergency receded. This gave wide scope to private economic decisions. Sweden debated at length Social Democratic proposals for a planned economy that would continue in modified form the strong role of the wartime state (see Lewin 1967, 1975). Nevertheless, it adopted a pragmatic policy of focusing state attention on issues of overall economic balance. In Norway, however, the strict postwar emergency measures prevailed until the end of the 1950s, and gradually evolved into a more flexible program of industrial and regional development. As economic recovery gained momentum, physical controls on labor, capital, and land were largely replaced by the budgetary policies that came to be the heart of the Keynesian formulas (Jörberg and Krantz 1976).

Denmark, Norway, and Sweden participated in the Marshall Plan (European Recovery Program 1947–52), which not only funneled substantial U.S. economic assistance to Western Europe but also stimulated sustained European economic cooperation. Finland's sensitive relations with the Soviet Union (which had walked out of the initial Marshall Plan conference in Paris in 1947) prevented direct participation. Sympathetic with Finland's plight, the United States provided discreet aid primarily through its Export-Import Bank. Within the Scandinavian countries, only the Communists dissented from the support given to closer Western economic cooperation. While some Social Democrats worried about possible restrictions on national economic policy resulting from multilateral collaboration, the legacy of international wartime cooperation, especially in Norway, was strong, the needs overwhelming, and the benefits enticing. Only when European economic integration became pressing in the mid-1950s did the Scandinavian countries draw back. The reluctance of Great Britain, still their main trading partner, to participate seriously provided a convenient excuse to maintain lower levels of collaboration. Concurrently, plans for a Scandinavian customs union had a prominent place on the Scandinavian foreign-economic policy agenda in the 1950s. Norway proved to be reluctant, and a regional arrangement was discarded in favor of the seven-nation European Free Trade Association (see Haskel 1976; Stråth 1978).

By the end of the recovery period, Nordic national economies still operated on different political premises. Norway, with its majority Labor government, remained committed to firm governmental direction of national economic activity. Planning remained the watchword, although controls had gradually been liberalized during the 1950s.

Sweden had gone through an intensive internal debate over the Social Democratic government's commitment to planning, but rigid direction was neither politically possible (the Social Democrats lacked a parliamentary majority) nor apparently necessary, given the power of fiscal instruments.

Denmark experienced a succession of minority governments. Between 1950 and 1953, a pragmatic nonsocialist minority coalition jettisoned most rationing and allowed free markets to function but with heavy excise taxes on luxuries (e.g., automobiles, gasoline, cosmetics, and the like). When the Social Democrats returned to power in 1953, they lacked a political majority for the ambitious economic policy goals of their postwar program. During the mid-1950s, the government groped for compromises to break the stop-go cycle that plagued Denmark. Economic expansion, especially in the growing industrial sector, required imported capital and raw materials. This caused international payment problems that forced the government to put on the economic brakes, which in turn stopped the expansion.

Finland's postwar economic policy was shaped by reconstruction. There was enormous war damage, particularly in Lappland. More than 400,000 Finns had to be resettled from territories, mainly in Karelia, taken by the Soviet Union. Finally, Finland had been saddled with heavy reparation payments of industrial goods to the Soviet Union between 1944 and 1952. This was set at a punitive level of $300 million (about 10–15 percent of Finland's GDP), and required rapid reconstruction of damaged industrial infrastructure.[4] Militant action by communist labor unions at times threatened the economic recovery, especially through strikes in 1947, but remarkably, Finland met its foreign obligations as well as domestic needs (Jussila, Hentilä, and Nevakivi 1999, pp. 227, 237–44; Jörberg and Krantz 1976, pp. 430–31).

Expansion (1955–73)

A period of unprecedented prosperity commenced in the mid-1950s for two reasons. First, the growth of the industrial economy and the relative decline of the agricultural sector made possible rapid increases in productivity. Second, a rapid and sustained growth of world trade, in part the result of freer trade, increased foreign demand for Scandinavian goods. In addition, at least in Sweden, innovations in economic policy seemed to provide new means to achieve higher rates of capital formation and lower rates of unemployment while improving the social-insurance system and the flexibility of the labor market.

The first Swedish innovation was the introduction in 1959, after a spirited and extended political debate (Molin 1965), of compulsory supplementary pensions for all wage earners (Allmänna Tillägspension, or ATP). Not only did the ATP system mark a major extension of the welfare state as described in Chapter 8, it also reduced barriers to labor mobility (changing jobs no longer affected your pension) and created a substantial source of investment funds. These funds were invested conservatively in national and local government bonds and housing, solving infrastructure problems, eliminating the housing shortage, and moving private capital from those areas toward investment in the productive sector. Modest ATP investment in corporate stock was permitted in 1974. (Demographic and economic changes—longer life spans, lower birthrates, and slower economic growth—undermined ATP's economics, and Sweden made major reforms to its pension system in the late 1990s [International Monetary Fund 1998, pp. 56–61].)

The second innovation was the implementation of the "active labor-market policy" in the 1950s and 1960s. The policy was designed to maintain full employment without overheating the economy and creating severe balance of payments deficits. Originated by the Swedish labor movement's two leading economists, Gösta Rehn and Rudolf Meidner, the active labor-market policy was a composite of retraining, rehabilitation, mobility, and aggressive job-placement services. Sweden's state-run employment service also promoted accelerating entry of women into the paid labor market (see Table 9.2) and managed the recruitment of foreign

Table 9.2

Labor Force as Percentage of Population Aged 15 to 64, by Gender, 1960–99 (average for period)

	MEN				WOMEN			
	1960-67	1970-73	1980-89	1990-99	1960-67	1970-73	1980-89	1990-99
Denmark	97.3	90.7	88.3	86.3	48.1	60.0	74.6	76.2
Finland	93.5	81.4	82.0	77.9	66.4	62.2	72.7	70.8
Iceland	90.6	94.1	92.5	90.3	45.8	46.0	64.3	78.9
Norway	90.6	88.0	87.3	83.8	36.8	44.9	67.8	72.9
Sweden	93.4	88.4	85.5	80.7	53.5	61.2	77.6	76.4
EU	93.3	89.4	81.4	78.8	43.5	43.3	50.9	57.3
US	88.2	85.3	84.5	85.2	43.9	49.8	63.7	70.1

Sources: OECD (1994, p. 35); OECD (2000, p. 39).

workers. The implications of this microlevel intervention are explored later in this chapter.

The Golden Sixties transformed both public and private Scandinavia. In the late 1950s, there was a consensus for growth. Fifteen years later, genuine affluence was widespread, but the consensus for growth seemed endangered by increasing inflation and environmental uncertainties. As was the case in several other advanced industrial societies, Scandinavian opinion seemed to be dividing into two cultures, which Ronald Inglehart (1977) termed *materialist* and *postmaterialist*. His was a more precise and empirical elaboration of a theme raised a half century earlier by an English social theorist, R. H. Tawney, of the "acquisitive society" (1920). Acquisitive or materialist citizens have a thirst for soaring private consumption and a hearty appetite for public programs. Many favor the Social Democratic principles of security and equality, but their support is predicated upon a growing economic pie. The postmaterialists are critical of consumerism and many of the norms of industrial society, both capitalist and socialist. Despite Karl Marx's derogatory remarks about the "idiocy of rural life," the young ecological socialists found the countryside an attractive alternative to the consumerist urban culture. They decried the environmental and cultural costs of affluent materialism and saw the material world as a fixed store of resources. Overconsumption (i.e., consuming more than one needs) costs the poor or less-affluent groups in society, the less-developed countries, and nature dearly. Before these conflicts could be resolved, however, the oil crisis of 1973 burst upon the scene and reminded Scandinavians of their dependence on international economic conditions for both prosperity and security.

Crisis and Adjustment (1974–89)

After the sudden oil-price increases of 1973, economic growth declined dramatically, except in Norway. There, higher oil prices spurred the exploitation of large offshore petroleum resources, providing an important alternative to stagnating traditional industries. Yet, even in Norway, the North Sea riches, which provided virtually full employment, could not guarantee balanced economic growth. In the 1980s Denmark's more modest offshore gas and oil helped restore economic growth. Over the next quarter century, recurring global recessions (1974–75, 1980–82, and 1990–92) highlighted economic instability.

In Denmark, Finland, and Sweden, stagflation (stagnation and inflation) threatened to undo two decades of increased economic prosperity and equality. Iceland continued to cope with Latin American rates of inflation and wildly fluctuating economic growth rates, but generally maintained nearly full employment. Ironically, the same social security programs developed to insure against individual and family economic difficulties became a barrier to economic management. Legislated programs dictated heavy automatic expenditures that increased rapidly. These costs increased budgets and tax rates to very high levels and limited policy flexibility. Payments to the unemployed and, in Sweden, to troubled firms ameliorated the impact of the crisis but seemed to close avenues of escape.

Countercyclical government spending could reverse the sharp but short postwar recessions, but in the 1970s the prolonged downturn produced huge budget deficits. Public spending, especially generous unemployment compensation, strained national economic resources and political consensus. The Swedes struggled to bridge the downturn by adding subsidies for inventory stockpiles to their usual countercyclical policies, which included emergency employment and investment funds. Although initially successful in maintaining domestic activity, prolonged international recessions and foreign competition made the program too expensive to continue beyond 1978 (Martin 1985).

Ironically, after the 1976 electoral victory of the first nonsocialist government in forty-four years, the Swedish response was directed by its earlier opponents, who resorted to an unlikely policy choice: socialism. The state assumed responsibility for restructuring the troubled shipbuilding and steel industries. During the six years of nonsocialist government (1976–82), more Swedish industry came under state control than during the previous four decades of socialist rule. When a banking crisis swept Sweden, Finland, and Norway in the late 1980s, again the state stepped in.

Although high by the standards of the decades of prosperity, Swedish unemployment following the oil crisis remained substantially below prevailing Western European levels. The Swedish emergency-employment system accounted for one of the lowest open unemployment rates among Western industrial countries. Sweden's arsenal of employment measures, although staggering under the rapid increase in clients in the 1970s, provided training, income security, and intangible psychological support to tens of thousands of citizens.

Swedish governments sought to increase investment in expanding industries, while trying to cushion the fall of such industries as shipbuilding, where long-term prospects were bleak. Only in the late 1970s, when wage restraint, currency devaluations, and structural changes once again made Swedish industry profitable, did industrial investments return to normal levels. Stagnant wages (in real terms) unleashed labor unrest, including, in 1980, Sweden's largest strike in two generations. The acceleration of inflation after six years of wage restraint (in part due to the second oil crisis of 1979–80) exhausted popular patience. This mediocre performance, coupled with growing disagreement among Sweden's nonsocialist parties, helped pave the way for the 1982 Social Democratic electoral victory.

Danish policies were largely in Social Democratic hands until 1982, although the nonsocialist agrarian Liberals governed during 1974 and briefly, in coalition with the Social Democrats, in 1978–79. All were minority governments that sought broad political support to respond to the deterioration in Denmark's economic position. Denmark, which imported nearly 100 percent of its energy in 1973, was hard hit by oil-price increases.[5] Unlike the Swedes, the Danes left adjustment to the market and to their excellent unemployment compensation system. Unemployment became the most visible sign of distress, and it was all the more painful because of its concentration among young and female wage earners. Public finances, after nearly two decades of internal fiscal balance, began to disintegrate under the impact of double-digit budget deficits. The foreign economic balance, always Denmark's most vulnerable economic account, collapsed and forced even the Social Democrats to apply harsh economic brakes.

Denmark adopted countercyclical measures more halfheartedly than did Sweden, in part because Denmark's domestic and international financial situation was significantly weaker. Unlike Sweden, Denmark had few economic emergency plans. There was little political support for any long-term economic recovery strategy and, not surprisingly, no such reform programs emerged. Political consensus was limited to short-term emergencies, or as in the case of energy conservation, areas of obvious immediate return. Taxes continued to climb, despite the rise of tax-protest parties. Denmark remained on a liberal course like most European Community countries, and paid for it by high unemployment levels, which exceeded 10 percent by the early 1980s.

Norway's oil boom was more than a fortunate windfall. It demonstrated dramatically the advantages of administrative and technological resources. First, three decades of sophisticated economic planning and policy had created a cadre of skilled administrators. Although petroleum extraction did not provide many jobs, there was an enormous initial infrastructure investment that benefited Norway's skilled-labor force and sophisticated industrial enterprises. Money borrowed against petroleum collateral propelled Norway ahead as the other European economies sputtered. As one Danish newspaper put it, mocking traditional Norwegian modesty, "prosperity was unavoidable." Problems appeared later: Inflation eroded Norway's nonpetroleum export industries, and the country became highly dependent on one product for much of its export earnings and public finance. By 1986, oil accounted for one-third of Norwegian exports and one-fifth of the national income. Still, these seemed to be minor difficulties compared to the structural changes and resource worries of most other industrial countries.

Adapting to Globalization (1990–present)

Economic globalization has been a gradual, ongoing process. It has involved three forces. The first is an ideological change—a move toward the neoliberal or "Washington consensus" that deregulation of regulated portions of the market economy, privatization of some public-sector function, and marketization of others is desirable—that really began in the early 1980s with the policies of Prime Minister Thatcher in Britain and President Reagan in the United States. The second has been an exponential growth in international capital flows as well as a continued expansion in the trade in goods and services. The third was the fall of the Berlin wall and inclusion of Eastern Europe and the former Soviet Union in the global market. While these changes occurred during the 1980s and into the early 1990s, the collapse of the Communist regimes in Eastern Europe in 1989–90 marks an appropriate watershed.

Although no Scandinavian political party, much less any government, has adopted the new Anglo-American neoliberal economic orthodoxy as its own, all have been influenced by it to a greater or lesser extent. All have explored deregulation (especially in financial markets), privatization (especially of telecommunications), and introducing market principles into some public services (especially transportation and some hospital services). These efforts have enjoyed mixed success. In general privatization of the telephone system has speeded installation of new service (waiting weeks to get telephone service had been one of the standard complaints of new residents) and accelerated the introduction of new technology. This has helped make Finland's Nokia and Sweden's L. M. Ericsson major players in the wireless communications market. On the other hand, deregulation of the banking system in Finland, Norway, and Sweden produced a severe banking crisis between 1988 and 1992 similar to the savings and loan deregulation debacle in the United States and with the same need for government bailouts of the sector.

Controls on capital movements in and out of the country were a key part of economic management through the 1980s, particularly in Sweden. In the 1970s, even buying dollar-denominated travelers checks in Sweden required complying with currency export restrictions. In the end of the 1980s, however, those controls were dismantled, in part because Swedish firms had become genuinely transnational in their activities. Integration into the global capital markets had many advantages, and offshore investment has become a key strategy both for the Norwegian national petroleum profits fund and for the individually invested component of the Swedish ATP pension system. It has also meant that the Swedish krona was a target for international speculation after its link to the European currency cooperation in 1991. Efforts to protect the krona by pushing up interest rates failed to stem the speculative tide that previously would have been controlled by capital import and export regulations. As described in Chapter 7, the Swedish krona had to be floated in 1992; it promptly lost about a quarter of its value against the German, British, and U.S. currencies. For better or worse, integration into the global capital markets strips national governments of what had once been a major tool of national economic management.

The collapse of the Soviet bloc in 1989 and of the Soviet Union itself in 1991 marked the end of an era. The Cold War was over, as was the separate COMECON trading system that included Eastern Europe and the Soviet Union. It also meant the end of the special Finnish trading relationship with the Soviet bloc that had provided a significant market (more than 20% of exports) for Finnish goods; the total collapse of this market and the 1990–92 global recession shot Finnish unemployment through the roof in the early 1990s, peaking at over 20 percent in 1994. Sweden was also affected in part as Finland's other major trading partner; its unemployment rate quadrupled from under 2 percent to about 8 percent between 1990 and 1994.

On the more positive side, the end of the Cold War freed Finland from Soviet-imposed restrictions on aligning itself with the European Union. The consequence was that both Finland and Sweden applied for European Union membership, held referenda on membership in 1994, and entered the EU in 1995. Norway, too, took EU membership to a second vote in 1994, but voters again rejected joining Europe.

By the turn of the century, all of the Nordic countries had returned to both public and private prosperity, in part because of the international economic cycle and in part because they had made major policy and structural reforms.

MAKING ECONOMIC POLICY IN SCANDINAVIA TODAY

The preceding section should dispel any myth of a triumphant Scandinavian march to socialism. The Social Democratic parties knew what they wanted—economic prosperity, equality, and democracy—but their plan to achieve those ends by socializing the means of production had to be laid aside out of consideration for their allies. Instead, they sought to achieve the same ends through a growing public sector and active state intervention to manage the market economy.

Clearly the economy should be managed to achieve democratic ends. But how are democratic goals defined at the macroeconomic level? Political democracy stresses the right to take part, but historically participation was not an issue in economic policy. Since the Depression, however, providing employment for those who sought it and fairer economic conditions have become a key goals of economic policy. The lack of work caused by unemployment, disability, or gender barriers has been addressed in Scandinavia as successive governments, regardless of political coloration, have sought to assure access to work to all citizens. Since the 1960s, this has particularly become an issue of guaranteeing work for women who wanted to enter the labor market. The degree of Scandinavian success in this regard can be seen in the higher labor force participation rates for women in Table 9.2. Scandinavian female labor-force participation rates have risen from roughly the OECD norm in the 1960s to 15 to 20 percentage points above the norm in the late 1990s as laggards Iceland and Norway have caught up with the rest of Scandinavia. Simultaneously the proportion of men in the labor force has contracted slightly because of extended secondary and postsecondary education, long-term unemployment, and early retirement schemes but continues to remain above the EU norm.

Political democracy also stresses political equality. The analog in the economy would be relative equality of wealth and, especially, income. This is not easily achieved in a modern economy. People obviously work at different rates, with different skills and different abilities. Productivity cannot be equal, even for a single individual over his or her entire life. Wealth, however, in all but subsistence economies, is more closely associated with social standing than with actual productivity. The question of relative equality in income hinges on how the products of production are distributed.

Another problem in defining democratic economic goals is the complication that arises when discussing the failure of economic systems to measure fully human activity. Only labor in the marketplace has a cash value. Yet all societies require unpaid labor. Consider, for example, the activities of the housewife. She often puts in a fourteen-hour day, but there is no cash value accorded to her labor. Some argue that the generosity of citizens in donating their time and skills and time is an accurate predictor of the quality of life in that society. Therefore, it is important when discussing various policies in different countries to remember that there are limits to the value of statistical and historical comparisons. Economics has cultural as well as technical dimensions.

This perspective reminds us that we all have three distinct sources of income. First, the market compensates us for our labor and for the savings that we and previous generations have accumulated. Second, society's laws, regulations and family relationships provide certain income guarantees, particularly for children. Finally, the state provides transfer payments (pensions, unemployment compensation, etc.) and services collectively to its citizens.

Framing Economic Policy Issues

The context for Scandinavian economic policies is not conceptually different from that of other Western industrial economies. The players and constraints are similar. Private decision makers include businesses, banks and other financial institutions, and private consumers; the public sector includes national, regional, and local governments, as well as some public enterprises that do not operate on a strictly commercial basis. The production of goods remains overwhelmingly in the private sector, while that of services is divided between the public and private sectors. Finally, there is the international economic system, which looms especially large for Scandinavia. It is only a slight exaggeration to say that the Scandinavian countries do not have national economies at all, but are small parts of an international economy. Like most small, advanced, industrial countries, they are highly dependent on foreign sources for raw materials, capital, and technology. They are equally dependent on exports to foreign markets.

Small open economies, such as those of Scandinavia, must react quickly to accommodate domestic policies to global economic and political developments. In the international arena, they are policy takers rather than policy makers. Their deviations from the policy norms of other Western economies must not reduce their competitiveness in the international market. Between 1995 and 2000 Denmark, Finland, and Sweden as partial or full members of the emerging Economic and Monetary Union (EMU) were obligated to fulfill and maintain specific "convergence criteria" regarding government deficits, debt, and inflation. For large industrial firms, such as Sweden's world-class automobile firms, Volvo and Saab (now largely owned by American automobile companies), and for small enterprises, global economic events are decisive constraints.

Economic policy is shaped by the same constitutional procedures and political necessities as other policies. It is both technical and political. Although Parliament is constitutionally supreme, public economic decisions lie primarily with the executive cabinet, and programmatic choices are also shaped by the involvement of corporatist interest groups. Let us examine the role of these three in the process of making economic policy.

Parliamentary Politics and Economics

The struggle for parliamentary supremacy in Scandinavia as elsewhere focused on the power of the purse; no taxes could be collected nor public funds spent without parliamentary approval. Parliament acquired the right to set the main direction of economic policy, but in practice it responds to governmental proposals and interest-group demands. As the public sector expanded, so too did the number and scope of political economic issues.

The Scandinavian economic policy debate occurs simultaneously at two levels. The first is an ideological and simplistic argument on *policy means* between those advocating collectivist or political decisions and those urging individualist or market solutions to economic problems. Scandinavia has demonstrated that there can be a middle way between the two views: using varying degrees of state intervention to make markets work better and to provide social security. In the past decade the ideological pendulum has swung toward market (i.e., private) solutions, without in practice shrinking the size and cost of the public sector. The second and more important political debate focuses on the *policy agenda*. This, too, is highly partisan, because policy making requires choices and priorities. While the ideological debate has become less vociferous, the debate over priorities, choices, and acceptable performance has become more critical. Although the agenda debate is more easily reduced to pragmatic options and compromises, there is a broad consensus from the Social Democrats and the nonsocialist parties that public spending and taxation also have their "limits to growth" (see Lindblom 1977).

The *budget cycle* (annual public spending and tax proposals) consumes much parliamentary time. Here political principles must confront practical considerations. Studies of the Swedish budgetary process described how what is called the annual budget in fact covers as much as four years. Original drafting and economic projections at the local and agency level commence at least eighteen months before the start of the fiscal year. Wish lists then go through the processes of administrative and political review before the government submits its budget bill to parliament five-and-one-half months before the start of the fiscal year, which, in Sweden, is July 1. Several months of parliamentary review and amendment ensue. A final budget is passed, typically by the end of May. The government then has a month to issue regulations and budgetary guidelines before spending starts. During the fiscal year, unforeseen situations may require additional funds (rarely do they result in less spending). After the fiscal year ends, there is a four-month auditing period. But with as much as 70 percent of expenditures required by legal entitlement, enforcement of budgetary ceilings is weak (Vinde and Petri 1978, pp. 70–76; OECD 1997a, p. 63). The other Nordic countries are similar, and all face a challenge in adjusting budgetary decisions to volatile economic conditions.

In each of the Scandinavian countries there is at least one parliamentary committee concerned with governmental spending programs (the budget) and one concerned with taxation (revenue). All of the functional policy committees must, of course, consider the economic and budgetary consequences of their programs, although their diligence in attending to this task may vary greatly. Even among the several committees concerned with economic policy, workloads and responsibilities differ. In Denmark, for example, the Political Economy Committee has light duties, while the Finance Committee has so enormous a workload that it is hard to see how it can give more than perfunctory attention to most budget items. In budget and taxation issues, as in most policy matters, the parliamentary strength of the government is a decisive factor in determining the role of parliamentary committees. Parliamentary scrutiny of budgetary and tax matters affords opposition parties time to gather detailed economic information, to question the means and ends of governmental policies, and to audit and evaluate the efficiency of programs and the civil service. If the government enjoys a formal parliamentary majority, committee work, especially on annual budgets, will be routine. When a minority government must forge a workable majority, committees concerned with economic policy become crucial forums for compromise. A consistent problem has been uneven communication and cooperation between the economic policy committees and those with functional policy responsibilities (Arter 1984, pp. 182–89).

Parliament's ability to inform, argue, and participate in the economic policy debate is hampered by the technical complexities of the issues. Government agencies have ample professional resources at their command, but economic expertise does not resolve policy disputes. "If all economists were laid end-to-end," George Bernard Shaw once remarked, "they would not reach a conclusion." Scandinavian members of parliament do not have significant research resources; the research staffs of parliamentary parties and select committees are also small. Governmental proposals and reports, which vary in quantity and quality among the Scandinavian countries, provide the most direct source of public information. Central banks and *ad hoc* or permanent panels of economic experts (exemplified by the Danish Economic Council, *Det økonomiske Råd*), supplemented by testimony and information given to parliamentary committees, provide independent information. Although some of the technical issues may not be easily accessible to the public, in recent decades the media have focused more on economic matters assisted by outside benchmarking agencies like the OECD and the International Monetary Fund plus the substantial research staffs of commercial banks, the employers' associations, unions, and the research staffs at universities and other research institutions.

Complicating Nordic economic and budgetary policy is the substantial decentralization of spending and taxing decisions to local and regional governments. These governments provide most health services, social benefits, primary and secondary education, and regional transportation. They have substantial independent taxing and spending authority while they are also required to meet national standards of service. Twenty to fifty percent of their revenue is transferred from the national treasury primarily to equalize the tax burdens and expenditures between richer and poorer regions and municipalities (OECD 1997b, pp. 171, 368, 410–11). These issues are negotiated between the various levels of governments with the municipal and county governments represented by their own organizations.

Thus, Parliament is but one of many actors in the budgeting and taxing process. It does define the distinction between *public* and *private* economic issues, and can make productive use of its inquiry and informational powers. Often, however, the Scandinavian parliaments ratify decisions hammered out between political parties, public bureaucracies, and interest organizations.

Executive Leadership and Economic Management

The cabinet, or the government, makes the most important decisions for the public sector. Through the budgetary process, long-term investment and policy commitments, and taxation policy, the national government shapes economic policy. These fundamental policies set the economic course and are the main instruments for managing overall economic policy. While faith in long-term planning or even fine tuning through Keynesian fiscal policy has waned, the Nordic governments still exercise close management of overall economic balance. As their economies have opened to European and global forces—and economic isolationism has never been a choice for the Nordic countries—national policies must be adjusted to outside forces. Together with monetary policies through the central banks, measures to stimulate during times of stagnation and to restrain during inflationary periods describe the course of economic management in modern Scandinavia. Open economies have, however, considerably less autonomy to pursue such policies at the national level.

Responding to the Great Depression, Nordic governments embraced pragmatic policies of countercyclical economic policy even before John Maynard Keynes's theories were formalized (1936). The various broad economic deals of 1933–35 united industrial labor, urban wage earners, and rural interests in coherent measures to stimulate the national economy while increasing social security. World War II and the postwar recovery period prolonged the sense of common crisis. The three principal economic emergencies of the twentieth century—World War I, the Great Depression, and World War II—engendered planning before it became a clear political issue. Ironically, much of the debate about planning came after the historical fact.

Economic planning was an important and recurring issue in Scandinavian politics into the 1980s. It has been debated in ideological, economic, and policy terms. Although definitions of planning vary widely, their common denominator is the substitution of centralized governmental decisions for decentralized private market forces. Most Nordic planning efforts were analogous to the French practice: "indicative planning" (i.e., goal setting) rather than the comprehensive, Soviet-styled "Five Year Plans." In practice, the term *planning* has been attached to a wide range of activities—from the mere collection and analysis of various economic forecasts, to the evaluation of the fiscal consequences of alternative economic policies, to energetic efforts to direct large sectors of the national economy through centralized infrastructure and investment planning.

The importance of planning in the Scandinavian economic-policy debate stemmed, in part, from its being a practical, rational substitute for the abstract ideological discussion on state ownership versus private ownership. It was also a matter of efficiency and a way to assure economic growth and full employment. Broadly accepted during the war, planning was emphasized by the Social Democratic parties as a means of economic recovery and development. Gradually it became a substitute for direct state ownership (nationalization) of industry, which had lost favor as an economic strategy among many leading Social Democrats (see Lewin 1967; Tilton 1987, 1990), except where such natural monopolies as the railroads existed, or where regional economic considerations suggested public investment, as in the iron mines of northern Sweden. Planning seemed to be another opportunity to find the middle way. Enterprises would remain largely in private hands and the free market would flourish, but the public interest would be reflected in planned economic priorities.

Planning procedures vary considerably among the Scandinavian countries. Norway and Finland had the most determined planning program. Severe war damage, particularly in the north, made planning, rationing, and other means of direct governmental control a necessity in the immediate postwar period. Following reconstruction, the focus of Norwegian planning changed. Strict physical planning yielded to politically guided indicative planning, which used conventional tools of fiscal, and, to a much lesser extent, monetary policy (Bergh 1977, pp. 11–99). With physical planning, permits were required to obtain raw materials, labor, and credit; permits were issued primarily for activities that were in accordance with economic plans. Indicative planning is a method both of encouraging informed decisions by public and private players and of favoring those activities (through tax or credit benefits) that are deemed conducive to the public good.

As the public sector grew particularly through new social policies, planning focused increasingly on the public sector broadly defined. By the 1980s governmental revenues accounted for nearly 60 percent of the GDP and although most of those funds were transferred to local and regional governments or to individual beneficiaries for spending decisions, the overall size and balance of public finance required systematic forecasting and planning. Nordic governments (and indeed most OECD states) currently project progammatic commitments and revenue estimates five or ten years forward. For example, the principal Norwegian planning document is the government's long-term program prepared by the Ministry of Finance in consultation with the other departments. With detailed forecasts and alternatives for the ensuing four-year period, the long-term plan is presented several months prior to the quadrennial parliamentary elections. This document is basically a prospectus of the current government's economic policy intentions for the next parliamentary term, presented with a solid statistical base and some discussion of the underlying economic and political assumptions.

The program is debated in parliament and usually provides a focus for the election campaign that follows. In practice, it does not formally commit the government and after the elections, either the new or the continuing government must reassess economic policies. At best, it requires that future economic policies be thought out and subjected to public scrutiny with the help of economists and the press. Forcing the government to put its economic cards on the table and the opposition to respond increases the possibility of broader and more focused participation. As a result, economic policy making also may be more effective and democratic.

Although the concept of economic planning remained popular in the abstract with the Swedish Social Democrats, it has not been a major instrument of economic policy during peacetime (Lewin 1975, pp. 282–302). As in Norway, the tendency in Sweden has been to rely more on reports forecasting the consequences of alternative policies. The purpose behind such reports is to provide a common basis for political debate and to anticipate the medium- (three to five years) and longer-term (ten to fifteen years) results of previous policy decisions. The average citizen is unlikely to pay much attention to these technical economic documents. The main interest organizations, however, have the technical expertise to evaluate the accuracy and consequences of the government's forecasts. The press—both popular and sophisticated—tries to interpret and disseminate the abstract economic data, while the political parties alert their constituencies (Lindbeck 1974, pp. 165–83). Hence, planning has evolved into a tool for democratic policy making. By making the economic and political assumptions driving current economic policy known, the Swedish government also broadens the debate, allows alternatives to emerge, and permits interested groups to mobilize for or against the policy.

Economic planning did not appear on the Danish policy agenda until the 1970s. This was in part a result of the weakness of the Social Democrats. Unlike their Norwegian and Swedish counterparts, they were far short of a parliamentary majority. Therefore, their economic policies required reliance on the center parties, whose liberalism eschewed centralized planning. The radical socialists (the Communists until 1960 and the Socialist People's party thereafter), who did favor planning, were an anathema to the Social Democrats until 1966. After the market revolution of the late 1980s and 1990s, the radical left remains the last bastion of faith in economic planning. The center and left has increasingly embraced regulation and cooperative European measures as means of taming market excesses.

During the past decade an increasingly important source of economic policy evaluation and debate have been private domestic and international organizations. The economic research departments of domestic corporatist organizations—the labor movement, industrial associations and even quasi-official agencies like the Danish Economic Council (*Det økonomiske Råd*)—provide independent assessments of national economic policies and performance. All of the Nordic countries face periodic assessments of their public and private economic situation by the International Monetary Fund, the OECD, and for Denmark, Finland, and Sweden, the Commission of the EU. These international agencies speak with considerable authority, but they are sensitive to the political concerns of their member governments and, of course, have no statutory authority. National and international private banks and financial institutions assess economic performance and credit worthiness.

Finally the quasi-autonomous central or reserve banks make key economic decisions. Sweden's Central Bank (*Riksbanken*) is the world's oldest existing bank, dating from 1668; Denmark's and Norway's banks stem from the early nineteenth century (Scott 1977, p. 263). Although in their early years the central banks were privately owned and performed commercial functions (such activities persisted in Denmark until the postwar period), they are today public institutions exclusively concerned with monetary policy (principally interest rates) and the stability of the national banking systems. Given the importance of monetary policy to all aspects of public and private finance, this is a major source of political and economic power. The central banks are today legally subordinated to parliamentary and governmental control, but their domestic autonomy in practice remains considerable. Parliament appoints the central banks' governing boards, while the government appoints the director for a set term. The central bank directors are known for their independent commentary on economic developments, and the professional bank staff provides another source of economic evaluation. Although a contemporary director could never act as independently as the conservative Nicolai Rygg did during his remarkable tenure at the Norges Bank from 1920 to 1947,[6] it is still an influential position (Hodne 1983, pp. 30, 136–37). In the age of the EMU and financial globalization, most small countries have very modest monetary independence.

With the renaissance of global capital markets after 1950 and the removal of nearly all capital controls (i.e., restrictions on the export or import of money) in the Nordic countries since the late 1980s, national central banks like their governments have lost autonomy while gaining resources. Nordic interest rates closely shadow those set by the new European Central Bank. Exchange rate policies have diverged, even among Scandinavian EU members. To date only Finland has fully joined the EU's Economic and Monetary Union (EMU); the Finnish markka was replaced by the Euro in 2002. The Danish krone has been firmly tied to the German mark or Euro since 1982, but Danish voters turned down the EMU in September 2000. Following the economic crisis in the early 1990s, Sweden's venerable Riksbank again has again received substantial autonomy to keep inflation at about 2 percent per year and to manage the country's floating currency.[7] Norway and Iceland also retained flexible exchange rates for their national currencies, which are pegged to baskets of their trading partners' currencies, but their monetary independence is limited.

Corporatist Participation

Democratic corporatism, like parliamentary politics, focuses on economic issues. Policies affecting wages and salaries, farm price supports, and fishing policies all involve regular consultation between the government and the appropriate interest organization. Corporatist policy making also consists of quiet and continuous bargaining among organizations, parties, and bureaucrats. The policy environment of the small Scandinavian societies is influential here. Although the outlooks of the professional staff of these organizations differ depending upon the interests they represent, they have similar academic training. A whole generation of Norwegian economists was influenced by the work of Ragnar Frisch, especially in the area of economic planning. Frisch was internationally known as one of the founders of econometrics as well as a strong advocate of state-led economic planning. Personal acquaintance is normal. There is continuity and a common interest in consensus, achieved in part through the emphasis on objectivity in investigating policy alternatives, which is so often emphasized as a Scandinavian characteristic. Recall Tom Anton's (1969) concise, four-word description of the policy process in Sweden: consensual, open, rationalistic, and deliberative (CORD). With modifications, these observations can be extended to the other Nordic countries as well. This emphasis on factualness and detail reinforces the consensual political system in which policy is made.

The degree to which corporatist organizations actually made public policy was historically crucial in the Nordic countries. To take the extreme case, in the highly centralized collective-bargaining process (described in detail in Chapter 10) interest organizations had created a means to make wage formation fundamentally a political decision. Not surprisingly, this has led to substantial governmental involvement in collective bargaining. In fact, it sometimes seems that collective bargaining is tripartite, with the government as much involved as labor and management. For example, the implementation of the solidaristic wage policy, which has substantially reduced wage differentials, was a far-reaching step toward income equality. But it is also a major policy departure that was settled in bargaining by the LO and the employers' federation of each of the three countries.

In an era that stresses markets, European economic integration and globalization, can democratic corporatism survive?

Democratic goals in economic management must coexist with strong commitments to the principles of a market economy and the collective assertion of public interests. Although relations with the EU have been especially controversial among economic interest organizations, corporatism, generous social programs, and taming of market forces are high on the agenda of many other EU states, especially Germany, France, the Netherlands, Belgium, and Austria. The role of foreign trade and international economic relations common to the small Scandinavian economies places additional restraints on national policy responses. These are detailed later in this chapter, but ironically Europeanization may be the most effective alternative to the extremes of globalization. Nevertheless, the Nordic tradition of a large public sector and of active state economic policy over the previous fifty years, as well as the corporatist decision-making process all ensure a collective pluralism; that is, a competitive bargaining process among nearly all social and economic groups. Walter Korpi (1978) has called the process "the democratic class struggle." This may be overly dramatic especially as traditional class consciousness has faded. Duels between opposing economists armed with computer printouts is not the usual portrayal of class struggle. The battle is tamed by consensus on economic realities. This, in turn, is largely the result of the democratic politics and egalitarian social policies of the welfare state. Small, open, and interdependent industrial countries cannot afford lengthy delusions.

POLITICAL ECONOMY AND THE WELFARE STATE

The economic reconstruction programs inaugurated during the Depression and after World War II have been honed in Scandinavia into macroeconomic policy tools sufficiently powerful and comprehensive to be models of applied Keynesianism.[8] When the economy turned down, automatic stabilizers, such as unemployment compensation (which approximates 90% of the average industrial wage) and income-related payments to families, maintained consumer purchasing power. Until the 1980s public works projects, special business investment accounts and other measures were used to soak up unemployment.

The reasons for public-sector growth are related to welfare needs, not economic management. But the result is to create a large sector where demand and employment remain constant in the short term, regardless of the economic cycle. In fact, as can be seen in Table 9.3, there has been a rapid growth in public-sector expenditures and employment since 1960. In 1965, the size of Scandinavia's public sector did not differ significantly from other Western European countries; thirty years later, it was significantly larger. Now the gap between the Nordic countries and other EU members has stopped growing, but public spending is 15 to 30 percentage points of GDP above the United States and public employment is more than twice that of the U.S. As we shall see, however, in economic terms social spending in Scandinavia diverges less from the EU and American norms than raw statistics indicate.

Scandinavian Keynesian policies ran into four serious obstacles in the postwar period. The first was inherent in Keynesianism itself: Inflating domestic demand not only reduced unemployment, it also increased inflation. The Social Democrats' goal of full employment could not be reached through simple demand-side Keynesianism without also achieving destructively high rates of inflation. The second obstacle lay outside the Keynesian model: In an internationalized economy, recessions and booms were also international. The tools suited to managing the domestic economy could prove insufficient in the face of international economic storms. The third obstacle was the general problem of financing very large public sectors without producing serious distortions in the economy. The fourth problem centers on efforts to resolve such financing problems by borrowing large sums on the international market. Let us look at each of these obstacles in turn.

Full Employment without Inflation

The problem with achieving full employment through expansionary macroeconomic policies is that this course creates substantial inflationary pressure before full employment is reached. Several Swedish economists, including most notably Gösta Rehn, drew the conclusion in the 1940s that

Table 9.3
Receipts and Outlays of Government as Percentage of GDP, 1960–99

	Average over period 1960-73 1974-79 1980-89 1990-99				Public sector employment % labor force 1996†
Denmark					
Receipts	35.4	45.2	52.0	54.3	30.5
Outlays	33.8	46.7	56.5	57.7	
Finland					
Receipts	32.6	41.7	44.8	50.7	25.1
Outlays	30.3	38.3	43.1	55.1	
Iceland					
Receipts	31.2	32.0	35.1	36.7*	
Outlays	29.6	33.6	36.5	38.9	19.8
Norway					
Receipts	40.2	48.4	50.3	50.9	30.6
Outlays	36.7	47.0	46.6	49.8	
Sweden					
Receipts	41.7	54.4	59.4	57.4	30.7
Outlays	38.9	54.4	62.9	63.2	

EU 15					
Receipts	34.4	39.5	43.0	43.8	NA
Outlays	35.6	43.8	48.6	49.5	
US					
Receipts	27.6	29.7	31.0	32.8*	13.2
Outlays	29.1	32.2	35.3	34.3	

*1996 or 1997 (last single year available). Receipts and expenditures are for all levels of government: national, regional, and local. *Receipts* include taxes and all sources of governmental income (e.g., rail tickets), and *outlays* include direct cash transfers to citizens and businesses (e.g., pensions and subsidies).

†Public employment consists of two components: traditional public administration and defense personnel and people employed in education, health care, and social service. These are overwhelmingly public in the Nordic countries, but often private in the United States. The traditional distinction between public and private has been clouded by trends toward privatizing the delivery of public services and public subsides for nominally privately provided service (e.g., about 45% of health care costs are paid by the public sector in the Untied States).

Sources: OECD (1999b, p. 72); OECD (2000, p. 68); and OECD (2001c, pp. 32–33).

the solution was not to rely on this course of action, but rather to couple a generally restrictive macroeconomic policy with an active labor-market policy of selective, microeconomic measures that focus on specific areas of high unemployment in individual industries or towns. Such measures, it was hypothesized, could also increase the flexibility of the labor market through the retraining and relocation of individual workers.

The policy was presented to the 1951 LO Congress. As it was developed in the 1950s and 1960s, the active labor-market policy called for the county and national labor-market boards (Arbetsmarknadsstyrelsen, or AMS) to provide not only employment services, but also training programs, relocation subsidies, rehabilitation, and comprehensive local labor-market planning. Regular labor-market board activities were coupled with regional development measures in 1965 to bring employment to high unemployment areas, while emergency employment measures at the municipal level, pioneered in the 1930s, were used with increasing sophistication.[9]

Swedish job-training programs are impressive both in size and in length. During the employment crisis of the 1990s, they absorbed more than one-third of those without work. Although they continue to provide training and economic support, their original goal of increasing economic modernization and mobility has faded (Flanagan 1987, p. 158). The universality of pension, health, and welfare benefits, which has decoupled benefits from individual jobs, also increased labor mobility. Special measures are used to deal with the problems of the disabled and others who might be considered difficult to employ. Direct wage subsidies are used to encourage the recruitment of the long-term unemployed and other less-competitive job seekers.

As a consequence of the active labor-market policy, until the 1980s unemployment occasioned by layoffs was treated as an opportunity. Municipalities and other public agencies are encouraged, through central government subsidies, to develop plans for major public-works projects. Such plans are put on the shelf until the need for them arises. While these projects have the same impact as make-work projects in putting the unemployed back to work, typically they also provide needed public facilities or reconstruction of the public infrastructure.

The assumption that such measures would be relatively short-term (covering business-cycle swings) proved unrealistic for the prolonged slowdown after 1975. Long-term unemployment spread Swedish activation measures to Denmark and later Finland. Table 9.4 shows the spread of such active labor market policies in the Nordic and Western European countries as opposed to the modest measures in Britain, Canada, and the United States. They have been greatly supplemented (especially for younger workers) with educational requirements and opportunities,

Table 9.4

Spending on Unemployment Policies, as Percentage of GDP, 1985–96

	1985	1990	1996	"Active" share (percent) of labor market policies (c. 1996)	Unemployment Compensation	
					Replacement Rate	Maximum Duration
Denmark	1.1	1.1	1.9	31	80	260 weeks
Finland	0.9	1.0	1.7	32	81	100 weeks
Norway	0.6	0.9	1.2	56	73	156 weeks
Sweden	2.1	1.7	2.4	51	85	60 weeks
EU	0.9	0.9	1.2	35	n/a	n/a
US	0.3	0.2	0.2	39	60	26 weeks

Notes: No information on Iceland (but minimal unemployment).
Replacement rate is the percentage of an insured average production worker's earnings replaced by unemployment compensation in the first month of unemployment. Insurance coverage in the Nordic countries is nearly universal, but in the United States often less than half the unemployed draw unemployment compensation primarily because of the short time frame. They are entitled, however, to other forms of income security (e.g., food stamps).
Sources: OECD (1998, pp. 7–8, 25); U.S. Social Security Administration (1999).

while older long-term unemployed have been removed from the labor market by early-retirement programs.

These measures accommodated major structural economic changes not without pain, but without severe hardship and community distress. Consider the Swedish response to the shipyard crisis. Before the international economic crisis of the 1970s, Sweden was the world's biggest per capita builder of ships. Swedish shipyards expanded rapidly in the 1960s, with specialization in very large oil tankers. But as demand for high-priced petroleum stagnated, the market for new tankers dried up and competition from Asian shipbuilders intensified. Initially the state acquired the ailing shipyards and sought to restructure some of them to smaller, more specialized work such as repairs and offshore petroleum industry. Unfortunately the crisis became permanent and led to massive closures with temporary employment and subsidy programs easing the transition along the Swedish west coast. Similar dilemmas befell the Danish and Finnish shipyards. New jobs appeared, especially in information and biotechnology, but they required a different workforce than the older, "metal-bashing" trades.

The problem of employing young entrants to the labor market, which is common to all Western industrial democracies, was exacerbated in Scandinavia as in many other European countries by high minimum wages (set by collective bargaining) and the job security laws. Those laws tended to reduce turnover and new openings. The Swedish response is symptomatic of the Swedish approach to employment policy: an age-specific program for teenage job seekers. Since 1984, AMS has been required to find or provide work for all eighteen- or nineteen-year-olds within three weeks of their registering as being unemployed. Denmark adopted similar legislation a few years later. That has required subsidized employment in the private sector and direct employment in the public sector. Both private-sector jobs (established by agreement between the labor market organizations and heavily subsidized by the government) and those in the public sector are specifically designed as make-work jobs. Such jobs may be of questionable utility for the society, but the Swedish view is that unless the young are incorporated into the labor market, some will suffer a permanent economic handicap with undesirable long-term social consequences. About one-half of those passing through the state program have gone directly into the open job market.

Although emergency measures have mitigated some of the economic and social effects of higher unemployment, they are expensive remedies for fundamental structural change in the economy and labor market. It has been a generation since rapid industrial growth could absorb employees into good and secure jobs. All of the Nordic countries have emphasized increased formal education to prepare young people for the demanding jobs of the future. Structural changes at home improved employment prospects in the late 1990s in large part because changes in collective bargaining (discussed in the next chapter) restored Nordic competitiveness in an increasingly European and global economy.

International Constraints

With between 32 and 39 percent of all national economic activity dependent upon exports, global conditions weigh heavily on economic developments and plans in the Nordic countries (see Chapter 7). There is, of course, room to maneuver. Anticipation of international developments and timely responses to them can produce at least short-term national advantages. The decision to build up domestic technical and managerial expertise in the petroleum sector has strengthened Norway's position. Denmark's more restrained industrial policies may have encouraged a faster restructuring of export industries. Finland's specialization in communications technology fueled its economic recovery in the 1990s. Sweden's ambitious countercyclical economic schemes collapsed in part because it did not provide for structural changes to meet new global economic conditions. Meanwhile Iceland's aggressive expansion of offshore economic zones (for fishing) and partial success in managing fish stocks have allowed it maintain a healthy fishing industry. Thus the Nordic states have prospered despite growing global dependency.

Interdependence remains a two-sided coin. When petroleum prices plunged in 1999 to under $11 per barrel, Norway's North Sea oil was no longer profitable. A year later oil was over $30 per barrel and gushing revenues threatened to overheat the economy. These swings have recurred regularly since 1974, and in part to avoid a boom-and-bust economy, Norway created a massive petroleum fund to invest much of the revenue offshore (i.e., in foreign capital markets) to insulate the Norwegian economy from such wild swings and to provide future resources when the petroleum reserves are depleted.

Since the 1950s there has been a growing distinction between those Scandinavian economic sectors that must compete on a world market where cost constraints are evident to both business and labor and those sectors that are protected by their nature or by public policy. Obviously, the public sector is one such protected area; international markets do not affect the labor costs for civil servants or their equivalents. The construction industry and much of the service sector are similarly not subject to international competition.[10] Agriculture and fisheries remain either nationally protected (Norway and Iceland) or through the EU Common Agricultural Policies (Denmark, Finland, and Sweden) (Ingebritsen 1998). All advanced industrial economies face the tension between wages in competitive and protected sectors as well as in those sectors where productivity increases are clearly visible and subject to greater technological innovation. In the Scandinavian countries, the coordinated wage-bargaining policies discussed in Chapter 10 permit a simple solution: The wage pattern is set in the competitive sector and that settlement is duplicated in the protected sector.

Financing Large Public Sectors: Taxation

Taxes are a highly visible aspect of Scandinavian economic policy. Not only have taxes been raised dramatically in the postwar period to pay for new public programs, but the tax law has been an instrument to encourage or discourage specific economic and social activity. Significant tax-law changes have accompanied the growth of the public sector. As a result taxes have become a major issue in the Scandinavian welfare states.

It is easier to discuss the direct impact of taxes on the Scandinavian economies than to discern their political and social consequences. A tax system usually boils down to two questions: (1) What is taxed? and (2) How high are the various taxes? The concise answers to these respective questions are "everything" and "very high."

Denmark, Finland, Norway, and Sweden are consistently among the five most heavily taxed OECD countries. In 1999, Nordic taxes ranged from 35 percent of the GDP in Iceland to 52 percent of GDP in Sweden. In the same year, the weighted average for EU states (which include Denmark, Finland, and Sweden) was 41 percent, while the U.S. level was 29 percent (OECD 2001a, p. 8).[11] Table 9.5 shows the distribution of tax revenue among tax sources in Scandinavia. There is significant national variation. No OECD country collects less of its taxes through social security contributions than Denmark. Only Turkey and New Zealand have placed as much weight on taxation of income and profits as Denmark.

Danish taxes focus on domestic incomes and consumption and may indirectly contribute to the lower labor costs of Danish firms. Unfortunately for politicians, Danish taxes are highly visible; that is, the taxpayer knows rather precisely how much is paid on income and property, and at least the rate of consumption taxes. Finnish, Norwegian, and Swedish taxes fit closely into the European pattern of placing greater weight on earmarked and less-visible social security contributions. Iceland benefits from its geographic position; people cannot easily cross a border to avoid consumption taxes. Denmark and Norway were notorious for their tax-protest parties in the 1970s, but tax reforms in the 1980s relieved some of the pressures and protest parties have generally moved to other issues. Unlike their American counterparts, antitax politicians in the Nordic countries are aggressively asked which public programs they intended to cut to pay for tax cuts.

Given the weight of taxes on consumption and the usually proportional local and regional income taxation, Scandinavian taxes are only modestly progressive. Recent tax reforms have lowered marginal tax rates while broadening the base. Capital gains are treated relatively lightly, as are

Table 9.5
Sources of Tax Revenues as a Percentage of Total Tax Revenue, 1998

Type of tax	personal income	corporate income	social security	property	goods and services
Denmark	51.6	5.6	3.9	3.6	33.2
Finland	32.3	9.0	25.2	2.4	30.7
Iceland	35.2	3.4	8.3	7.1	45.9
Norway	27.3	9.7	23.3	2.4	37.2
Sweden	35.0	5.7	33.5	3.7	21.6

EU*	23.9	8.7	32.7	5.4	28.8
US	40.5	9.0	23.7	10.6	16.2

*Weighted average. *Social security* includes compulsory wage taxes for social and health programs.
Source: van den Noord and Heady (2001, p. 10).

business taxes, provided enterprises channel significant sums into internal investment. The result is a high level of taxation on average citizens. Norwegian petroleum taxes (which fall on petroleum consumers and firms) may counteract this slightly, but such revenues have thus far proven highly volatile because they are dependent upon world petroleum prices and offshore investment.

High taxes are a Scandinavian fact of life given the consensus on social and other public expenditures. How such taxes should be raised, and the unintended economic and social consequences of high taxes are recurring political issues. In 2000 a single Dane with an average industrial wage (roughly equivalent to $30,000 per year) typically paid 37 percent of his or her total income in national and local income taxes. A professional couple with two children and with two incomes (about $80,000) would pay about 41 percent in income taxes (Denmark, Ministry of Taxation, 2001). All post–income tax household expenditures, of course, are subject to the ubiquitous VAT and, often, to excise taxes as well.

Economists of various political persuasions have objected to the distortion of economic activity as a larger number of taxpayers have faced high marginal taxes. Before the reforms of the past fifteen years, Denmark furnished the most extreme cases. The most amazing involved tax-advantaged, limited partnership leasing schemes for coastal cargo ships that turned thousands of landlubbers who couldn't tell the difference between port and starboard into ship owners. The most costly was the fact that the tax deductibility of interest on real-estate and consumer loans combined with high marginal tax rates made housing loans completely insensitive to interest rates. That insensitivity fueled a real-estate boom that drove up housing prices and housing costs. Although housing loans are still subsidized through tax deductions, the subsidy has been essential cut in half for newer home buyers. Tax shelters, loopholes, and outright tax fraud (particularly *black labor*, or working off the books) remain problems but less so as EU tax policies and rates have become more similar. Not only is the loss of revenue substantial, but such practices also encourage an unquantifiable but serious demoralization of economic society.[12]

Tax reform was implemented in Denmark, Norway, and Sweden in the 1980s. Following an international trend, marginal tax rates have been lowered (by 10–15 percentage points at the top) in return for reductions in popular tax loopholes and deductions, especially for interest on private loans; this broadened the tax base. Most of the Nordic countries have simplified their tax and benefits systems to make their generous social benefits generally taxable. Hence benefits that go to high-income people are clawed back at 50 to 60 percent tax rates while low-income recipients pay modest income taxes on pensions and benefits. The tax base has been widened, usually by reducing deductions (especially for interest on private loans) and by increasing social security taxes; these are much less visible to the taxpayer (although not for independent small businesses, which have the greatest opportunity to hide income) and raise less political resistance (Steinmo 1993, pp. 185–92).

A significant tax innovation in several of the Nordic countries during the past decade has been so-called Green Taxes. These are excise taxes on consumption that has a negative environmental impact. Typically they focus on energy that releases carbon dioxide and other wastes into the atmosphere. The Nordic countries have traditionally taxed consumption heavily, especially anything smacking of luxury and/or immorality. Alcohol, tobacco and gasoline are notoriously walloped. Green Taxes replace earlier puritanism with environmental activism. They have retarded consumption and encouraged energy efficiency while helping these small countries reduce their CO_2 emissions.[13]

Tax reform can reduce irrational economic behavior, but the bills still must be paid. Burdens have been redistributed, but not reduced. High social security taxes are borne by businesses in the first instance, but eventually by society as a whole. To hire a young unskilled worker in Sweden or Norway costs a firm not only the starting wage of more than $9 per hour, but an additional cost of $3 per hour in social security and related fees. In the end, the tax issue leads to the question of whether Scandinavia can afford its public sector and especially the lavish social expenditures that account for so large a proportion of the costs of the welfare state.

Beyond Fiscal Crisis

Scandinavian taxes were high enough to be disruptive, but not high enough to cover government expenditures during the oil crisis. Tax revenues remained stagnant or rose slowly, while expenditures expanded rapidly.

Between 1960 and 1990, governmental expenditures in Denmark, Finland, and Sweden soared at more than twice the Western European rate. In Norway they grew slightly less than average, albeit from a high base (see Table 9.3). Tax revenues kept pace until the oil crisis. Revenues began to lag badly behind expenditures in Denmark and Sweden in the late 1970s. This reflects the fall of growth rates in Denmark and Sweden after 1973 and continuing, oil-fired rapid growth in Norway. The results was growing public domestic and foreign debt not only to finance investment, as in Norway, or to bridge a recession, as in Sweden, but to finance current public and private consumption. This made substantial sense in terms of Keynesian economics, but the size of the deficits was unsustainable in the long run. Public debt continued to soar into the 1990s as a bank crisis swept across Finland, Norway, and Sweden, and economic shocks plunged Finland and Sweden into a severe crisis between 1990 and 1993.

Small, trading economies cannot ignore indefinitely the need to respond, and as policy changes took hold in the 1990s (and the world economy improved after 1992) the disastrous plunge was reversed. By the end of the decade levels of public indebtedness in the Nordic countries fell to less than 60 percent of GDP, the acceptable standard (so-called convergence criteria) adopted by the EU.

The solution has been fiscal restraint, currency adjustments (especially in Iceland, Norway, and Sweden), and economic growth. All of the Nordic countries have run surpluses both in their public budgets and international current (trading) accounts after 1995. Indeed Norway's large petroleum earnings have been partially diverted into the Petroleum Fund invested in foreign securities to prevent excessive domestic demand and the preserve some of the funds for future needs. The fund's assets grew rapidly from 47.8 billion Norwegian krone (approximately $6.5 billion) at the end of 1996 to 609 billion krone (approximately $82 billion) at the end of 2002 (Norges Bank 2003). This soaring fortune makes it hard politically to restrain public spending or demands for tax cuts as evidenced by the debates in the September 2001 Norwegian parliamentary elections.

DOES ECONOMIC POLICY HAVE A FUTURE?

The Scandinavian welfare state is not a theoretical design; it is a pragmatic solution. Its dynamics change as new needs and opportunities are placed on the policy agenda. Scandinavians are not alone in discovering that the welfare state is an expensive proposition. Throughout its history, opponents have concentrated their attack on the cost to taxpayers, business firms, and society at large. Cost and affordability have been nearly the sole domestic critiques of the Scandinavian welfare states.

With the recent improvements in public finances and foreign debts as well as the five good years (1995–2000), the Nordic states can meet their promises in social expenditures in the near term. Pessimistic assessments of the "fiscal crisis of welfare state" have receded (see Lindbeck 1994 versus Lindbeck 1997) but have certainly not disappeared. All of the Nordic states are highly dependent on the European economies as well as global developments. Demographic pressures, especially the rising proportion of elderly, will continue to put pressure on public expenditures. With political support for higher taxes unlikely, they must rely increasingly on economic growth, productivity, and increasing public-sector reallocations and efficiencies for fiscal balance. The lessons of the recent crisis must not be forgotten.

Social programs will compete fiercely with other public spending for meager additional resources. Improvements will have to come through better administration of existing programs or through reallocation among them. Economic policies will have to be smarter, for they will not be able to count as much on economic growth. Privatization of public enterprises has continued with mixed results. Efforts to use market mechanisms within the public sector have also advanced despite political and especially labor union skepticism.

As small countries in an increasingly internationalized economy, Scandinavians are finding that the tools used successfully in the past will not necessarily work in the future. The Scandinavian welfare states share the common interdependence of modern international economic relations. As discussed in Chapter 7, the Nordic countries have managed globalization reasonably well. The EU (and the EEA for Iceland and Norway) provides a bulwark against some of the excesses of globalization. When there is a Euro-consensus on economic and social policy (a major theme in EU politics during the past decade), the smaller member states gain substantial weight in decisions. The convergence criteria have thus served more as a resource for political flexibility than as a restraint. Although the EU is frequently blamed for intrusion into domestic politics, one can argue that it provides a more solid economic and policy foundation for much of the Nordic welfare agenda.

Because of the organizational aspects of Scandinavian politics, economic policy is probably more pluralistic there than in most other democracies. Constitutional bodies, including parliament and the ministries; quasi-autonomous agencies such as the central bank; and the nominally private corporatist sector of business and commercial associations, labor unions, and grassroots organizations, are all significant. Consensual political values permeate the process of managing the economy. Most but not all of this policy culture is compatible with the EU. Consensus is not assured either domestically, regionally or globally. There must be leadership, vision, and effective communication. With few exceptions major groups can at least participate in the process to reach political accommodation. Nevertheless, in each of the five countries, there is ample evidence that conflict is not merely a historical memory. Policy confrontations remain part of Nordic politics: relations with the European Union, pension reforms,[14] budget allocations (especially in the health and social sectors), to name a few contentious continuing issues. Even in Scandinavia, the buck has to stop somewhere. Policy decisions remain political. To paraphrase the late Olof Palme's phrase, "politics is to choose."

NOTES

1. For example, the total labor costs for the average Swedish industrial worker in 1999 was approximately 275,000 Swedish krona (about $27,000) including social-insurance taxes. In constant prices, it had risen from 76,000 Swedish krona in 1940, 126,000 in 1960, and 249,000 in 1980. This does not take into account nonmonetary gains, such as improved public services, shorter working hours,

longer holidays, and so forth. But note the slowdown after 1980. Swedish Institute (1996 and 2000).

2. Although Finland was part of the Russian Empire and, thus, a belligerent in World War I, its young men were excused from the Russian draft, and Finnish units did not fight. Some young Finns went to Germany, where they were trained for military action as part of the German-sponsored Jäger (light infantry) corps. These units would be important in the Finnish civil war following independence in 1917 and the Russian Bolshevik Revolution. Finland was, however, affected by various blockades and wartime economic restrictions (Jussila, Hentilä, and Nevakivi 1999, pp. 90–91).

3. These "Stockholm school" economists anticipated John Maynard Keynes's theory justifying countercyclical fiscal policy. Keynes himself anticipated his theory by calling for government stimulation of the sluggish British economy in the 1928 Liberal party manifesto. Like Keynes, most of the Stockholm school were politically active and saw the need to respond to a crisis without waiting for theoretical justification (see Lundberg 1985 and Pekkarinen 1989).

4. The Finnish reparations bill to the Soviet Union through 1952 was $226.5 million in 1938 prices, or about $600 million in then-current prices. This was about 10 to 15 percent of Finnish GDP. By comparison the notorious reparation burden thrust on Germany after World War I was less than 3 percent of GDP (Jörberg and Krantz 1976, pp. 430–32). Although the reparation payments were a severe hardship on Finland (despite some Soviet concessions after 1947) in the immediate postwar years, they forced economic and industrial modernization and paved the way to a profitable and normal trade relationship with the USSR (and other Eastern European communist regimes) until the Soviet collapse in 1990. Even the Soviets were impressed with the quality and promptness of Finnish reparations. This may have encouraged a more moderate line in Moscow, which prevented the Finnish Communists from attempting a coup in 1948.

5. The higher petroleum price spurred development of Denmark's North Sea sector, which by the mid-1980s began to produce significant quantities of oil and, especially, gas. In addition Denmark undertook large investments in energy conservation, efficiency, and alternative production, producing a world-class wind generation industry. By 1990 Denmark was essentially energy self-sufficient. Unlike the political restraint in economic restructuring, the Danish state was quite active in the energy sector.

6. Rugg's tenure took him through fourteen governments and regimes, including the historic rise of the Labor party as well as the infamous period of German occupation and collaboration (under Vidkun Quisling) during World War II.

7. Sweden continues to pursue a determined "cheap krona" policy, which has assisted it greatly in regaining international competitiveness over the past decade. Over the past twenty years, the Swedish krona has fallen by about 40 percent in relation to the U.S. dollar and about 25 percent in relation to the EURO-12 currencies (plus Denmark). This has accelerated its economic revival but lowered its relative standard of living.

8. For a concise analysis of Nordic Keynesianism through the late 1980s, see Pekkarinen (1989). He notes that Finland has a much weaker Keynesian tradition than the other Nordic countries. Over the past decade as Finland has become an

ordinary West European economy and a full member of the EU and EMU, this deviation has become smaller.

9. For a comprehensive English description of Swedish labor-market policy, see Jangenäs (1985); for historical developments, see Öhman (1974); for Rehn's own retrospective analysis, see Rehn (1985). More concise are Flanagan (1987) and Vartiainen (2001).

10. With the public sector alone accounting for about one-third of overall employment (in Sweden, 39%) and major parts of the private sector also protected from foreign competition, this noncompetitive sector is of vital importance to incomes policy. Excessive wage increases in the sheltered sector can make it difficult to maintain a competitive export sector or to curb public expenditures. See Lindbeck (1997), Martin (2000), and Bosworth and Rivlin (1987). Since 1985 many formerly protected sectors (e.g., finance, telecommunications) have been opened to global competition.

11. These figures vary slightly from those in Table 9.3, which reflect the growth in total government receipts. Total government receipts include the revenue from public enterprises, such as utilities, fees for services, and so on. Still, paying an electric bill to a public utility is politically different from paying a tax.

12. An anecdote related by a prominent Danish politician illustrates the dilemma. He needed to have several rooms painted in his house. The painter's bid was the standard $18 per hour rate, which, after income and value-added taxes, would leave him with about $5 per hour. He offered to paint "off-the-books" for $6 per hour. The politician could not afford the legal price and would not be an accomplice to tax fraud. The result: He painted the rooms himself.

13. Gasoline, tobacco, and alcohol taxes can quadruple the retail price. Automobiles are heavily taxed with special excises and then the VAT is placed on the both the product price and excises. Value-added and sales taxes are typically 20 to 25 percent in the Nordic countries. CO_2 and some other environmental taxes are rebated to businesses and farmers, which reduces their impact considerably.

14. All of the Nordic countries have adjusted their old-age pension systems for demographic realities. Their tendency has been to supplement basic public pensions with public and private contributory pensions. Over time these will in fact relieve fiscal demands on social security programs. The major Swedish pension reform of 1998 was much more consensual than the confrontation over supplementary pensions in 1958–60 and Wage Earner Funds between 1985 and 1994.

CHAPTER 10

From Industrial Conflict to Workplace Democracy

[T]he Nordic countries have not yet reached anything close to a stable equilibrium in their class relations, at least as these are reflected in the labor market. The labor movements continue to be forces which are not only adapting to but are also changing these societies.
—Walter Korpi, 1981

Within the life span of the generation now passing from the scene, the "fortified poorhouse"—Zeth Höglund's characterization of Sweden on the eve of World War I—has been replaced by widely shared affluence. We have discussed the role of public policy and welfare state measures in this process. But it is also a consequence of the ways in which the unique strength of Scandinavian labor organizations and the Scandinavian system of collective bargaining have changed the society. Those are the subjects of this chapter.

The Scandinavian countries are characterized by the strongest trade union movements in the world. Today they organize between 55 and 90 percent of all blue-collar and white-collar workers, compared to 30 to 40 percent in the rest of Europe and 14 percent in the United States. In the rest of the West, as the service sector grew in importance relative to industry, unionization declined. In Scandinavia, it grew. Even American multinational corporations that pride themselves on being nonunion, like IBM and Toys R Us, are unionized in Scandinavia.

Historically the blue-collar unions provided the bulk of Social Democratic voters in Denmark, Norway, and Sweden. In the 1930s through the 1960s, they mobilized the political muscle for welfare state reforms. In the labor market, they raised working-class wages and benefits and shortened hours to achieve middle-class levels and to reduce economic inequality. Union-sponsored housing cooperatives built modern apartments in the suburbs to replace the city slums. Union travel agencies brought the Mediterranean sun within reach for the Scandinavian working class in the February darkness.

With virtual universal union organization, the system of collective bargaining has become a key component of the development of national prosperity. Labor and employers' organizations play a central role in Scandinavian public policy formation. Their primary political role is not lobbying parliament, providing manpower and money to political campaigns, subsidizing the party press, applying extraparliamentary pressure on the government from the streets, or supplying Royal commissions with members and expert witnesses, although they do all these things. It is rather that, collectively, they make national economic and social policy. When the majority of all wage and salaried employees are members of trade unions, and when basic contractual provisions are bargained at the national level between national labor and employer federations or at the industrial level between sectoral groups of unions and employers, as is usual in Scandinavia, the contract is no longer a private agreement. It is the cornerstone of national economic policy.

When collective bargaining is universal and centralized as it is in Scandinavia, it is simply too important to be left to private organizations. Instead, bargaining the national or major industrial sector contract is a tripartite affair, involving the government as well as labor and employers' organizations.

The contract shapes practically every aspect of the labor market policy. Wage formation, wage differentials, rates of reinvestment, and general distribution of such social benefits as vacations and work week reductions are influenced or set by national or sectoral contracts. National or sectoral contracts impact the rate of inflation and national competitiveness. The government's labor market policies, which are designed to promote full employment and flexibility in the labor market, form the context within which these contracts are hammered out. No longer an independent arena in which labor and management could fight it out, collective bargaining became a public process, as political as parliament itself, in which the adversaries at the bargaining table represented their members' long-term interest in the shape of and success of the economy, as well as their short-term interests in higher wages or higher profits.

The Scandinavian industrial relations system is part of the explanation for the generally good economic performance of the Scandinavian countries. The degree of labor peace that the system has encouraged—despite virtually universal unionization—has meant that crippling strikes and lockouts have been few and far between. The national full employment

policy, which has been the cornerstone of national economic poli
the high levels of government support for retraining and unempl
compensation mean that Scandinavian unions have been more supportive
of technological innovation than have unions elsewhere, because their
members are, to a very substantial extent, protected against its adverse
consequences. Full employment itself, in a growing, vital economy, both
holds down the costs of the welfare state and creates the resources to
finance it. The unions' success in raising the general wage level and in
narrowing wage differentials has reduced the degree of income inequality
generated in the marketplace, and helps limit the need for redistribution
through the public sector. In short, the system of industrial relations is a
key part of the Scandinavian welfare state model.

Prior to taking power in the 1930s, the Danish, Norwegian, and Swedish
Social Democrats assumed that when they won power, they would deal
with economic inequality at its source by the state taking control of the
means of production, and that workers' organizations would have a direct
role in running industry. Instead, the result of the historic compromise of
the 1930s was that the welfare state, broadly defined to include a managed
capitalistic economy, became the surrogate for socialism. Workers' organizations continued their classic role of seeking more—higher wages and
benefits and shorter hours—within the new context. The old goals could
now be pursued either through collective bargaining or through state action. Because of their dominance in the trade unions, the Social Democrats
in these three countries were able to do both simultaneously.

Historically Finland and Iceland clearly differed from the core Scandinavian model, particularly from World War I into the 1960s. They were
distinguished by strong communist factions within the unions and a far
more adversarial form of labor relations that reflected political needs as
much as wage demands. However, both have increasingly converged with
the core Scandinavian labor relations model after World War II, particularly since 1968 in Finland and since 1990 in Iceland. Differences within
the broader Scandinavian community remain, but the five national models
look increasingly similar.

Despite the relative success of the labor-relations system in Scandinavia,
it has never been without substantial strains and challenges. Some have
been internal. The growth of the public sector and of the private service
sector eclipsed numerically the manufacturing and construction workers
who were the core of the Social Democratic constituency, and the unions
had to transform themselves and their policies to serve these new constituencies. At the same time, frustrated in their drive to maximize their
members' pay by their responsibility for national economic policy, unions
turned to face the question of inequality in authority on the job and in
ownership and control of corporations. These questions, largely neglected
between the 1930s and 1960s, were again put on the agenda in the 1970s.

They resulted not only in controversy, but also in impressive reforms democratizing the economy from the shop floor to the boardroom.

While the blue-collar unions continue to have more political influence than their white-collar counterparts, over time the numerical balance has shifted toward the white-collar and professional unions. Today each country has a powerful white-collar union federation and a strong professional union federation (characterized by its members' university and professional training) along side the blue-collar federation. The white-collar federations have gradually become increasingly Social Democratic, reflecting the class backgrounds of the new white-collar workers, and the professional unions have become more militant. Doctors, nurses, economists, professors, and even army officers have been found on the picket lines.

Other strains and challenges, however, were external, especially as economic globalization became a crucial issue in the 1980s and 1990s. With increasing exposure to international competition, role of centralized bargaining was reconsidered. There was a transition from generally negotiating a single national contract to bargaining several sectoral, industrywide agreements. This has undercut the push toward wage equality across the entire labor market and created greater flexibility in wage rates to respond to international conditions. Otherwise, it has altered more the form than the substance of Scandinavian industrial relations.

As we look forward into the new century, globalization poses new challenges. How should Scandinavian labor handle the growing importance of transnational corporations? Should unions themselves turn to international or at least European-wide collective bargaining? If capital moves to lower wage areas, must labor concern itself with ensuring adequate capital reinvestment, especially in the geographic periphery that makes up such a large part of Scandinavia? Or must unions accept an end to full employment? In short, how must unions change to protect their members' interest in the new global economic order?

THE POLITICS OF LABOR MARKET ORGANIZATION

The historical prerequisite for Social Democratic political dominance in Denmark, Norway, and Sweden has been the party's political hegemony in a powerful, unified trade union movement. The nineteenth-century pioneers of the labor movement liked the metaphor that walking requires two legs: The party was the one, the unions, the other. The party represented the working class in the political arena by fighting for its political rights against the representatives of the old order; the unions represented the working class by fighting for its economic rights against employers. The organic connection between party and unions proved crucial in creating and developing the welfare state and in the labor market.

Scandinavian trade unions are set apart by their strength. They organize between 55 percent and 90 percent of all wage and salaried employees. As can be seen in Table 10.1, the Nordic unions have increased their organizational percentages throughout the postwar period, especially in Finland, which was playing catch-up. This is particularly striking in relation to other European and American unions. (Note that the Scandinavian figures in Table 10.1 are not fully comparable with those elsewhere. Finnish and Norwegian organization percentages are exaggerated by the inclusion of retired and student members not in the labor force; this reflects the fact that being a union member is a matter of identification for

Table 10.1
Trade-Union Density in Selected Western Nations, 1950–97 (union membership as a percentage of the gainfully employed)

	1950	1960	1970	1980	1990	1995	1997
Denmark	55.5	61.8	62.6	87.8	88.9	93.2	89.9
Norway		57.2	57.9	64.4	70.3	72.5	71.3
Sweden	67.3	70.7	66.6	78.2	82.4	87.5	86.4
Finland	33.1	34.4	57.4	80.9	87.6	95.5	95.6
Iceland					88.0*	86.2	84.1
Austria	66.3	65.8	63.6	59.6	56.2	49.1	46.6
Belgium	43.3	51.6	54.9	75.7	77.6	85.0	
France	30.2	19.2	21.0	17.1	9.2	8.6	
Germany	40.8	38.7	37.7	40.6	38.5	35.5	33.4
Italy	43.8	28.5	38.5	49.0	39.2	38.0	
Netherlands	44.2	44.2	39.8	39.4	29.5	30.2	28.9
United Kingdom		44.5	48.5	54.5	38.1	32.1	30.2
United States	22.0	23.6	22.6	22.0	16.1	14.9	14.5
Canada	29.5	32.3	32.6	30.5	33.1		31.5

Note: Scandinavian and European union data express total reported union membership divided by the gainfully employed. Although the percentages are consistent from year to year, they overstate Norwegian and Finnish union membership relative to the other Scandinavian countries by including retirees and unemployed union members; comparable density figures for 1997 are 55 percent and 78 percent for Norway and Finland, respectively.
*1993.
Sources: Waddington and Hoffman (2000, pp. 54–55); *Statistical Abstract of the United States* (various years). (Washington, D.C.: U.S. Bureau of the Census); *Canada Year Book, 1992* (Ottawa: Statistics Canada); M. C. Urquhart and K. A. H. Buckley, editors, *Historical Statistics of Canada* (Toronto: Macmillian Company of Canada, 1983); Akyeampong (1999, p. 23); Statistics Iceland, 2001, *Labour Market Statistics 2000,* http://www.hagstofa.is/talneafn/vinna2000/english/labour 2000.htm, Table 7.1.8.

life, not just a matter of convenience in working years. A more accurate number in 1997 was that 78 percent of the labor force in Finland and 55 percent in Norway were unionized. Danish and Swedish rates are a couple of percentage points high because of the inclusion of unemployed union members.) In contrast, only 10 to 50 percent of blue- and white-collar workers are organized elsewhere in Europe, except Belgium, which matches Scandinavian rates; most European countries fall in the 30 to 40 percent range. In the United States only about 14 percent are organized.

The high rates of organization in Scandinavia reflect the fact that white-collar and professional unions organize close to the same portion of their potential constituency as the blue-collar unions do. The reasons are two. First, Scandinavian unions have a strong organizational culture, combining strong shop floor organization with well-staffed national unions. Second, they administer the national unemployment compensation systems in every country except Norway (which is the principal reason why union density in Norway lags behind the others) and Iceland; Icelandic labor law, however, requires preferential hiring for union members, which has helped membership to 85 percent of the labor force. As a consequence of union provision of unemployment compensation, unionization rates went up sharply among white-collar workers in the 1970s when unemployment threatened. In other countries (except Belgium, which has the same system as the Scandinavian countries), unionization rates fall during economic downturns; in Scandinavia, they go up.

Scandinavian unions are also uniquely centralized. There is a single blue-collar trade union federation in each country. In Denmark, Norway, and Sweden, it is known as Landsorganisationen, or LO (literally, "The National Organization," and no one asks which). There is a single white-collar federation in each country, except Finland, which has two, and a single federation for professionals with academic training. Today, there are no significant organizational division along religious or political lines as in France and Italy, although Finland had both Social Democratic and Communist federations for a decade in the 1950s and 1960s. The national blue-collar federation has bargaining competence; Iceland is the only exception where bargaining power is in the hands of the sectoral federations of unions within the national federation. While there are clear political differences within unions between the Social Democrats and those to their left, today all parties' supporters pledge allegiance to the principle of labor unity, which means in practice that the dominant Social Democrats have been able to speak for a unified blue-collar and white-collar trade-union movement.

Employers' central organizations developed between 1896 and 1902 in Denmark, Norway, and Sweden, and in 1907 in Finland, contemporaneously with the national trade union federations. Only in Iceland did employers lag labor; Icelandic employers' organizations were not united until 1934. Scandinavia employers organize close to the same proportion of employers as Scandinavian unions organize workers. They too have centralized bargaining power. Today they are split between public sector and private sector employers. In the private sector, the Danes, Icelanders, Norwegians, and Swedes have a single employers' organization although each has sectoral organizations within it. The Finns have two employers' organizations: one for employers in manufacturing, transportation, and construction and the other for employers in the private service sector. The misleading convention in English is to refer to them as "employers' confederations," which suggests much less central power than in fact exists.

Although the patterns of labor organization and industrial relations in Denmark, Finland, Iceland, Norway, and Sweden are substantially similar today, that was not the case historically. (A chronology of key events is provided in Fig. 10.1.) The range of differences among trade unions was vast. First, they varied in strength. Although Danish unions stood off the employers in their great trial of strength in 1899, Swedish unions went down to disastrous defeat in a similar test in 1909, and the Finnish unions were crushed in 1918 when perhaps as much as a sixth of their membership were killed in the civil war, executed, or died of hunger or disease in the concentration camps that followed. Second, they varied in organizational form, from the continuing predominance of craft unionism in Denmark and Iceland to the industrial unionism of Norway and Sweden to a mixed form in Finland. (Craft unionism—organization on the basis of the training you have in your trade rather than on the basis of the industry you work in—however, characterizes the unions for academically trained professionals throughout Scandinavia). Third, they varied in ideology, from the stalwart reformism of the Danish and Swedish unions to the revolutionary syndicalism in the Norwegian unions at the end of World War I and the Communist dominance of Icelandic and Finnish unions in much of the postwar period. Despite this range of historical differences, there has been a substantial convergence since the 1930s in terms of the structure of labor relations and in the relationship between the labor market organizations and the state.[1]

The Development of the Labor Movement

Scandinavian labor organization began first in Denmark and was shaped both by the well-developed craft guilds and by Denmark's proximity to the continent. Abolition of the guilds' legal monopolies (1862) followed the beginning of industrialization in the 1850s, but the guild traditions of collective action and social cohesion did not disappear with their legal monopoly. The journeymen's sickness and burial societies persisted, and the guild masters' organizations continued virtually intact; these were the seed for unions and employers' associations, respectively.

Figure 10.1
The Development of Scandinavian Industrial Relations

S 1846/64			
D 1862	Abolition of guild		
F 1868	Monopolies		
N 1869			
		1870s D	Initial organization
		1880s N & S	of local unions
		1890s F & I	
D & S 1898	Establishment of	1896 D	
N 1899	national union	1900 N	Establishment of
F 1907	federation	1902 S	Employers
I 1916		1907 F	Confederation
		1934 I	
D 1898	Basic Agreement		
N 1935	negotiated	1915 N	Legislated
S 1938		1928 S	framework for
F 1944		1938 I	labor relations
I 1942	Establishment of		
S & F 1944	main white-collar	1945 S	Works Councils
D 1952	union federation	1946 F & N	established
N 1977		1946 F & N	
		1947 D	
		1973 D, N, S	Employee board
			seats mandated
		1976 S	Workplace
		1979 F	codetermination
N 1980s			
D late 1980s	Decentralization		
S 1990s	of collective	1991 F	Employee board
F early 1990s	bargaining		seats mandated

D = Denmark, F = Finland, I = Iceland, N = Norway, and S = Sweden

Union organization grew with explosive rapidity in all those skilled trades where there had been guilds; within five years from the onset of union organization in 1870–71, there were reasonably strong unions in all the major Danish guild trades. The structure of the Danish craft unions was strong enough to absorb the influx of new workers into industry. The craft unions' social insurance schemes (sickness, travel and unemployment, and burial insurance) reduced economic insecurity for their members, and guaranteed union survival when strikes were lost. Moreover, although strikes by the unskilled could be broken by a combination of physical force and importing strikebreakers, strikes by the skilled depended more on the ability to control the supply of skilled labor by group cohesion reinforced by social insurance than it did on picket lines. Danish craft unions regularly used their control of travel benefit funds, which were the precursors of unemployment-compensation benefit funds, to require all unmarried journeymen to leave town and to seek work elsewhere for the duration of the strike, and gainfully employed unions members were expected to contribute substantial sums (one day's pay per week was not uncommon) to support the families of married journeymen for the duration of the strike.

The extent of Danish craft organization (by 1890 some of the smaller crafts had achieved 100% organization in the cities) was such that labor faced management with some degree of equality. This was so at least in part because Danish firms were small. Moreover, contemporary evidence from the late 1880s and 1890s suggests that the overwhelming majority of owners had themselves been apprenticed in the trades. The craft union model was so clearly successful that the unskilled unions imitated it. By the turn of the century, the union that organized the unskilled male brewery works in Copenhagen (the strongest Danish unskilled union) provided social insurance matching that of the skilled trades. In 1907, state financial support for union unemployment-insurance systems enabled unskilled unions that were organizing workers who were worse-paid than those in other unions to provide some insurance benefits as well. As a consequence, when the Danish Social Democrats hosted the Socialist International Congress in 1910, they could legitimately claim to have the strongest union movement in the world. The party and the trade unions were, of course, seen as two legs of the same movement.

Union organization in Sweden and Norway lagged behind Denmark's. The guild structure of the traditional crafts persisted equally long (guild monopolies were abolished in 1846 in Sweden in favor of compulsory craft associations, which persisted until 1864; in Norway guild monopolies were abolished in 1869). Craft unions were organized in the old guild trades in both countries in the 1870s and 1880s. Yet, in neither Norway nor Sweden were the traditional manufacturing trades as significant as in Denmark, and guild organization had been far weaker. The craft unions, when they emerged, were smaller. Industrialization also lagged behind that of Denmark, beginning a decade or more later in Sweden and about the turn of the century in Norway, and it was based primarily on the exploitation of such natural resources as minerals, timber, wood pulp, chemicals, and hydroelectric power, rather than on the mechanization of artisan workshops.

The new Swedish and Norwegian industrial workers were predominantly unskilled. They were recruited from agriculture, they lacked the traditions of guild collective action, and their economic reserves, individually and collectively, were small. When they attempted to organize to raise wages, they faced a solid phalanx of employers and provincial administrators. In Sweden, the first act of this drama was the 1879 Sundsvall strike of unorganized sawmill workers against wage reductions, which was put down with bayonets and prison sentences for the leaders of the rebellion. The last act was not played until the 1931 "massacre in Ådalen," as an official Swedish trade-union history characterizes it (Landsorganisationen 1973, p. 19), when the military turned machine guns on unarmed strikers the year before the Social Democratic assumption of power. The use of the military was atypical, but the antagonism and the bitter economic desperation were not.

The consequences of the geography of industrialization should not be overlooked. Every major industrial dispute in Denmark affected Copenhagen and raised the emotional temperature of the capital's working-class majority. By contrast, the most bitter industrial conflicts of Swedish and Norwegian labor history were played out far from Stockholm and Oslo, which, in the early years of industrialization, remained more administrative capitals than industrial ones. The use of military force to break strikes in the two Northern countries did not carry with it the same implicit threat to political stability as it did in Denmark.

Although the bases for trade-union organization were different in the three countries, the union representatives, who met in a series of Scandinavian workers' conferences beginning in Gothenburg in 1886 and continuing regularly until 1912, perceived themselves to be much alike. Most of those who participated in the meetings were skilled craftsmen who shared a common background. A large portion of the founding generation in the skilled unions of all three Scandinavian countries had worked as itinerant journeymen abroad. They were bound together by common traditions and by the new Social Democratic ideology that espoused labor as the source of all value in society. Scandinavian labor conferences called regularly for extending and strengthening trade-union organization to provide the support necessary to meet employers on the basis of parity. Some of their recommendations, such as the establishment of city central trade councils (1886 Gothenburg conference) and national trade union federations (1897 Stockholm conference), were quickly followed. Others, most notably the establishment of pan-Scandinavian trade unions, had less impact.

The establishment of local unions in the 1870s and 1880s was followed by the formation of national unions in the 1880s and 1890s and by national union federations in 1898–99 in Denmark, Norway, and Sweden. The employers responded in kind with the establishment of branch and industry organizations in the early 1890s, and with national federations in 1896 in Denmark, 1900 in Norway, and following a political general strike for universal suffrage, in 1902 in Sweden.

Finland, then under Russian rule, and Iceland, then under Danish rule, lagged behind the core Scandinavian states in economic development and labor organization. Both were far poorer and even more agricultural than Sweden and Norway. The manufacturing sector in 1900 in Finland is said to have employed the same proportion of the labor force as manufacturing did in Sweden in 1850 and in the 1700s in Denmark (Knoellinger 1960, p. 28)—and that was after the industrial workforce had almost tripled in the previous fifteen years. Sawmills and the forest industry drove Finnish industrialization in the pre–World War I period; together they employed 40 percent of industrial workers in 1910.

Iceland was even more overwhelmingly rural and agricultural. As late as 1860, 80 percent of its population was employed in agriculture and only 3 percent lived in towns. One indication of Icelandic backwardness: A major labor demand of 1900 was for payment of workers in cash, rather than in food. Parliament actually legislated cash payment for labor in 1901. The Icelandic equivalent of industrialization was the mechanization of the fishing fleet, which began in 1902 with an installation of a paraffin-burning, two-horsepower motor on the Stanley, a six-oar rowboat. It was astonishingly rapid. By 1930, half the population of the country had moved to coastal fishing towns.

Labor organization also lagged in both. Finnish guild monopolies continued in the skilled trades of the cities until 1868, not dissimilar from the rest of Scandinavia. However, legal restrictions implemented in the 1879 Trades Act severely limited workers' rights to collective action and to strike. Although initial union organization dates to the Helsinki typesetters in the 1880s, and local unions were formed outside Helsinki in the 1890s, union membership in the whole country comprised no more than seven to eight thousand at the turn of the century (Knoellinger 1960, p. 44). Finnish union ties were primarily with the Danes, Swedes, and Germans, following the old routes of journeymen's travels in the skilled trades, and craft unions were the norm.

That all changed, however, with the Finnish General Strike in October–November 1905. Influenced by their Russian colleagues, Finnish workers, too, created Red guard units that allied themselves with the Russian sailors' units at the Helsinki naval base. The strike swept away the archaic four estate parliament that had endured under Czarist rule, replacing it with a parliament elected by universal suffrage—including women who also won about 10 percent of the seats—for the first time in Europe. In the euphoria engendered by the strike, Social Democratic party membership quintupled between 1904 and 1906, and the new industrial unions established for the unskilled in the sawmills, woodworking, and paper industries became the largest unions founding the Finnish Federation of Labor in 1907. The first democratic election held under these rules in 1907 produced a sweeping victory for the Social Democrats, who won 40 percent of the parliamentary seats, leapfrogging their Danish, Norwegian, and Swedish counterparts. However, Finnish unions were not able to institutionalize these political gains in organizational strength, in part because the poverty of the largely unskilled work force limited the unions' ability to develop the benefit societies that were the backbone of continuing union organization among the skilled. The Finnish employers, who organized a national federation in 1907, also appear in retrospect to have been more antagonistic to unionization than their Scandinavian counterparts, and the Russian administration lacked any sympathy for unions.

Iceland had a far more liberal legal regime for unions under the Danes. Continuing craft union organization dates to the Reykjavik typographers in 1897. But skilled workers were few and far between in agricultural Iceland. Continuing organization of the unskilled began with the formation of Dagsbrun (Daybreak) in Reykjavik in January 1906; by the end of the year it had organized about a quarter of the male workforce of the city. It won its first major strike (with the Danish contractor building the Reykjavik harbor) in 1913. A Reykjavik general women's union Framsokn (Progress) followed in 1914. The Seamen's Union, destined to become the strongest Icelandic union followed in 1915 and the Icelandic Labor Federation in 1916 at the same meeting at which the Icelandic Labor party was formed. A single employers' federation followed in 1934. The Labor Federation and Labor party remained organizationally unified until 1942.

From Conflict to Compromise

The test of strength between unions and employers was not long in coming in Denmark, where unionization was most advanced. In 1898, the national craft unions followed the Stockholm labor-conference decision, organizing the national labor federation, De samvirkende Fagforbund (DsF), now known as Landsorganisation (LO). The employers' association, Dansk Arbejdsgiverforening (DA), organized in the Copenhagen building trades in 1896, achieved comparable national scope with the affiliation of the metal trades employers' and provincial employers' associations in 1898. This organizational arms race culminated in a general labor conflict the next year.

The direct cause of the conflict, like that of World War I, was trivial. Seven carpenters' locals in Jutland rejected a contract proposal. The employers called a national lockout of carpenters and, on May 24, 1899, expanded it to a general national lockout. The Great Lockout started as a great adventure. It was summer. Workmen used to putting in ten-hour days, six days a week, had time for their children. The unions held picnics and ran lectures for members. But the national lockout dragged on for sixteen long weeks. Picnics ceased. Family savings were exhausted. The lectures became bitter. Union resources were drained, despite heavy strike levies on working members. The unions escaped disaster through shipping thousands of journeymen abroad to find work (which elicited a sympathy blacklist of locked-out Danish craftsmen by employers in northern Germany), through financial aid from foreign unions, and through direct assistance from sympathetic farm families who provided food for the locked-out workers and who took in their children for the duration of the lockout. The lockout ultimately exhausted the employers as well. It ended with an agreement in September 1899 between the DA and the DsF that has set the pattern of labor relations until the present day.

The *September Agreement* set the rules for conducting industrial conflicts. It limited the means and scope of conflict, imposed strict rules concerning authorization and notice of strikes and lockouts, and required that the central organizations, DA and DsF, assume the responsibility for enforcing the rules on their affiliates. Employers won union agreement that their right "to direct and allocate work" was absolute. Both sides agreed to accept court decisions as final in cases of breach of contract that could not be resolved by negotiation (a special labor market court was established by a separate agreement).

Although these specific provisions were generally those demanded by DA when it initiated the lockout, unions could and did live with them. The September Agreement restricted the unions' past strike practices (although the unions maintained the intention of overturning the agreement as soon as the balance of power shifted in their favor), but they won one notable concession: formal employer recognition of the right of workers to organized, bargain, and strike. Although strikes and lockouts were hardly a thing of the past in Denmark, industrial conflict would henceforth be within the limits of agreed-upon rules, and the survival of organized labor would never be at stake. Moreover, the exhaustion of 1899 continued to shape employers' and unions' attitudes toward conflict: Massive tests of strength offered little possibility of gain, while the costs were known and heavy. Danish labor relations were considerably more peaceful after 1899 than those in Norway and Sweden, not to mention Finland and Iceland.

The pattern of development was notably different in the other four countries. There rapid industrialization was followed by cycles of rapid union growth among unskilled workers after the turn of the century alternating with equally rapid contraction following lost strikes or, in the most extreme case, the decimation of union activists in the Finnish civil war and its aftermath.

In Sweden, the great test of strength came in 1909 after a series of successful but bitter strikes in the preceding four years. A series of small strikes and lockouts culminated July 26 in a general lockout, and the LO responded with a general strike on August 4. Despite the élan with which the general strike began, the circumstances were fundamentally different from those in Denmark a decade earlier. Unskilled workers predominated in union ranks. They lacked the personal resources to endure a long strike, despite financial support from abroad, and their unions had little of the benefit infrastructure that had served the Danish skilled unions well in 1899. Employers made massive use of strike breakers, some of whom were students recruited from universities and university-preparatory high schools. Strike breakers enjoyed special legal protection in Sweden under an 1889 statute. It was class war.

The outcome was a disastrous defeat for labor. As winter came on, the last strikers went back to work on the employers' terms on November 13. Union membership plummeted to one-half of what it had been. It took the Swedish unions the better part of a decade to recover. They did, however, reorganize. LO Congress decisions in 1912, 1917, and 1922 required the consolidation of craft unions along industrial lines; by 1923, 60 percent of the Swedish unions' members belonged to one of seventeen industrial unions (Hansson 1927).

Sweden's unenviable record of labor conflict resumed as the unions recovered during World War I. The imposition of general legislation to regulate industrial relations in 1928, including the establishment of a labor court, provoked protest strikes, rather than labor peace. However, industrial conflict began to subside after the Social Democrats took power in 1932. In 1936, parliament legislated the right of workers to organize and bargaining collectively. It eased further after the unions and employers reached agreement on basis rules for labor relations in the Saltsjöbaden Agreement of 1938, which paralleled the Danish September Agreement of 1899.

In Norway, where employers were even better organized in relation to labor, the government took a far more active role on the side of the employers than in either Denmark or Sweden. It stepped into a major conflict in 1911 and proposed, as an outgrowth, legislation for compulsory mediation and arbitration. The labor movement opposed the latter, threatening a political general strike in 1914 if the government insisted on passing the measure with that provision. The act as passed in 1915 provided for the establishment of a labor court, like that in Denmark, to rule on all matters concerning interpretation of valid agreements, and, before conflicts could start, for compulsory mediation in all disputes at contract renewal. Either employers or unions could reject the mediator's proposal, and there was no provision for compulsory arbitration (i.e., the imposition of a binding settlement by a third party). Compulsory arbitration, however, was imposed repeatedly as an emergency measure (in 1916–21, as a consequence of World War I; in 1922–23, as an outgrowth of a general strike against wage reductions; in 1927–29; and again from the end of World War II to 1952 for the sake of reconstruction). The unions opposed compulsory arbitration during all but the last period, and construction workers staged a bitter, illegal, but widely supported strike against the arbitration result for six weeks in 1928. Despite compulsory arbitration, between the end of World War I and the Labor party's assumption of power in 1935, Norway compiled the worst record in Scandinavia for industrial warfare.

World War I reshaped the Norwegian labor movement. Despite their neutrality—only Finland (as part of Russia) was a quasi-belligerent—all the Scandinavian countries were affected by severe shortages during the last years of the war. Suffering was borne unequally. So-called goulash barons became rich by selling supplies to the belligerents, while, during the winter of 1917–18, food shortages and economic dislocation produced increasing radicalism in union ranks and among the unemployed. *Syndicalism*—direct action by workers to "expropriate the expropriators" through strikes, boycotts, and even sabotage without regard for contracts—gained increasing support. While the syndicalist wave ultimately ebbed in Denmark and Sweden, in Norway it overwhelmed the conventional unions.

In the journeyman painter Martin Tranmæl, Norwegian revolutionary syndicalism had a leader of stature. Tranmæl, like many Norwegians, had emigrated to the United States, and his experience there with the syndicalist Industrial Workers of the World (IWW) helped shape his views. Under Tranmæl's astute leadership, the left wing captured the Labor party in 1918, and the syndicalists won control of the union federation in 1920. They used it to reorganize the movement along industrial-union lines between 1920 and 1924. Tranmæl led the united Norwegian labor movement into the Communist International in 1919. With an ideology of revolutionary syndicalism, the Norwegians fit the Bolshevik model badly and withdrew from the Comintern in 1923. The Labor party remained resolutely revolutionary in the 1920s. The first Norwegian Labor government, under Christopher Hornsrud, took office in 1928 proclaiming its desire to transform Norway into a socialist society. It fell after eighteen days.

Ultimately pragmatism triumphed. In 1927, the Labor party removed the "dictatorship of the proletariat" from its party program. Its 1933 program tempered revolutionary phraseology with the pragmatism of a party seeking to win power through elections. It fought the 1933 election under the unrevolutionary but timely slogan, "Work for Everyone." Labor's 1933 victory paved the way to power in 1935; in the same year, a general agreement between unions and employers, comparable to the Danish 1899 September Agreement, was reached.

In Iceland, poverty and economic backwardness exceeding those elsewhere in Scandinavia provided fertile soil for labor radicalism, but a general acceptance of the legitimacy of collective bargaining kept labor conflict within bounds. Iceland passed legislation providing mediation in labor disputes in 1925. The Depression strained civility, however. In 1932, unemployed demonstrators, led by the Communists, defeated the Reykjavik police, the closest thing to a military force in that island nation, in an all-out battle. The Labor and Farmers parties won the elections in 1934, and formed their first joint government. In 1938, they passed legislation to regularize conditions for strikes and lockouts and to establish the primacy of collective agreements over individual contracts. It went beyond the Danish, Norwegian, and Swedish basic labor agreements, however, to forbid the employment of strikebreakers (Karlsson 2000, p. 301) and to provide employment preferences for unionized workers under closed shop agreements. The 1938 Industrial Relations Act also provided for union organization by trade (craft unionism) rather than by firm or industry.

The economic crisis of the 1930s was exacerbated in Iceland by the outbreak of the Spanish Civil War, which closed a major market for Icelandic fish. In 1938, the Labor party split, and the Icelandic Communist party allied itself with the Social Democratic left in the Socialist party. When the Labor party and labor federation were divided organizationally in 1942, the Socialists captured control of the Labor Federation. A second Social Democratic schism in 1958 led to the formation of the People's Alliance, an even broader left-wing party that continued to dominate the unions. In the postwar period, Icelandic union militancy was sustained by a continual round of strikes to recover wage losses to inflation. It wasn't until 1990—after Mikhail Gorbachev's policies in the Soviet Union had rendered the Cold War division of the labor movement irrelevant—that the Icelandic unions assumed a Scandinavian-style role in incomes policy, actually breaking the back of the inflationary spiral that had characterized the entire postwar period in Iceland (see Table 9.1).

The situation was very different in Finland. The 1917–18 civil war and its aftermath split the labor movement for three generations. Both the Social Democrats and the unions were largely unified in supporting the "Reds." Symptomatic of that unity was the fact that only two of the ninety-two Social Democrats elected to parliament in 1917 were permitted to return to parliament after the Civil War. The others had fled to Russia (40), or, been executed (5), or, had been put in concentration camps (45) by the "Whites." While casualties in the civil war numbered between 3,000 and 5,000 dead on each side, the victorious Whites celebrated by executing some 8,000 of their opponents and confining another 80,000 in concentration camps where another 12,000 died from hunger and disease. A special Tribunal of High Treason sentenced 67,000 of them to prison terms and more than 500 to death (Jussila, Hentilä, and Nevakivi 1999, pp. 111–12, 121). To put these numbers in context, on the eve of the civil war at the end of 1917 Finnish unions, which provided the bulk of the Red troops, had 157,000 members, up from 42,000 at the beginning of the year. Twenty-five thousand dead, not to mention the thousands who fled to Russia, was devastating.

The aftermath of the civil war crushed the Finnish labor movement organizationally as well as physically. Finnish employers, having been on the winning side, generally successfully opposed unionization and collective bargaining. Strike breakers were provided by the Vientirauha Oy, organized by White activists, which claimed 34,000 members; labor conflicts were considered by many on both sides to be the continuation of the civil war by other means (Jussila, Hentilä, and Nevakivi 1999, p. 152). The Finnish Social Democratic party was reconstituted with the leadership drawn from those who had not participated in the civil war and rapidly regained three-quarters of its prewar strength. Communist-led organizations claimed most of the rest until their complete suppression in 1930. However, Finnish unionization rates between 1919 and 1938 averaged only 8 percent—compared to 34 percent in Denmark, 30 percent in Sweden, and 19 percent in Norway (Korpi 1981, p. 314). Not until the Winter War between Finland and the Soviet Union in 1940 did employers accept labor's right to unionize and to bargain collectively. This was established by the January Agreement in 1940 and solidified by the Basic Agreement of 1944, which paralleled similar agreements of the 1930s in Norway and Sweden and the Basic Agreement of 1899 in Denmark.

With the legal framework in place, Finnish unionization rates rose rapidly in the 1950s and 1960s, catching up with the other Scandinavian countries by 1970. However during this period, the cleavage between the Social Democrats and the Communists continued to divide the Finnish unions and weaken labor politically at a time when it could otherwise have dominated the government. This division took organizational form as well after the bitter strikes of 1956; from 1960 to 1969 when the Finns had two labor federations. Only with the decline of the importance of this division after the Finnish joint Social Democratic and Communist coalition government in 1966 did Finnish industrial relations begin to move toward the more general Scandinavian model, although it remained substantially more strike prone than the Scandinavian norm. And with the decline of this division, the Social Democrats began to play a more dominant role in government, again converging on the Scandinavian norm.

Thus interwar developments in labor relations depended primarily on whether a framework for collective bargaining had been established early (Denmark and, to a lesser extent, Iceland). When that was not the case, labor conflict could be astonishingly bitter since it often revolved around whether workers could organize and bargain collectively. That was the situation in Norway and Sweden until the advent of Social Democratic governments in the early 1930s. In Finland collective bargaining was the exception until the crisis of the Winter War with the Soviet Union in 1940 led employers and unions to agreement. Even the Finnish civil war receded in importance when there was a new war to fight.

Organizing the Changing Labor Force

From their origins through the 1930s, Scandinavian unions organized skilled workers in the crafts and unskilled workers in industry, construction, and transportation. They struggled mightily to organize agricultural workers. Unions had a foothold in the public sector in the railroads and telephone companies, which were state-owned, but organized few civil servants. In the private service sector, they had only a tenuous existence.

In organizational terms, the story of the postwar period in Scandinavia has been the mass organization of the public sector and of the private service sector. Given the different gender composition of the labor force in the public and service sectors from manufacturing, this also led to the feminization of the labor movement.

Unlike the interwar period when the right to organize was still contested, in the postwar period, every Scandinavian country had established a framework for collective bargaining. After World War II, workers' rights to organize were never challenged systematically. As a consequence, white-collar and service sector organization proceeded gradually through the 1950s and 1960s. It was most advanced in Sweden, where white-collar unionization accelerated after 1936 legislation provided organizing rights in the private sector; state and municipal employees won the right to organize (but not to strike) in 1937 and 1940, respectively. The white-collar unions created their own national federation in 1944, *Tjänstemännens centralorganisation* (TCO), combining a private sector federation dating to 1931 and a public sector federation founded in 1937. TCO's two hundred thousand members at its formation in 1944 comprised an estimated 30 to 40 percent of all white-collar employees (Forsebäck 1976, p. 21). Swedish public sector employees, including police and military, got the right to strike in 1966. Similar, but numerically smaller, white-collar federations were organized in Finland in 1944, Denmark in 1952, and Norway in 1977; the Icelandic salaried employees' federation dates to 1942. Professional unions federations quickly followed: *Sveriges akademikers centralorganisation* (SACO) was organized in 1947, and comparable professional federations were established in Denmark, Finland, and Norway in 1950. The professional unions generally are based on the craft union principle that education determines which union you belong to, rather than the industrial union principle that what sector you are employed in determines which union you belong to, even in Sweden and Norway where industrial unionism is otherwise virtually universal.

The explosive growth of white-collar and professional unions' membership occurred in the 1970s when unemployment first became a substantial threat for white-collar workers. Eligibility for unemployment compensation in Denmark, Finland, and Sweden (as well as Belgium, where similar growth took place) virtually requires union membership. The jump in overall union membership in Table 10.1 (12 percentage points in Sweden, 13 percentage points in Finland, and 25 percentage points in Denmark, contrasted to 6 percentage points in Norway) between 1970 and 1980 reflects this reality.

The impact of white-collar and professional union growth on the overall union movement has been dramatic. Consider the Swedish case. Today, of the top ten Swedish unions, only two are blue-collar, private sector manufacturing unions. Eight are white-collar, including five TCO unions. Six have female majorities. Half have the majority of their members in the public sector. In 1945, LO unions accounted for 79 percent of Swedish union membership; in 1999, they accounted for 55 percent. Between 1945 and 1999, TCO and SACO membership grew from 15 percent to 43 percent of total union membership. Independent unions account for the remainder (Kjellberg 2000, pp. 532–35).

This change in the groups organized meant a feminization of the union movement. In Sweden, in 1999, unionization rates were 78 percent among men and 83 percent among women. Women comprised 52 percent of union members (Kjellberg 2000, p. 570). In Finland, unionization rates among women are 82 percent; among men, 75 percent. Fifty-one percent of union members are women (Kauppinen and Waddington 2000, p. 191). This feminization has had substantial impact on union political goals. It is beginning to affect the gender composition of union leadership as well: Wanja Lundby-Wedin was elected as the first woman to lead the Swedish LO in 2000 and Liv-Gerd Valla was elected as the first woman chairman of the Norwegian LO in 2001; both came from public sector unions.

In short, in organizational terms, the Scandinavian unions have transformed themselves in step with the transformation of the economy and the labor force. They have kept pace with the growth of the service and public sectors, growing both numerically and in percent of the labor force throughout the postwar period. That is virtually a unique accomplishment in the West, and it affects both political decisions and wage formation in the market.

STRUCTURING LABOR RELATIONS

Industrial relations is a method of managing industrial conflict, not resolving it. It assumes that conflicts of interest between labor and capital are sufficiently severe and permanent to require a system of state-sanctioned regulation. Although the origins of current labor-relations practices in Scandinavia can be traced back to the guild period, the current rules[2] date to private agreements between national labor and employers' organizations reached in 1899 in Denmark, 1935 in Norway, 1938 in Sweden, and 1944 in Finland, and to legislation in 1938 in Iceland. The agreements of those years, which codified and extended existing practices, laid down the basic framework for bargaining, ratifying, interpreting, and enforcing collective agreements, calling strikes and lockouts, and otherwise structuring the relations between workers' organizations, on the one hand, and their employers, on the other. The general structure created was subsequently extended to accommodate the organization of salaried employees and collective bargaining in the public sector. But despite the rapid growth in the numbers covered in both public-sector and white-collar agreements, the negotiations between the LO and the employers' confederations in the private manufacturing sector remain fundamental: They provide the pattern for white-collar and public-sector agreements that are otherwise insulated from international competition.

While similar provisions govern labor relations in other Western democracies, the structure of Scandinavian labor relations is distinguished by three attributes: (1) its rules rest principally on private agreements between unions and employers, not legislation; (2) its form is highly centralized; and (3) it has provided an arena, second only to the state, for the Social Democratic effort to restructure society.

The Danish September Agreement set the pattern for current Scandinavian collective-bargaining rules by being an agreement between private parties not involving government legislation. The Norwegian Basic Agreement of 1935, the Swedish Saltsjöbaden accord of 1938, and the Finnish Basic Agreement of 1944 were similarly reached by the labor and employers' organizations. By contrast, the comparable U.S. rules were laid down by legislation in the Wagner Act in 1935. The parties to the September Agreement and the subsequent Norwegian, Swedish, and Finnish agreements formally recognized each other's right to exist. Employers accepted the unions' right to organize and bargain collectively; unions recognized the employers' managerial prerogatives to direct work. Voluntary agreement on the rules of the game is conducive to industrial peace. Both sides agreed on self-regulation, including the rules governing the calling of strikes and lockouts, and both central organizations agreed to enforce the provisions of the agreement among their own members. The rivalry in the unions between the Communists and Social Democrats, however, in Finland and Iceland militated in the opposite direction.

Centralized Bargaining

Employers were interested in centralizing contract bargaining to avoid being picked off one by one. The Great Lockout of 1899 in Denmark had originated in employer efforts to block the standard union practice of extracting a good contract from one employer and then proceeding to strike the next while the first was open for business. The employers' federations were as oriented to industrial conflict as the unions: They provided for support payments to member firms during strikes and for heavy fines for those who broke ranks to sign contracts while other companies remained strike bound. Employer organizations pushed for broader contracts, and industry-wide bargaining became common in Denmark, where, by 1910, employers' associations were as well organized as the unions. The other countries gradually followed suit.

In the postwar period, contracts have varied between industry-wide bargaining and coordinated national bargaining between the national trade-union federation and the national employers' association. The extent of organization of both workers and employers has meant that wage levels, hours, vacations, and the like have frequently been set for the majority of employees in the country in a single round of negotiations. In Denmark and Norway, contracts are subject to membership ratification votes in both trade unions and the employers' organizations. In Sweden, however, a membership vote is not required. The contract, once ratified, is legally binding and is enforced through a system of labor courts. Disputes about existing labor contracts go to the labor court, not to regular courts or to industrial action. The Danish labor court was established in 1910 on the basis of an agreement between the unions and the employers. The Norwegian and Swedish courts were established by statute in 1915 and 1928, respectively, over the protest strikes of the unions. Labor courts followed in 1938 in Iceland and 1946 in Finland. The courts have subsequently been accepted by the labor unions as legitimate. The labor courts are tripartite, with representatives of unions, employers, and the public.

The concept of a basic national contract is foreign to U.S. and British trade unionists and employers alike. The British and American pattern has been to bargain on a plant-by-plant or company-by-company basis. Bargaining contracts for entire industries is rare; bargaining a single national contract for all unionized workers is simply inconceivable. In fact, neither the AFL-CIO and its British counterpart, the Trades Union Congress, nor the national employers' associations—the National Association of Manufacturers in the United States and Confederation of British Industries, respectively—have any bargaining mandate at all.

In rounds of fully centralized Scandinavian bargaining, there are three levels of agreements: national, industrial sector, and plant. The national contract typically sets rates of across-the-board wage increases, hours, and holidays. Other benefits do not generally enter into negotiations because the health-insurance and pension packages that are central concerns in U.S. bargaining are covered by governmental programs in Scandinavia. Frequently, government mediators play a role in hammering out the final agreement. The national agreement is then fleshed out by industry-specific bargaining. Finally, there are plant negotiations about local issues. Basic wages and hours are not supposed to be an issue at the industry or plant level, although piece-rate and bonus schedules, which account for most wage drift, are bargained there. When there is no national contract, bargaining is decentralized to the sectoral level, and the sectoral framework is fleshed out by plant agreements. Note that there is almost no bargaining at the company level, which is a common focus for U.S. labor relations.

Danes, Norwegians, and Swedes developed national contract bargaining at varying points in time, but it became the predominant bargaining form in the 1950s through the 1970s. The Finns joined their ranks in 1968. It became a key component of Social Democratic incomes policies during this period. Since 1980 and particularly in the 1990s, however, there has been increased pressure for decentralized bargaining without a national framework agreement, although with sectoral coordination. Iceland, however, which has bargaining at the level of sectoral union federations within the national federation, developed a more coordinated national bargaining system in the 1990s. We will return to this change in the final section of this chapter.

In general this system has been conducive to labor peace. In the postwar years, there was generally less labor conflict in Denmark, Norway, and Sweden than in other Western countries—despite the far higher levels of unionization. (See Table 10.2.) Finland and Iceland, with union movements divided politically, had substantially higher rates of labor conflict. In the 1990s, Western labor conflict rates have fallen as unionization rates have declined. Scandinavian rates seem higher by contrast, reflecting both higher labor organization rates and the impact of decentralizing collective bargaining from a single national contract to several sectoral contracts.

Consequences of Centralized Bargaining

Scandinavian collective bargaining, whether national or sectoral, is more centralized, more comprehensive, more integrated into national economic policy, and more political than the Western pattern. Close relationships between trade unions or business organizations on the one hand and governing parties on the other are hardly unusual. But the degree of cooperation between Social Democratic governments and Social Democratic–led trade unions in Scandinavia far exceeds similar ties between government and interest organizations in other countries. This degree of cooperation has meant the integration of the national wage contract into national economic policy. While some elements of governmental involvement have been official, particularly in Norway and in the tripartite bargaining among government, unions, and employers in Sweden, the policy has been all the more effective because it has been largely

Table 10.2
Days Lost through Strikes and Lockouts per 1,000 Employees in Selected Western Nations, 1960–99

	Annual Averages				
Country	1960-67	1968-73	1974-80	1982-86	1990-99
Denmark	500	730	186	570	173
Norway	135	17	120	300	81
Sweden	25	52	20	10	51
Finland	285	1180	844	740	169
Iceland	1185	1463	1086	866	296
Belgium	150	430	450		29
France	315	288	312	150	77
Germany	25	70	76	130	11
Italy	1120	1975	1806	1040	159
Netherlands	45	105	60		22
United Kingdom	230	925	1055	970	29
United States	850	1408	930	310	40
Canada	710	1715	1980	15	220

Note: Danish and Swedish figures before 1974 and 1971, respectively, cover only manufacturing and are not directly comparable to other figures. The Icelandic data may not be completely comparable with the other countries but are internally consistent.

Sources: 1960–80: International Labour Organization data covering mining, manufacturing, construction, and transportation from Great Britain, Department of Employment *Gazette*, as cited in Barkin (1983, p. 387). 1982–86: Data covering mining, quarrying, manufacturing, construction, transportation, and communications as cited in Great Britain, British Information Service, *Survey of Current Affairs*, vol. 18, no. 8 (August 1988), p. 275. 1990–99: International Labour Organization data covering all industries and services as cited in Great Britain, National Statistics, *Labour Market Trends*, vol. 109, no. 4 (April 2001), p. 196; Akyeampong (1997, p. 52). We have calculated the Icelandic numbers from Iceland 1997, Tables 3.11 and 3.18, at http://www.hagstofa.is/talnaefn/LH_2001/TOFLUR/03/L0101301.xls and L010319.xls.

informal, resting on a government-union consensus, not on governmental decree. The replacement of this consensus by legislation in the 1970s and 1980s was both a sign and a source of strain; its collapse in the 1990s will be discussed in the last section of this chapter.

Centralized bargaining and a high degree of organization make it possible to impose incomes policies through national negotiations. The Scandinavians in general have been reasonably successful in carrying out the kind of long-term incomes policy that is the dream of every European finance minister. Part of the reason for that success has been at the trade unions' own initiative. It was the unions (beginning in Sweden in the late 1930s in theory, and in the 1960s in practice) that pushed for the solidaristic wage policy in national bargaining. This policy trades wage restraint among the highest-paid for higher increases for the poorest-paid workers (Meidner 1974). It has reduced pay differentials by raising the wages of women and unskilled workers relative to the pay of skilled males. As a consequence, the Scandinavian countries top the OECD countries in wage equality.

The solidaristic wage policy restrains wages in the most advanced, profitable sectors, increasing profits and the rate of capital formation; its obverse is that wage increases in the technologically less-advanced, low-profit sectors, such as textiles and shoes, have ruthlessly eliminated these industries, freeing labor for the competitive, export-oriented sector. (See Fig. 10.2.) Relatively low wage differentials, of course, increase labor mobility. So too does the fact that benefits, provided through the public sector, are virtually identical in all sectors of the economy. The solidaristic wage policy has been a conscious policy of industrial renewal, redeploying labor and capital from the least advanced to the most advanced economic sectors at a more rapid rate, and with less government interference than otherwise would have been the case.

The windfall profit the solidaristic wage policy creates in the most profitable sectors and companies, however, poses a serious problem for the unions. The purpose of unions, after all, is not increasing profits for the

Figure 10.2
How the Solidaristic Wage Policy Works

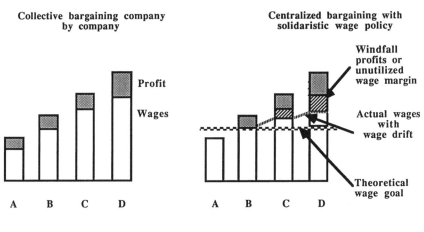

COMPANIES   COMPANIES

Source: From *Modern Welfare States: Politics and Policies in Social Democratic Scandinavia*, Eric S. Einhorn and John Logue. 1989. Praeger Publishers (Westport, CT). Reprinted with permission.

owners of corporations. The Swedish unions' efforts to recapture part of this surplus profit through establishing wage-earner funds (often called the "Meidner plan" after its author, trade union economist Rudolf Meidner) became one of the biggest political hot potatoes of the last quarter of the twentieth century. Many believe that the wage-earner fund proposal, which raised the specter of trade union control of the economy, was partly responsible for the Social Democratic election defeat in 1976, ending more than four decades of Social Democratic government. The Social Democrats enacted a much more modest, regionalized version of the wage-earner funds after returning to power in 1982. (For a discussion of the fund debate and results, see Hancock and Logue 1984.) Carl Bildt's conservative government eliminated the regional funds during its tenure in the early 1990s.

The windfall profits created for the most efficient firms and sectors remain a byproduct of the solidaristic wage policy. However, as we will explore at the end of this chapter, the transition from national collective bargaining to sectoral bargaining has increased wage differentiation and, presumably, cut the windfall.

Making Incomes Policies Work

In the 1960s and 1970s, incomes policies, or government planning and control of the rates of market-income growth, were a popular theoretical answer to how to maintain balanced growth in advanced capitalist market economies with full employment and without inflation (see Flanagan, Soskice, and Ulman 1983). How can inflationary wage increases be avoided when the economy is at or close to full employment and the union movement is strong?

One choice is for the government to dictate wage and price increases, and to impose confiscatory taxes on growth in income from capital. Such policies have been used with some success in liberal democracies under wartime conditions, but the evidence from that experience suggests that government dictation is sustainable only during a national emergency. Under more normal conditions, wage and price freezes have had a very short life expectancy.

Incomes policies offer a more consensual mechanism to achieve the same goal. In theory, at least, labor and employers agree to conduct themselves in a fashion that maximizes collective long-term economic gains, rather than seeking to maximize individual short-term gains that are eaten up by the inflation that collectively they generate. The peculiar configuration of the Scandinavian labor market, with its high degree of organization, centralized bargaining, and a nearly permanent government–trade union link, created the ability to conduct an effective incomes policy. Social Democratic dominance of government guaranteed that the rules would not be changed in midstream, and the Social Democratic–trade union link gave the government the credibility to control earned income without taking extraordinary steps against increases in income from capital. Capital income could be controlled by taxes. Last but not least, centralization of bargaining provided the perfect mechanism for reaching and maintaining a consensus.

The high degree of organization and the centralization of bargaining not only provided a potent tool for national economic policy, it created the necessity for using that tool. The extent of organization guarantees that wage earners will keep pace with inflation, or perhaps do better. There is no mass of nonunionized workers in Scandinavia to dampen the flames of inflation through declining real wages and declining consumption. Similarly, the centralization of bargaining means that the alternative to a successful conclusion of negotiations is a general strike and lockout. It is the deterrence theory of labor relations: Labor conflict becomes so expensive that no one can afford it.

The government is not a neutral bystander in this process. The pattern of contract negotiations has been susceptible to bargaining between government and trade unions, in which tax cuts or increased social benefits were traded for wage restraint. In countries in which marginal tax rates for production line workers can approach 50 percent, every krona in better benefits is worth two in wage increases. The Scandinavian dependence on exports plays a crucial role in the desire to hold the rate of wage increases at or below the rate of wage increases of major trading partners in order to maintain the export position. Reduction of business taxes has been used similarly to win employer agreement.

Incomes policies were most successful in Scandinavia when they were informal, that is, when they were based on unofficial coordination between Social Democratic governments and Social Democratic–led trade unions. It was rational for the trade unions to accept this policy that postponed benefits given the guarantee provided by Social Democratic political dominance. Noninflationary growth offers members a chance to do more than play catch up with inflation, and a successful incomes policy means that no other group will be able to grab a bigger share. As a result, unions can still serve their members' interests without a fixation on maximizing gains in any given bargaining round. Social Democratic control of government guaranteed unions that what was won at the bargaining table would not be lost on the floor of parliament in higher taxes, reduced social benefits, or increased unemployment. It offered the possibility of nonwage compensation for wage restraint. It also extended the unions' time perspectives: Current restraint can be a rational trade-union policy when the likelihood of greater future benefits for members is high.

The political and economic developments of the last quarter of the twentieth century called the stability of the informal Scandinavian incomes policy into question. The problem was most obvious in Denmark where the government imposed the 1975, 1977, 1979, and 1985 national contracts by legislative action. Those actions were a sign of the collapse of the consensus that was the foundation of the informal incomes policy. The compression of income differentials had reached the point that it undercut skilled workers' support for the solidaristic wage policy, while shifting governmental constellations undermined the reliability of agreements reached between the unions, the employers, and the government. Meanwhile, employers pushed for greater flexibility in setting wages by sector. Government imposition of contracts was also indicative of the increased coercion necessary to carry out the incomes policy. The consequence was a move in the 1990s to decentralize wage bargaining from a single national contract to several sectoral contracts that provided greater flexibility.

Ironically Iceland—the only country without an incomes policy—introduced one with labor, employers and government coordination in 1990 to break the inflationary spiral of that had plagued the country during the postwar period. Seeing wage gains eaten up by inflation and governmental devaluations of the Icelandic kronur, unions struck to recover losses, leading to more inflation. Union militants saw themselves in constant conflict with both employers and the government. The fact that the Social Democrats were usually a minority partner in the government and the unions were largely Communist-led exacerbated this conflict. Only after the Gorbachev and the end of the Cold War did Icelandic unions, employers, and government collaborate to bring the inflationary spiral under control; symptomatically, however, the government of the time included both the People's Alliance (which includes the Communists) and Social Democrats as well as the agrarian Progressive party.

Incomes policies remain necessary in Scandinavia. The combination of a high degree of organization and wage-maximizing unions would rapidly price Scandinavian goods out of the world market, even with the higher unemployment of the 1990s. The swing from national bargaining to sectoral bargaining in the 1980s and 1990s was dictated in part by a desire for freer wage formation and more responsiveness to market forces, both opposite the aims of incomes policy. However the results of sectoral bargaining were higher rates of wage increases and inflation, as unions leapfrogged each other. Governments found themselves trying to coordinate decentralized negotiations to avoid these undesirable outcomes.

For the bourgeois parties, the dilemma is clear. When they win governmental power, they cannot pursue an incomes policy against union opposition without massive coercion. Yet to woo the unions while strong-arming the employers is to risk their political base. Social Democrats governments have more credibility with the unions and more power within them than do bourgeois governments.

Yet that is finite as well. Thus the Swedish Social Democratic government collapsed briefly in 1990 over trying to legislate an incomes policy with LO and SAF support that, among other things, banned strikes; the rank-and-file union outcry unraveled backbench support, and forced the resignation of the Social Democratic finance minister. The debacle paved the way for the Conservative assumption of power after the 1991 election. Even for the Social Democrats neither credibility nor power are inexhaustible resources. It is ultimately Social Democratic supporters who are the objects of governmental coercion, and their opponents' supporters who are the beneficiaries.

As long as trade unions are autonomous and democratic (i.e., more than tools of the party or state, and responsive to member opinion), a long-term incomes policy can succeed only when it is consensual. When there is little real growth to distribute, when wage differentials within the labor market have been compressed, and when the need of those outside the labor market is no longer so pressing, one must look elsewhere to seek distributive justice.

It is in this context that the discussion of *industrial democracy*, or the redistribution of power and ownership in the firm, acquired immediacy in the 1970s and 1980s and lifelong training and education became important in the 1990s.

INDUSTRIAL DEMOCRACY: DEMOCRATIZING THE CORPORATION

In the days before World War I, when Social Democrats were orthodox Marxists, they assumed that political democracy would automatically bring in its wake labor majorities in parliament. These majorities would proceed to build the New Jerusalem that the Social Democratic evangelists had preached in the mines and the mills. The means to transform the old society into the new was simple: socialize industry, which then would be managed for and by the workers.

Political democracy itself was only one milestone for Scandinavian Social Democrats on the road to a democratic society. As political democracy was "steered into the harbor," as Swedish Social Democratic leader Hjalmar Branting put it in the final parliamentary debate on constitutional revision in 1918, the party proclaimed its dedication to achieving "our socialist and democratic ideals fully and completely" (Alsterdal and Sandell 1970, p. 119). Political democracy was indeed important. But it, like other milestones, not only marked a distance traversed, but it also indicated the miles still to be covered. Branting, like other Scandinavian Social Democrats of his generation, pursued without apology the reforms that were on the common agenda of Liberals and Social Democrats: universal suffrage, the eight-hour day, and the reform of the poor laws. "But we have never," said Branting, "lost sight of our goal, which lies beyond a bourgeois society, and which points toward a socialist order" (Alsterdal and Sandell 1970, p. 123).

Thus, the first Branting government, which took office in March 1920, established commissions to examine both socialization of the means of production and industrial democracy. In Sweden today, it is fashionable on the intellectual left to see both commissions as efforts by the mainstream Social Democratic leadership to bury the radical demands of the working class in royal commissions that deliberated interminably. The Socialization Commission did, in fact, set something of a record for longevity by not finishing its work until 1941. (For a discussion of the content of the work of the Socialization Commission, see Tilton 1987.) But for Branting and the other members of the dominant mainstream of Swedish Social Democracy, the aim was clear: to begin to examine how goals, still far beyond reach, might someday be achieved. When the goal might be reached was an open question. What the goal was, however, was not.

Placing a Democratic Economy on the Political Agenda

Democratizing decision making in the economy was raised as a political issue in Europe at three principal junctures. It came up in the immediate aftermath of World War I with the establishment of workers' councils in factories during the revolutions in Eastern and Central Europe; in the aftermath of World War II in the general push for the establishment of works councils throughout Western Europe; and again after 1968 in the events that began in May that year with the student-worker alliance in France and then spread throughout the rest of Europe, reaching as far north as the northern Swedish mines of Kiruna and Gällivare.

Since 1968, practically all Western European countries have grappled with how to expand democracy into economic life. From the shop floor to the corporate boardroom, employees have won new rights. These new employee rights have brought a substantial measure of workplace democratization in Scandinavia. As has been the case repeatedly in the last fifty years, the Scandinavian democracies—especially Sweden—have been on the cutting edge of reform. Although we focus on Sweden in the discussion that follows, Denmark, Finland, and Norway have undertaken similar, if less comprehensive, reforms.[3]

The initial push in the immediate aftermath of World War I yielded no more than commission hearings in Sweden, and not even that in Denmark and Norway. (In Finland the civil war destroyed labor's institutional power for a generation.) Universal suffrage brought not the expected Social Democratic majorities, but a period of shifting minority governments. Through the 1920s, weak Social Democratic minority governments (1924–

26 in Denmark; 1920, 1921–23, and 1924–26 in Sweden; and 1928 in Norway) existed only on the sufferance of centrist parties.

When the Social Democrats took office under more stable circumstances during the Depression, it was in alliance with the liberals and farmers, and Social Democratic continuity in government depended on a tacit understanding that socialization of the means of production would be held in abeyance. In any case, dealing with the immediate problems of the Depression was a sufficiently demanding agenda to absorb Social Democratic energies. After World War II, however, agreements establishing works councils, or plant committees with management and employee representation, were negotiated in 1945 in Sweden, 1946 in Norway, and 1947 in Denmark; they were legislated in Finland in 1946. But in the workaday world that resumed following the heady summer of liberation in Denmark and Norway, the works councils came to play a far smaller role than their proponents had assumed they would. Their powers were only consultative, and union ability to bargain far-reaching local influence receded as employers, sensing the cold winds of the Cold War at their backs, did not hesitate to use the managerial prerogatives to "lead and direct work" enshrined in paragraph 32 of the Swedish Employers' Confederation's statutes (and accepted as part of the standard national labor contracts) and in paragraph 4 of the Danish September Agreement to block any employee intrusions in management.

What put workplace democracy back on the agenda was the strike at the iron mines of Kiruna, above the arctic circle in the north of Sweden, in the winter of 1969–70. As one of the few industries in Sweden in state hands, the iron ore mines paid high wages; LKAB (Luossavåra Kiirunavåra Aktiebolaget is always known by its acronym) was an enlightened employer. But that strike in the dark of the Arctic winter became a symbol that high wages and the benefits of the welfare state were not enough. The unauthorized strike, which broke out on December 9, 1969, as a protest against newly negotiated piecework rates in the newest and most efficient of the three LKAB mines, quickly took on a political character directed as much against the existing system of labor relations as against the company. In a country where wildcat strikes were a rarity, Kiruna gave evidence that something was seriously amiss.

The LKAB strike rearranged the Social Democratic and trade union agenda. The joint Social Democratic–trade union equality commission chaired by Alva Myrdal stressed in its 1969 report not what had been achieved in terms of equality but what remained to be done. The place where inequality was most thoroughly entrenched in everyday life was on the job (Myrdal 1971, pp. 106–7). The Swedish trade union federation took up and acted on the question at its 1971 convention, adopting its Industrial Democracy program (Landsorganisationen 1972). From there the issue went with the trade unions' imprimatur to the Social Democratic party, which put it on its legislative agenda. In 1975, the party enshrined the goals of "guaranteeing the wage earners influence on their work places and firms and . . . expanding their participation in the formation of capital and administration of collective savings" as a third stage of democratization in its party program (Swedish Social Democratic Party 1975, p. 17).

Workplace Reform

Since that winter of arctic discontent in 1969–70, a series of workplace reforms that were adopted through unilateral action by management, change in union structure, collective bargaining, and legislation have transformed the exercise of authority in the workplace. The process of reform was piecemeal and incremental rather than revolutionary. No single piece of legislation is genuinely radical, except perhaps not the highly controversial wage-earner fund proposal that was finally passed in much moderated form in 1983. But more than a quarter century of piecemeal, incremental reforms, taken together, yielded a substantial transformation of authority in working life that extends democracy into the enterprise.

Together these reforms have democratized factories and offices in three ways:

1. They have altered production processes to reduce monotony and increase job satisfaction;
2. they have expanded individual rights in the workplace; and
3. they have provided considerable collective influence for employees in company decision making.

The first reforms, which began about 1970, were undertaken by management. Inspired by the pioneering work of Einar Thorsrud (Emery and Thorsrud 1969) in the 1960s in Norway, Swedish companies sought to redesign jobs to fit workers, rather than trying to redesign workers to fit jobs. Major departures included extending the work cycle, reducing repetition, and, in some notable cases, replacing the assembly line with team assembly. At Saab's Södertalje engine plant outside Stockholm, the assembly line was replaced by engine assembly in groups of three who set their own pace; each worker learned to assemble the engine by himself or herself. Volvo's Kalmar plant used the team concept for final assembly.

Because of the basic labor market context, both Swedish managers and unions had strong reasons to pursue improved job satisfaction. The solidaristic wage policy produced more equal wage levels throughout the economy, government programs equalized health and pension benefits, and the unemployment rate in the early 1970s was low (about 2.5%). In addition to increased turnover and absenteeism, the consequence of full employment was that workers could easily change jobs: They could choose *where* they want to work. The consequence of the excellent sick-pay system (90% of wages up to a ceiling roughly equal to the average industrial wage) was that workers had some choice in *whether* they wanted to work. This combination produced a substantial expansion in individual freedom. It also meant that the employer who wanted to maintain a stable, competent labor force needed to replace dirty, exhausting, and monotonous jobs with more pleasant and satisfying ones.

Swedish unions also were much more interested in influence on the job than their U.S. counterparts. The high Swedish tax rates diminished the value of wage increases for employees because half of any wage increase ended up in government coffers. Moreover, the excellent welfare state eliminated the need to bargain such basic benefits as health and dental care, sick pay, supplemental unemployment benefits, and pensions. As a result, unions' priorities shifted toward nonmonetary benefits, such as satisfaction on the job.

By the late 1970s, job redesign had ceased to be experimental. A sign of the times was the publication by the Swedish Employers' Confederation of a report entitled *Job Reform in Sweden: Conclusions from 500 Shop Floor Projects* (1975). In a country of Sweden's size, five hundred plants and departments represents a significant portion of production capacity. Old plants, like Volvo's main Torslanda works in Gothenburg, were retrofitted in the 1970s to draw the least-expensive lessons from job redesign experiments elsewhere; and new plants constructed in the 1980s, such as Volvo's Malmö and Saab's Uddevalla assembly plants, were designed around the new patterns of work organization.

Between 1973 and 1976 an unprecedented series of legislative measures opened Swedish companies' management to employee influence. Legislation in 1973 provided for putting two employee representatives on all corporate boards on a trial basis; the system was made permanent in 1976. Separate 1973 legislation also required companies to set aside 20 percent of their pretax profits in special funds to improve the physical work environment at the plant level; employee representatives were accorded veto rights over the projects proposed for the use of this money. In 1974, a safety steward system was established that accorded safety stewards the legal right to shut down production to force the correction of immediate safety hazards. Meanwhile, the law on security of employment provided employees with protection against discharge without cause and made provision for advance notice of layoffs and a general system of severance pay when notice was not provided. In addition, a fourth supplemental pension fund was created that was empowered to invest in common stock. In 1975, legislation provided employees the rights to educational leave, to paid maternity and paternity leaves, and, for foreign-born workers, to Swedish-language instruction on company time. Also, a contractual agreement provided unions access to company books. Finally, in 1976, the *co-determination law* (generally referred to as the MBL [Medbestämman-delagen]) passed parliament; it took effect in 1977 and accorded unions veto rights on subcontracting and substantial rights of contract interpretation. It obligated companies to provide employees with full information and to negotiate with employee representatives prior to making major changes in the company. It also abrogated contractual provisions that limited the issues that could be bargained, such as the employers' absolute right to manage. The effect of the MBL was to extend collective bargaining to include everything from investment decisions, to building plants abroad, to hiring department managers.

Although Danish, Finnish, and Norwegian workplace reforms have not been as comprehensive as the Swedish, they have still been significant. All three countries, like the Swedes, developed works councils in the immediate aftermath of World War II; the powers of these councils were broadened in Norway in 1966. In the 1960s, the joint LO-NAF Cooperation Council in Norway took a leading role in encouraging job redesign while the practice was still experimental. Safety-steward systems generally comparable to that of Sweden were established in 1975 in Denmark and in 1977 in Norway. There is no equivalent of the MBL in either country, although there are some similar tendencies in the Norwegian cooperation agreement of 1978 and the Danish technology agreements of 1981 and 1986. Finland's 1979 law on plant cooperation committees, enacted by a Social Democratic–led government, parallels the MBL. Employee representatives were added to company boards in Norway in 1973 (one-third of the board), in Denmark in 1973 and 1979 (two representatives, and one-third of the board, respectively), and Finland in 1991 (one-quarter of the board).

The Impact of Workplace Reforms

Today, for the average employee in Sweden or the other Scandinavian countries, the expansion of individual rights is the most crucial aspect of workplace democratization. In addition to such specific rights as paid maternity or paternity leaves and leaves of absence for education, legislation provides a generally high level of protection against arbitrary firings, and about as much job security as can be provided within a capitalistic market economy. Once workers have passed through their probationary period, they have substantial legal rights to their job. The safety-steward system offers considerable protection for the individual against immediate hazards on the job, and contractual agreements in a number of industries require plant doctors to devote one-half or more of their time to the prevention of industrial diseases and accidents. Equally important for individual rights in many industries has been the demise of Taylorism, with its emphasis on hierarchy, control, and the division of the labor into the small and highly repetitive tasks that characterize the assembly line, as a management philosophy.

Influence on actual decision making in the firm is not an individual question so much as a collective matter. In the Swedish system, it is the union that represents the employees collectively both on the company board and in the MBL negotiations. Of the two, the latter is unquestionably the most important. Through the MBL information procedures, employees have full access to company records, while the MBL bargaining procedures mean that employee representatives are involved in discussing all important decisions. The company obligation to bargain does not include the obligation to reach agreement, and management can ultimately impose its decision if it chooses. However, the process of informed discussion and bargaining often produces compromise and consensus decisions.

One additional consequence of workplace democratization has been an increase in the activity and competence of union locals, which, in Sweden, historically had less shop floor presence than their U.S. equivalents. The safety-steward system increased the number of union representatives by at least one-third in most plants, and the excellent training program for safety stewards created a broad circle of workers who were well informed on health and safety issues. The various measures providing rights for immigrant workers brought many of them into active participation in the local union. Finally, and most importantly, the MBL negotiations radically expanded the scope of union activity. All of this has created more activity in union locals and made them more representative than they were previously.

The Whole is Greater than the Sum of the Parts

None of the Scandinavian work-life reforms is in itself revolutionary. Other democratic nations have enacted more sweeping measures in particular areas of democratizing the corporation. West Germany's system of codetermination provides German unions and workers with half of the seats on corporate boards. Some Italian and French judges clap executives in jail for health and safety violations, which is more draconian than the Swedish safety-steward system. A number of U.S. Employee Stock Ownership Plans (ESOPs) offer workers the possibility of far greater capital accumulation in and, perhaps more significantly, greater control of their firms than was ever proposed in any of the various wage-earner fund proposals in Sweden, much less the version finally enacted.

Sweden has become a model for democratizing working life not because of any single reform; rather it is a model because of the scope and comprehensiveness of the reforms as a whole. To put it simply, the whole of Sweden's workplace reforms is greater than the sum of the parts.

The thrust of the Swedish reforms is to restructure authority relationships in the economic sphere, to replace the pattern of managerial absolutism established during the industrial revolution with a far more democratic pattern. One cannot visit many Swedish plants without realizing that twenty-five years of reforms have had a cumulative impact, especially on the shop floor. Plant-level managerial practices that were the norm in 1970 (secrecy in decision making, lack of employee consultation, failure to inform employees) are virtually extinct today. A more open, more participatory and democratic style has taken its place. Part of this is the direct result of the law. But a bigger part seems to be a cultural revolution in attitudes among both management and labor. That does not happen overnight.

Workplace democracy, like all forms of democracy, requires a change in attitudes and behavior. "You can't *force* people to do something like this," Göran Johansson, then metalworkers' local chairman at the big SKF ball bearing plant in Gothenburg, responded to complaints that reforms were moving too slowly in 1978, the year after the MBL went into effect. "They have to have a chance to think it out, to change their roles. There's a risk in making this kind of change too quickly. All you get then is the appearance of change, an illusion. We [management and labor] need respect for each other as individuals, and that takes time" (interview, May 25, 1978).

The MBL and safety-steward systems amounted to forced schooling in cooperation for both labor and management. Within a decade of the passage of both reforms, union local leaders and stewards had become conversant with the basic problems of the economics of their own plants and industries. They too faced the trade-off between short-term gains through wage increases and long-term gains through capital improvements. Plant managers learned that they had a new constituency: their employees. It was a constituency that is far more knowledgeable—and far closer—than stockholders. The plant manager found himself responsible not only to the company president (and thus, indirectly, to the board and to the shareholders), but also to his employees. Employee goals have not taken precedence over stockholders goals at the company level, but some balance has been achieved in the plant.

That balance has surprisingly little to do with wages, but a great deal to do with working conditions, style of management, and reinvestment. Reinvestment was Johansson's priority. "What do we need influence for?" he asked rhetorically. "To see that capital is used to provide secure jobs. We just can't trust the management to do that by itself."

Increasing workers' influence on management has changed some of the rules of the game. It altered the behavior and attitudes of supervisors, plant managers, company investment planners, and union local leaders alike. Workers still work, and managers still manage, but they do so in a new environment. The lines of class conflict, once so obvious in the plant, have lost their clarity. The unions have traded the certainty of the old adversary relationship for influence and for the compromise that this entails. Management has traded its dictatorial authority for a role of leadership. Although neither group is entirely comfortable with the outcome, the overall impact of workplace reform is judged positively by both.

Because of the protections and the influence that the reforms have provided, employees and their unions are rather more sympathetic to change than their counterparts in the United States and Great Britain. Consider the question of the introduction of new technology on the job. The guarantees that the Swedish employment-security law provides to the individual, the excellent unemployment-compensation system, the general provision of health and welfare benefits through the public sector, the constant availability of additional training, and the narrow wage differentials all combine to reduce employees' resistance to new technology. If workers are replaced by robots, there is a substantial certainty that they will suffer little hardship and will end up with another job, probably in the same company, that pays similar wages and identical benefits. Moreover, employee influence on the introduction of new technology through MBL negotiations and through the safety-steward system has meant that new technology has, on the whole, brought more obvious benefits in the workplace in Sweden than elsewhere. As a consequence, it is not particularly surprising that Swedish industry has moved more rapidly to embrace new technologies in the workplace than has industry in the United States.

More generally, the impact of democratization on company efficiency and profitability in Sweden seems positive as well. There seems to be little question that Sweden's democratization of work life has increased employee motivation and satisfaction just as it has increased employee input into decisions. There is no one-to-one correlation, but the pattern is clear. Although decisions may take longer to make, they are carried out more swiftly and with greater unanimity because of the consultative process that precedes them.

INDUSTRIAL RELATIONS IN THE ERA OF GLOBALIZATION

Economic globalization in the 1980s and 1990s altered the context for labor relations. As small, open economies, Scandinavians had long faced substantial international competition. But the centralized system of wage bargaining and the active labor-market policy had treated the national contract as a portion of national economic policy. It led the Scandinavians to willingly relinquish jobs in low-wage industries, such as textiles and shoes, while redeploying capital and labor to higher-wage industries.

The solidaristic wage policy, however, assumed that the nation was an appropriate unit for making economic policy. Globalization has called that assumption into increasing doubt.

At the same time, the triumph of neoliberal theory in Great Britain under Prime Minister Thatcher and in the United States under President Reagan in the 1980s suggested alternatives to the Social Democratic policy consensus in Scandinavia. As it captured the international policy high ground in the International Monetary Fund and World Bank, it exerted still greater appeal as the "Washington consensus." This alternative, which emphasized markets and downplayed government, was particularly attractive to a new generation of Scandinavian conservatives who had not been shaped by World War II and the development of the postwar consensus. Younger Social Democratic politicians and economists began to talk approvingly of entrepreneurship, markets, and privatization.

In the labor market this justified a reconsideration of the role of centralized bargaining and a transition from generally negotiating a single national contract to bargaining several sectoral, industry-wide agreements. This has undercut the push toward wage equality across the entire labor market and created greater flexibility in wage rates to respond to international conditions. The increase in unemployment and in involuntary, contingent and part-time labor ran counter to long-standing Scandinavian trade union policies. The rapid expansion of multinational corporations through purchase of existing workplaces in Scandinavia forced managers to serve two masters: national law that required consultation and negotiation and international corporate culture that often seemed to seek unlimited freedom of action. Although union members provided the largest bloc of anti–European Union voters in Denmark, Finland, and Sweden, which joined the EU (as well as Norway, where voters rejected the EU), EU regulation and European union cooperation emerged as a primary union response.

Decentralizing Bargaining

Given the problems that centralized national wage negotiations caused for the unions—excess profits for owners in the most advanced industrial sectors and firms and wildcat strikes to increase wage drift between contracts—it is ironic that the movement away from centralized national bargaining was pushed by conservative governments and by the employers' federations. This seems to reflect a rather un-Scandinavian cause: the triumph of ideology over pragmatism. Scandinavian conservatives have never embraced the neoliberal economic policy agenda in full, but they did embrace it in the 1980s and 1990s in the labor market. What was needed, they argued, was greater flexibility, more economic incentives, and less imposed equality. This philosophy, they argued, required decentralized bargaining.

The blue-collar union leadership certainly disagreed with this reasoning, but it offered them a way out of the vicious spiral of increased membership opposition to incomes policies that expressed itself in wildcat strikes. Besides, how could incomes policies be carried out successfully without long-term Social Democratic government? Occasional rounds of decentralized bargaining had always been a safety value for the unions—like wage drift—in the otherwise centralized system. So the unions had little reason to oppose strenuously the push for decentralization.

Centralized bargaining had put the blue-collar union federation LO and the private employers' federation at the center of the bargaining process. They negotiated the pattern-setting agreement, which was followed by the service sector and public sector. (A good rationale for this procedure was the overall national wage settlement was based on what exporters and the import-competitive sector could afford.) A major contributing factor to the decentralization of bargaining was the declining importance of the private manufacturing sector in the overall union movement. For example, by the middle of the 1990s, the LO-SAF sector comprised less than a third of all Swedish union members (Kjellberg 2000, p. 549). The increased importance of white-collar and professional unions altered the constellation of bargaining partners.

The trend toward decentralized bargaining began in Norway in the early 1980s. The Conservative governments of Kåre Willoch (1981–86), the first of the new wave of quasi neoliberal Scandinavian conservative cabinets, ended the incomes policy effort. Employers decentralized negotiations to industrial sectors. The result was a sharp increase in wage drift (which rose to 70% of pay increases), increased inflation, and a deterioration of competitiveness. Employers fought back in the 1986 bargaining round with a disastrous general lockout. The employers also lost the conflict, for which they had been ill-prepared, giving up large wage increases and a reduced work week (37.5 hours) and retention of guarantees for less well paid workers. It also contributed to the fall of the Willoch government, to the Labor party's return to power, and a resumption of more centralized coordinated bargaining in the 1990s.

Despite the Norwegian example, Danish employers forced decentralized bargaining in the late 1980s under a Conservative-led government; the Swedish employers' federation announced in 1990 that it would not continue to bargain a central contract (although the government successfully coordinated sectoral bargaining until 1995); and Finnish employers forced decentralization in 1991–93 under an agrarian Center government. The collapse of the Soviet Union, a major Finnish export market, drove unemployment up to close to 20 percent, yet decentralized bargaining produced large real wage increases at the bottom of the Finnish recession.

The largely uncoordinated 1995 Swedish round also produced high wage increases and a high level of conflict despite the highest unemployment rate since the 1930s.

The consequence was a general move to coordinated sectoral agreements, although the Finns returned to centralized bargaining in the 1995 and 1997. Although initial experience with sectoral bargaining was uniformly bad from a national economic standpoint, sectoral bargaining did provide greater flexibility for both sides. For employers, it provided some flexibility to respond to global pressures. For unions, it recognized the increased importance of white-collar and professional unions, and defused wage discontent in the most competitive sectors of the economy among workers who had borne the costs of the labor-market-wide policy of wage solidarity. Sectoral solidarity remained, but decentralization permitted greater wage gains in these sectors. OECD wage figures, however, suggest that decentralization did little to increase wage inequality in Scandinavia: From 1980 to the early 1990s, wage inequality increased modestly in Sweden and Denmark but decreased in Finland and Norway (Clayton and Pontusson 1998, p. 73).

In practice, sectoral agreements are typically bargained between subgroups of the national employers' federation and cartels or bargaining councils of unions, often drawn from more than one union federation. Sectors can also undergo easy redefinition, increasing flexibility. Thus, for example, the Swedish engineering sector bargaining council in the 1992 negotiations included Metall, the metalworkers union from LO; SIF, the salaried industrial employees' union, from TCO; and CF, the civil engineers' union from SACO. In 1997 this bargaining council was extended to cover all of manufacturing by the addition of five more LO unions.

The jury is still out on the utility of national versus sectoral agreements. The push for sectoral agreements seems to have increased strikes and lockouts, especially in Norway in the 1980s. It has certainly stopped the tendency toward greater wage equality that was built into the national bargaining rounds. On the other hand, decentralized bargaining also appears to have increased the rate of wage increases—not the employers' intent in initiating it—and inflation. The consequence has been that the governments have repeatedly tried to coordinate sectoral bargaining to achieve incomes policies, though with less success than in the period of national contract bargaining.

Declining Employment Security

From the Great Depression until the 1990s, full employment was the single most important policy goal of Social Democratic governments and Social Democratic–led unions. But despite their efforts, the last quarter of the twentieth century was a period of rising unemployment. Danish unemployment rose to European levels after joining the European Community in 1973 and during the energy crisis of 1974–75. A whole generation of less skilled, less educated young people found themselves marginalized economically despite repeated governmental initiatives and continual union wage restraint. Danish unemployment finally started to fall in the latter part of the 1990s.

In the early 1990s, after Sweden opened her capital markets and the Soviet market collapsed, both Sweden and Finland saw unemployment jump to levels not seen since the 1930s, reaching Danish levels in Sweden and doubling them in Finland. The integration of both countries into the European Union meant more harmonization with European policy measures that lacked the Scandinavian emphasis on full employment.

Only Norway and Iceland, outside the EU, remained unaffected by the secular rise in unemployment. Both, however, had employment cycle problems of their own. The Norwegians found themselves trapped in an economic cycle driven by oil prices. Icelanders were equally dependent on fishing stocks. Both, however, have unemployment rates significantly lower than other Western countries—and this is in spite of the fact that Iceland has one of the longest average working weeks (fifty-four hours for men and forty-four hours for women in 1998) in the industrial world.

The reappearance of unemployment as a major issue posed an identity crisis for the unions. For a century, the moral superiority of the working class over the decadent bourgeoisie had rested on its labor. Now suddenly, despite retraining programs and early pension schemes, labor was in surplus. Is paying workers to stay home the equivalent of paying farmers to leave land fallow? Is it conservation? Or is it demoralizing and destructive?

While Icelanders regulated both income and unemployment through lower pay and lots of overtime hours when fish were plentiful and lower pay and fewer hours in bad fishing seasons, the other Scandinavian countries lacked such easy adjustment strategies. They found themselves turning instead to an emphasis on reformulating union goals to include improving skills, life time learning, and supporting technological change. The outstanding example was Norway. Responding to the need to moderate wage increases without merely pushing up company profits, the Norwegian labor federation conference in 1997 committed itself to comprehensive vocation training, lifelong learning, and secondary school for all employees. Subsequent bargaining rounds have been characterized by these issues.

A second troublesome issue stemming from the lack of work was the growth of part-time and contingent work. Given the emphasis that Scandinavian unions accorded job security in the past, this, too, was seen as undermining labor rights. As temporary and contingent employment grew, the problem worsened. What does the labor movement have to offer the new class of marginalized proletarians who lie outside the now legislated employment security guarantees? If labor market flexibility is key to global competitiveness, what can labor do at the national level? Despite union efforts to push organization rates up, unionization rates among temporary employees only crept up from 62 to 65 percent in Sweden between 1987 and 1999; in Norway, where the unions do not control the unemployment compensation system, only 21 percent of private sector, temporary workers held a union card in the mid 1990s.

Internationalizing Capital and Labor

Since the Danish September Agreement in 1899, Scandinavian labor agreements and labor legislation have rested on the assumption that the nation was the appropriate unit for regulating labor relations. For the first three-quarters of the twentieth century, that was an accurate perception. During the last quarter, however, it became increasingly questionable. Capital became ever more mobile. Foreign multinational corporations merged with or bought Scandinavian national champions outright. Consider Sweden, once the Scandinavian economic powerhouse. In the 1990s, for every Swedish firm that expanded internationally like L. M. Ericsson or Electrolux, two or three vanished. Swedish ASEA merged with Swiss Brown-Bovari; the company headquarters moved to Switzerland. The Swedish chemical company Nobel was bought by Dutch Akzo; Akzo Nobel is headquartered in the Netherlands. In the auto industry, General Motors bought Saab car manufacturing in 1995, and Ford bought Volvo's car manufacturing in 1999; key Swedish auto decisions now get made in Detroit. Volkswagen bought Scania Trucks. Only Volvo Trucks remains Swedish owned and managed. The Swedish Astra pharmaceuticals merged with English Zeneca in 1999; the headquarters are in London. Swedish pharmaceutical giant Pharmacia merged with American Upjohn in 1995; guess where the headquarters are. After all, why would a non-Swedish-owned multinational company remain headquartered in peripheral Sweden?

The replacement of national employers with multinational firms undercuts the basis of national employers' organizations. From a union perspective, it means a shift of bargaining power from firms committed to the national stage to those that have no compunctions about pulling up their stakes and moving elsewhere in the world in search of greater profits.

The globalization of capital demands the globalization of the labor movement, and Scandinavian unions have been in the forefront of that effort. They founded the Nordic union confederation *Nordens fackliga samorganisation* in 1972 and were major participants in founding the European Trade Union Confederation (ETUC) in 1973.

So far there has been little coordinated bargaining between national unions and multinational corporations inside the EU. The ETUC has been a lobbying organization vis-à-vis the European Union's organizations and an international labor forum, not a bargaining organization. Sectoral federations, like the European Metalworkers' Federation, lack bargaining power, but could in time provide significant bargaining coordination. The EU Directive on European Works Councils provides for information and consultation in transnational European corporations, but is far weaker in its requirements than the Swedish MBL. It provides, however, a forum for international union cooperation vis-à-vis transnational corporations.

The largest single globalization issue in the future for the Scandinavian unions doubtlessly will be anchoring capital and jobs. The Scandinavian countries are geographically peripheral to Europe, and the northern parts of Finland, Norway, and Sweden are doubly so. Why invest there? Their citizens do so because that's where they live. Multinational corporations lack that motivation. They generally need special reason to invest in high wage areas. In this context, it is worth noting that Swedish wages have ratcheted down comparatively to German, French, and Dutch wages since Sweden abandoned capital controls in the 1980s. Unions are likely to find that control of capital is too important to leave to the capitalists.

In short, the challenges of the future for labor seem daunting. So did those of the past. Yet Scandinavian unions succeeded beyond their counterparts elsewhere. The Danish Social Democrats and unions optimistically started the century publishing a volume called *Socialdemokratiets Århundrede* [The Social Democratic Century] (1900). As it turned out, they were right.

NOTES

1. The most comprehensive work in English on the history of Scandinavian labor relations remains that of Walter Galenson (1952b); for more detail, see his treatment of Norwegian (1949, pp. 7–121) and Danish (1952a, pp. 7–93) labor history. For the development of Finnish labor relations, see Knoellinger (1960, pp. 1–126). Almost nothing on Icelandic labor history is available in English, except the brief treatment in Karlsson (2000, pp. 297–301); those who read Danish will find Einarsson (1979) useful. More contemporary developments are discussed in comparative terms by Korpi (1981) and Galenson (1986). There is a good discussion of Swedish white-collar unionism in Wheeler (1975) and of 1980–85 developments in Sweden in Flanagan (1987). For recent surveys, see the chapters on Denmark (Lind 2000), Finland (Kauppinen and Waddington 2000), Norway (Dølvig 2000), and Sweden (Kjellberg 2000) in Waddington and Hoffman (2000).

2. For a more extensive discussion of the structure of collective bargaining see Forsebäck (1976) on Sweden, Dorfman and Christensen (1975) on Norway, and Christensen and Nielsen (1967) on Denmark. For those who read Swedish, Bruun et al. (1990) provides an excellent and more recent comparative treatment of labor law in Denmark, Finland, Norway, and Sweden.

3. For a broad comparative treatment of the push for industrial democracy in the Nordic countries, see Gustavsen (1981). For a historical survey of Swedish developments, see Schiller (1974). Swedish reforms of the 1970s are surveyed and analyzed in Gunzburg (1978) and Hancock and Logue (1984). The principal efforts to frame the issue in a theoretical perspective in Sweden have been the quasi-Marxist works of Abrahamsson and Broström (1980) and, specifically on wage-earner funds, Meidner (1978). For a theoretical analysis reaching similar conclusions from a liberal democratic perspective, see Dahl (1985). For a comparative Nordic perspective, see Flodgren (1990).

PART IV

The Model Appraised

CHAPTER 11

Scandinavian Welfare States and Their Critics

The Swede has accepted a patterned and organized existence, because in return he has been given comfort and security. He wants nothing else; he sees nothing beyond his Welfare State. "Given the choice between Welfare and Liberty," says the editor of a liberal newspaper, "I would choose welfare every time." The price of contentment in Sweden is absolute conformity. . . . Personality has been suppressed, the collective worshipped at the expense of the individual. Given the European ethos, this might be expected to arouse rebellion. But not among the Swedes. They love their servitude.

—Roland Huntford (1971).

We are no longer satisfied with our welfare system. There's a lack of confidence in democracy. We were used to having very good schools, hospitals, care for the aged. But now we see that the quality of these basic institutions is not so good.

—Harald Stanghelle (2001)

To much of the world, it is Sweden that epitomizes the Social Democratic welfare state, and it is Sweden that has served as the lightning rod for both praise and criticism. To Marquis Childs in the 1930s, Sweden offered "the middle way" between "the absolute socialization of Russia and the end development of capitalism in America," which Childs at that time judged to have "worked to the end of blind self-destruction" (1936, p. 161). To Hudson Strode in the 1940s, Sweden was "model for a world" (1949). Richard Tomasson (1970) described it as the "prototype of modern society," and Henry Milner (1989) saw it as "Social Democracy in practice." Analyses of contemporary welfare states always include Nordic cases (see Lange, Golden, and Wallenstein 1995; Glyn 2001; and Pierson 2001). Academic studies tend to be more balanced than journalistic accounts, but they increasingly focus more on Nordic problems than solutions.

THE WELFARE STATE UNDER FIRE

In the last thirty years, critiques of the Scandinavian welfare states have become harsher. *Time* magazine looked at Sweden and heard "Cries and Whimpers in Socialism's Showcase," which were detailed in a cover story on "Sweden's Surrealistic Socialism" (*Time* 1976, p. 6). English journalist Roland Huntford (1972) judged Swedes to be "new totalitarians" who were in the process of establishing an amateurish but effective brave new world of socially engineered conformity that left little room for initiative, innovation, or individuality. Danish journalist Mogens Berendt, who inveighed against "the Sweden of prohibitions," reported approvingly that Frenchmen, demonstrating against Mitterrand's reforms in 1982, carried placards proclaiming "NO to the Swedish model!" (1983, p. 158).

Although Huntford's, Berendt's, and *Time*'s jaundiced views of Sweden can be dismissed as journalistic polemics, the more considered but similarly dark views of Per Olov Enquist (1984), Arne Ruth (1984), and especially Assar Lindbeck (1994 and 1997) and Bo Rothstein (1998) demand our attention. These critics sympathize with the aims and principles of Swedish policies. Nevertheless, they see problems as well as triumphs. For Enquist, the "strong society" of the Social Democratic vision, which was meant to sustain the weak, has instead become the "guardian society" that knows what is good for its citizens better than they do. Ruth sensed in Sweden "a malaise . . . reminiscent of the thirties." Lindbeck and his collaborators based their detailed critique of the Swedish model on a thorough economic and political analysis that suggested that political institutions were failing to maintain the legitimacy and effectiveness of social programs.[1] Rothstein emphasized the collapse of the corporatist model that built on trust and moderation between government, employers and employees. The more radical "economic democracy" goals of Olof Palme's Social Democrats after 1968 led to a breakdown of "organized social capital."

Sweden is not the only focus for criticism. In recent years Denmark and Norway have received their fair share of critical comment as well. Willy Martinussen described Norway as "the distant democracy" (1977). Bent Rold Andersen (1984a), a former Danish Social Democratic minister of social affairs and a strong supporter of the welfare state, looks at the question from an even broader perspective by questioning the future of all the

Scandinavian welfare states in his book *Kan vi bevare velfærdsstaten?* (*Can We Maintain the Welfare State?*).

Like beauty, the success of the Scandinavian welfare states seems to be in the eye of the beholder. Some see them as a model to be emulated. Others find them opprobrious. Is it a sign of the times or a temporary aberration of intellectual fashion that there are today more of the latter and fewer of the former? Certainly, the number of critics inside and outside of Scandinavia could indicate that the welfare states are in crisis. Then again, the criticism could be an indication that the welfare states are reaching maturity and now have a record to defend rather than only an agenda to pursue.

The Scandinavian welfare states have come to the end of a road that began more than seventy years ago when the Social Democrats took power. The basic structures of the industrial welfare state, which provide real guarantees of economic security despite old age, sickness, disability, and unemployment, were completed by the mid-1970s. More could be done to extend them, and there is no shortage of reform proposals in Scandinavia. But, fundamentally, the edifice is complete; what remains is decoration, regular maintenance, and periodic checks to determine whether the foundations of the welfare state are still structurally sound.

Two new challenges have appeared in the past thirty years: responding to the needs of women seeking to combine careers with families and integrating non-European immigrants into the social and economic mainstream. Much progress has been made on gender issues, but the immigration/integration issues remain highly controversial. Finally the fundamental economic issue—can the Nordic countries afford their generous welfare states—remains open.

Under these circumstances, the critics, whether foreign or domestic, deserve a careful hearing. In their diagonoses, we may glimpse a future cure. Moreover, with the completion of the basic structure of the welfare state, it is time to rethink some fundamental issues. As long as unemployment, poverty, and a destitute old age were the common lot, it was an act of arrogance to suggest that the welfare state might destroy individual incentives or undercut individual freedom. However, since the welfare state has effectively banished both the reality and the fear of poverty and hunger, we now have the luxury of addressing more philosophical concerns.

The modern Scandinavian debate about what lies beyond the welfare state centers on thirty- to forty-year-old stock criticisms that have been refined to fit today's world. The consequence is a level of sophistication in discussion that permits interesting conclusions, including some convergence in arguments by critics from the Right and Left. This convergence is made possible by the persistent Scandinavian consensus on the basic structure of the welfare state. Unlike the American or British right, Scandinavian conservatives do not advocate efforts to roll back the welfare state. Moreover, the basic structure of the economy is accepted by the Social Democrats.

Many of the criticisms of the welfare state were laid out more than fifty years ago. The Right attacked welfare measures for undermining social morality, undercutting the efficiency of the capitalist system, and being inimical to individual freedom. The Left quickly replied that nothing was more inimical to individual freedom than hunger, poverty, disease, and economic dependence. It was hypocritical, the Left said, to speak of morality in an economic system built upon avarice, or of efficiency in a system that automatically produced cataclysmic economic crashes.

Nevertheless, the Left also offered criticisms of the welfare state. The welfare state's transfer payments and social services treated only the symptoms of social ills, not the underlying causes. Moreover, it was unsuccessful in reducing inequality and promoted centralization and bureaucratization that was, for want of a better term, inimical to individual freedom. Middle-aged "new leftists" in the social science departments of universities and in government ministries have found themselves in the uncomfortable position of arguing, to crib Churchill's line on democracy, that the welfare state was the worst of all possible systems—except for the alternatives.

Moral Criticisms

All social criticism is rooted in moral indignation, even when cloaked in the objectivity of statistics. A critic's moral and political views can often be determined by looking at which statistics are marshaled to support his or her position. Still, to couch one's moral indignation in supposedly unbiased social criticism may occasionally seem naive.

Sin, Sex, and Suicide

Such may be the case with the sin, sex, and suicide syndrome. It has always been more popular among American critics than among Scandinavians, who, when they are confronted with it, generally reply with little grace that they are at least as moral as Americans. But such ill-tempered responses do not quell the perennial interest in the topic. There is no question that Scandinavians drink, fornicate, and commit suicide, although not universally and not necessarily in a causal sequence. The question is to what degree these activities that offend the commentators are related to the welfare state.

Perhaps the most prominent expression of this view grew out of a 1959 *Saturday Evening Post* article about Sweden that linked welfare measures to alcoholism, suicide, and crime (Wyden 1959), which was widely disseminated through the *Reader's Digest*. President Dwight D. Eisenhower picked up this frightening example of "Swedish decadence" in 1960 to warn against the consequences of an expanded domestic welfare policy in the United States.[2] A decade later, Roland Huntford (1972, pp. 325–37) argued that the sexual liberation side of social engineering helped to make Swedes love their servitude.

Yet despite such claims, evidence about the relationship between social ills and the welfare state is fairly clear. Herbert Hendin's solid study of suicide rates (1964) found grounds other than the welfare state, such as family and small-group dynamics and religious concerns, for the higher suicide rates in Scandinavia. The causal link is further weakened by the fact that Norway, which shares similar welfare institutions with Denmark and Sweden, does not share their high suicide rates. Clearly the widespread abuse of alcohol predates the welfare state and persists in spite of an active antialcohol policy, particularly in Sweden. The relative failure of Swedish policy in this area seems to attest to the limits of social engineering. And as for sex, well, that may say more about the frustrations of the critics than about Scandinavia. Incidence rates of sexual activity among teenagers in Scandinavia seem comparable to U.S. rates for the same age group, but the incidence of unwanted pregnancy is lower in Scandinavia. And although the attitude toward public nudity is clearly more relaxed in Denmark and Sweden than in the United States or Great Britain, nudity is not directly linked to sex. Sexually transmitted diseases, particularly the HIV/AIDS epidemic are more problematic; Danish STD and HIV statistics are comparable to those in the United States, while Sweden, and especially Norway and Finland have much lower rates.

Today, to relate sin, sex, or suicide to the welfare state seems a bit quaint. In the Nordic countries, as throughout the West, moral attitudes have changed significantly over the past generation. The causes seem to be affluence, popular culture, and changing attitudes toward personal freedom, not the provision of welfare state services, such as health care and child care, or transfer payments, such as sick pay.

Despite suggestions to the contrary by some critics, Scandinavian governments do not refrain from offering their citizens moral guidance. In fact, there is a degree of paternalism in Scandinavian governmental policies that offends right-wing critics of a more libertarian bent (see, e.g., Berendt 1983, pp. 127–48). These attempts by government to regulate the behavior of citizens as if they were children who needed to be looked after is particularly obvious in Sweden, where the government periodically exhorts its citizens to improve their nutrition, pay more attention to their children, and so on. Mandatory seat-belt laws and continual propaganda against combining drinking and driving particularly irritate those who see the automobile as the last frontier of human freedom. Governmental propaganda is indeed intrusive. On the one hand, it reflects a tradition of paternalism. On the other, it is a reflection of the government's desire to hold down public expenditures.

Diminished Social Solidarity

Although it is easy to debunk the moralists' sin, sex, and suicide argument, the welfare state does present serious moral problems. The most basic is this: By transferring responsibility for dealing with all social ills to the society (the state), the welfare state diminishes the reciprocal responsibility of each individual for his or her family, neighbors, and workmates. It atomizes society, destroying a significant portion of the social fabric simply by making it unnecessary. Admittedly, this development is one that is common to all urban, industrial societies, and it is related to housing patterns, social and geographic mobility, and above all, to housewives' entry into the labor force. However, it has more serious implications in Scandinavia because of the extent to which the Scandinavian welfare state was grounded on the reciprocal responsibility of the agrarian and labor movements.

"We lived on air and love, because that was all there was in abundance. And we dreamed of a new and just society" is how Swedish actress Birgitta Kadfeldt (1986) recalled her youth, which was spent in Gothenburg in the midst of mass unemployment during the 1930s. But

when we baked bread in the tenement in Masthugget [a working-class Gothenburg district] back then . . . it was a matter of course to share with other families who happened to be worse off. Today you don't even ask how your neighbors or acquaintances are doing. Take care of yourself and to hell with the others is the gospel we live by. Can you understand how we got to be this way?

The answer to Kadfeldt's question, we fear, is that the pervasive sense of social solidarity, or reciprocal responsibility, that underpinned the precursors of the welfare state—the mutual-insurance societies, that provided health, burial, and old-age insurance for workers, artisans, and farmers— has become more abstract as it has become more distant. When it is the "strong state," and not the small group, that takes care of its own, one's personal obligation is diminished. If paying your taxes provides home assistance for elderly Mrs. Hansson next door, then why inquire whether she needs a ride to the store or wants to have dinner on Friday?

By providing its benefits on an individual basis, the welfare state diminishes what Bent Rold Andersen describes as the "social network" that previously furnished many social services (1984a, 1984b). What has happened can be stated bluntly. In the past, to the extent that they were provided at all, social services were provided for the elderly and for children by housewives. Because working-class families usually required two incomes to survive, few working-class wives had the option of not working. While there were few latchkey children in middle-class neighborhoods in 1930 or 1950, in working-class districts, two-year-olds were often cared for during school hours by their six-year-old siblings. The elderly were similarly left to their own resources. As a result, the Social Democrats sought to provide not only social services for their constituency but to provide quality services as well. In fact, the quality of the services they provided was so high that the programs were as attractive to the middle class as they were to the working class. The labor shortage of the 1960s added impetus to the expansion of these programs. By the mid-1970s, the cultural pressures on middle-class women to drop out of the labor force when their children were under school age collapsed as tax incentives, smaller families, superb day care, modern technology, and the ideology of the women's movement combined to pull women out of the home (cf Table 9.2). In younger middle-class families living in urban areas, the housewife became an endangered species.

As the housewife disappeared, the demand soared for such programs as day care and after-school care for children, assistance for the elderly, and other social services previously provided on the basis of mutual obligation (and without pay) within the family. Many of the new careers open to women have been in staffing the so-called caring professions that were previously provided by family and neighbors. Moreover, as the older generation, which was used to providing services for family, friends, and workmates, passes on, the demands on the welfare state increase. Even without increasing the quality of service, the welfare state has to work harder at maintaining the existing level of service in the face of growing demands. This suggests the distressing conclusion that the costs of the welfare state will rise over the long term without a concomitant increase in actual well being (see Gress 2001, esp. pp. 289–91).

In effect, the welfare state has provided through collective means the guarantees that permit the individual to exist as an individual. Ties to family and friends may be emotionally satisfying, but they are no longer required for material security. It is ironic that the collectivist means that conservatives always feared would destroy individualism have, in fact, encouraged it. And it is equally ironic that this individualism seems to lead to an atomized society that puts greater pressure on welfare services than did the more organic society that it has replaced. It is worth noting, however, that societies with less adequate welfare systems have experienced much the same atomization. Moreover, in those cases it has probably produced more of a decline in real social welfare than it has in Scandinavia.

Absorbing Immigration

Unprecedented immigration from non-European countries to Scandinavia since the 1960s has further strained the solidaristic roots of the Nordic welfare state. Recent economic immigrants have been religiously and culturally far more different from the Scandinavian societies that received them than their predecessors were. They were also far more numerous than the political refugees who fled the Nazis, the Soviets, or, in more recent years, Latin American dictatorships for Scandinavian havens. Most immigrants have become productive, tax-paying residents and supportive consumers of social services. They face, however, widespread prejudices that some of the immigrants, particularly recent refugees, are social refugees seeking to exploit the collective generosity of the Nordic countries. Although data on such issues is incomplete and tentative (in part because many of the refugees are required to live on social benefits rather than work), it is clearly harder for many Scandinavians to support their "foreign" neighbors than their native fellow citizens.

This cultural conflict has undermined some of the support that universal welfare provisions have otherwise enjoyed. Solidarity rested, after all, on the small group cohesion of the workplace or the village extended, first, to your class and, then, to your nation. The sudden appearance of significant groups with very different cultural norms in the midst of your neighborhood—who worshiped differently, who saw themselves as distinctive, who slaughtered their animals differently, and occasionally slaughtered their daughters as well when they "shamed their family" by rejecting arranged marriages[3]—strains social bonds. To a unique degree, however, the attractive, universalistic provisions of the Scandinavian welfare states rested on the assumption that small group solidarity could be writ large. Are the differences with immigrant groups too great? Or does this just require a generation for assimilation?

Efficiency and Inefficiency in Market Economies

There is no question that the Scandinavian welfare states directly and indirectly impinge on the capitalist-market economy. The most direct impact is interference in the market to limit the impact of the economic cycle. Normally, one would expect countercyclical intervention in the market to protect the least efficient producers from the consequences of their inefficiency (i.e., bankruptcy). But, in Scandinavia, high rates of unionization and the unions' solidaristic wage policy, which increases the wages of the worst off, have all but ended subsidies to inefficient businesses through low wages (see Chapter 10).

The indirect impacts of the welfare state on the economy are more difficult to analyze. Still, the argument itself is clear enough:

1. The welfare state reduces the need for personal savings. Individuals consume more and save less with the expectation that the state will provide for sickness, old age, or any sudden catastrophe. The result is a low savings rate, which with demographic changes (fewer workers and more

retirees), has severe economic implications for both the public and private sectors.

2. The growth of the public sector drains what savings there are from the private sector into the public sector. Investment that ought to create manufacturing jobs goes instead into building nursery schools. The public sector, lacking a market mechanism, is inherently less efficient in its investments. The result is the long-term misallocation of resources.

3. Welfare benefits are so high that they reduce individual incentives to work. Why should you stand on the assembly line at all when you can collect almost as much on unemployment compensation? Why not skip work today, call in sick, and collect 90 percent of your pay anyway?

4. Paying for the welfare state in Scandinavia requires levels of taxation so high that, over time, the tax code has become a primary force in shaping all economic behavior. That inevitably produces huge and sometimes bizarre misallocations of resources.

The overall result of this unfortunate combination of forces is inefficiency. The dynamism of the capitalist economy is sapped by the welfare state, which depends on a strong economy for its resources. One need not be a conservative to concede the logic of this argument. But how does it work in practice?

Are Savings Rates Too Low?

It is easy to demonstrate that the Scandinavian countries, except Norway, have some of the lowest rates of household savings in the world. So does the United States, but that is for reasons other than the munificence of the American welfare system. In general, the Scandinavian answer has been to raise the rate of collective savings, which are needed anyway to pay the costs of the welfare system and future public-sector development. Private-sector collective savings has been stimulated by the lenient taxation of retained business earnings, a move that also encourages self-financing and more recently by tax-advantaged private pension schemes that cover nearly all salaried employees. Public-sector collective savings includes impressive pension funds, substantial public infrastructure investment, and, in Norway, an enormous Petroleum Fund (about $83 billion in January 2003, or roughly $18,000 per man, woman, and child) to stretch out the country's North Sea windfall. Because it is the rate of savings, and not whether it is individual or collective, that determines what is available for reinvestment, it is hard to argue that the lack of household savings per se is a serious problem. Moreover, the ending of international financial restrictions has led to significant foreign investment in Nordic advanced technology sector, especially electronics, biotechnology, and telecommunications as well as Scandinavian investment abroad.

Does the Public Sector Drain the Private Sector?

If we in the United States are plagued by what John Kenneth Galbraith once described as "public squalor amid private affluence" (1976), Scandinavian countries might be expected to exhibit the opposite: public splendor amid struggling private enterprises. At least that might be the expectation of those who consider private-sector–public-sector relations to be a zero-sum game (i.e., capital invested in nursery schools cannot be invested in new production equipment).

This argument has some intuitive appeal. However, there seems to be little evidence to support it when we compare long-term rates of economic growth with the size of the public sector in the OECD countries (cf. Tables 9.1 and 9.3). There are a number of good reasons why large public sectors may increase rather than decrease the rate of private-sector growth, all of which involve a long-term rather than short-term view of efficiency.

First, the stability and size of public-sector demand cushion the impact of the market on private-sector sales. This means economic downturns have less effect on private-sector production. Second, major portions of the Scandinavian public sector actually provide services to or reduce the costs of private-sector producers. For example, the massive Swedish labor market programs reduce job-training costs for business and dramatically improve the efficiency of the labor market. Expensive, high-quality day-care programs keep professional women, in whom society has an immense investment, in the labor market while their children are small. The importance of such public programs to the private sector becomes readily apparent whenever day-care employees go on strike. A third reason why large public sectors increase the rate of private-sector growth is by increasing the availability of human resources. By increasing the education and opportunities for the working class and for women, welfare state programs have made possible better use of human resources and a more efficient market economy. The emphasis on lifelong education through voluntary evening programs and massive union- and business-run programs on the job clearly do both.

Have Individual Incentives Diminished?

There is no question that the welfare state has diminished certain incentives. The existence of decent systems of sick pay diminishes the incentive to go to work when ill, and may also lower the threshold at which workers decide that they are sick.[4] Similarly, the existence of good unemployment compensation eliminates the incentive to take jobs that pay extremely low wages. It may also diminish the speed and enthusiasm with which the unemployed seek work. The efficient Scandinavian employment services automatically provide job referrals, and now force the unemployed to be less choosy. Other similar examples can be cited.

It is far from clear that these factors undermine the efficiency of the economy. Take comprehensive national health insurance as an example. The Nordic countries spend about 40 percent less on health care than the United States and have far better health statistics. The general availability of sick pay and free health care in Scandinavia, which almost certainly leads to more screening of ailments in the early, less expensive stages, is probably part of the reason. The bulk of better health statistics, however, almost certainly stems from the better access to health care.

On the other hand, generous social benefits may change attitudes and deter economic efficiency in the long run. Until they were tightened (by both nonsocialist and Social Democratic governments in the 1990s) the generous Danish system of unemployment compensation, for instance, unquestionably encouraged a significant number of Danish university graduates (and young people in general) to stay unemployed—to continue being unemployed French teachers and historians, fields in which job openings are few, rather than taking jobs for which they were not directly trained but for which they are qualified. Of course, such program-specific behavior can be discouraged simply by modifying the program. Today there are stricter work or training requirements for the young.

Are Taxes a Disincentive?

For almost fifty years, Scandinavian Social Democrats have sought to use the tax system, which financed the welfare state, as a redistributive mechanism in itself. For the same length of time, the bourgeois parties have tenaciously defended tax deductions that benefited their supporters. These deductions grew in importance and cost as marginal tax rates (i.e., the tax on additional earnings) increased. Eventually, the high marginal tax rates reached the increasingly prosperous working class. By the end of the 1970s, manual workers often lost two-thirds of overtime income to income taxes, and, by 1980, the Scandinavians had managed to produce the worst of all possible tax worlds: a system that combined very high nominal marginal individual income tax rates (which topped at 85% in Sweden) with open-ended deductibility of interest for private debt and a variety of other, freely chosen deductions.

Not surprisingly, this opened a veritable Pandora's box of undesirable consequences. There was a regular erosion of the tax base, a compensating compression of the progressive tax rates, which pushed more people into higher brackets, and a secular increase in household debt that was completely insensitive to interest rates. Mogens Glistrup, the iconoclastic tax lawyer and evader who erupted onto the Danish political scene at the head of the second-largest parliamentary party in 1973, suggested that the tax records be burned in the midsummer's eve bonfires, which was the traditional means of ridding the country of witches. The proposal had some merit. The economic dislocations that this system produced were extraordinary. But they were not the result of the tax system's disincentives. Individuals did not stop working because marginal rates were high. Instead they rushed for the nearest tax shelter. It reaffirms one's belief in human rationality to discover that, when their marginal rates are equal, the ordinary citizen is as capable of utilizing arcane tax loopholes as the average U.S. millionaire. It does little, however, for the efficiency of the economy.

This is one area in which the critics of the existing structure of the welfare state have converged. The Social Democrats abandoned their effort to use the tax system to increase equality, and the Conservatives and the other bourgeois parties abandoned their valiant fight to protect every tax loophole possible, irrespective of its socially undesirable consequences. The two sides agreed to disagree on the aggregate level of taxes and agreed to agree on broadening the tax base by slashing deductions while reducing progression. Excise taxes were moved to environmentally degrading activities, such as consuming fossil fuels. These reforms started in the early 1980s and made the Nordic tax systems more compatible with European and global trends (Haskel 1987; Steinmo 1993). The critics were right. It simply took ten years to put the reforms in place.

Nordic social, educational, and health services are expensive, however, and tax burdens remain high. As Table 9.3 indicates, the gap between Scandinavia and the rest of the European Union is no longer growing. What appears to be crucial to avoid distortion of individual behavior by the tax system is that the tax base be broad, marginal tax rates be capped, and income be taxed at similar rates regardless of source. Few Scandinavians would argue that they are under taxed. On the other hand, the tax and welfare system seem fundamentally fairer today to most people than they were perceived to be in the 1970s and 1980s.

The neoliberal argument against the Scandinavian welfare states rests upon assumptions not unlike those above: They reduce the efficiency of the market economy and hence reduce the overall welfare of their citizens. Certainly that has, on occasion, been an unintended consequence of individual programs. But minor changes in those programs to correct these flaws seem to be successful. Throwing the baby out with the bath water has rarely been a good strategy.

The Persistence of Inequality

The traditional criticism from the Left was that the welfare state treated only the symptoms of the capitalistic illness and, worse, for this reason, did an inadequate job of ameliorating them.

The growing absolute impoverishment of the working class was an article of faith for Marxists who experienced the Depression. Not only had the Social Democrats sold out socialism for a mess of welfare pottage, but it was not even enough to compensate for the rising absolute and relative deprivation of the working class (see Nørlund 1959a, 1959b). The problem with this argument was that, like many other criticisms based on articles of faith, it was demonstrably false. Scandinavian welfare state programs did not exist in a vacuum. They were embedded in managed capitalist economies that were not prone to ever-greater crises, and they were pushed by unions that were successful in winning real, long-term wage increases for workers. Moreover, they raised the living standards of those outside the labor market.

On the other hand, empirical evidence seemed to confirm the equally hoary belief that capitalism led automatically to the concentration of economic power. The argument was made most forcefully in Scandinavia by C. H. Hermansson (1959, 1971), who became chairman of the Swedish Communist party in 1964. Hermansson, extending Rudolf Hilferding's (1910) arguments on financial capitalism, surveyed the interlocking directorate of banks, insurance companies, and financial holding companies through which "Sweden's fifteen families" controlled Swedish industry. Because political power was thought to flow from economic power, the growing concentration of economic power that Hermansson documented in Sweden called into question the future of democracy.

In the same period—the 1950s and 1960s—the standard Social Democratic critique of the welfare state emphasized its incompleteness. Bent Hansen (1969), who would later become a Danish Social Democratic social welfare minister, and Gunnar and Maj-Britt Inghe (1967) in Sweden pointed out where the welfare state fell short. At the end of the 1960s, this line of argument was incorporated into a more systematic critique of the welfare-capitalist amalgam that the Social Democrats had created.

During the end of the 1960s and early 1970s, as the final major income security programs were put in place, first the Swedes and then the Norwegians and Danes established commissions to examine the persistence of inequality in spite of the welfare state. This heralded a revival of leftist politics in the Nordic countries. The first and most remarkable of these commissions was the joint Swedish Social Democratic–trade union commission chaired by Alva Myrdal. Established in June 1968 at the party congress, the Myrdal Commission absorbed the lessons of the French student-worker revolt. Its 1969 report (Myrdal 1971) devoted one-half of one chapter to the successes of the welfare state and eight chapters to the failure of the Swedish welfare state to achieve genuine equality for all Swedes. That report was followed in Norway in 1972 and in Denmark in 1976 by the establishment of governmental commissions to investigate the degree and causes of social, economic, educational, gender, and political inequality.

The persistence of gross inequality, as documented in the Myrdal report and its Norwegian (Norway 1976) and Danish (Denmark 1982) successors, confirmed that, while the welfare state clearly raised the living standards of the worst-off and provided a genuine guarantee of material security for all, the welfare state had done less to equalize opportunity than had been believed, and far less to equalize results. While equality of opportunity—especially in open access to education and for women—enjoyed broad support, equality of results was a subject of great controversy. More than any other subject, this threatened the welfare state consensus (see Heckscher 1984, pp. 227–53).

The drive for greater equality that has developed from the left-wing criticism of the welfare state over the last thirty years has provided a focus for political action without providing satisfactory intellectual solutions to two crucial underlying questions: At what level does the trade-off between equality and efficiency yield a lower standard of living for those who are less equal? And do Scandinavians want economic equality among families or among individuals?[5]

Instead, debate has focused on the obvious political point: The acceptable level of inequality in society is a matter of the political balance of forces. In parliamentary politics, the argument has been waged around the edges of the welfare state. Battles have been fought in Denmark and Sweden over marginal reductions in income replacement ratios during periods of sickness or unemployment and whether sick pay should start on the first, second, or third day of illness. Inside the unionized sector, where the solidaristic wage policy has significantly lessened inequality by reducing wage differentials between skilled and unskilled workers and between the private and public sectors, the unions that organize skilled workers in industries with high-profit levels have finally rebelled against further reduction of wage differentials. The result is that the systematic reduction of wage differentials, which began as a union policy in the 1950s and 1960s, came to a halt in the 1980s and 1990s.

Scandinavians have never really addressed the question of whether desired economic equality is equality among households or among individuals. While family programs assumed the former, changes in the tax code in the 1970s assumed the latter. This lack of harmony in policies almost demands a dysfunctional outcome. It reduces tax revenues and increases the demand for welfare services without actually raising the level of social welfare. Alone among Western industrial democracies, the Nordic countries tax income on an individual basis exclusively. The consequence is that the marginal tax rate for a second wage earner is approximately one-third lower than if the same money were earned as additional income by the first wage earner.[6] Not surprisingly, much of the exceptionally high demand for day care in Scandinavia comes from women who simply cannot afford to stop working while their children are small because no amount of overtime or pay raises for their husbands can maintain the family's after-tax income.

At a different level, increased immigration and the growth of the global economy call into question the whole project of reducing inequality at the national level. Can islands of relative equality be maintained in small nations on the northern periphery of Europe? Will they inevitably be inundated by the rising tide of global inequality, including rising CEO salaries like those in the United States and competition from the Third World countries that pay near-starvation wages to industrial workers? Long standing Scandinavian development aid seems only to be a drop in the bucket. However here again, collective action within the European Union seems to offer an alternative.

Treating Symptoms, Not Causes

Between 1935 and 1975, there was a clear sense that welfare programs were producing improvements in the level of welfare in society. Since the mid-1970s, however, there has been a growing suspicion that, despite significant growth in welfare spending, both absolutely and as a percentage of GDP, there has been little or no increase in social welfare. Some Social Democrats have succumbed to the queasy feeling that maybe the bourgeois parties were right that welfare programs were somehow socially destructive. Others have tended to think that leftist critics were right when they charged that the welfare state was treating the symptoms of capitalism, but ignoring the illness itself. Perhaps, they thought, it was time to deal with the root of inequality: the private ownership of the means of production.

Between 1968 and roughly 1985 the neo-Marxist Left argued that the welfare state increasingly was less a means to satisfy real needs and more a means to absorb the social costs of capitalistic production. This was true both in terms of training the required sophisticated labor force (Andre Gorz's "wider reproduction of labor") and in terms of dealing with the damaged labor force resulting from the capitalistic system. Speed-ups in production relegated older workers to a marginal position and wore the young out early. The introduction of hundreds of new chemicals in the workplace every year guaranteed a continued epidemic of occupational cancer and other diseases. Care of the disabled, the sick, and those forced out of the labor market all made the irrationalities of capitalistic production more tolerable. Society picked up the costs; the capitalists harvested the benefits.

Given the continual, probably accelerating, change in the methods of production, there seemed no limit to the demands on the welfare state posed by the economic system. Like a conscientious squirrel, it seemed the welfare state could run faster and faster on the treadmill without ever making any progress.

The answer offered by the more pragmatic of these critics was prevention within the existing economic system. Regulation to prevent the victimization of workers, especially of women and children, has its roots in the protective legislation of the nineteenth century. But the proposed preventive regulation was different. Consider the implications of the workplace reforms discussed in Chapter 10. The occupational health and safety system, established in Sweden beginning in 1974 and subsequently replicated in Denmark and Norway, transferred primary responsibility for health and safety on the job from government inspectors to union safety stewards who were given far-ranging powers. Their powers included substantial influence on investment decisions to force the incorporation of health and safety considerations in new equipment purchases and building construction, and the draconian authority to shut down plant operations (with full pay) until immediate dangers were eliminated. To take another example, the Swedish MBL, or codetermination law, abolished the concept of managerial prerogatives and opened all business decisions, from hiring department heads to investment decisions to advertising campaigns, to collective bargaining. Such developments created positions of countervailing power inside businesses, making them more responsive to employee interests, within the constraints of the market, and less likely to engage in behavior that increased welfare costs.

Not only did the redesigned union-management relations in the plant tend to encourage measures that reduced demands for welfare, but on some occasions labor and management agreed that companies should assume welfare obligations previously shouldered by the society (see Einhorn and Logue 1982, pp. 46–47). The initial version of the wage-earner fund called for making employees co-owners of the earnings their companies retained. That version, as discussed in Chapter 10, proved politically unpalatable to other parties, and the Swedish Social Democrats modified the plan virtually beyond recognition before finally passing it in 1983. The Conservative government phased it out between 1991 and 1994. The idea, however, was attractive to many and, ironically, was partially recycled in the 1999 Swedish pension reform that allowed employees to control part of their pension funds. Over time such funds may convert the capitalistic system from a machine that automatically created economic inequality into one that creates capital for workers and capitalists alike. That kind of economic system would require far less redistribution and a far smaller public sector to achieve the same welfare ends.

INDIVIDUAL FREEDOM AND COLLECTIVE RESPONSIBILITY

The question of the welfare state and individual freedom is inherently speculative. The quick answer to the simplistic conservative claim that the welfare state is inimical to individual freedom is that poverty, hunger, disease, and economic deprivation are even more hostile. Discussions about individual freedom become interesting only after everyone has been clothed, fed, and housed.

The Scandinavian welfare states have abolished not only hunger, poverty, and deprivation, but also the fear of those scourges. In this fashion, the welfare state has created a basis for the extension of personal, social, and economic freedoms. The growth of the welfare state has historically paralleled the expansion of individual freedom, at least in democratic societies. In the final verdict, the welfare state must be judged as compatible with individual freedom, in spite of various opinions to the contrary.

The current debate on welfare and freedom revolves around the issue of whether the means to the former diminish the latter. The principal avenues of the creation of welfare have been centralization and bureaucracy. Local governmental units have been consolidated to improve their capacity to provide welfare services in Denmark, Norway, and Sweden. Unions have been stripped of employment-service functions to make the labor market more flexible and efficient. In Denmark, the neighborhood-based health insurance societies have been nationalized into a government-run (as well as government-funded) system.

The consequence has been a radical reduction in welfare services administered by elected or appointed officials and a concomitant increase in bureaucracy and hierarchy. For some, this threatened to create a tyranny of the experts who owed their position to education (Dich 1973); they were not citizens' servants but their superiors. A sign of the times is the Danish statistical classification of children in day care into three groups: "taken care of in day care centers," "taken care of by [approved] day nurses," and "not taken care of" (i.e., left in the hands of their untrained parents) (Danmarks Statistik, *Statistiske Efterretninger*, 1982, p. 376).

If in fact much of the increase in welfare utilization in the last two decades stems simply from higher rates of utilization associated with a generational cultural change (see Logue 1986), then the long-term prognosis for the Scandinavian welfare state is one of growing fiscal strain unrelated to actual need. The size of the Scandinavian public sectors (50–60% of the GDP) has reached a level where further increases, absent corresponding growth in the private sector, are probably not politically feasible. Of necessity the Nordic countries have accepted that the welfare state has grown to its political and perhaps economic limits. A way must be found to restrict the growing cost of welfare.

The introduction of means tests and other measures of bureaucratic control offer an obvious, but unpleasant, way to cut welfare demand without reducing the material living standards of the worst off. Such measures are expensive to administer. And while they would certainly restrict middle-class use of welfare programs, they would also mean a loss of political support for the welfare state.

Another way of restricting the increasing costs of the welfare state is politically more feasible, but morally less attractive than means testing. The level of transfer payments or the quality of social services could be reduced for all. That seems likely for old-age pensions, where the universal element is expected to grow more slowly than the earnings-related portion. Unfortunately, such a move would affect most severely those who are in greatest need of assistance from the welfare state.

A third and more attractive alternative, however speculative, is to expand on the decentralization process begun in the 1970s and 1980s. If there is any area in which there is a convergence of criticism from the Left, the Right, and the Center, it is the issue of decentralization. Attacks on bureaucracy are always popular, even when the bureaucracy is vital to and successful in achieving popular goals. Careful plans for a small scale, ecologically balanced, and popular democratic society appeared in the wake of the energy and environmental crisis of the 1970s (cf Åkerman 1979; Meyer, Petersen, and Sørensen 1978). Although these decentralized utopias are economically more radical than most conservatives will find comfortable, the pursuit of a more organic sense of community is a familiar conservative theme. In the past decade policies allowing for greater administrative autonomy in the public service sector as well as the privatization and partial deregulation of some services have begun to test these theories. The push, explicit in both plans, for the maximum feasible degree of decentralization and participation in the governance of enterprises and of cities will disturb those on both the right and left who believe that there is only one right way to organize a society. The re-creation, on a modern technological basis, of a society that is both decentralized in decision making and human in scale would lead to a far more diverse society than has typified the Scandinavian countries in the past. It would, however, require a relaxation of strict national standards to permit more community choice, and that would make the state a less effective instrument for carrying out social transformation.

The greatest virtue of a radical decentralization of the administration of welfare programs is that it may replicate, in a modern economic and social context, that sense of reciprocal responsibility within the group that underlay the Scandinavian welfare state in its origins. Scenarios for decentralization of responsibility for welfare to smaller communities, whether in the workplace (as in occupational health and safety) or in neighborhoods or towns (as in the Åkerman and the Meyer, Petersen, and

Sørensen plans), offer some prospect of reversing the atomization of society, with the increased demand for welfare that it entails, and for reversing the decline in social solidarity that otherwise threatens to make the attractive, noncoercive, and universalistic features of the Scandinavian welfare state a one-generation phenomenon.

NOTES

1. Lindbeck et al. initially undertook their analysis as an official public report under the nonsocialist Bildt government in 1992–93. For a different perspective, see Korpi and Palme (1998).

2. Speaking at a candidates' breakfast in Chicago in July 1960, Eisenhower discussed the danger of political extremes. He referred to a "fairly friendly European country" that suffered from twice the U.S. rate of drunkenness, and he denounced nations that showed a "lack of moderation discernible on all sides." In contrast, "the great middle road" was most likely to succeed (*New York Times*, July 28, 1960, p. 1:8). It was an ironic twist for Sweden, a country so often portrayed as embodying "the middle way." Despite Eisenhower's coyness in not naming the country, the Norwegian newspaper *Verdens Gang* helpfully suggested that if Ike was concerned with drunks and suicides, he must have been referring to Sweden. Meanwhile, offended Swedish officials criticized Eisenhower for his ignorance of Swedish conditions. Commentary continuing the tempest provided considerable midsummer entertainment. Eisenhower eventually apologized.

3. The most prominent case in point is that of Fadime Sahindal, a twenty-six-year-old Kurdish immigrant to Sweden, who was raised in Uppsala, Sweden, and was killed in 2002, apparently for "shaming her family" by rejecting their choice of husband. Before her death, she had been an icon of cultural transition on television, on public platforms, and, in November 2001, before the Swedish parliament.

4. After all sick days used to care for sick children are omitted, Danish sick-pay statistics, for example, yield the bizarre finding that young adults have a higher incidence of illness than the old ones (see Jensen 1980, p. 57; Sundbo et al. 1982, pp. 100–107; and Dansk Arbejdsgiverforening 1981–83). For a discussion of this and other peculiar findings that suggest a major generational shift in behavior, see Logue (1986, pp. 268–70). Tightening Swedish sick-pay rules—requiring employees to absorb the first day of sick-leave—in 1992 resulted in a dramatic fall in sickness-related absenteeism by almost 50 percent. Some wags suggested that the health minister responsible be awarded the Nobel Prize in medicine for the instantaneous improvement in Swedish national health.

5. The question of the trade-off between equality and the overall level of prosperity in society is discussed most rigorously by John Rawls (1971) in his theory of distributive justice. His solution, the "difference principle," permits deviations from equality provided that these deviations cause a cumulative improvement in the absolute standards of living of those who are worst-off. In a sense, the Scandinavian welfare states that the Social Democrats engineered with their combinations of managed capitalistic economies and redistributive public-sector programs are real-world exercises in the Rawlsian difference principle. Dynamic

capitalistic economies simultaneously generate inequality and the wealth that funds redistributive public-sector programs to combat inequality. The practical problem for the Rawlsian model of justice is to maintain both the redistributive principle in the public sector and long-term political support for redistribution. The fact that most Scandinavian programs are available to all, rather than being means-tested, has maintained political support, but has gradually reduced redistribution as the comfortably well-off have come to regard welfare programs as suitable for the middle class.

6. This is after the tax reforms of the 1980s and early 1990s. Previously the second earner might have a marginal tax rate 50 percent of the full-time worker.

CHAPTER 12

The Future of the Scandinavian Model

With all its faults, the welfare state [remains] the most humane and civilized system ever created.

—Olof Palme

At some rare moments a nation pauses to reflect on its future. Such moments usually occur in periods of decline and crisis. . . . Today Sweden is experiencing its most serious crisis since the 1930s. How Sweden works to overcome the crisis will mark the country for decades to come. The form the solution will take is still an open question.

—Assar Lindbeck et al., 1994

Among the characters Selma Lagerlöf describes in her 1891 novel *Gösta Berling's Saga*, the fate of Kevenhüller is particularly poignant. He forsakes the privileges of noble birth in Germany to improve mankind's lot with his mechanical inventions. He wanders through Europe learning the secrets of the tiniest watch and the largest mill. Kevenhüller finally comes to Värmland in Sweden, where a chance meeting with a wood nymph in Karlstad changes his life. She repays his kindness to her by granting him the ability to make whatever he chooses—once. Frustrated by his inability to replicate his inventions, Kevenhüller ultimately destroys each and goes mad.

Is the success of the welfare state in its attractive Scandinavian variant a phenomenon that, like Kevenhüller's inventions, cannot be replicated? Although the institutions of the welfare state are relatively permanent, the international economic situation, the domestic political party constellation, and the cultural context within which those institutions operate are anything but static. The changing environment requires the re-creation of the model in every generation.

There is much to build on. Both Scandinavian political institutions and welfare state policies have not only flourished in good times, they have also stood the test of the economic difficulties of 1975–95. The Scandinavians have come through the period without the virulent rightist protest seen in France, the urban rioting in Great Britain, and the relative impoverishment of a significant portion of the population that has occurred in the United States. Despite substantial economic strain and policy problems, the Scandinavian welfare states have weathered both national and international economic storms with relative consensus about institutions and policies. They are not, however, unchanged.

The consensus on political institutions remains firm. Parliamentary democracy has not been seriously challenged since World War II. Subsequent constitutional reforms (including new constitutions in Denmark, Finland, and Sweden) have made little change in the institutional structure of politics; even the abolition of the upper houses of the Danish and Swedish parliaments occurred after they had ceased to be politically significant. Generally the new constitutions updated the old by codifying recent practices, although the Finnish constitutional reform of 2000 curtailed some Presidential power in favor of a more parliamentary government. Although minority and coalition governments have been the rule rather than the exception, the consequence has been the development in all major parties of a willingness to compromise that has ultimately made them all responsible, to a greater or lesser degree, for current Scandinavian policies. Judgments of the success of political institutions, however, are always relative. Recall Winston Churchill's qualified praise for democracy as "the worst form of government except all those other forms that have been tried from time to time."

What passes as a cause for concern in Scandinavia might be considered ideal elsewhere. That is certainly true of the structures of Scandinavian democracy. The multiparty parliamentary system has stood the strain of the economic difficulties. New parties in Denmark and Norway have been accommodated within the patterns of parliamentary bargaining. A homegrown, democratic, radical socialist opposition on the Social Democrats' left has survived the demise of Leninist-style Communism. Indeed, in Sweden, radical socialists have supported the Social Democratic minority government for nearly a decade, while in Finland the Social Democrats governed with the post-Soviet Left Alliance, centrists, and Conservatives from 1994 to 2003. Here is a rainbow coalition that actually wins elections! Even the protest parties of the right in Denmark and Norway have begun to participate in the usual parliamentary give and take. Greater cabinet instability in Norway and Sweden reflects the end of Social Democratic hegemony and the conversion of elections into genuine contests about alternative governments. It does not reflect a pernicious decay in democratic practice.

Political participation rates in Scandinavia are high. Rates of election turnout (which vary between 65% and 80% in Finland, 75% and 85% in Norway, and between 85% and 90% in Denmark, Iceland, and Sweden), and party membership are high in comparison to other democracies, but lower than a generation ago. Participation through membership in interest organizations far exceeds that in other democracies. Rates of involvement in grassroots political organizations are also among the highest in the world. Surveys indicate that political resources are more widely distributed in Scandinavia than in most other democracies. Conversely, rates of political violence and other indicators of instability are low. The assassination of Prime Minister Olof Palme in 1986 remains an anomaly. More disturbing is the rise of violent crime with immigrants disproportionately the perpetrators and victims.

The Scandinavian political systems have been reasonably successful in incorporating previously excluded groups into political life. Granting the right to vote in local elections and the right to hold local office to resident noncitizens has drawn them into party and political life. Perhaps most impressive has been the recruitment of women to political office. Between 1965 and 2000 the proportion of women in Nordic parliaments rose from roughly 10 percent to about 40 percent (cf Table 4.1). The proportion of women cabinet ministers, mayors, and ranking civil servants continues to increase sharply, and Norway's Gro Harlem Brundtland was prime minister three times before retiring from Norwegian politics to become the Director of the World Health Organization (cf Bergqvist et al. 1999). In 2000 Finland's new President Tarja Halonen became the ranking female political figure in Scandinavia, and she was joined in 2003 by Prime Minister Anneli Jäätteenmäki.

Further, the development of more direct forms of citizen participation and the elaboration of the ombudsman system have provided additional channels for citizen control of government (see Chapter 4). The most cruelly divisive issue of postwar Scandinavian politics—membership in the European Union—was decided by referenda in Denmark, Finland, Norway, and Sweden; the same was the case with the key issues of the supplemental-pension system (1958) and nuclear power (1980) in Sweden. Direct democracy is still restrained, and there are no provisions for well-financed, citizen-led initiative ballots that challenge representative government in Switzerland and many American states. Despite the fears of Crozier, Huntington and Watanuki (1975), Brittan (1977) and Lindbeck et al. (1994) that excessively broad participation in the policy process will lead to inadequate, unbalanced, and inconsistent responses to pressing problems (if not to a paralysis of ungovernability), Scandinavian democracy looks very good when judged by external standards. Nor do Scandinavians take democracy for granted; recurring studies of democratic procedures and "democratic audits" have become the norm.

Agreement in Scandinavia on basic lines of policy remains reasonably firm. The postwar Keynesian consensus on economic policy continues: Private enterprise is the main engine of economic growth; the state assures social investment and overall economic balance; and the welfare state guarantees substantial economic and social security to all. After 1973, sluggish economic growth in Denmark and Sweden (and briefly in Norway) placed severe economic demands on income-security programs, but none of the alternative governing coalitions proposed significant changes in basic welfare state policies. Recurring economic crises in all of the Scandinavian countries between 1989 and 1994 brought greater changes. Labor markets became more flexible, the public sector cautiously pursued outsourcing and privatization, and social spending was restrained. None of these measures rolled back the welfare state in any fundamental area, but the political and economic agenda now emphasizes growth, productivity, and efficiency more than redistribution, equality, and security. Without adopting the American winner-takes-all approach, Scandinavia pursues a sustainable welfare state.

Yet there are signs of strain. The Scandinavian countries, like much of the democratic West, are prone to recurrent bouts of malaise that have political, economic, and social dimensions. Political optimism returned in the 1990s with the sudden end of the Cold War, the collapse of Soviet-style communism, and the new democratic regimes of a dozen Central and Eastern European states. German reunification was acceptable under the fully democratic constitution of the Federal Republic, and the Nordic countries embraced their long-captive Baltic sister-states. Democratic government and a strong Western orientation in Central Europe relieved historic geopolitical tensions and allowed Finland to become a fully normal Scandinavian and Western European state. On the other hand, the collapse of Yugoslavia and the ensuing wars and humanitarian outrages demonstrated that Europe was not yet a continent of democracy, peace, and moderation. The severe economic contractions in Sweden and Finland after 1990 following banking crises, the mediocre economic performance of the 1980s, and the collapse of Finnish exports to the Soviet bloc strengthened economic pessimism. This was further heightened by concerns about environmental dangers, energy crises, and the North–South economic gulf. Finally, there appeared a distinct social pessimism that grew from the uncomfortable discovery that social programs did not eliminate need, social expenditures grew more rapidly than predicted, and successful reforms transformed rather than solved problems. Disenchantment with the affluent society and fear about the economic consequences of slower economic growth undermined the policy consensus to some degree, and the influx of non-Scandinavian immigrants and, more importantly, their visibility as a new dependent group has raised social tensions.

Moreover, the internal dialectic between goals and means in policy implementation has also become a source of strain. The expansion of the sphere of governmental activity to implement the policies adopted by parliament has created a larger bureaucracy on the one hand and, on the other, subordinated heretofore independent organizations to the state in a form of neocorporatism. While the neocorporatist solutions may be more advantageous to members of interest organizations than anything they could achieve through independent activity, the neocorporatist form has also alienated members of those organizations. Growing bureaucracy and neocorporatism have increased the distance between citizens and their government. Citizens are more likely, therefore, to act as self-interested individuals rather than as responsible members of a community. The results are an erosion of the solidarity on which the Scandinavian welfare states have been based and a decline in support for the corporatist institutional arrangements that have been an integral part of the welfare states (see Olson 1995). Let us examine these two problems in greater detail.

SOLIDARITY OR EGOTISM?

There are many reasons why the Scandinavian welfare states have been particularly successful. The homogeneity of Scandinavian populations, small size of the nations, and consistency of policy during half a century of predominantly Social Democratic government are just a few. In addition, a key role was played by the concept of solidarity, a cultural value enshrined in the secular theology of the two great democratic popular movements of nineteenth-century Scandinavia: the agrarian and labor movements.

Solidarity, a term rarely heard in the "liberal market" democracies (i.e., the United States, Britain, and Canada), as we have noted means "common responsibility or reciprocal obligation" (Anonymous [C. M. Olsen] 1911, p. 74). In large countries with both social and ethnic heterogeneity, solidarity seems an improbable concept except at the local level or during national emergencies such as war. In Scandinavia, however, reciprocal obligation was the foundation for the myriad farmers' cooperatives and trade-union benefit societies that sprang up during the fifty years before World War I. There was no question about the material benefits and economic security that such organizations provided for members and their families. There were good, rational, self-interested reasons for belonging.

But, to the Scandinavian popular movements, solidarity had more than an instrumental value. It also held a moral status that gave the working-class movement claim to higher ethical values than the self-seeking greed and avarice of bourgeois society. Solidarity helped define "the special ethics built on a feeling of solidarity, a willingness to sacrifice, a subordination to common economic and political goals," according to K. K. Steincke (1920, p. 9). As Social Democratic minister of social affairs, Steincke drafted the Social Reform Act of 1933, which laid the foundation for the modern Danish welfare state. Steincke thought solidarity offered the working class the prospect of creating a higher social order based on "cooperation and reciprocal aid" (1920, p. 5).

A generation steeped in the solidaristic values of the popular movements laid the foundations of the welfare state in Scandinavia. And it was a generation that had been shaped by the privation of the Depression and had grown to adulthood during World War II that first inherited its benefits. Under the Social Democratic tutelage of the postwar reconstruction period, the class-specific values of the labor movement seemed to take root in other social strata as well. That may be why conservative leaders of the 1940s felt an affinity for the welfare state. John Christmas Møller, a conservative who served as foreign minister in the Danish liberation government in 1945, responded to the new nationalism of the Social Democrats with an emphasis on consensualism and solidarity. That is also why such a thoughtful elder statesman as Gunnar Heckscher, Swedish Conservative party leader in the late 1950s and early 1960s, could espouse Social Democrat Per Albin Hansson's *folkhemmet* (a home for all the people) as the ideal for Swedish society (Heckscher 1984). It was not because they sought to steal the heroes, myths, and symbols of their opponents. It was because for them, as for the Social Democrats, the good society embodied communitarian values.

There is a great deal of evidence that the solidaristic values of reciprocal obligation and responsibility upon which the Scandinavian welfare states were based were generation specific. As Bo Rothstein (1998) and others have noted, these values constituted an essential component of Scandinavian "social capital." They had been fostered in an atmosphere of small-group cohesion toughened by the Depression and World War II. Institutionalized in the welfare state, they were professionalized and bureaucratized and, ultimately, diminished. A growing egotism seems to be taking their place sharpened by the immigration and the growth of multiculturalism.

The problem posed by affluence and acquisitiveness is not limited to Scandinavia. It is a focus for broader critiques of Western industrial society (see Bell 1976; Galbraith 1976; Lasch 1979). It is hard to fault Scandinavians with being especially egoistic or acquisitive. Indeed, there is less private wealth and public squalor in Scandinavia than in other Western industrial societies. Yet growing egotism and acquisitiveness may have more deleterious effects in systems premised on solidarity than in those that assume individuals will pursue self-aggrandizement, such as the United States.

The success of the welfare state in guaranteeing material security has, in time, brought a transformation of attitudes. The completion of the major structures of the welfare state has led to a diminution of the political returns on reforms. Election results since the early 1970s suggest that the Social Democratic half century of hegemony that was associated with the creation of the welfare state is over. The welfare state has succeeded, and in doing so has become the common property of all political parties, even when nonsocialist governments tamper with it at the margins. But citizen satisfaction seems more closely correlated with the rate of improvement in welfare state benefits than with benefits levels or general success (Zetterberg 1981). As the girl asked her true love on the thirteenth day of Christmas, "What did you bring me today?"

To some extent the critics are right. There is a price paid in personal liberty for collective goods. Payment of taxes to support public programs is rarely voluntary. Societies require obligations from which emigration is the only escape. But this is a fundamental political and cultural fact that most Scandinavians (indeed most Western Europeans) are willing to accept considerable constraint on individual liberty for the sake of group and national welfare. Liberty, like wealth or security, is a fungible concept. Civil liberties defined as "no restraint" are not enough. As Daniel Bell (1976) first suggested, even U.S. libertarians saw religion, education, and culture rather than government as the source of necessary and beneficial restraints. The resurgence of conservatism in the United States in part reflects a classical American distrust of governmental intervention and fears that secularism has destroyed social constraints. Scandinavian conservatism (which is generally less conservative on social issues than Americans expect) is more narrowly focused on economic issues and the question of social-policy burdens. In practice, the libertarian issue is far less prominent in Scandinavia despite serious intellectual discussion (see Andersen 1984b; Heckscher 1984, pp. 227–53). Concerns about bureaucratic restraints and democratic deficits have turned from the nation-state to international organizations like the EU or the processes of globalization.

More disturbing is the evidence for a marked generational shift in the use of welfare state benefits that are not means tested. This has pushed take-up rates sharply higher (see Logue 1986), producing a number of curious anomalies including that cited in Chapter 11: In Denmark, the take-up rate for sick pay indicates that the young are sick more often than the old, and sickness seems to have become more common among the young today than it was in the past. Sweden saw a dramatic fall in illness-related absenteeism when it modestly tightened criteria for sick-leave pay in 1992.

Bent Rold Andersen (1984a, 1984b) has argued more generally that welfare measures that undercut what he calls "the social network" of extended family, friends, and neighbors have led to escalating demands for state services. Although these factors have pushed costs up sharply, there is little evidence that the increased expenditures have raised the actual well-being of the population. The limits in solidaristic systems have been those of group cohesion and self-restraint by individual members. The crisis—if that term is warranted at all—in the Scandinavian welfare model is that this small-group solidarity breaks down over time when transferred to the societal plane, and the egotism that has replaced it is hard to control without doing damage to the attractive universalism of Scandinavian social programs.

The economic cost of programs based on the demanding norm of social solidarity is also a fundamental question. Can Scandinavian economies support the current programs and the promises made to future generations and still remain internationally competitive? This is partially a political issue. Since the 1980s there have been incremental cuts (the so-called cheese-slicer approach of repeatedly shaving very small amounts off extensive programs). These have unleashed strong protests, particularly when they confront activist constituencies (students, labor, and such essential public employees as nurses and doctors). The affordability of the welfare state is a common theme of Social Democratic and conservative skeptics alike (see Andersen 1984a, 1984b; Heckscher 1984; Lindbeck 1997). EU pressures through the so-called convergence criteria have forced tighter fiscal discipline on Denmark, Finland, and Sweden.[1]

The costs of solidarity rise with the growth of dependent groups relative to the economically active. Demographic changes, which are beyond the direct control of public policy, have an obvious impact on future expenses. However, there is often a lag in recognition of the political implications of such changes. Consider the rise in the number of the retired and what it means in terms of pension costs. Although the Scandinavian pension age has historically been relatively high (sixty-seven), it has dropped significantly in the past twenty-five years as a result of general reductions and, especially, early-pension schemes designed to make jobs available for the young. Early retirement has become the rule: In 1980 nearly 70 percent of Norwegian males still worked at age sixty-five; now only 30 percent do (Reegård 2001, p.4). The recent reform of the Swedish pension system coupled with growing private employee retirement schemes may alleviate some of the pension burden, but rising health care costs for the elderly along with institutional and home assistance for the very aged loom ahead.

Cultural changes associated with the transformation of women's roles have imposed a greater burden on welfare state programs in Scandinavia than elsewhere. Again, the cause is the overarching norm of solidarity—solidarity with women seeking gainful employment and with the children who, in the past, were principally their mothers' responsibility. The rapid rise in labor market participation rates for women (see Table 9.2) gives evidence of greater economic equality, but it also increases the cost of the open-ended commitment to subsidized day care and after-school care. The availability of this care and significant transfer payments to low-income single parents have reduced the economic reasons for maintaining bad marriages. In this area, as in the others discussed above, what may be good for the individual is also costly for the society.

A growing cultural pluralism—multiculturalism—has strained the basis for solidarity. Homogeneity is difficult to assess as a factor in politics. Cultural differences are often subjective; the passion of the debate on the relative role of the two Norwegian languages, for instance, is entirely incomprehensible to outside observers. Hence the impact of new immigrant groups from outside Northern Europe is difficult to predict. Foreign workers were recruited for specific jobs. They earned their own way and tended to establish social contacts through their jobs and unions. Refugees are more difficult to integrate because many consider their stay temporary, their educational background may make retraining difficult, and their status is subject to internal political debate. Although immigrants and refugees in Scandinavia are still fewer in number than in many larger EU states (e.g., Germany, France, or Britain), their presence increasingly dominates political, social, and cultural debates. Anti-immigrant passions, especially in Denmark and Norway, which have a smaller proportion of immigrants than Sweden, rose sharply in the 1990s, and extremist parties continue to appeal to such sentiments. For the first time since the 1930s, racial and ethnic slurs are part of the Scandinavian political dialogue. There is less restraint in denouncing "foreign" beneficiaries of the welfare state than native, but the rhetoric has unmistakable echoes of earlier "poor law" debates. Whether such issues will affect the traditionally broad support for the universalistic welfare state remains unclear.[2]

Yet there is still a strong political consensus supporting the welfare state. No party, not even the extreme ones, wishes to change the fundamental welfare programs of income security, health, and education. Even the Progress and Danish People's parties of Norway and Denmark have reversed their initial attack on the welfare state to concerns about abuses (by immigrants and refugees) that divert resources from the elderly and other native clients. There is discussion of strategies for rationalizing the programs, including competition, privatization, user fees, and compulsory savings. There is also support for experimentation, including comparing the economic, political, and social costs and benefits of alternative approaches (such as comparing the Swedish active labor policy with the Danish system of virtually permanent unemployment compensation). Can decentralization and local experimentation produce a more accountable and effective welfare state?

CORPORATIST INSTITUTIONS UNDER STRAIN

We who concern ourselves with the politics of the small, homogeneous, and well-governed Scandinavian countries have often justified our interest by invoking the metaphor that the Scandinavian countries are a sociopolitical laboratory in which the common problems of industrial society can be diagnosed and solved. This has always been, in some ways, a dubious proposition. The Scandinavian countries have been in the forefront of the development of many programs common to industrial democracies, but the principal cause, surely, has not been the metaphorical laboratory situation but the very real Social Democratic dominance of the political scene. Social Democratic political success is owed in no small measure to the relatively consistent and efficacious economic policy that corporatism, or the incorporation of economic interest organizations into making and implementing public policy, has made possible.

The element of consensualism in Scandinavian political life is not a consequence of some bizarre cultural compulsion to compromise. Scandinavian rulers executed their opponents, peasants stoned their kings, hussar regiments sabered demonstrators, kings deposed parliamentary governments, and soldiers machine-gunned strikers. Consensualism is engrained in the social science literature as a characteristic of Scandinavia (e.g., Rustow 1955; Elder, Thomas, and Arter 1982) primarily because, at two key modern-history junctures, the Scandinavians avoided serious political violence. The first was when the king and the conservatives conceded parliamentary supremacy and democratic suffrage. Repression had been tried and failed. One did not need to be particularly farsighted to read the handwriting on the wall in 1918 when Swedish conservatives grudgingly accepted political democracy, or in 1920 when the Danish king tried to reestablish his prerogative to appoint his own cabinet and then abandoned the effort in the face of the threat of a general strike. (The fact that the Finns fought a civil war instead set their political development apart from that of the rest of Scandinavia.) The second historical juncture, of course, was in the 1930s as Social Democratic governments elsewhere in Europe collapsed or were destroyed. In that context, Scandinavian Social Democrats chose to minimize their risks and to undertake that historic compromise with the Agrarians and Liberals that postponed socialism but guaranteed farm price supports, emergency work or unemployment compensation for the unemployed, and a fundamental reform of the poor laws that in time became the welfare state. This compromise enabled the Social Democrats to retain power, which they used to achieve what they described as the second stage of democratization: social democracy.

The pattern of compromise begun in the 1930s has subsequently been broadened to encompass other groups, including business organizations and their political representatives, and deepened to draw such component organizations of the popular movements as labor unions and farmers' organizations into closer coordination with state decisions. This gave such organizations influence but, at the same time, obligated them to join in implementing the common decision. It clipped their wings as protest organizations and put their leaders in the incongruous situation of seeming to represent government interests among their own members as much as they represented their members' interests in government. Because the legitimacy of leaders in the democratic interest organizations of Scandinavia stems from their support among members, the situation clearly becomes problematic for them.

Consider the transformation of party-union-state ties in the transition from the struggle for political democracy to that for social and to economic democracy. In the phase of achieving political democracy, the role of the party was paramount in the political sphere; the role of the unions was to seek satisfaction of members' economic demands by means of independent action. Party and unions represented the same class and were considered two legs of the same movement but operated in different spheres. Both stood in opposition to the state, which was considered an instrument of ruling-class oppression under both the old conservative and new liberal bourgeois regimes.

During the fifty years of constructing social democracy, party-union-state relations were transformed. Achieving Social Democratic aims in this stage rested on the use of state power. The state was not to expropriate the expropriators and then wither away, as in the classical Marxist model. Instead, its responsibilities were expanded to include the obligation to provide for the welfare of its citizens. This was an obligation that dwarfed the traditional tasks of the state. The implicit compromise between Social Democrats and Liberals and Agrarians traded socialism in its traditional form for the *strong society,* the state of all the people. The slogans of the time make the transformation of the Social Democratic attitude very clear. In Social Democratic terminology, Sweden *det befästa fattighuset* became *folkhemmet Sverige;* that is, Sweden "the fortified poorhouse" became the "people's home." The Danish class state was recharacterized as *Danmark for folket,* or a "Denmark for the people." In this context, the state ceased to be the tool of the class opponent and became the agent of transformation in the hands of the party. The unions found their immediate demands on behalf of their members tempered by the recognition that living standards could be raised more rapidly through economic growth with public sector redistribution than through industrial strife, and through a combination of state programs and union benefits, not just through contract bargaining. The former necessitated corporatist coordination; the latter justified it.

Finally, in the ongoing phase of economic democratization, there is strong pressure not only to transform authority relations in the workplace and patterns of ownership in the macroeconomic sphere but also to sub-merge the residual antagonism between capital and labor in an overarch-ing common interest. National unions and employers' organizations are uncomfortable with the implications of this pressure, but there is little question at the plant level that the consequence of growing worker par-ticipation in decision making has been to create a substantial community of interest between local management and local unions.

Harbor no illusions about corporatist institutions. In both classic fascist ideology and modern democratic practice, the attraction of corporatism lies in the degree of control accorded the state. Interest organizations are subordinated to the *common good,* however and by whomever that may be defined. Even when corporatism has been a consequence of the de-mand for participation (see Ruin 1974), it becomes a synonym for the subordination of group interests to the general interest. Comprehensive interest representation and effective policy bargaining—collective ac-tion—delayed the "ossification" of political and economic institutions that some feel has been a danger to advanced industrial societies (see Olson 1982, 1995).

Interpreting Scandinavian Corporatism

The empirical studies of recent decades amply document the role of interest groups in making and implementing governmental policy in a variety of European nations, including both traditionally divided socie-ties, such as the Belgian, Dutch, and Austrian, and traditionally homo-geneous ones, such as the Scandinavian. Although the evidence for the existence of corporatist structures is simply overwhelming in Denmark, Norway, and Sweden (see Johansen and Kristensen 1982; Schwerin 1980, 1982; Ibsen and Jørgensen 1978; Ruin 1974), the historical derivation of corporatist patterns in Scandinavia was fundamentally different from that on the European continent. In Scandinavia, corporatist institutions reflect not the balance sought in a segmented society, but the political hegemony of well-organized, democratic popular movements: agrarian and labor. There is a parallel to the European segmented societies in that the Scan-dinavians sought to limit conflict. However, given Social Democratic he-gemony in political office, theirs was a corporatism that reflected restraint more than balance. As the building of the welfare state became the Scan-dinavian Social Democrats' surrogate for socialism, the need for steady economic growth, best achieved by coordinating public and private de-cisions, became clear: This argued for including all those integral to car-rying out economic policies in decisions.

How should corporatism in Scandinavia be interpreted? One view, honed to a very sharp edge by Anglo-American journalists and Scandi-navian conservatives, is that it represents an end-run around representative democratic institutions by powerful special-interest organizations, principally trade unions (Huntford 1972; Meyerson 1982). As a consequence of the alliance between Social Democratic unions and Social Democratic governments, the unions have attained a position of undeserved and illegitimate influence in a variety of institutions far removed from their proper sphere of interest; they are involved in such extraneous matters as university curriculum, cultural policy, and international affairs. It reflects, for those who adhere to this view, a power grab by union bosses, ratified by rabidly prounion Social Democratic or timid bourgeois administrations.

The converse of this argument is advanced by radicals of a syndicalist persuasion who are concerned exclusively with labor organizations. To them, the incorporation of unions in making state policy, particularly incomes policy, represents an abandonment of members' interests. The argument can be couched in terms of betrayal of members by an oligarchical leadership (see Wechselmann 1975) or in more sophisticated and less-polemical terms (see Dencik 1976; Ibsen and Vangskjær 1976). In either case, corporate incomes policies are seen to sacrifice working-class interests to promote an illusion of class harmony.

A third line of argument suggests that corporatist institutions represent a subordination of heretofore independent and representative organizations to the dictates of the state for reasons basically in accord with members' interests. The state is at once the domestic economic umpire regulating how conflict is conducted and the captain of the national economic team seeking to achieve optimal growth and balance. It can be demonstrated that the development of corporatist institutions in the labor market in Denmark have altered the nature of the members' referendum on the contract, transforming it over time from a vote on the contents of the contract into a vote on the system of wage bargaining itself (see Chapter 10). But in this view there are no villains to blame for the alteration of democratic and participatory institutions into mechanisms for ratifying centralized, coordinated policy decisions. The right to vote "Yes" remains, but that to say "No" is muted. And one can make a good argument that the No's should be muted so long as the overriding goal of national economic policy is maintaining economic growth.

Today, effective decision making in some areas of public policy requires bargaining between representative governments of the traditional sort and large private interest organizations, if only to achieve the degree of consensus necessary to avoid those organizations' sabotaging the policy. The alternative, overt coercion, is more destructive of representative, democratic institutions, especially when the coerced are large organizations with many members. Furthermore, the direct involvement of interest organizations is legitimized by the fact that, in some fields, making any policy at all requires the surrender of some jealously protected rights. This is most obvious in the labor market, where wage and incomes policies demand the abridgment of free collective bargaining. European and global economic integration has strengthened the need for national consensus.

The structure of corporatist decision making exacerbates some of these strains on the welfare state. Not only do interest groups see particular programs as their own (and that is surely the case in liberal systems as well), they have a particular claim to them in that they have bargained for them and made concessions to the state (and often to other groups) to have them established. They feel a contractual right to "their" programs, that government can tamper with only at the risk of other portions of the original bargain coming unraveled. Moreover, the government is dependent upon their future cooperation.

A particular problem is posed by the strong public-sector unions, that are not only frequently involved in corporatist consultations of the normal sort but also make particular claims for expertise in their professional capacity. The professionalization of services that were once provided by the family or by the local small group (e.g., union locals) makes the alteration of programs already in place more difficult. It also creates a strong lobby for expansion of such services that is not obviously related to the needs of recipients. To take the extreme case, the radical expansion of day-care facilities for children under two is obviously not a product of rising demand among the "under-twos" for an escape from the parental nest. It is more likely, as Bent Rold Andersen (1984a, pp. 122–23) argues, a product of housing costs and other economic pressures. However, there is a strong organizational lobby for day-care expansion and none for containing prices of owner-occupied homes for young families with small children.

Finally, centralized coordination of decision making has become a cause of political malaise in those groups, such as trade unions, in which participatory democracy was significant in the past. Even excellent performance of corporatist policies (e.g., export growth and economic expansion derived from corporate incomes policies) no longer yields as much political support as in the past. That is due in part to the fact that generational increases in take-up rates consume the resources that might otherwise be available to establish new programs. In any case, the Scandinavian welfare states are essentially complete: The end is accepted enthusiastically, but the means are a cause of increasing dissatisfaction.

Corporatism as a Democratic Structure

Grounded as they are in popular organizations with long democratic traditions, can corporatist institutions in Scandinavia offer the potential for expanding popular representation and participation into spheres traditionally governed by nondemocratic decision or into those outside the scope of conscious decision making altogether?

For corporatism to serve this function several conditions must exist. First, practically all members of society must belong to collective action organizations (Olson 1982). With their high rates of organization among blue- and white-collar workers, employers, farmers, fishermen, and other sole proprietors, the Scandinavian countries approximate this situation. Second, the collective must represent the individual member's interest. At one time Scandinavian interest groups organized in culturally, economically, and politically homogeneous groups. As they have grown, that homogeneity has declined. This is clear in politics. Blue-collar union members are voting for nonsocialist parties in significant numbers. Even more dramatically (as shown in Chapter 5), highly educated, well-paid public employees are voting socialist. Group identifications that hark back to the first decades of industrialism are increasingly inadequate. But even though Scandinavian economic interest organizations today are broader than the popular movements that they remain affiliated with, a strong argument can be made that they continue to be good representatives of their members' common interests, even as that area of commonality shrinks.

Moreover, as Peter Katzenstein (1985) suggests, the extent of organization in the comprehensive corporatist systems of small states means that interest organizations take a broad rather than a narrow perspective. The state must supervise and regulate the corporate bargaining process in the national interest. Robert Dahl holds out hope that centralized bargaining by inclusive organizations "can help to create a tendency toward convergence of functional or particular interests and more general interests, and therefore toward agreement on a social compact that is in the general interest" (1982 p. 71). This formal bargaining process by inclusive organizations, Dahl suggests, could approximate the "functional parliament" proposed by the guild socialists.[3] This common perspective leads to greater flexibility and cooperative adjustment for the common national interest (Katzenstein 1985, pp. 191–211). This may be unduly optimistic, but structural changes and increases in productivity in the Nordic countries are at least equal to the Western European average.

Corporatist centralization of power in society also offers avenues for democratic control that are absent in noncorporatist centralized systems because corporatist structures maintain a pattern of interest representation that is absent when the governmental bureaucracy itself is not obliged to deal with organized groups. Consider, for example, the position of the unemployed, an obviously disadvantaged group, in a corporatist system where unemployment insurance is administered through the trade unions (as is the case in Denmark, Finland, and Sweden) under rules set nationally, as contrasted to that in the United States. In these Scandinavian countries, the unemployed remain organized in the groups that administer the compensation funds and, should they be treated arrogantly, have immediate recourse to their elected union officials, a more direct and effective recourse than protesting the behavior of a governmental employee to your congressman or state legislator.

The point of this example is that while corporatism has been a tool of centralization, it currently offers an element of democratic control and offers prospects of decentralization and democratization in the future more easily than is the case in noncorporatist centralized systems, such as those of France or Great Britain. It is precisely the nongeographic nature of corporatist interest representation that makes it of such utility. Corporatist bodies provide an avenue for representation vis-à-vis the functional areas of governmental policy that cannot be duplicated in noncorporatist systems. Although it is surely possible, for example, to decentralize the administration of unemployment compensation from the state to the county or city, it is far from clear that this would make the system more responsive to the unemployed. Nor is it clear that society would like to accomplish that anyway. The interest of the unemployed is in bridging the period between jobs with the smallest possible loss of income and dignity. But is this the interest of employers? The desperation of the unemployed holds down wages. Both interests are represented, although hardly equally, in the legislatures that oversee the unemployment-compensation system.

As it developed, the modern state took on tasks that are unrelated to its geographical subunits. Many had been performed (inadequately, to be sure) previously by private organizations. Although geographical decentralization makes a lot of sense in terms of urban planning, hospital care, elementary schools, or home help for the elderly, it makes little sense in terms of farm price supports or employment policy. In other policy areas, both geographical and functional decentralization may make equal sense.

There has been a push for decentralization of many tasks of the central government to geographical subunits in Scandinavia, as indicated in Chapter 4. The more visionary of the critiques of modern Scandinavia discussed in Chapter 11, such as Åkerman's and Meyer, Petersen and Sørensen's, anticipate a return to smaller geographical communities. The ecological socialism embraced by the Nordic Left has much the same emphasis on local sustainable community.[4] But there are many tasks in modern society not susceptible to local resolution but susceptible to functional decentralization.

The limits of conventional representative democracy are those inherent in centralized administration. Corporate channels of interest representation that are internally democratic and representative can offer an attractive supplement: a functional democratization of modern industrial society. And it may relieve some current strains on the Scandinavian welfare systems.

Toward Functional Democracy?

To predict that the Scandinavians will muddle through strains and crises shows a distressing lack of dramatic vision. They probably will. Yet there are compelling and converging grounds why the expansion of what could be called *functional democracy* in the Scandinavian context would be a better way to ameliorate a variety of the increasing stresses described above. When representative institutions abandon their mandate to the professional lobbies in the new areas of state authority, and when the incorporated interest organizations are threatened with the fate of becoming transmission belts for centralized decision, a devolution of authority to lower levels in incorporated interest organizations is increasingly appropriate. A return to the solidarity of the smaller group and to the responsibility to friends and family that imposes on the individual probably would reduce financial strains on some welfare programs as well. Although decentralizing authority to smaller geographical units conflicts with the need for economies of scale (indeed, all of the Scandinavian nations save Iceland consolidated local government a generation ago to produce units large enough to provide adequate social services), a decentralization of authority over individual functions faces fewer of these problems.

The basic rule of functional democracy is to divide policy areas into components best dealt with by those most directly involved with them. Functional democracy permits the combination of economies of scale in government or the economy, with the flexibility of democratic control of particular decision areas by organizations based not on geography but on common interests, such as those shared by employers', workers', and farmers' organizations.

Consider, for example, the area of working life, where something like functional democracy has advanced in Sweden and the other Scandinavian countries. The solution to the problems of inequality in authority most compatible with traditional representative democracy and private industry is the election of employee representatives on corporate boards, as in the German system of codetermination. Swedes did, in fact, put worker directors on corporate boards in 1973, but did so without faith in the efficacy of this measure. More effective were measures expanding rights of collective bargaining to include what had previously been managerial prerogatives and providing full information on company affairs to employees (the Employee Participation Act—Medbestämmandelagen, or MBL—passed in 1976) and measures that radically expanded the influence of worker-safety representatives on plant working conditions (the

Work Environment Acts of 1974 and 1978). The impact of these measures in practical democratization has been uneven, just as one would expect with functional democracy. In practice, management's control of many areas of decision making, such as product development, marketing, long-term planning, and the like, has been unaffected. In other areas, however, employee influence has become decisive, as in many aspects of shop-floor management, including foremen's practices and health and safety issues. As a consequence of democratization, there is more commonality of interest between management and labor, at least at the plant level.

Functional democracy in working life has positive implications for the long-term sustainability of welfare program expenditures. For example, besides protecting the unemployed, elderly, sick and disabled, the welfare state relieves industry of the burden of providing for those groups through generous unemployment compensation, early retirement programs for those with occupational ailments, and disability payments. Functional democracy seems to reduce costs. It appears, for instance, that the democratization of the enforcement of occupational health and safety standards in Sweden, that have put enforcement in the hands of those most immediately affected, has had more preventive impact on the incidence of occupational injuries and disease than efforts at strict government enforcement by authorities in other countries.

Moreover, the functional democratization of working life creates greater scope for the development of solidarity inside the workplace. Consider, for example, the rehabilitation work groups established in the body plant in Saab's main auto plant in Trollhättan. The replacement of the traditional welding and metal-finishing line with team production essentially transferred control of the production process to the blue-collar workforce. Production workers quickly realized that team production provided the flexibility to permit a "rehabilitation team," which made for a softer, earlier reentry into production for workers who have been injured or seriously ill and which permitted women in the latter stages of pregnancy to work at a slower place, delaying the start of their maternity leave. The union pushed the issue successfully in local negotiations. The workplace community voluntarily assumed the portion of the responsibility for individual welfare that the company had been happy to dump on the society at large. Solidarity in the small group is not an ideological catchword; it has concrete meaning. Similarly, increasing democracy on the job increases job security. The standard U.S. practice of allowing heavy overtime for the employed while thousands in the industry are still on indefinite layoff could never survive democratic decision marking that included those who are laid off. This underlines the need for relatively permanent membership in functional democratic institutions.

There is, however, little question that such measures at the level of the firm reduce labor market flexibility. The rise in Finnish and Swedish unemployment in the early 1990s was simply not susceptible to microlevel, functional democratic solutions. It required a more fundamental economic restructuring to strengthen their international competitiveness. Given Scandinavia's high wage labor force, technical innovations, increases in productivity, moderate wage demands, financial liberalization, and a more positive attitude toward entrepreneurship (especially in high-technology products) seem essential for global competitiveness.

Until the late 1980s the organized, corporatist channels of influence in state policy expanded the scope of democratic decisions. Organizations of new groups, such as students, or around new issues, such as nuclear power, have created new communities, which have been given stable roles by their co-optation into the Scandinavian political system. Ultimately, they seem to have served to democratize certain functions of society. It is striking that the participatory wave of 1968 had its most restricted impact on those parliamentary institutions that were the object of its protest. Its greatest impact has come in democratizing decisions that had been matters reserved for such experts as city planners and developers, university professors, and nuclear engineers, or matters entirely outside the political sphere, such as corporate investment decisions. Far from replacing representative democracy with direct democracy, the process the rebels set in motion has supplemented representative democracy with functional democracy in those very areas in which the corporatism, co-optation, and coordination that the rebels railed against was strongest. Yet corporatist channels seem to have been unable to handle the new issues related to globalization. In Sweden especially significant groups have abandoned two generations of interest group representation. In 1991 the Swedish Employers Association (SAF) quit numerous tripartite commissions. Nevertheless, corporatism still moderates the interaction between important economic and policy elites. The negotiated economy still functions if only because labor, employers, and government cannot avoid it. Yet with the EU influencing an ever greater range of policy issues, corporatism must adapt to Europeanization and globalization (Blom-Hansen 2000, pp. 158, 173, 177).

NATION-STATES IN A GLOBAL ERA

With increasing economic globalization, the nation-state is becoming an ever less effective unit for making and implementing economic policy. Education policy, cultural policy, home care policies for the elderly, and so on, can still be made in Helsinki or Copenhagen, but the ability of small nations to shape their own macroeconomic policy is in clear decline. In the global economy, small nations—like those of Scandinavia—are simply too small to pursue independent economic policies. Sweden, for example, ran a very successful and independent economic policy from the 1930s through the 1960s at the national level, because the nation-state was still the appropriate unit for economic management. As late as the 1970s, its efforts to run a full-employment policy consciously counter to the international economic cycle (the "production for inventory" scheme) still seemed plausible. But what worked in the 1930s and 1950s in Sweden didn't work in the 1970s and 1980s. The 1990s saw the Swedish Central Bank do valiant battle against currency speculation and lose. Even Norway with its petroleum bonanza has found national economic management increasingly difficult.

Social Democratic welfare state policies in Scandinavia have rested upon the ability of the national government to manage the national economy. If this has ceased to be possible, what are the choices for economic policy?

The first is the neoliberal, global market. Privatize, deregulate, reduce the public sector, and the invisible hand of the market will maximize economic growth and individual prosperity is the mantra. Few in Scandinavia espouse this model in its totality, for it is clear that small, high-wage countries, high-tax countries are likely to see fewer economic benefits and more economic disruptions than their less highly paid, less highly taxed brethren elsewhere.

The second is shifting decisions from the Scandinavian capitals to Brussels. While the European Union may look like part of the globalization process, in fact it represents a collective response to it. Unlike the Scandinavian nation-states, the EU is a sufficiently large economic unit to make effective policy. With its external tariffs, large scale agricultural subsidies, substantial economic development program, common monetary policy, and fiscal convergence, the EU offers an alternative model of carefully controlled international economic integration. On the other hand, the EU suffers—at least in Scandinavian eyes—from a continuing democratic deficit that makes citizen input and citizen control extremely difficult.

The third is developing local and/or regional economic policy tools. While these are still in their infancy, outlying Scandinavian regions, which are under more pressure from globalization than the capitals and other major industrial and commercial cities, have to consider whether they should continue to rely on national policies.

In fact, what is emerging melds all three with existing national policy tools. A limited amount of privatization and deregulation has encouraged competition in some sectors, particularly telecommunications, and increased international capital flows. Some economic policy decision making has moved south to Brussels. Outlying regions are beginning to develop their own investment funds and local economic development policies. Some national policy making, including Swedish monetary and exchange rate policies, continues to be jealously guarded.

THE SCANDINAVIAN FUTURE

"Nothing is harder to predict," the Danish sage Robert Storm Petersen noted, "than the future." Still, attempting to do so can clarify current issues in Scandinavia. Because the Scandinavian countries serve as an early-warning system for the problems of advanced industrial societies, they may provide some illumination of the route ahead for the rest of us.

The patterns of future Scandinavian development can be glimpsed in the present lines of political conflict. The classical Left-Right economic division continues to characterize the party system and much of the Scandinavian political debate, but the virulence of economic conflict has declined as consensus has grown around the welfare state and state management of a capitalistic market economy. Europeanization and globalization are trends that dominate every dimension of the Scandinavian welfare states, but their responses have been proactive and varied.

The classical economic conflict between Left and Right, however, remains strong in one area. As liberals and Social Democrats have pushed through equality of opportunity for the children of the working class and for women, they have discovered that equal opportunity can produce startlingly unequal results. Measuring inequality of results has become a social science growth industry in Scandinavia. The effort to achieve more equal results, and not just an adequate standard of living, for all has explosive implications that make many Social Democrats as uncomfortable as conservatives. The latter object in the abstract; individuals are innately unequal, they maintain. The former worry about concrete cases. They are happy with equal results for everyone who works, but what about the lazy and the free riders? Still, the primary reason for inequality of results is inequality of points of departure. The fight about leveling the playing field for children of rich and poor alike still raises passions. This issue is not abstract. For example, does expansion of private health insurance and even of hospitals and clinics—a widespread trend of the past decade—provide additional resources or increase inequality of access? It may do both. Does the growth of private pension programs reinforce and sustain public pensions or does it undermine support for the latter just as costs are about to soar?

New issues excite debate. Three will continue to shape Scandinavian politics in the next several decades. Each involves what we have called *qualitative politics,* that is, the renewed importance of ideological and value-oriented issues in the administrative and distributional politics of advanced industrial societies. None is well articulated by the existing configuration of the party system; each cuts across bloc lines and divides some parties internally. None is strong enough to cause a fundamental realignment of the party system, but all are likely to have substantial effect on the direction of change in Scandinavian policies.

The first is the issue of immigration and multiculturalism that we have discussed at considerable length throughout of this book. The attractive hospitality to refugees—economic as well as political—that characterized the Scandinavian countries when such refugees were few has become politically costly as they became many. As we noted earlier in this chapter, for the first time since the 1930s, racial and ethnic slurs have become part of the Scandinavian political dialogue from the new Right in parliament in Denmark and Norway as well as from skinheads in the streets. That has provoked a verbal reaction from all other parties in parliament and a violent reaction from young anarchists, militant immigrants, and direct action groups in the streets. This issue has the potential to produce major polarization, especially in an economic downturn, if the established parties do not deal with it successfully.

The second revolves around the division between "materialist" and "postmaterialist" attitudes articulated by Ronald Inglehart (1977) and others concerned with postindustrial politics. In simple terms, it is the argument between those urging continued economic growth, technological innovation, and cultural rationalism, usually with strong globalization and EU sympathies, versus the qualitative demands of the Greens and some elements of the old left, who claim that small is beautiful and that ecological and human goals should replace narrow acquisitive interests in those countries with enormously high living standards. There is a strong echo of nineteenth-century rural romanticism in these postmaterialist claims. With the fading of socialist models elsewhere, essential anticapitalistic and anti-industrial, even antitechnology, sentiments could forge a common, alternative platform.

Green parties have been organized throughout Scandinavia, but have had trouble making headway because the old parties quickly seized upon their issues. There is considerable agreement among most Scandinavians that environmental protection and nonmaterialist cultural values deserve support. The primary exponents of the Green position have been the agrarian parties on the right and the Socialist Peoples', Socialist Left, and former Communists on the left, although the Greens themselves won modest parliamentary representation in the 1983 Finnish, 1988 Swedish, and 1999 Icelandic elections. The sharpest confrontation was over nuclear power in Sweden, where nostalgic rural romanticism meshed with countercultural utopianism to yield the strange antinuclear alliance between the agrarian Center and the Left Communist parties. Antinuclear parties stressed the issue in the 1999 and 2003 Finnish elections with modestly positive results. Simple division on such issues is hampered by the industrialization of agriculture (chemical requirements of which make it one of the principal environmental polluters in Scandinavia) and the diffusion of advanced industrial establishments into smaller towns.

The radical environmentalist models for shrinking modern Scandinavia have encouraged experimentation with the development of communes of the counterculture into permanent living arrangements. This is the principal manifestation of communitarian postmaterialism. Far more significant, however, have been the individualistic manifestations of post-materialism. The most obvious has been the significant decline in working hours since 1970, and the spread of part-time work (both from economic and from environmentalist considerations), which amounts to a kind of national work-sharing program. The choice of leisure over income reflects a strong postmaterialist tendency in Scandinavian political culture. Although consumption of public and private goods has shown little tendency toward monastic austerity, there is little doubt that the relatively high degree of economic equality in the Scandinavian countries and the relative security provided by the welfare state create a hospitable climate for postmaterialist ideas. Unfortunately it conflicts with the need to improve productivity in both the public and private sectors. For example, the endemic problem of health care waiting lists reflects shortages of doctors, nurses, and other health care workers. Increased leisure for them has meant less adequate or convenient health care for many.

The third new issue likely to be of lasting import involves decentralization of a different sort. To put it schematically, it counterposes state decision making versus market choice. This dimension is clearest on such questions of collective management in conjunction with state planning and political decisions as setting credit priorities or special subsidies for export, research, or training, where there has been a renewed interest in using the market mechanism. This state-versus-market perspective no longer coincides as it once did with the historical Left-Right dimension. Centralized state management of the economy still has appeal because of the assumptions of rational management, economies of scale, and equality of treatment for employees, clients, and citizens. Norwegian distrust of centralized political power, for instance, has not prevented a strong faith in state enterprises, such as the state oil company, or in strong indicative economic planning. In Scandinavia, the Right and the Left accept the premise that national health care systems, for example, can achieve economies of scale, contain costs, and improve health by preventive screening. Until recently, few Scandinavians would have argued that a competitive, privatized system would achieve equally desirable results in terms of total cost or health. Now both private health insurance—often to shorten waiting time for noncritical treatment—as well as private clinics and services are expanding rapidly. Many argue that the public sector is simply run too lean; a more affluent society may be willing to pay extra for convenience. Yet almost no one envies the severely unequal access and astoundingly expensive American system, which costs 30 to 50 percent more as a share of GDP than the Scandinavian systems do.

Modern managerial theory and technology, however, has challenged the hierarchical model in both public and private enterprise, encouraging greater competition and private choice in both spheres. This has had least impact in terms of public provision of social services, reflecting the generally high level of satisfaction with the quality of what the public sector provides in this area. The one notable exception is private education in Denmark, which flourishes thanks to a uniquely liberal voucher system that pays for about 80 percent of the cost of private schools that meet basic quality criteria. Perhaps this will extended into other social and public services. But, in some other areas, such as energy production, the Scandinavian countries are awash with thousands of new producers: windmills owned individually and cooperatively, village heating plants running off methane gas made from manure, farm heating systems fueled with agricultural waste, and so on. It may not be quite what Prime Minister Thatcher or President Reagan envisioned when they talked about expanding the market sector, but it is the Scandinavian variant on that theme.

What is most ironic, given the usual conservative enthusiasm for privatization, is that its greatest successes in Scandinavia have come through trade-union power. Union strength has kept labor "law" a semiprivate matter determined principally by way of collective bargaining, not parliamentary legislation. The legislated labor market reforms of the 1970s provided a framework for private bargaining, not rigorous government regulation. A powerful argument can be made that codetermination in the workplace offers an attractive, flexible, and private alternative to governmental microregulation and the bureaucratic control that that entails. Privatization need not always be a conservative strategy nor need it mean sacrificing public interest on the altar of private avarice. Indeed, the old Marxist dream of the withering away of the state constitutes a total privatization in which public and private interests become synonymous. That is not on the agenda in Scandinavia or anywhere else, but the private sector need not be reserved only for the privileged.

These competing alternatives suggest that ample opportunity remains in Scandinavia for experimentation. Investment versus compensation, centralized control versus decentralization, and growth versus encouragement of new cultural attitudes are likely to define the focus of Scandinavian policy debates of the near future. We have no crystal ball to reveal the outcome of that debate. We have, however, the experience of the past: Scandinavian conservatives have recognized that preserving what was best in the old society required continuous, cautious change, while Scandinavian radicals have recognized that, in small, dependent countries, idealism cannot lose contact with international reality. This pertains to the welfare state as well.

Where are the Social Democratic architects of the welfare state in this futuristic speculation? For many Scandinavian Social Democrats, the welfare state has been a surrogate for socialism; some saw the growth of the public sector as virtually synonymous with progress. Still, the welfare state has principally been a means to an end, not the end itself. As such, it has always been open for reconsideration. While the Social Democrats offer no qualitatively different alternative to their own creation, they too have become critics. Too much of the growth in the public sector stems from increased utilization of social programs by those for whom they are an optional benefit rather than from satisfying real needs. Centralized, bureaucratic administration, necessary for efficient pursuit of welfare state goals, has increasingly become a target of discontent, despite the fact that the actual administration of much of the welfare state was transferred from the national to county and municipal governments in the 1970s. Still, and more important, new programs are not necessarily frills. Providing adequate child care for working parents—there are hardly any other kind—or social integration of immigrants and other marginalized groups remain pressing concerns.

Pragmatism and flexibility, rather than dogma, have always characterized the Scandinavian Social Democratic middle way. That was true in the struggle for political democracy, in constructing the welfare state, and, most recently, in the push for economic democracy. As the report presented to the 1986 Swedish trade-union congress, *Fackföreningsrörelsen och välfärdsstaten* (The Trade Union Movement and the Welfare State), concluded with substantial clarity of vision, Sweden is the world's first nation to approach the end of a developmental stage in which increasing human welfare requires

the massive expansion of the resources of society [i.e., the public sector]. In the next stage, the prerequisites for welfare have basically been changed because the resources exist. Now the issue is how we can best use them (Landsorganisationen 1986, p. 172).

Exactly how best to use them is still the question for the Scandinavian welfare states in the new century.

NOTES

1. The EU's Economic and Monetary Union convergence criteria restrict government deficits, inflation, and public debt. This forces a modicum of fiscal discipline on all EU states. The Nordic countries have been well within the limits since about 1995.

2. Immigrants and especially refugees are overrepresented among nonelderly social security beneficiaries, which reflects their lower socioeconomic (and educational) status, non–Northern European gender roles—women remain at home—

and especially their extended and larger family structures. Complicating matters are the severe restrictions placed on refugees entering the workforce and systematic discrimination against even educated immigrants. Immigrants are underrepresented among elderly social security and pension recipients, which are two very costly programs.

3. Dahl's conclusion on this point is far reaching: In Scandinavia "a significant degree of control over crucial economic decisions, which in conventional democratic theory should remain with the citizens' representatives in parliament and cabinet, has plainly been transferred to a kind of non-elected parliament of industry. . . . This shift of power away from the elected representatives looks to be irreversible. . . . I find it hard to resist the conjecture that we are witnessing a transformation in democracy as fundamental and lasting as the change from the institutions of popular government in the city-state to the institutions of polyarchy in the nation-state"(1982, p. 80). Deregulation and privatization along with the pressures of globalization have accelerated this flow of power away from national governments.

4. Sustainability has become a mantra of the Nordic left and environmental movements, which often overlap. It is free of the archaic class-warfare vocabulary but still challenges industrial, consumerist capitalism. Its implications are obviously vague; what is "sustainable" and what policies are required to achieve sustainability?

PART V

Appendixes

APPENDIX A

Popular Vote in Scandinavian Parliamentary Elections

Table A.1
Elections to the Danish Parliament, 1918–2001 (in percent)

Year	Turn-out	PP/DPP	Con	Agr Lib	ChrP	RL	Lfj	CD	SD	SPP	CP	LS	O
1918	75.5		18.3	29.4		20.7			28.7				3.0
1920a	80.6		19.7	34.2		11.9			29.3				4.9
1920b	74.9		18.9	36.1		11.5			29.9				3.6
1920c	77.0		17.9	34.0		12.1			32.2		0.4		3.4
1924	78.6		18.9	28.3		13.0	1.0		36.6		0.5		3.7
1926	77.0		20.6	28.3		11.3	1.3		37.2		0.4		1.7
1929	79.7		16.5	28.3		10.7	1.8		41.8		0.2		0.7
1932	81.5		18.7	24.7		9.4	2.7		42.7		1.1		0.7
1935	80.7		17.8	17.8		9.2	2.5		46.1		1.6		5.0
1939	79.2		17.8	18.2		9.5	2.0		42.9		2.4		7.2
1943	89.5		21.0	18.7		8.7	1.6		44.5		#		5.5
1945	86.3		18.2	23.4		8.1	1.9		32.8		12.5		3.1
1947	85.8		12.4	27.6		6.9	4.5		40.0		6.8		1.8
1950	81.9		17.8	21.3		8.2	8.2		39.6		4.6		0.3
1953a	80.8		17.3	22.1		8.6	5.6		40.4		4.8		1.2
1953b	80.6		16.8	23.1		7.8	3.5		41.3		4.3		3.2
1957	83.7		16.6	25.1		7.8	5.3		39.4		3.1		2.7
1960	85.8		17.9	21.1		5.8	2.2		42.1	6.1	1.1		3.7
1964	85.5		20.1	20.8		5.3	1.3		41.9	5.8	1.2		3.6
1966	88.6		18.7	19.3		7.3	0.7		38.2	10.9	0.8		4.1
1968	89.3		20.4	18.6		15.0	0.7		34.2	6.1	1.0	2.0	2.0
1971	87.2		16.7	15.6	2.0	14.4	1.7		37.3	9.1	1.4	1.6	0.2
1973	88.7	15.9	9.2	12.3	4.0	11.2	2.9	7.8	25.6	6.0	3.6	1.5	0.0
1975	88.2	13.6	5.5	23.3	5.3	7.1	1.8	2.2	29.9	5.0	4.2	2.1	0.0
1977	88.7	14.6	8.5	12.0	3.4	3.6	3.3	6.4	37.0	3.9	3.7	2.7	0.9
1979	85.6	11.0	12.5	12.5	2.6	5.4	2.6	3.2	38.3	5.9	1.9	3.7	0.4
1981	83.3	8.9	14.5	11.3	2.3	5.1	1.4	8.3	32.9	11.3	1.1	2.7	0.2
1984	88.4	3.6	23.4	12.1	2.7	5.5	1.5	4.6	31.6	11.5	0.7	2.7	0.1
1987	86.7	4.8	20.8	10.5	2.4	6.2	0.5	4.8	29.3	14.6	0.9	1.4	3.8
1988	85.7	9.0	19.3	11.8	2.0	5.6		4.7	29.8	13.0	0.8	0.6	3.4
1990	82.9	6.4	16.0	15.8	2.3	3.5	0.5	5.1	37.4	8.3	1.7*		3.0
1994	84.2	6.4	15.0	23.3	1.9	4.6		2.8	34.6	7.3	3.1		1.0
1998	86.0	9.8+	8.9	24.0	2.5	3.9		4.3	35.9	7.6	2.7		0.4
2001	87.2	12.6+	9.1	31.2	2.3	5.2		1.8	29.1	6.4	2.4		0.0

Notes: PP—Progress party (Fremskridtspartiet) and DPP—Danish People's party (Dansk Folkeparti); Con—Conservative People's party (Det konservative Folkeparti); Agr Lib—agrarian Liberal party (Venstre); ChrP—Christian People's party (Kristeligt Folkeparti); RL—Radical Liberals (Det radikale Venstre); LfJ—League for Justice (Georgists) (Retsforbundet); CD—Center Democrats (Centrum-Demokraterne); SD—Social Democrats (Socialdemokratiet); SPP—Socialist People's party (Socialistisk Folkeparti); CP—Danish Communist party (Danmarks kommunistiske Parti); LS—Left Socialists (Venstresocialisterne): O—Other parties.

#The CP was outlawed during World War II.

*Unity List (Enhedsliste) includes CP and LS.

+ Thereof Progress party 2.4 percent and Danish People's party 7.4 percent in 1998; Progress party 0.6 percent and Danish People's party 12.0 percent in 2001.

Sources: Denmark. Danmarks Statistik (1985, pp. 38, 58–67); Danmarks Statistik (1987b, pp. 4–5); *Statistiske Efterretninger: Befolkning og valg* (1988: 6, pp. 2, 23; 1990: 19, pp. 5, 8, and 24; 1994: 11, pp. 4, 8, and 25); 1998: *Nordic Statistical Yearbook 2000* (pp. 118 and 122); and www.indenrigsministeriet.dk.

Table A.2
Elections to the Finnish Parliament, 1907–2003 (in percent)

Year	Turn out	FP	YFP	Con	SwdPP	Lib	RP	Chr L	Agr Cen	SD	G	FPDU /LA	Other
1907	70.7	27.3	13.6		12.6				5.8	37.0			3.6
1908	64.4	25.4	14.2		12.7				6.4	38.4			2.8
1909	65.3	23.6	14.5		12.3				6.7	39.9			2.9
1910	60.1	22.1	14.4		13.5				7.6	40.0			2.3
1911	59.8	21.7	14.9		13.3				7.8	40.0			2.2
1913	51.1	19.9	14.1		13.1				7.9	43.1			2.0
1916	55.5	17.5	12.5		11.8				9.0	47.3			1.9
1917	69.2	30.2*			10.9				12.4	44.8			1.8
1919	67.1			15.7	12.1	12.8			19.7	38.0			1.6
1922	58.5			18.2	12.4	9.2			20.3	25.1		14.8	0.1
1924	57.4			19.0	12.0	9.1			20.2	29.0		10.4	0.2
1927	55.8			17.7	12.2	6.8			22.6	28.3		12.1	0.4
1929	55.6			14.5	11.4	5.6			26.2	27.4		13.5	1.5
1930	65.9			18.0	10.8	5.8			27.3	34.2		1.0	2.8
1933	62.2			16.9	10.4	7.4			22.5	37.3			5.4
1936	62.9			10.4	11.2	6.3			22.4	38.6			11.1
1939	66.6			13.6	10.1	4.8			22.9	39.8			8.8
1945	74.9			15.0	8.4	5.2			21.4	25.1		23.5	1.5
1948	75.3			17.0	7.7	3.9			24.2	26.3		20.0	0.8
1951	74.6			14.6	7.6	5.7			23.3	26.5		21.6	0.9
1954	79.9			12.8	7.0	7.9			24.1	26.2		21.6	0.4
1958	75.0			15.3	6.7	5.9		0.2	23.1	23.2		23.2	2.4
1962	85.1			14.6	6.4	5.9	2.2	0.8	23.0	19.5		22.0	5.6
1966	84.9			13.8	6.0	6.5	1.0	0.4	21.2	27.2		21.2	2.6
1970	82.2			18.0	5.7	5.9	10.5	1.1	17.1	23.4		16.6	1.6
1972	81.4			17.6	5.4	5.2	9.2	2.5	16.4	25.8		17.0	1.0
1975	73.8			18.4	5.0	4.3	3.6	3.3	17.6	24.9		18.9	4.1
1979	75.3			21.7	4.6	3.7	4.6	4.8	17.3	23.9		17.9	1.7
1983	75.7			22.1	4.9		9.7	3.0	17.6	26.7	1.4	14.0	0.6
1987	72.1			23.1	5.6	1.0	6.3	2.6	17.6	24.1	4.0	9.4	6.1
1991	68.4			19.3	5.8	0.8	4.8	3.1	24.8	22.1	6.8	10.1	2.4
1995	68.6			17.9	5.5	0.6	1.3	3.0	19.8	28.3	6.5	11.2	5.7
1999	64.6			21.0	5.1	0.2	1.0	4.2	22.4	22.9	7.5	10.9	4.8
2003	69.6			18.6	4.6		1.6	5.3	24.7	24.5	8.0	9.9	2.8

Notes: FP—Finnish party (Suomalainen Puolue), also know as the Old Finns (Vahasuomalaiset), 1906–17; YFP—Young Finnish party (Nuorsuomalainen Puolue), 1906–17; Con—National Coalition (Kansallinen Kokoomus); SwdPP—Swedish People's party (Svenska Folkepartiet/Ruotsalainen Kansanpuolue)—includes Swedish Left (Svenska Vänstern) and, since 1948, Åland Coalition (Ålandsk Samling); Lib—National Progressive party (Kansallinen Edistyspuolue), renamed Finnish People's party (Suomen Kansanpulue) in 1951 and Liberal People's party (Liberaalinen Kansanpuolue) in 1966; RP—Finnish Smallholders party (Suomen Pientalonpoiken Puolue), renamed Finnish Rural party (Suomen Maaseudun Puolue) in 1966 and True Finns since 1999; ChrL—Christian League (Suomen Kristillinen Liitto); Agr Cen—Agrarian League (Maalaisliitto), renamed Center party (Keskustapuolue) in 1965 and Finnish Center (Suomen Keskusta) in 1988; SD—Social Democrats (Suomen Social Demokraattinen Puolue); G—Greens (Vihreät Liitto); FPDU/LA—Finnish People's Democratic Union (Suomen Kansan Demokraatinen Liitto) and predecessor Communist parties in the 1920s and, since 1990, Left Alliance (Vasemmistoliitto).
*Joint FP and YFP vote.

Sources: Macke and Rose (1991, pp. 109–29); Jussila, Hentilä, and Nevakivi (1999, pp. 367–68); Finnish Council of State History Page, http://www.vn.fi/vn/english/index.htm.

Table A.3
Elections to the Icelandic Parliament, 1916–1999 (in percent)

Year	Turn out	Ind. Party	LP	Prog Party	SD	Women List	ULL	Green	CPI/ PA	Other
1916	24.3	63.6		29.6	6.8					
1916	49.2	70.3		12.9	6.8					10.0
1919	45.4	71.1		22.2	6.8					
1922	41.1	33.0		27.1	17.2	22.7				
1923	70.9	53.6		26.6	16.2					3.7
1926	45.9	39.4	9.4	25.0	22.7	3.5				
1927	71.5	42.5	5.8	29.8	19.0					2.8
1930	70.5	48.3		31.4	20.3					
1931	78.3	43.8		35.9	16.1				3.0	1.2
1933	70.1	48.0		23.9	19.2				7.5	1.3
1934	81.5	42.3		27.3	21.7				6.0	1.7
1937	87.9	41.3		31.0	19.0				8.4	0.2
1942	80.3	40.6		27.6	15.4				16.2	0.2
1942	82.4	40.7		26.6	14.2				18.5	
1946	87.4	39.5		23.1	17.8				19.5	0.1
1949	89.0	39.5		24.5	16.5				19.5	
1953	89.9	40.4		27.9	15.6				16.0	
1956	92.1	46.9		20.1	18.3				19.2	
1959	90.6	42.5		29.7	12.5				15.2	
1959	90.4	39.7		25.7	15.2				16.0	
1963	91.1	41.4		28.2	14.2				16.0	
1967	91.4	37.5		28.1	15.7		3.7		13.9	
1971	90.4	36.2		25.3	10.5		8.9		17.1	
1974	91.4	42.7		24.9	9.1		4.6		18.3	0.4
1978	90.3	32.7		16.9	22.0		3.3		22.9	2.2
1979	89.3	35.4		24.9	17.4				19.7	2.5
1983	88.6	38.5		18.5	19.3	5.5			17.2	1.1
1987	90.1	38.1		21.8	15.4	10.2			13.3	·
1991	87.5	39.8		21.3	15.5	8.3			14.4	0.7
1995	87.4	37.1		23.3	18.5	4.9			14.3	1.1
1999	84.1	40.7	4.2	18.5	26.8*			9.1		0.7

Notes: IndP—Independence party (Sjalfstaedisflokkur) includes Home Rule party (Heimastjornaflokkur), Hardline Independence party (Sjalfstaedisflokkur "thversum"), and Moderate Independence party (Sjalfstaedisflokkur "langsum") in the elections of 1916–22, and includes the breakaway groups Commonwealth (Thjodveldismenn), Republic party (Lydveldisflokkir), and, in the elections of 1987 and 1991, the Citizens party (Borgaraflokkur); LP—Liberal party (Frjalslyndiflokkur); CPI/PA—Communist party of Iceland (Kommunistaflokkur), later United Socialist party and People's Alliance. In 1938, the Communist party merged with a Social Democrat splinter group to form the United Socialist party (Sosialistaflokkur). In 1956, the People's Alliance (Althyudubandalag) was formed by the United Socialist party and another Social democrat splinter group. It was joined by the

National Preservation party in 1963; ProgP—Progressive party (Framsoknarflok-kur) (formed by merger of two farmers' parties, Baendaflokkur and Ohadir Baen-dur, after 1916 election) includes the breakaway Farmers party (Baendaflokkur) in 1934 and 1937, National Preservation party (Thjodvarnarflokkur) in 1953–59, and the National party (Thjodarflookur) in 1983 and 1987; SD—Social Democrats (Althyduflokkur) includes Social Democratic Federation (Bandalag Jafnathar-manna) in 1983 and People's Movement in 1995; WL—Women's List (Kvennalista in 1920s, and Samtök um Kvennalista since 1983); ULL—Union of Liberals and Leftists.

*Alliance of Social Democrats, People's Alliance, and Women's List.

Sources: Macke and Rose (1991, pp. 206–23); Esaiasson and Heidar (2000, pp. 449–50, Tables A2.5–A2.6).

Table A.4
Elections to the Norwegian Parliament, 1906–2001 (in percent)

Year	Turn-out	PP	Con*	Agr Cen	ChrP	Lib#	Labor	CP	SPP /SV	O
1906	61.1		32.8			49.9	16.0			1.3
1909	62.9		41.5			34.1	21.6			2.8
1912	64.5		33.2			40.0	26.3			0.6
1915	59.2		29.0			37.2	32.1			1.7
1918	59.7		30.4	4.7		31.6	31.6			1.7
1921	67.9		33.4	13.1		20.1	30.5+			2.8
1924	69.8		32.5	13.5		18.6	27.2+	6.1		2.0
1927	68.0		25.5	14.9		17.3	36.8	4.4		1.5
1930	77.6		30.0	15.9		20.2	31.4	1.7		0.8
1933	76.4		21.8	13.9	0.8	17.1	40.1	1.8		4.6
1936	84.0		22.6	11.6	1.4	16.0	42.5	0.3		5.7
1945	76.4		17.0	8.1	7.9	13.8	41.0	11.9		0.3
1949	82.0		17.8	7.9	8.5	13.5	45.7	5.8		0.7
1953	79.3		18.8	9.0	10.5	10.0	46.7	5.1		0.0
1957	78.3		18.9	9.3	10.2	9.6	48.3	3.4		0.0
1961	79.1		20.0	9.3	9.6	8.9	46.8	2.9	2.4	0.1
1965	85.4		21.1	9.9	8.1	10.3	43.1	1.4	6.0	0.0
1969	83.8		19.6	10.5	9.4	9.4●	46.5	1.0	3.5	0.1
1973	80.2	5.0	17.4	11.0	12.2	6.9●	35.3	11.2▲		0.9
1977	82.9	1.9	24.8	8.6	12.4	4.6●	42.3	0.4	4.2	0.8
1981	82.0	4.5	31.7	6.7	9.4	4.4●	37.2	0.3	4.9	0.8
1985	84.0	3.7	30.4	6.6	8.3	3.6●	40.8	0.2	5.5	1.0
1989	83.2	13.0	22.2	6.5	8.5	3.2	34.3		10.1	1.7
1993	75.8	6.3	17.0	16.7	7.9	3.6	36.9		7.9	3.7
1997	78.0	15.3	14.3	7.9	13.7	4.5	35.0		6.0	3.4
2001	75.1	14.6	21.2	5.6	12.4	3.9	24.3		12.5	5.5

Notes: Before the introduction of proportional representation in 1921, a two-ballot system of plurality election in single-member districts was used. For the 1906–18 elections, the figures reported here are parties' percentages of the first-ballot vote. PP—Progress party (Fremskrittspartiet); ran as Anders Lange's party in 1973; Con— Conservatives (Høyre); Agr Cen—agrarian Center party (Senterpartiet); ChrP— Christian People's party (Kristelig Folkeparti); Lib—liberals (Venstre); Labor—Labor party (Det norske Arbeiderparti); CP—Communist party (Norges Kommunistiske Parti); SPP—Socialist People's party (Sosialistisk Folkeparti; SV—Socialist Left party (Sosialistisk Venstreparti) in 1977 and thereafter; O—Other parties.

*Includes Independent Liberals (Frisinnede Venstre).

#Includes Labor Democrats (Arbeiderdemokrater).

+ Includes the Labor party's right wing (Norges Sosialdemokratiske Arbeider-parti), which polled 9.2 percent in 1921 and 8.8 percent in 1924.

●Includes the wing of the Liberals which supported membership in the European Community (Det nye Folkepartiet), which polled 3.4 percent in 1973, 1.4 percent in 1977, and, as Det liberale Folkepartiet, 0.5 percent in 1981 and 0.5 percent in 1985.

▲Socialist Electoral Alliance (Sosialistisk Valgforbund) included the CP and SPP.

Sources: Norway, Statistisk Sentralbyrå, *Stortingsvalget*, vols. 1907–36; Statistisk Sentralbyrå, *Stortingsvalget* 1985 vol. 1 (1986), Table 2; Norges offisielle Statiskikk, *Statistisk Årbok 1991*, p. 396; and *Nordic Statistical Yearbook 2000*, pp. 120, 129. 2001: http://www.ssb.no/emner/00/01/10/stortingsvalg, Table 2.

Table A.5
Elections to the Swedish Parliament, 1911–2002 (in percent)

Year	Turnout	ND	Con	Cen	ChrD	Lib	EP	SD	OS	CP/VpK	O
1911	57.0		31.2			40.2		28.5			0.1
1914a	69.9		37.7			32.2		30.1			0.0
1914b	66.2		36.5	0.2		26.9		36.4			0.0
1917	65.8		24.7	8.5		27.6		31.1	8.1		0.0
1920	55.3		27.9	14.2		21.8		29.7	6.4		0.0
1921	54.2		25.8	11.1		19.1		36.2	3.2	4.6	0.0
1924	53.0		26.1	10.8		16.9		41.1		5.1	0.0
1928	67.4		29.4	11.2		15.9		37.0		6.4	0.1
1932	68.6		23.5	14.1		11.7		41.7	5.3	3.0	0.7
1936	74.5		17.6	14.3		12.9		45.9	4.4	3.3	1.6
1940	70.3		18.0	12.0		12.0		53.8	0.7	3.5	0.0
1944	71.9		15.9	13.6		12.9		46.7	0.2	10.3	0.4
1948	82.7		12.3	12.4		22.8		46.1		6.3	0.1
1952	79.1		14.4	10.7		24.4		46.1		4.3	0.1
1956	79.8		17.1	9.4		23.8		44.6		5.0	0.1
1958	77.4		19.5	12.7		18.2		46.2		3.4	0.0
1960	85.9		16.5	13.6		17.5		47.8		4.5	0.1
1964	83.9		13.7	13.2	1.8	17.0		47.3		5.2	1.8*
1968	89.3		12.9	15.7	1.5	14.3		50.1		3.0	2.6#
1970	88.3		11.5	19.9	1.8	16.2		45.3		4.8	0.4
1973	90.8		14.3	25.1	1.8	9.4		43.6		5.3	0.6
1976	91.8		15.6	24.1	1.4	11.1		42.7		4.8	0.4
1979	90.7		20.3	18.1	1.4	10.6		43.2		5.6	0.8
1982	91.4		23.6	15.5	1.9	5.9	1.7	45.6		5.6	0.3
1985	89.9		21.3	12.4+		14.2	1.5	44.7		5.4	0.5
1988	86.0		18.3	11.3	2.9	12.2	5.5	43.2		5.8	0.7
1991	86.7	6.7	21.9	8.5	7.1	9.1	3.4	37.7		4.5	1.0
1994	86.8	1.2	22.4	7.7	4.1	7.2	5.0	45.2		6.2	1.0
1998	81.4		22.9	5.1	11.8	4.7	4.5	36.4		12.0	2.6
2002	79.0		15.1	6.2	9.1	13.3	4.5	39.9		8.3	2.9

Notes: ND—New Democrats (Ny Demokrati); Con—Conservatives (Högern), renamed Moderata Samlingspartiet (Moderate Unity party) in 1969; Cen—agrarian Center party (Centerpartiet), called Bondeförbundet (Farmer's party) prior to 1957; ChrD—Christian Democrats (Kristdemokratiska Samhällspartiet); Lib—Liberal People's party (Folkpartiet; Liberalerna); EP—Environmental party, the Greens (Miljöpartiet de gröna); SD—Social Democrats (Socialdemokraterna); OS—Other socialist parties—include Left Socialists (Vänstersocialisterna) in the 1917–21 elections and Socialists (Socialisterna) in the 1932–44 elections; CP—Swedish Communist party (Sveriges Kommunistiska Parti), renamed Left party; VpK—Communists (Vänsterpartiet Kommunisterna) in 1967 and Left party (Vänsterpartiet) in 1990; O—Other parties.

*Common Conservative, Liberal, and Center slate 1.5 percent; Common Liberal and Center slate 0.3 percent.

#Common Conservative, Liberal, and Center slate 1.7 percent; Common Liberal and Center slate 0.9 percent.

+Joint Center and Christian Democratic slate.

Sources: Sweden, Statisiska Centralbyrån 1980, Table 1; Sweden, *Från Riksdag & Departement* 1988: 30, p. 3; Sweden, Statistiska Centralbyrån, *Statistisk Årsbok 1992*, pp. 387–88; *Nordic Statistical Yearbook 2000*, pp. 120, 130; Sweden, Riksdag: http://www.val.se/flash/OOR/00.html (accessed September 16, 2003).

APPENDIX B

Distribution of Parliamentary Seats

Table B.1
Party Distribution of Seats in the Danish Folketing,* 1918–2001

Year	Total	PP/ DPP	Con	Agr Lib	ChrP	RL	Lfj	CD	SD	SPP	CP	LS	O
1918	139		22	44		32			39				2
1920	139		28	48		17			42				4
1920	.139		26	51		16			42				4
1920	148		27	51		18			48				4
1924	148		28	44		20	0		55		0		1
1926	148		30	46		16	2		53		0		1
1929	148		24	43		16	3		61		0		1
1932	148		27	38		14	4		62		4		1
1935	148		26	28		14	4		68		2		6
1939	148		26	30		14	3		64		3		8
1943	148		31	28		13	2		66		-		8
1945	148		26	38		11	3		48		18		4
1947	148		17	49		10	6		57		9		-
1950	149		27	32		12	12		59		7		-
1953a	149		26	33		13	9		61		7		-
1953b	175		30	42		14	6		74		8		1
1957	175		30	45		14	9		70		6		1
1960	175		32	38		11	0		76	11	0		7
1964	175		36	38		10	0		76	10	0		5
1966	175		34	35		13	0		69	20	0		4
1968	175		37	34		27	0		62	11	0	4	-
1971	175		31	30	0	27	0		70	17	0	0	-
1973	175	28	16	22	7	20	5	14	46	11	6	0	-
1975	175	24	10	42	9	13	0	4	53	9	7	4	-
1977	175	26	15	21	6	6	6	11	65	7	7	5	-
1979	175	20	22	22	5	10	5	6	68	11	0	6	-
1981	175	16	26	20	4	9	0	15	59	21	0	5	-
1984	175	6	42	22	5	10	0	8	56	21	0	5	-
1987	175	9	38	19	4	11	0	9	54	27	0	0	4
1988	175	16	35	22	4	10		9	55	24	0	0	-
1990	175	12	30	29	4	7		9	69	15	0	0	-
1994	175	11	27	42	0	8		5	62	13		6+	1
1998	175	17#	16	42	4	7		8	63	13		5	-
2001	175	22#	16	56	4	9		0	52	12		4	-

Note: For party abbreviations and sources, see Table A.1.

*Members elected in European Denmark only. In addition, the Faeroe Islands elected one member until 1947 and two members since then. Since 1953, the uni-cameral Danish parliament has also included two representatives from Greenland.

#Thereof Progress party 4 and Danish People's party 13 in 1998; Danish People's party 22 in 2001.

+ Unity List in this and subsequent elections.

Table B.2
Party Distribution of Seats in the Finnish Parliament, 1907–2003 (seats)

Year	Total	FP	YPF	Con	Swd PP	Lib	RP	ChrL	Agr Cen	SD	G	FPDU/ LA	Other
1907	200	59	26		24				9	80			2
1908	200	54	27		25				9	83			2
1909	200	48	29		25				13	84			1
1910	200	42	28		26				17	86			1
1911	200	43	28		26				16	86			1
1913	200	38	28		26				18	90			0
1916	200	33	23		21				19	103			1
1917	200	32	24		21				26	92			5
1919	200			28	22	26			42	80			2
1922	200			35	22	15			45	53		27	0
1924	200			38	23	17			44	60		18	0
1927	200			34	24	10			52	60		20	0
1929	200			28	23	7			60	59		23	0
1930	200			42	21	11			59	66			1
1933	200			18	21	11			53	78			5
1936	200			20	21	7			53	83			2
1939	200			25	18	6			56	85			2
1945	200			28	15	9			49	50		49	0
1948	200			33	14	5			56	54		38	0
1951	200			28	15	10			51	53		43	0
1954	200			24	13	13			53	54		43	0
1958	200			29	14	8		0	48	48		50	3
1962	200			32	14	13	0	0	53	38		47	2
1966	200			26	12	9	1	0	49	55		41	7
1970	200			37	12	8	18	1	37	51		36	0
1972	200			34	10	7	18	4	35	55		37	0
1975	200			35	10	9	2	9	39	54		40	2
1979	200			47	10	4	7	9	36	52		35	0
1983	200			44	11	0	17	3	38	57	2	27	1
1987	200			53	13	0	9	5	40	56	4	16	4
1991	200			40	12	1	7	8	53	48	10	19	0
1995	200			39	12	0	1	7	44	63	9	22	3
1999	200			46	12	0	1	10	48	51	11	20	1
2003	200			40	9	0	3	7	55	53	14	19	0

Note: For party abbreviations and sources, see Table A.2.

Table B.3
Party Distribution of Seats in the Icelandic Parliament, 1916–99

Year	Total	IndP	LP	ProgP	SD	WL	ULL	Green	CPI/PA	Other
1916	6	5		1	0					
1916	34	25		6	1					2
1919	34	24		10						
1922	3	1		1		1				
1923	36	21		13	1					1
1926	3	1		1	1					
1927	36	13	1	17	4					1
1930	3	2		1						
1931	36	12		21	3					
1933	36	17		14	4					1
1934	49	20		18*	10					1
1937	49	17		21**	8				3	
1942	49	17		20	6				6	
1942	52	20		15	7				10	
1946	52	20		13	9				10	
1949	52	19		17	7				9	
1953	52	21		18#	6				7	
1956	52	19		17	8				8	
1959	52	20		19	6				7	
1959	60	24		17	9				10	
1963	60	24		19	8				9	
1967	60	23		18	9		1		9	
1971	60	22		17	6		5		10	
1974	60	25		17	5		2		11	
1978	60	20		12	14				14	
1979	60	21		17	10				11	1
1983	60	23		14	10##	3			10	
1987	63	25+		13	10	6			8	1
1991	63	26		13	10	5			9	
1995	63	25		15	11++	3			9	
1999	63	26	2	12	17▲			6		

Notes: 1916, 1922, 1926, and 1930 were special supplementary elections. For party abbreviations and sources, see Table A.3.
*Of the eighteen seats, Farmers party received three seats.
**Of the twenty-one seats, Farmers party received two seats.
#Of the eighteen seats, National Preservation party received two seats.
##Of the ten seats, Social Democratic Federation received four seats.
+Of the twenty-five seats, Citizens party received seven seats.
++Of the eleven seats, Popular Movement received four seats.
▲Alliance of Social Democrats, People's Alliance, and Women's List.
Sources: Macke and Rose (1991, pp. 206–23); Esaiasson and Heidar (2000, pp. 449–50, Tables A2.5–A2.6).

Table B.4
Party Distribution of Seats in the Norwegian Storting, 1918–2001

Year	Total	PP	Con*	Agr Cen	Chr PP	Lib#	Labor	CP	SPP/ SV	Others
1918	126		50	3		54	18			1
1921	150		57	17		39	37+			0
1924	150		54	22		36	32+	6		0
1927	150		31	26		31	59	3		0
1930	150		44	25		34	47	0		0
1933	150		31	23	1	25	69	0		1
1936	150		36	18	2	23	70	0		1
1945	150		25	10	8	20	76	11		0
1949	150		23	12	9	21	85	0		0
1953	150		27	14	14	15	77	3		0
1957	150		29	15	12	15	78	1		0
1961	150		29	16	15	14	74	0	2	0
1965	150		31	18	13	18	68	0	2	0
1969	150		29	20	14	13	74	0	0	0
1973	155	4	29	21	20	31	62		16●	0
1977	155	0	41	12	22	2	76	0	2▲	0
1981	155	4	53	11	15	2	66	0	4	0
1985	157	2	50	12	16	0	71	0	6	0
1989	165	22	37	11	14	0	63	0	17	1
1993	165	10	28	32	13	1	67	0	13	1
1997	165	25	23	11	25	6	65	-	9	1
2001	165	26	38	10	22	2	43		23	1

Note: For party abbreviations and sources, see Table A.4.

*Includes Independent Liberals 1918–36.

#Includes Labor Democrats 1918–36.

+ Includes eight seats won by the Labor party's right wing, Norway's Social Democratic Labor party in 1921 and 1924.

‡Includes one seat won by the New People's party, the pro-EC wing of the Liberal party.

●Socialist Electoral Alliance included CP and SPP.

▲Socialist Left party in this and subsequent elections.

Table B.5
Party Distribution of Seats in the Swedish Riksdag, 1918–2002

Year	Total	ND	Con.	Agr Cen	ChrD	Lib	EP	SD	CP/ VpK	Others
1918	380		145	14		107		102	12*	0
1921	380		108	49		87		126	10*	0
1922	380		103	39		79		143	16*	0
1925	380		109	41		68		156	6	0
1929	380		122	44		63		142	9	0
1933	380		108	54		47		162	9#	0
1937	380		89	58		43		178	12#	0
1941	380		77	52		38		209	4	0
1945	380		69	56		40		198	17	0
1949	380		47	51		75		196	11	0
1953	380		51	51		80		189	9	0
1957	381		55	44		88		185	9	0
1959	382		61	54		70		190	7	0
1961	383		58	54		73		191	7	0
1965	384		59	54	0	69		191	10	1
1969	384		57	59	0	60		204	4	0
1970	350+		41	71	0	58		163	17	0
1973	350		51	90	0	34		156	19	0
1976	349		55	86	0	39		152	17	0
1979	349		73	64	0	38		154	20	0
1982	349		86	56	0	21	0	166	20	0
1985	349		76	43	1	51	0	159	19	0
1988	349		66	42	0	44	20	156	21	0
1991	349	25	80	31	26	33	0	138	16	0
1994	349	0	80	27	15	26	18	161	22	0
1998	349	-	82	18	42	17	16	131	43	0
2002	349	-	55	22	33	48	17	144	30	0

Note: For party abbreviations and sources, see Table A.5.

*Includes Left Socialists.

#Includes Socialists.

+ This and subsequent elections are to the unicameral parliament.

APPENDIX C

Governing Parties and Coalitions

Table C.1
Danish Governments since World War I

Year	Party Composition	Prime Minister
1913-16	Radical Liberal	C. Th. Zahle (RL)
1916-18	National Unity: Radical Liberal- Agrarian Liberal-Conservative- Social Democratic*	C. Th. Zahle (RL)
1918-20	Radical Liberal-Social Democratic*	C. Th. Zahle (RL)
1920	Caretaker government	M. P. Friis
1920-24	Agrarian Liberal	Niels Neergaard (Agr Lib)
1924-26	Social Democratic	Thorvald Stauning (SD)
1926-29	Agrarian Liberal	Th. Madsen-Mygdal (Agr Lib)
1929-40	Social Democratic-Radical Liberal*	Thorvald Stauning (SD)
1940-43	National Unity: Social Democratic- Radical Liberal-Agrarian Liberal- Conservative*	Thorvald Stauning (SD)(40-42) Vilhelm Buhl (SD) Erik Scavenius (RL)
1943-45	German military rule	
1945	Liberation coalition of all parties*	Vilhelm Buhl (SD)
1945-47	Agrarian Liberal	Knud Kristensen (Agr Lib)
1947-50	Social Democratic	Hans Hedtoft (SD)
1950-53	Agrarian Liberal-Conservative	Erik Eriksen (Agr Lib)
1953-57	Social Democratic	Hans Hedtoft (SD) (1953-55) H. C. Hansen (SD)
1957-60	Social Democratic-Radical Liberal- League for Justice*	H. C. Hansen (SD) (1957-60) Viggo Kampmann (SD)
1960-64	Social Democratic-Radical Liberal	Viggo Kampmann (SD) (1960-62) Jens Otto Krag (SD)
1964-68	Social Democratic	Jens Otto Krag (SD)
1968-71	Radical Liberal-Agrarian Liberal- Conservative*	Hilmar Baunsgaard (RL)
1971-73	Social Democratic	Jens Otto Krag (SD) (1971-72) Anker Jørgensen (SD)
1973-75	Agrarian Liberal	Poul Hartling (Agr Lib)
1975-78	Social Democratic	Anker Jørgensen (SD)
1978-79	Social Democratic-Agrarian Liberal	Anker Jørgensen (SD)
1979-82	Social Democratic	Anker Jørgensen (SD)
1982-88	Conservative-Christian People's- Agrarian Liberal-Center Democrats	Poul Schlüter (Con)
1988-90	Conservative-Agrarian Liberal- Radical Liberal	Poul Schlüter (Con)
1990-93	Conservative-Agrarian Liberal	Poul Schlüter (Con)
1993-94	Social Democratic-Radical Liberal- Center Democrats-Christian People's*	Poul Nyrup Rasmussen (SD)
1994-96	Social Democratic-Radical Liberal- Center Democrats	Poul Nyrup Rasmussen (SD)
1996-01	Social Democratic-Radical Liberal	Poul Nyrup Rasmussen (SD)
2001-	Agrarian Liberal-Conservative	Anders Fogh Rasmussen (Agr.Lib)

*Majority government.

Table C.2
Finnish Governments since World War I

Year	Party Composition	Prime Minister
1917	Social Democrat-Young Finnish-Finnish Party-Agrarian-Swedish People's*	Oskari Tokoi (Social Democrat)
1917-18	Young Finnish Party-Finnish Party-Agrarian-Swedish People's*	Pehr Svinhufvud (Young Finnish)
1918	Finnish Party-Young Finnish Party-Agrarian-Swedish People's*	Juho Paasikivi (Finnish Party)
1918-19	National Coalition-Liberals-Swedish People's*	Lauri Ingman (National Coalition)
1919	Liberals-Agrarian-Swedish People's	Kaarlo Castren (Liberal)
1919-20	Liberals-Agrarian	Juho Vennola (Liberal)
1920-21	National Coalition-Agrarian-Swedish People's-Liberals*	Rafael Waldemar Erich (Liberal)
1921-22	Liberals-Agrarian	Juho Vennola (Liberal)
1922	Non-party	Aimo Cajander
1922-24	Agrarian-Liberals	Kyosti Kallio (Agrarian)
1924	Non-party	Aimo Cajander
1924-25	National Coalition-Liberals-Agrarian (5.31.24-11.22.24)-Swedish People's (11.22.24-3.31.25)	Lauri Ingman (National Coalition)
1925	National Coalition-Agrarian	Antti Tulenheimo (National Coalition)
1925-26	Agrarian-National Coalition	Kyosti Kallio (Agrarian)
1926-27	Social Democrat	Väinö Tanner (Social Democrat)
1927-28	Agrarian	Juho Sunila (Agrarian)
1928-29	Liberals-National Coalition	Oskari Mantere (Liberal)
1929-30	Agrarian-National Coalition*	Kyosti Kallio (Agrarian)
1930-31	National Coalition-Agrarian-Liberals-Swedish People's*	Pehr Svinhufvud (National Coalition)
1931-32	Agrarian-National Coalition-Liberals-Swedish People's*	Juho Sunila (Agrarian)
1932-33	Liberals-National Coalition-Swedish People's	Toivo Kivimäki (Liberal)
1933-37	Agrarian-National Coalition-Liberals	Kyosti Kallio (Agrarian)
1937-39	Liberals-Social Democrat-Agrarian*	Aimo Cajander (Liberal)
1939-41	Social Democrat-Agrarian-Liberals-National Coalition-Swedish People's*	Risto Ryti (Liberal)
1941-43	Liberals-Agrarian-Social Democrat-National Coalition-Swedish People's-Patriotic People's Movement*	Johann Rangell (Liberal)

(continued)

Table C.2 (*continued*)

Year	Party Composition	Prime Minister
1943-44	National Coalition-Social Democrat-Agrarian-Swedish People's-Liberals*	Edwin Linkomies (National Coalition)
1944	National Coalition-Social Democrat-Agrarian-Swedish People's-Liberals*	Antti Hackzell (National Coalition)
1944	National Coalition-Social Democrat-Agrarian-Swedish People's-Liberals*	Urho Castren
1944-46	People's Democratic League-Social Democrat-Agrarian-Swedish People's-Liberals*	Juho Paasikivi
1946-48	People's Democratic League-Social Democrat-Agrarian-Swedish People's*	Mauno Pekkala (People's Democratic League)
1948-50	Social Democrat	Karl August Fagerholm
1950-53	Agrarian-Swedish People's-Liberals (3.17.50-1.17.51)-Social Democrat (1.17.51-7.9.53)*	Urho Kekkonen (Agrarian)
1953-54	National Coalition-Liberals-Swedish People's	Sakari Tuomioja
1954	Agrarian-Social Democrat-Swedish People's*	Ralf Törngren (Swedish People's)
1954-56	Agrarian-Social Democrat*	Urho Kekkonen (Agrarian)
1956-57	Social Democrat-Agrarian-Liberals-Swedish People's*	Karl August Fagerholm (Social Democrat)
1957	Agrarian-Liberals-Swedish People's (7.2.57-11.29.57)	Veino Johannes Sukselainen (Agrarian)
1957-58	Non-party	Rainer von Fieandt (non-party)
1958	Social Democrat-Liberals	Reino Kuuskoski
1958-59	Social Democrat-Agrarian-National Coalition-Liberals-Swedish People's*	Karl August Fagerholm (Social Democrat)
1959-61	Agrarian-Swedish People's	Veino Johannes Sukselainen (Agrarian)
1961-62	Agrarian	Martti Miettunen (Agrarian)
1962-63	Agrarian-Social Democrat-National Coalition-Liberals-Swedish People's*	Ahti Karjalainen (Agrarian)
1963-64	Non-party	Reino Lehto (non-party)
1964-66	Agrarian-National Coalition-Liberals-Swedish People's*	Johannes Virolainen (Agrarian)
1966-68	Social Democrat-People's Democratic League-Agrarian-Workers and Smallholders' Party*	Rafael Paasio (Social Democrat)
1968-70	Social Democrat-People's Democratic League-Agrarian-Workers and Smallholders' Party-Swedish People's*	Mauno Koivisto (Social Democrat)

(*continued*)

Table C.2 (*continued*)

Year	Party Composition	Prime Minister
1970	Non-party	Terra Aura (non-party)
1970-71	Agrarian Center-Social Democrat-People's Democratic League (7.14.70)-Liberals (7.14.70) Swedish People's (7.14.70)*	Ahti Karjalainen (Agrarian Center)
1971-72	Non-party	Terra Aura (non-party)
1972	Social Democrat	Rafael Paasio (Social Democrat)
1972-75	Social Democrat-Agrarian Center-Liberals-Swedish People's*	Kalevi Sorsa (Social Democrat)
1975	Non-party	Keijo Liinamaa (non-party)
1975-77	Agrarian Center-Social Democrat (11.30.75-9.29.76)-People's Democratic League (11.30.75-9.29.76)-Swedish People's-Liberals*[1]	Martii Miettunen (Agrarian Center)
1977-79	Social Democrat-People's Democratic League-Agrarian Center-Liberals, Swedish People's*	Kalevi Sorsa (Social Democrat)
1979-82	Social Democrat-People's Democratic League-Agrarian Center-Swedish People's*	Mauno Koivisto (Social Democrat)
1982-87	Social Democrat-People's Democratic League (2.19.82-5.6.83)-Agrarian Center-Rural (5.6.83-4.30.87)-Swedish People's*	Kalevi Sorsa (Social Democrat)
1987-91	National Coalition-Social Democrat-Swedish People's-Rural*	Harri Holkeri (National Coalition)
1991-95	Agrarian Center-National Coalition-Swedish People's-Christian League*	Esko Aho (Agrarian Center)
1995-2003	Social Democrat-National Coalition-Swedish People's-Left Alliance-Greens*	Paavo Lipponen (Social Democrat)
2003-	Agrarian Center-Social Democrat-Swedish People's*	Anneli Jäätteenmäki (Agrarian Center)

Notes: Miettunen was a majority government from November 11, 1975, to September 29, 1976. From September 29, 1976, to May 15, 1977, Miettunen was a minority government.

*Majority government.

Sources: Bidwell (1973, pp. 48–53); Jussila, Hentilä, and Nevakivi (1999, pp. 362–66); Finnish Ministry of Justice, Finnish Council of State History Page, http://www.vn.fi/vn/english/index.htm.

Table C.3
Elections for Finnish President since World War I

Year	Turn-out	Con	Swd PP	Lib	RP	ChrL	AgrCen	SD	FPDL /LA	Others
Indirect election through electoral college, 1925-1988 (in percent of vote)										
1925	39.7	22.7	12.6	11.0			19.9	26.2		6.7
1931	47.1	21.6	9.0	17.7			20.0	30.2		1.5
1937	57.8	21.6	10.2	11.0			16.6	30.7		9.8
1950	63.8	22.9	8.9	5.4			19.6	21.8	21.4	0.1
1956	73.3	17.9	6.9	4.5			26.9	23.3	18.7	1.7
1962	81.4	13.1	6.7	8.0			31.7	13.1	20.5	6.8
1968	69.9	21.2	5.7	5.0	11.8		20.7	15.5	17.0	3.7
1978	64.3	14.7	3.9	2.9	4.7	8.7	19.4	23.3	18.0	4.3
1982	81.4	18.7	3.8	1.8	2.3	1.9	16.8	43.1	11.0	0.5
1988	77.6	20.0			4.0		21.7	39.4	9.6	5.1
Direct Election of President by Popular Vote, 2nd ballot (in percent of votes)										
1994	78.7	46.6						53.9		
2000	80.2						48.4	51.6		

Finnish Presidents since 1919

Period in office	President	Party
1919-25	K.J. Ståhlberg	Liberal
1925-31	L. Relander	Agrarian
1931-37	P.E. Svinhufvud	National Coalition
1937-40	K. Kallio	Agrarian
1940-44	R. Ryti	Liberal
1944-46	Marshal Mannerhein	Non-party
1946-56	J.K. Paasikivi	National Coalition
1956-82	U. Kekkonen	Agrarian Center
1982-94	M. Koivisto	Social Democrat
1994-2000	M. Ahtisaari	Social Democrat
2000-	T. Halonen	Social Democrat

Sources: Macke and Rose (1991, pp. 109–29); Bidwell (1973, pp. 9–10); Finnish Council of State History Page, http://www.vn.fi/vn/english/index.htm.

Table C.4
Icelandic Governments since World War I

Year	Party Composition	Prime Minister
1917-20	Home Rule Party-Hardline Independence Party-and Progressive Party*	Jon Magnusson (Home Rule)
1920-22	Home Rule Party	Jon Magnusson (Home Rule)
1922-24	Independence Party	Siggurdur Eggerz (Independence)
1924-26	Conservative Party*	Jon Magnusson (Conservative)
1926-27	Conservative Party*	Jon Thorlakson (Conservative)
1927-32	Progressive Party	Trygvi Thorhalsson (Progressive)
1932-34	Progressive Party-Independence Party*	Ásgeir Ásgeirsson (Progressive)
1934-42	Progressive Party-Social Democrats (7/34-4/38)* Progressive Party (4/38-4/39) Progressive Party-Independence Party -Social Democrats (4/39-5/42)*	Hermann Jónasson (Progressive)
1942-43	Independence Party	Ólafur Thors (Independence)
1943-44	Caretaker	Björn Thordarson (no party)
1944-47	Independence Party-United Socialists, -Social Democrats*	Ólafur Thors (Independence)
1947-49	Social Democrats-Independence Party, -Progressive Party*	Stefán Jóhann Stefánsson (Social Democrat)
1949-50	Independence Party	Ólafur Thors (Independence)
1950-53	Progressive Party-Independence Party*	Steingrímur Steinthórsson (Progressive)
1953-56	Independence Party-Progressive Party*	Ólafur Thors (Independence)
1956-58	Progressive Party-People's Alliance-Social Democrats*	Hermann Jónasson (Progressive)
1958-59	Social Democrats	Emil Jónsson (Social Democrat)
1959-63	Independence Party-Social Democrats*	Ólafur Thors (Independence)
1963-70	Independence Party-Social Democrats*	Bjarni Benediktsson(Independence)
1970-71	Independence Party-Social Democrats*	Jóhann Hafstein (Independence)
1971-74	Progressive Party-People's Alliance-Union of Liberals and Leftists*	Ólafur Jóhannesson (Progressive)
1974-78	Independence Party-Progressive Party*	Geir Hallgrímsson (Independence)
1978-79	Progressive Party-People's Alliance-Social Democrats*	Ólafur Jóhannesson (Progressive)
1979-80	Social Democrats	Benedikt Gröndal (Social Democrat)
1980-83	Independence Party-Progressive Party-People's Alliance*	Gunnar Thoroddsen(Independence)
1983-87	Progressive Party-Independence Party*	Steingrímur Hermannsson (Progressive)
1987-88	Independence Party-Progressive Party-Social Democrats*	Thorsteinn Pálsson (Independence)
1988-91	Progressive Party-Social Democrats-People's Alliance	Steingrímur Hermannsson (Progressive)
1991-95	Independence Party-Progressive Party-Social Democrats*	Davíð Oddsson (Independence)
1995-present	Independence Party-Progressive Party*	Davíð Oddsson (Independence)

*Majority government.

Sources: Robin Bidwell, editor. 1973. *Bidwell's Guide to Government Ministers. Volume 1: The Major Powers and Western Europe, 1900–1971.* Portland, OR: Frank Cass and Company Limited, 48–53. *The Political Reference Almanac,* http://www.polisci. com/world/nation/IC.htm. Jonsson, Elias Snaeland. 1994. *The Republic of Iceland 50th Anniversary.* Reykjavik, Iceland: Linden hf. RÁÐUNEYTI 1917–2001 (Icelandic Prime Ministers: 1917–2001). http://www.althingi.is/~hlodver/ran.html. Skrif-stofa Alþingis: 23. apríl 2001.

Table C.5
Norwegian Governments since World War I

Year	Party Composition	Prime Minister
1913-20	Liberal (1913-18,* minority 1918-20)	Gunnar Knudsen (Lib)
1920-21	Conservative	Otto B. Halvorsen (Con)
1921-23	Liberal	Otto Blehr (Lib)
1923-24	Conservative	Otto B. Halvorsen (1923)
		Abraham Berge (Free Lib)
1924-26	Liberal	Johan Ludwig Mowinckel (Lib)
1926-28	Conservative	Ivar Lykke (Con)
1928	Labor	Christopher Hornsrud (Labor)
1928-31	Liberal	Johan Ludwig Mowinckel (Lib)
1931-33	Agrarian	Peder Kolstad (Agr) (1931-32)
		Jens Hundseid (Agr)
1933-35	Liberal	Johan Ludwig Mowinckel (Lib)
1935-40	Labor	Johan Nygaardsvold (Labor)
1940-45	National Unity Government in exile (London) Labor-Liberal-Conservative-Agrarian*	Johan Nygaardsvold (Labor)
1940-45	German military government (Oslo)	
1945	Liberation coalition of all parties*	Einar Gerhardsen (Labor)
1945-63	Labor (1945-61,* minority 1961-63)	Einar Gerhardsen (Labor)(1945-51)
		Oscar Torp (Labor) (1951-55)
		Einar Gerhardsen (Labor)(1955-63)
1963	Conservative-Liberal-Christian People's-Agrarian	Jon Lyng (Con)
1963-65	Labor	Einar Gerhardsen (Labor)
1965-71	Conservative-Liberal-Christian People's-Agrarian*	Per Borten (Agr)
1971-72	Labor	Trygve Bratteli (Labor)
1972-73	Christian People's-Agrarian-Liberal#	Lars Korvald (ChrP)
1973-81	Labor	Trygve Bratteli (Labor) (1973-76)
		Odvar Nordli (Labor) (1976-81)
		Gro Harlem Brundtland (Labor) (1981)
1981-83	Conservative	Kåre Willoch (Con)
1983-86	Conservative-Agrarian Center-Christian People's (1983-85*, minority 1985-86)	Kåre Willoch (Con)
1986-89	Labor	Gro Harlem Brundtland (Labor)
1989-90	Conservative-Agrarian Center-Christian People's	J.P. Syse (Con)
1990-97	Labor	Gro Harlem Brundtland (Labor)
		Thorbjørn Jagland (Labor)(1996-7)
1997-2000	Liberal-Agrarian Center-Christian People's	Kjell Magne Bondevik (Chr. P)
2000-01	Labor	Jens Stoltenberg (Labor)
2001-	Christian People's-Liberal-Conservative	Kjell Magne Bondevik (Chr.P)

*Majority government.
#The Liberal ministers were drawn from the anti–European Community segment of the party; the Liberal party split on the issue.

Table C.6
Swedish Governments since World War I

Year	Party Composition	Prime Minister
1917-20	Liberal-Social Democratic*	Nils Edén (Lib)
1920	Social Democratic	Hjalmar Branting (SD)
1920-21	Caretaker government	Louis De Geer (1920-21)
		Oscar von Sydow (1921)
1921-23	Social Democratic	Hjalmar Branting (SD)
1923-24	Conservative	Ernst Trygger (Con)
1924-26	Social Democratic	Hjalmar Branting (SD) (1924-25)
		Richard Sandler (SD)
1926-28	Liberal	G. C. Ekman (Lib)
1928-30	Conservative	A. Lindman (Con)
1930-32	Liberal	G. C. Ekman (Lib) (1930-32)
		Felix Hamrin (Lib)
1932-36	Social Democratic	Per Albin Hansson (SD)
1936	Agrarian	Axel Pehrsson i Bramstorp (Agr)
1936-39	Social Democratic-Agrarian*	Per Albin Hansson (SD)
1939-45	National Unity: Social Democratic, Agrarian, Liberal, and Conservative*	Per Albin Hansson (SD)
1945-51	Social Democratic	Per Albin Hansson (SD) (1945-46)
		Tage Erlander (SD)
1951-57	Social Democratic-Agrarian*	Tage Erlander (SD)
1957-76	Social Democratic (minority 1957-58, 1964-68; majority 1958-60,* 1968-70*)	Tage Erlander (SD) (1957-69)
		Olof Palme (SD)
1976-78	Agrarian Center-Conservative-Liberal*	Thorbjörn Fälldin (Agr Cen)
1978-79	Liberal	Ola Ullsten (Lib)
1979-81	Agrarian Center-Conservative-Liberal*	Thorbjörn Fälldin (Agr Cen)
1981-82	Agrarian Center-Liberal	Thorbjörn Fälldin (Agr Cen)
1982-91	Social Democratic	Olof Palme (SD) (1982-86)
		Ingvar Carlsson (SD)
1991-94	Conservative-Agrarian Center-Liberal-Christian Democrat	Carl Bildt (Con)
1994-	Social Democratic	Ingvar Carlsson (SD) (1994-96)
		Göran Persson (SD)(1996-

*Majority government.

Elections to the European Parliament, 1979–99

Table D.1
Elections to the European Parliament, 1979–99

Denmark

	1979 Pct.	1979 Seats	1984 Pct.	1984 Seats	1989 Pct.	1989 Seats	1994 Pct.	1994 Seats	1999 Pct.	1999 Seats
Social Democrats	21.9	3	19.4	3	23.3	4	15.8	3	16.5	3
Radical Liberals	3.2	0	3.1	0	2.8	0	8.5	1	9.1	1
Conservatives	14.1	2	20.8	4	13.3	2	17.7	3	8.5	1
Center Democrats	6.2	1	6.6	1	7.9	2	0.9	0	3.5	0
Socialist People's	4.7	1	9.2	2	9.1	1	8.6	1	7.1	1
June Movement							15.2	2	16.1	3
People's Movement against EU	21.0	4	20.8	4	18.9	4	10.3	2	7.3	1
Agrarian Liberals	14.5	3	12.5	2	16.6	3	19.0	4	23.4	5
Progress Party	5.8	1	3.5	0	5.3	0	2.9	0	0.7	0
Danish People's									5.8	1
Others	8.7	0	4.0	0	2.7	0	1.1	0	2.0	0
Total	100.1	15	99.9	16	99.9	16	100.0	16	100.0	16
Turnout	47.8		52.0		45.6		53.0		50.4	

Sweden

	1994 interim Seats	1995 Pct.	1995 Seats	1999 Pct.	1999 Seats
Social Democrats	11	28.1	7	26.0	6
Conservatives	5	23.1	5	20.8	5
agrarian Center Party	2	7.2	2	6.0	1
Liberal Party	1	4.8	0	13.9	3
Christian Democrats	1	3.9	0	7.6	2
Environmental Party	1	17.2	4	9.5	2
Left Party	1	12.9	3	15.8	3
Others	0	2.7	0	0.5	0
Total	22	100.0	22	100.1	22
Turnout		41.7		38.9	

Finland

	1996 Pct.	1996 Seats	1999 Pct.	1999 Seats
Social Democrats	21.5	4	17.9	3
Left Alliance	10.5	2	9.1	1
National Coalition	20.2	4	25.3	4
Center Party	24.4	4	21.3	4
Swedish People's	5.8	1	6.8	1
Liberal Party	0.4	0		
Christian League	2.8	0	2.4	1
Greens	7.6	1	13.4	2
Others	7.0	0	4.0	0
Total	100.2	16	100.2	16
Turnout	57.7		30.1	

Note: Pct. = percent

Sources: Denmark's Statistisk, Statistisk tiårsoversigt 1994, p. 30; Swedish News, September 20, 1995; Nordic Statistical Yearbook 2000, pp. 131–34.

References

In general, where English translations are available of Scandinavian-language materials, we have cited the English versions. The other translations in the text are by the authors.

Aardal, Bernt, Henry Valen, Hanne Marthe Narud, and Frode Berglund. 1999. *Velgere i 90- årene.* Oslo: NKS-Forlaget.

Abrahamsson, Bengt, and Anders Broström. 1980. *The Rights of Labor.* Beverly Hills: Sage. (Translation of *Om arbetets rätt: Vägar till ekonomisk demokrati.* Stockholm: AWE/Gebers, 1979)

Adema, Willem. 1998. "Uncovering Real Social Spending." *The OECD Observer* 211: 20–23.

———. 2001. "Net Social Expenditure" (2nd ed.). *Labour Market and Social Policy Occasional Papers,* no. 52. Paris: OECD, Directorate for Education, Employment, Labour, and Social Affairs.

Adler-Karlsson, Gunnar. 1967. *Functional Socialism: A Swedish Theory for Democratic Socialization.* Stockholm: Prisma. (Original Swedish title: *Funktionssocialism.* Stockholm: Prisma, 1967)

Åkerman, Nordal. 1979. "Can Sweden be Shrunk?" *Development Dialogue* 2: 71–114.

Akyeampong, Ernst B. 1997. "A Statistical Portrait of the Trade Union Movement." Statistics Canada, *Perspectives* 9(4).

———. 1999."Unionization: An Update." Statistics Canada, *Perspectives* 11(3).

Allardt, Erik, et al., editors. 1981. *Nordic Democracy.* Copenhagen: Det danske Selskab.

Alsterdal, Alvar, and Ove Sandell, editors. 1970. *Hjalmar Branting: Socialism och demokrati.* Stockholm: Prisma.

al-Wahab, Ibrahim. 1979. *The Swedish Institution of Ombudsman: An Instrument of Human Rights*. Stockholm: Liber.

Andenæs, Johannes. 1949. "Norge: Utviklingen av det politiske demokrati i Norge." In *Nordisk demokrati,* edited by H. Koch and A. Ross, pp. 58–72. Copenhagen: Westermann.

Andersen, Bent Rold. 1984a. *Kan vi bevare velfærdsstaten?* Copenhagen: AKFs Forlag.

———. 1984b. "Rationality and Irrationality of the Nordic Welfare State." *Dædalus* 113: 109–39.

Andersen, Johannes, Ole Borre, Jørgen Goul Andersen, and Hans Jørgen Nielsen. 1999. *Vælgere med Omtanke. En analyse af Folketingsvalget 1998*. Århus: Systime.

Anderson, Stanley V. 1967. *The Nordic Council: A Study in Scandinavian Regionalism*. Seattle: University of Washington Press.

Anonymous [C. M. Olsen]. 1911. *Ned med de Samvirkende Fagforbund! Et Par Ord af en Fagforeningsmand*. Copenhagen: Bording.

Anton, Thomas J. 1969. "Policy-Making and Political Culture in Sweden." *Scandinavian Political Studies* 4: 90–102.

Arter, David. 1984. *The Nordic Parliaments: A Comparative Analysis*. New York: St. Martin's Press.

———. 1999. *Scandinavian Politics Today*. Manchester: Manchester University Press.

Artis, Michael, and Sylvia Ostry. 1986. *International Economic Policy Coordination*. London: Routledge & Kegan Paul for the Royal Institute of International Affairs.

Bagehot, Walter. 1867. *The English Constitution*. Garden City, NY: Doubleday/ Dolphin reprint.

Baldwin, Peter. 1990. *The Politics of Social Solidarity: Class Bases of the European Welfare State 1895–1975*. Cambridge: Cambridge University Press.

Barkin, Solomon, editor. 1983. *Worker Militancy and Its Consequences: The Changing Climate of Western Industrial Relations,* 2nd ed. New York: Praeger.

Barnes, Hilary. 2000. "Sweden: Wanja Tackles Wage System." *Financial Times,* 4 December.

Bell, Daniel. 1976. *The Cultural Contradictions of Capitalism*. New York: Basic Books.

———. 1960. *The End of Ideology: On the Exhaustion of Political Ideas in the Fifties*. Glencoe, IL: The Free Press.

Berendt, Mogens. 1983. *Tilfældet Sverige*. Copenhagen: Chr. Erichsen.

Bergh, Trond. 1977. "Norsk økonomisk politikk, 1945–1965." In *Vekst og velstand: Norsk politisk historie, 1945–1965,* edited by Trond Bergh and Helge Pharo, pp. 11–50. Oslo: Universitetsforlaget.

Berglund, Sten, and Ulf Lindström. 1978. *The Scandinavian Party System(s)*. Lund: Studentlitteratur.

Berman, Sheri. 1998. *The Social Democratic Moment: Ideas and Politics in the Making of Interwar Europe*. Cambridge: Harvard University Press.

Bergqvist, Christina, et al. 1999. *Equal Democracies? Gender and Politics in the Nordic Countries*. Oslo: Scandinavian University Press.

Beveridge, William H. 1942. *Social Insurance and Allied Services*. London: HMSO.

Bidwell, Robin, editor. 1973. *Bidwell's Guide to Government Ministers. Volume 1: The Major Powers and Western Europe, 1900–1971*. Portland, OR: Frank Cass.

Blaustein, Albert, and Gisbert Flanz, editors. 1971 and later. *Constitutions of the Countries of the World*. Dobbs Ferry, NY: Oceana.

Blom-Hansen, Jens. 2000. "Still Corporatism in Scandinavia? A Survey of Recent Findings." *Scandinavian Political Studies* 23(2): 157–81.

Bogason, Peter. 1987. "Capacity for Welfare: Local Governments in Scandinavia and the United States." *Scandinavian Studies* 59(2): 184–202.

Borre, Ole. 1984. "Critical Electoral Change in Scandinavia." In *Electoral Change in Advanced Industrial Democracies: Realignment or Dealignment?* edited by R. J. Dalton, S. C. Flanagan, and P. A. Beck, pp. 330–64. Princeton, NJ: Princeton University Press.

Borre, Ole, and Jørgen Goul Andersen. 1997. *Voting and Political Attitudes in Denmark: A Study of the 1994 Election*. Århus: Aarhus University Press.

Borre, Ole, Hans Jørgen Nielsen, Steen Sauerberg, and Torben Worre. 1974. *Vælgerskreddet 1971–73. Arbejdspapir fra interviewundersøgelse*. Århus: offset.

Bosworth, Barry P., and Alice M. Rivlin, editors. 1987. *The Swedish Economy*. Washington, D.C.: Brookings Institution.

Brittan, Samuel. 1977. *The Economic Consequences of Democracy*. London: Temple Smith.

Bruun, Niklas, et al. 1990. *Den Nordiska Modellen: Fackföreningarna och Arbetsrätten i Norden—Nu och i Framtiden*. Stockholm: Liber.

Buksti, Jakob A., and Hans Martens. 1984. "Interesseorganisationer i EF. Euroorganisationernes Rolle og Betydning for Danske Interesseorganisationer i EF-Politiken." In *Dansk Udenrigspolitisk Årbog 1983,* edited by Christian Thune and Nikolaj Petersen, pp. 61–93. n.p. Dansk Udenrigspolitisk Institut, Jurist-og Økonomforbundets Forlag.

Caiden, Gerald E., editor. 1983. *International Handbook of the Ombudsman: Country Surveys*. Westport, CT: Greenwood Press.

Carstairs, Andrew M. 1980. *A Short History of Electoral Systems in Western Europe*. London: George Allen & Unwin.

Castles, Francis. 1978. *The Social Democratic Image of Society: A Study of the Achievements and Origins of Scandinavian Social Democracy in Comparative Perspective*. London: Routledge & Kegan Paul.

Childs, Marquis W. 1936. *Sweden: The Middle Way*. New Haven, CT: Yale University Press.

Christensen, C. Ove, and Villy Nielsen. 1967. *Arbejdsret*. Copenhagen: AOF/ Fremad.

Christensen, Peter Munk, and Hilmar Rommetvedt. 1999. "From Corporatism to Lobbyism? Parliament, Executives and Organized Interests in Denmark and Norway." *Scandinavian Political Studies* 22: 195–220.

Clayton, Richard, and Jonas Pontusson. 1998. "Welfare-State Retrenchment Revisited: Entitlement Cuts, Public Sector Restructuring, and Inegalitarian Trends in Advanced Capitalist Societies." *World Politics* 51: 67–98.

Crozier, Michel, Samuel P. Huntington, and Joji Watanuki. 1975. *The Crisis of Democracy*. New York: New York University Press.

Dahl, Robert A. 1971. *Polyarchy*. New Haven, CT: Yale University Press.

———. 1982. *Dilemmas of Pluralist Democracy*. New Haven, CT: Yale University Press.

————. 1985. *A Preface to Economic Democracy.* Berkeley: University of California Press.

————. 1989. *Democracy and its Critics.* New Haven: Yale University Press.

Dahl Jacobsen, K. 1967. "Politisk fattigdom." *Kontrast* 3: 6–10.

Damgaard, Erik. 1975. "The Political Role of Nonpolitical Bureaucrats in Denmark." In *The Mandarins of Western Europe,* edited by Mattei Dogan, pp. 275–92. New York: Wiley.

————. 1997. "Strong Scandinavian Parliaments," *Extensions* (Spring): 13–16.

————. 2000. "Conclusion: The Impact of European Integration on Nordic Parliamentary Democracies." *Journal of Legislative Studies* 6: 151–69.

Damgaard, Erik, editor. 1984. *Dansk demokrati under forandring.* Copenhagen: Schultz.

————. 1990. *Parlamentarisk Forandring i Norden.* Oslo: Universitetsforlaget.

Dansk Arbejdsgiverforening. 1981–83. *MLM-Fraværsstatistik.* Copenhagen: offset.

Den Danske Bank. 2002. *Nordisk Makrofokus.* København: Den Danske Bank. (February).

Dencik, Peter. 1976. "Inkomstpolitik—dess bakgrund och politisk-ekonomiska effekter." *Nordisk Tidskrift for Politisk Ekonomi* 4: 117–35.

Denmark. 1982. Lavindkomstkommissionen. *Lavindkomstkommissionens Betænkning.* Betænkning nr. 946. Copenhagen: Direktoratet for statens indkøb.

————. 1985. *Folketingsvalget den 10. Januar 1984.* Copenhagen: Danmarks Statistik.

————. 1987a. Danmarks Statistik. *Folketingsvalget den 8. September 1987. Uddrag.* Copenhagen: Danmarks Statistik.

————. 1987b. *Statistisk årbog 1987.* Copenhagen: Danmarks Statistik.

Denmark. 2000. "Hvad dækker en LO-families betaling af skatter og afgifter?" www.skat.dk/tal/oversigter/diverse/LO-familie.php3. (December).

————. Ministry of Taxation. 2001. "Familietypeeksempler." www.skat/tal/statistik/famtype_6_99–02.php3 (April).

Derry, Thomas K. 1973. *A History of Modern Norway, 1814–1972.* London: Oxford University Press.

————. 1979. *A History of Scandinavia.* Minneapolis: University of Minnesota Press.

Dich, Jørgen S. 1973. *Den herskende klasse.* Copenhagen: Borgen.

Dølvig, Jon Erik. 2000. Norwegian Trade Unionism between Traditionalism and Modernisation. In *Trade Unions in Europe: Facing Challenges and Search for Solutions,* edited by Jeremy Waddington and Reinar Hoffman, pp. 183–214. Brussels: ETUI.

Dörfer, Ingemar. 1997. *The Nordic Nations in the New Western Security Regime.* Washington, D.C.: Woodrow Wilson Center Press.

Dorfman, Herbert, and Jan Christensen. 1975. *Labor Relations in Norway,* 3rd ed. Oslo: Norwegian Joint Committee on International Social Policy.

Downs, Anthony. 1957. *An Economic Theory of Democracy.* New York: Harper and Row.

Einarsson, Olafur R. 1979. "Islandsk arbejderbevægelses historie 1887–1971—En oversigt." *Meddelelser om Forskning i Arbejderbevægelsens Historie,* 12 (April): 25–31.

Einhorn, Eric S. 1975. *National Security and Domestic Politics in Post-War Denmark. Some Principal Issues, 1945–1961,* Odense, Denmark: Odense University Press.

———. 1977. "Denmark, Norway, and Sweden." In *Government Secrecy in Democ-racies*, edited by Itzhak Galnoor, pp. 255–72. New York: Harper and Row.

Einhorn, Eric S., and John Logue. 1982. *Democracy on the Shop Floor? An American Look at Employee Influence in Scandinavia Today.* Kent, OH: Kent Popular Press.

———. 1988. "Continuity and Change in the Scandinavian Party Systems." In *Parties and Party Systems in Liberal Democracies*, edited by Steven Wolinetz, pp. 159–202. London and New York: Routledge.

———. 1999. "Scandinavia: Still the Middle Way?" In *Europe Today: National Poli-tics, European Integration and European Security*, edited by Ronald Tiersky, pp. 197–238. New York: Rowman & Littlefield.

Elder, Neil, A. H. Thomas, and D. Arter. 1982. *The Consensual Democracies? The Government and Politics of the Scandinavian States.* Oxford: Martin Robinson.

Eliasen, Kjell. 1981. "Organizations and Pressure Groups." In *Nordic Democracy*, edited by Eric Allardt et al., pp. 609–26. Copenhagen: Det Danske Selskab.

Elmér, Åke. 1969. *Från Fattigsverige till välfärdsstaten. Sociala förhållanden och social-politik i Sverige under nittonhundratalet*, rev. ed. Stockholm: Aldus/Bonniers.

Emery, Fred E., and Einar Thorsrud. 1969. *Form and Content in Industrial Democracy.* London: Tavistock.

Enquist, Per Olov. 1984. "The Art of Flying Backward with Dignity." *Dædalus* 113 (no. 1): 61- 73.

Erikson, Robert. 1985. "Welfare Trends in Sweden Today." *Current Sweden* no. 330. Stockholm: Swedish Institute.

Esaiasson, Peter, and Knut Heidar, editors. 2000. *Beyond Westminster and Congress: The Nordic Experience.* Columbus, OH: Ohio State University Press.

Esping-Andersen, Gösta. 1985. *Politics against Markets: The Social Democratic Road to Power.* Princeton, NJ: Princeton University Press.

———. 1999. *Social Foundations of Postindustrial Economies.* Oxford: Oxford Uni-versity Press.

Federspiel, Søren. 1978. "Fagforeningsinternationalen og DsF til 1914." In *Årbog for arbejderbevægelsens historie 1978*, edited by Erik Christensen, Jens Chris-tensen, Niels Senius Clausen, and Peter Søndergaard, pp. 6–54. Copenha-gen: SFAH.

Flanagan, Robert J. 1987. "Efficiency and Equality in Swedish Labor Markets." In *The Swedish Economy*, edited by Barry P. Bosworth and Alice M. Rivlin, pp. 125–74. Washington, DC: Brookings.

Flanagan, Robert J., David W. Soskice, and Lloyd Ulman. 1983. *Unionism, Economic Stabilization, and Incomes Policies: European Experience.* Washington, D.C.: Brookings Institution.

Flodgren, Boel. 1990. "Företagsdemokrati—medbestämmande." In Bruun et al. 1990, pp. 61–141.

Forsebäck, Lennart. 1976. *Industrial Relations and Employment in Sweden.* Stockholm: Swedish Institute.

Furniss, Norman, and Timothy Tilton. 1977. *The Case for the Welfare State.* Bloom-ington: Indiana University Press.

Galbraith, John Kenneth. 1976. *The Affluent Society.* 3rd rev. ed. Boston: Houghton Mifflin.

Galenson, Walter. 1949. *Labor in Norway*. Cambridge, MA: Harvard University Press.

——. 1952a. *The Danish System of Labor Relations*. Cambridge, MA: Harvard University Press.

——. 1952b. "Scandinavia." In *Comparative Labor Movements*, edited by Walter Galenson, pp. 104–72. New York: Prentice-Hall.

——. 1986. "Current Problems of Scandinavian Trade Unionism." In *Scandinavia at the Polls*, edited by Karl H. Cerny, pp. 267–96. Washington, D.C.: American Enterprise Institute.

Glyn, Andrew, editor. 2001. *Social Democracy in Neoliberal Times: The Left and Economic Policy since 1980*. Oxford: Oxford University Press.

Gorz, Andre. 1967. *Strategy for Labor: A Radical Proposal*. Boston: Beacon Press. (Translation of *Stratégie Ouvrière et Néocapitalisme*. Paris: Editions du Seuil, 1964)

Gourevitch, Peter. 1978. "The Second Image Reversed: The International Sources of Domestic Politics." *International Organization* 32: 881–912.

——. 1989. "Keynesian Politics: The Political Sources of Economic Policy." In *The Political Power of Economic Ideas*, edited by Peter A. Hall, pp. 87–106. Princeton: Princeton University Press.

Greider, William. 1997. *One World, Ready or Not: The Manic Logic of Global Capitalism*. New York: Simon & Schuster.

Gress, David. 2001. "The Nordic Countries." In *European Politics in the Age of Globalization*, edited by Howard J. Wiarda, pp. 218–302. Fort Worth, TX: Harcourt College Publishers.

Greve, Bent. 2000. "Denmark." In *Social Security and Solidarity in the European Union*, edited by Joos P. A. van Vugt and Jan M. Peet, pp. 35–49. Heidelberg: Physica-Verlag.

Gunzburg, Doron. 1978. *Industrial Democracy Approaches in Sweden*. Melbourne: Productivity Promotion Council of Australia.

Gustavsen, Bjørn. 1981. "Industrial Democracy." In *Nordic Democracy*, edited by Erik Allardt et al., pp. 324–58. Copenhagen: Det Danske Selskab.

Hall, Peter A. 1989. *The Political Power of Economic Ideas*. Princeton: Princeton University Press.

Hancock, M. Donald, and John Logue. 1984. "Sweden: The Quest for Economic Democracy." *Polity* 17(2): 248–70.

Hansen, Bent. 1969. *Velstand uden velfærd*. Copenhagen: Fremad.

Hansen, Hans. 1999. *Elements of Social Security*. Copenhagen: Danish National Institute of Social Research (report 99:14).

Hansson, Sigfrid. 1927. *Die Gewerkschaftsbewegung in Schweden*. Amsterdam: Verlag Internationaler Gewerkschaftsbund.

Haskel, Barbara G. 1976. *The Scandinavian Option: Opportunities and Opportunity Costs in Postwar Scandinavian Foreign Policies*. Oslo: Universitetsforlaget.

——. 1987. "Paying for the Welfare State: Creating Political Durability." *Scandinavian Studies* 59(2): 221–53.

Heckscher, Gunnar. 1984. *The Welfare State and Beyond: Success and Problems in Scandinavia*. Minneapolis: University of Minnesota Press.

Heclo, Hugh, and Henrik Madsen. 1987. *Policy and Politics in Sweden*. Philadelphia: Temple University Press.

Heidenheimer, Arnold, Hugh Heclo, and Carolyn Adams. 1983. *Comparative Public Policy*. New York: St. Martin's Press.

Hendin, Herbert. 1964. *Suicide and Scandinavia*. New York: Grune and Stratton.

Hermansson, Carl Henrik. 1959. *Koncentration och storförtag*. Stockholm: Arbetarkulturs Förlag.

———. 1971. *Monopol och storfinans—De 15 familjerna*, 3rd ed. Stockholm: Rabén and Sjögren.

Hilferding, Rudolf. 1910. *Das Finanskapital: Eine Studie über die jüngste Entwicklung des Kapitalismus*. Vienna: I. Brand.

Higley, John, Karl Erik Brofoss, and Knut Grøholt. 1975. "Top Civil Servants and the National Budget in Norway." In *The Mandarins of Western Europe*, edited by Mattei Dogan, pp. 253–74. New York: Wiley.

Hodne, Fritz. 1983. *The Norwegian Economy 1920–1980*. New York: St. Martin's Press.

Höglund, Zeth, Hannes Sköld, and Fredrik Ström. 1913. *Det befästa fattighuset*. Stockholm: Fram. Reprinted in 1979.

Holmberg, Sören. 1984. *Väljare i förändring*. Stockholm: Liber.

———. 2000. *Välja parti*. Stockholm: Norstedts Juridik.

Huntford, Roland. 1972. *The New Totalitarians*. New York: Stein and Day.

Ibsen, Flemming, and Henning Jørgensen. 1978. *Fagbevægelse og stat*. Ålborg: Ålborg Universitetsforlag.

Ibsen, Flemming, and Kai Vangskjær. 1976. "Indkomstpolitiske erfaringer i Danmark—Helhedsløsningen i 1963." *Nordisk Tidskrift for Politisk Ekonomi* 4: 136–69.

Iceland. 1997. *Icelandic Historical Statistics* (CD Rom). Reykjavik: Statistics Iceland.

Ingebritsen, Christine. 1998. *The Nordic States and European Unity*. Ithaca, NY: Cornell University Press.

Inghe, Gunnar, and Maj-Britt Inghe. 1967. *Den ofärdiga välfärden*. Stockholm: Tidens Förlag-Folksam.

Inglehart, Ronald. 1977. *The Silent Revolution: Changing Values and Political Styles among Western Publics*. Princeton, NJ: Princeton University Press.

International Monetary Fund. 1998. *Sweden: Selected Issues*. (Staff Country Report No. 98/124). Washington, D.C.: IMF.

Jakobson, Max. 1998. *Finland in the New Europe*. Westport, CT: Praeger.

James, Harold. 1989. "What is Keynesian About Deficit Financing? The Case of Interwar Germany." In Hall, pp. 231–62.

Jangenäs, Bo. 1985. *The Swedish Approach to Labor Market Policy*. Stockholm: Swedish Institute.

Jensen, Mogens Kjær. 1980. *Sociale problemer og ydelser 1966–1977*. Copenhagen: Socialforskningsinstituttet.

Johansen, Lars Nørby, and Ole P. Kristensen. 1982. "Corporatist Traits in Denmark 1946–76." In *Patterns of Corporatist Policy Making*, edited by Gerhard Lehmbruch and Philippe C. Schmitter, pp. 189–218. London: Sage.

Jones, W. Glyn. 1986. *Denmark: A Modern History*. London: Croom Helm.

Jörberg, Lennart, and Olle Krantz. 1976. "Scandinavia." In *The Fontana Economic History of Europe: Contemporary Economies* 6(2), edited by Carlo M. Cipolla, pp. 337–459. London: Collins/Fontana.

Jussila, Osmo, Seppo Hentilä, and Jukka Nevakivi. 1999. *From Grand Duchy to a Modern State: A Political History of Finland since 1809.* London: Hurst.

Kadfeldt, Birgitta. 1986. Interview in *Metallarbetaren,* no. 36: 28–29.

Karlsson, Gunnar. 2000. *The History of Iceland.* Minneapolis: University of Minnesota Press.

Katzenstein, Peter. 1985. *Small States in World Markets.* Ithaca, NY: Cornell University Press.

Kauppinen, Timo, and Jeremy Waddington. 2000. "Finland: Adapting to Decentralization." In *Trade Unions in Europe: Facing Challenges and Search for Solutions,* edited by Jeremy Waddington and Reinar Hoffman, pp. 183–214. Brussels: ETUI.

Kenilworthy, Lane. 1999. "Do Social-Welfare Policies Reduce Poverty? A Cross-National Assessment." *Social Forces* 77(3): 1119–39.

Keohane, Robert O., and Joseph S. Nye. 2001. *Power and Interdependence,* 3rd ed. New York: Longman.

Kjellberg, Anders. 2000. "The Multitude of Challenges Facing Swedish Trade Unions." In *Trade Unions in Europe: Facing Challenges and Search for Solutions,* edited by Jeremy Waddington and Reinar Hoffman, pp. 183–214. Brussels: ETUI.

Kleinman, Mark. 2002. *A European Welfare State? European Union Social Policy in Context.* New York: Palgrave.

Knoellinger, Carl Erik. 1960. *Labor in Finland.* Cambridge, MA: Harvard University Press.

Knudsen, Tim, editor. 1993. *Welfare Administration in Denmark.* Copenhagen: Institute of Political Science, University of Copenhagen.

———. 1995. "Statsministeriet: enevælde eller parlamentarisk kontrol med forvaltningspolitikken?" In *Demokratiets mangfoldighed: Tendenser i dansk politik,* edited by Morten Madsen, Hans Jørgen Nielsen, and Gunnar Sjöblom, pp. 290–302. København: Politiske Studier.

Koblik, Steven, editor. 1975. *Sweden's Development from Poverty to Affluence, 1750–1970.* Minneapolis: University of Minnesota Press.

Koch, H., and A. Ross, editors. 1949. *Nordisk demokrati.* Copenhagen: Westermann.

Korpi, Walter. 1978. *The Working Class in Welfare Capitalism.* London: Routledge and Kegan Paul.

———. 1981. "Labor Movements and Industrial Relations." In *Nordic Democracy,* edited by Erik Allardt et al., pp. 308–23. Copenhagen: Det Danske Selskab.

Korpi, Walter, and Joakim Palme. 1998. "The Paradox of Redistribution and Strategies of Equality: Welfare State Institutions, Inequality, and Poverty in the Western Countries." *American Sociological Review* 63: 661–87.

Kuhnle, Stein, 1981a. "The Growth of Social Insurance Programs in Scandinavia: Outside Influences and Internal Forces." In *The Development of Welfare States,* edited by Peter Flora and Arnold J. Heidenheimer, pp. 125–50. New Brunswick, NJ: Transaction.

———. 1981b. "Welfare and the Quality of Life." In *Nordic Democracy,* edited by Erik Allardt et al., pp. 399–415. Copenhagen: Det Danske Selskab.

———. 1996. "International Modeling, States, and Statistics: Scandinavian Social Security Solutions in the 1890s." In *States, Social Knowledge, and the Origins of Modern Social Policies,* edited by Dietrich Rueschemeyer and Theda Skocpol, pp. 233–63. Princeton, NJ: Princeton University Press.

Kuhnle, Stein and Liv Solheim. 1985. *Velferdsstaten—vekst og omstilling.* Oslo: TANU.

———. 1991. *Velferdsstaten—vekst og omstilling,* 2nd ed. Oslo: TANO.

Kurzer, Paulette. 2001. *Markets and Moral Regulation: Cultural Change in the European Union.* New York: Cambridge University Press.

Kvavik, Robert B. 1974. "Interest Groups in a 'Cooptive' Political System." In *Politics in Europe,* edited by Martin O. Heisler, pp. 27–89. New York: McKay.

———. 1976. *Interest Groups in Norwegian Politics.* Oslo: Universitetsforlaget.

Landsorganisationen. [Sweden.] 1972. *Industrial Democracy: Programme Adopted by the 1971 Congress of Swedish Trade Union Confederation.* Stockholm: LO.

———. 1973. *Steg för steg.* Stockholm: LO-Prisma.

———. 1986. *Fackföreningsrörelsen och välfärdsstaten: Rapport till 1986 års LO-kongress från LOs utredning om den offentliga sektorn.* Stockholm: LO.

Lane, Robert. 1985. "From Political to Industrial Democracy?" *Polity* 17: 623–48.

Lange, Peter, Miriam Golden, and Michael Wallerstein. 1995. "The End of Corporatism?" In *The Workers of Nations: Industrial Relations in a Global Economy,* edited by Sanford Jacoby, pp. 76–100. New York: Oxford University Press.

Lasch, Christopher. 1979. *The Culture of Narcissism.* New York: Norton.

Lauwerys, Joseph A., editor. 1958. *Scandinavian Democracy.* Copenhagen: Det danske Selskab.

Lehmbruch, Gerhard, and Philippe C. Schmitter, editors. 1982. *Patterns of Corporatism Policy-Making.* London: Sage.

Lewin, Leif. 1967. *Planhushållningsdebatten.* Stockholm: Almqvist & Wiksell.

———. 1975. "The Debate on Economic Planning in Sweden." In *Sweden's Development from Poverty to Affluence, 1750–1970,* edited by Steven Koblik, pp. 282–302. Minneapolis: University of Minnesota Press.

———. 1994. "The Rise and Decline of Corporatism: The Case of Sweden." *European Journal of Political Research* 26: 59–79.

Lijphart, Arend. 1984. *Democracies.* New Haven, CT: Yale University Press.

Lind, Jes. 2000. "Still the Century of Trade Unionism." In *Trade Unions in Europe: Facing Challenges and Search for Solutions,* edited by Jeremy Waddington and Reinar Hoffman, pp. 183–214. Brussels: ETUI.

Lindbeck, Assar. 1974. *Swedish Economic Policy.* Berkeley: University of California Press.

———. 1997. "The Swedish Experiment." *Journal of Economic Literature* 30: 1273–1319.

Lindbeck, Assar, et al. 1994. *Turning Sweden Around.* Cambridge: MIT Press.

Lindblad, Ingemar, Krister Wahlbäck, and Claes Wiklund. 1984. *Politik i Norden: En jämförande översikt,* 3rd ed. Stockholm: Liber.

Lindblom, Charles. 1977. *Politics and Markets.* New York: Basic Books.

Lindhagen, Jan. 1972. *Socialdemokratins program,* 2 vols. Stockholm: Tiden.

Lipset, Seymour Martin. 1960. *Political Man.* Garden City, NY: Doubleday.

Lipset, Seymour Martin, and Stein Rokkan. 1967. "Cleavage Structures, Party Systems and Voter Alignments: An Introduction." In *Party Systems and Voter Alignments: Cross-National Perspectives,* edited by Seymour Martin Lipset and Stein Rokkan, pp. 1 64. New York: Free Press.

Logue, John. 1982. *Socialism and Abundance: Radical Socialism in the Danish Welfare State.* Minneapolis: University of Minnesota Press.

———. 1984. "SF efter 25 år—Stadig et arbejderparti?" In *Socialisme på Dansk,* edited by Erik Christensen and Aage Frandsen, pp. 202–14. Århus: SP Forlag.

———. 1986. "Scandinavian Welfare States between Solidarity and Self-Interest." In *Futures for the Welfare State,* edited by Norman Furniss, pp. 265–91. Bloomington: Indiana University Press.

———. 1992. "Of Maastricht, Social Democratic Dilemmas, and Linear Cucumbers." *Scandinavian Studies* 64(4): 626–40.

Logue, John, and Eric S. Einhorn. 1988. "Restraining the Governors: The Nordic Experience with Limiting the Strong State." *Scandinavian Political Studies* 11(1): 45–67.

Lorenz, Einhart. 1972, 1974. *Arbeiderbevegelsens historie: En innføring,* 2 vols. Oslo: Pax.

Lundberg, Erik. 1985. "The Rise and Fall of the Swedish Model." *Journal of Economic Literature* 23: 1–36.

Lundestad, Geir. 1980. *America, Scandinavia and the Cold War 1945–49.* Oslo: Universitetsforlaget.

Macke, Thomas T., and Richard Rose. 1991. *The International Almanac of Electoral History,* 3rd ed. Washington, D.C.: Congressional Quarterly.

Madeley, John. 1998. "The Politics of Embarrassment: Norway's 1997 Election." *West European Politics* 21(2): 187–94.

Madsen, Morten, Hans Jørgen Nielsen, and Gunnar Sjöblom. 1995. *Demokratiets Mangfoldigheder: Tendenser I Dansk Politik.* København: Politiske Studier.

Marshall, T. H. 1965. *Class, Citizenship, and Social Development.* New York: Anchor / Doubleday.

Martin, Andrew. 1985. "Wages, Profits, and Investment in Sweden." In *The Politics of Inflation and Economic Stagnation,* edited by Leon N. Lindberg and Charles S. Maier, pp. 403–66. Washington, D.C.: Brookings Institution.

———. 2000. "The Politics of Macroeconomic Policy and Wage Negotiations in Sweden." In *Unions, Employers, and Central Banks: Macroeconomic Coordination and Institutional Change in Social Market Economies,* edited by Torben Iversen, Jonas Pontusson, and David Soskice, pp. 232–66. Cambridge: Cambridge University Press.

Martin, John. 1998. "What Works Among Active Labour Market Policies. Evidence from OECD Countries' Experience." *Labor Market and Social Policy Occasional Papers no. 35.* Paris: OECD.

Martinussen, Willy. 1977. *The Distant Democracy: Social Inequality, Political Resources and Political Influence in Norway.* New York: Wiley. (Translation of Fjerndemokratiet. Oslo: Gyldendal Norsk Forlag, 1973)

Meidner, Rudolf. 1974. *Samordning och solidarisk lönepolitik.* Stockholm: Prisma.

Meidner, Rudolf, in collaboration with Anna Hedborg and Gunnar Fond. 1978. *Employee Investment Funds: An Approach to Collective Capital Formation.* London: George Allen & Unwin. (Translation of *Löntagerfonder.* Stockholm: Tiden, 1975)

Mellbourn, Anders. 1979. *Byråkratins ansikten: Rolluppfatningar hos svenska högre statstjänstemän.* Stockholm: Liber.

Meyer, Niels I., K. Helveg Petersen, and Villy Sørensen. 1978. *Oprør fra midten.* Copenhagen: Gyldendal. (Translated as *Revolt from the Center.* London: Marion Boyars, 1981)

Meyerson, Per-Martin. 1982. *The Welfare State in Crisis: The Case of Sweden.* Stockholm: Federation of Swedish Industries.

Milner, Henry. 1989. *Sweden: Social Democracy in Practice.* Oxford: Oxford University Press.

Molin, Björn. 1965. *Tjänstepensionsfrågan: En studie i svensk partipolitik.* Gothenburg: Akademiförlaget.

Moses, Jonathon W., and Torbjørn Knudsen. 2001. "Inside Out: Globalization and the Reorganization of Foreign Affairs Ministries." *Cooperation and Conflict* 36(4): 355–80.

Myrdal, Alva, editor. 1971. *Towards Equality.* Stockholm: Prisma. (Translated and abridged from *Jämlikhet.* Stockholm: Prisma, 1969)

Nielsen, Hans Jørgen. 1970. "Voting Age of 18 Years." *Scandinavian Political Studies* 5: 301–5.

Nilson, Sten Sparre. 1978. "Scandinavia." In *Referendums: A Comparative Study of Practice and Theory,* edited by David Butler and Austin Ranney, pp. 169–92. Washington, D.C.: American Enterprise Institute.

Nordic Council. 1997. *Nordiska Samarbetsorgan.* Stockholm: Nordiska Rådet.

Nordstrom, Byron J. 2000. *Scandinavia since 1500.* Minneapolis: University of Minnesota Press.

Norges Bank. 2003. "Statens petroleum fond—nøkelltall for 1996–2002." http://www.norges-bank.no/petroleumfond/tall/hovedtall2000/index.html. Accessed March 31, 2003.

Nørlund, Ib. 1959a. "Er nordisk kapitalisme noget for sig selv?" *Tiden* 20(2): 66–76.

———. 1959b. "Om forringelsen af arbejderklassens stilling." *Tiden* 20(5): 207–11.

Norway. 1976. *Levekårsundersøkelsen: Sluttrapport.* Norges Offentlige Utredninger 1976:28. Oslo: NOU.

———. 1982. *Maktutredningen: Slutrapport.* Norges Offentlige Utredninger. NOU 1982:3. Oslo: Universitetsforlaget.

Norway. Norges Offisielle Statistikk. 1991. *Statistisk årbok 1991.* Oslo: Statistisk Centralbyrå.

Norway. Statistisk sentralbyrå. 2002. "Valgundersøkelsen 2001: Rekordmange skiftet parti." http://www.ssb.no/emner/00/01/vund/main.htm.

Öhman, Bendt. 1974. *LO and Labour Market Policy since the Second World War.* Stockholm: Prisma. (Translation of *LO och arbetsmarknadspolitiken efter andra världskriget.* Stockholm: Prisma, 1974)

Olsen, Erling. 1962. *Danmarks økonomiske historie siden 1750.* Copenhagen: Gad.

———. 1984. "The Dilemma of the Social-Democratic Labor Parties." *Dædalus* 113, (2): 169–94.

Olsen, Johan P. 1983. *Organized Democracy: Political Institutions in a Welfare State— The Case of Norway.* Oslo: Universitetsforlaget.

Olsen, Johan P., and James G. March. 1995. *Democratic governance.* New York: The Free Press.

Olsen, Johan, Paul Roness, and Harald Sætren. 1982. "Norway: Still Peaceful Coexistence and Revolution in Slow Motion?" In *Policy Styles in Western*

Europe, edited by Jeremy Richardson, pp. 47–79. London: George Allen & Unwin.

Olson, Mancur. 1982. *The Rise and Decline of Nations.* New Haven, CT: Yale University Press.

———. 1995. "The Devolution of the Nordic and Teutonic Economies." *The American Economic Review* 85(2): 22–27.

Organization for Economic Co-operation and Development (OECD). 1981. *Economic Surveys: Sweden.* Paris: OECD.

———. 1994. *Historic Statistics, 1960–82.* Paris: OECD.

———. 1996. *Economic Surveys: Denmark.* Paris: OECD.

———. 1997a. *Economic Surveys: Sweden.* Paris: OECD.

———. 1997b. *Managing Across Levels of Government.* Paris: OECD.

———. 1998. *Social Expenditure Database, 1980–1996.* Paris: OECD.

———. 1999a. *Benefit Systems and Work Incentives.* Paris: OECD.

———. 1999b. *Historic Statistics, 1960–97.* Paris: OECD.

———. 2000. *Historic Statistics, 1970–99.* Paris: OECD.

———. 2001a. Economics Department. "Tax Policies in OECD" (Working paper 2001/29).

———. 2001b. *OECD in Figures: Statistics of the Member Countries.* Paris: OECD.

———. 2001c. *Economic Outlook*, no. 69 (June 2001)

Ørvik, Nils. 1953. *The Decline of Neutrality 1914–1941.* Oslo: Grundt Tanum.

Østerud, Øyvind, editor. 1999. *Mot en ny Maktutredning.* Oslo: Ad Notem Gyldendal.

Pateman, Carole. 1970. *Participation and Democratic Theory.* Cambridge, England: Cambridge University Press.

Peaslee, Amos, editor. 1965. *Constitutions of Nations*, 3rd ed. The Hague: Nijhoff.

Pedersen, Mogens N. 1987. "The Danish 'Working Multiparty System': Breakdown or Adaptation?" In *Party Systems in Denmark, Austria, Switzerland, the Netherlands and Belgium*, edited by Hans Daalder, pp. 1–60. New York: St. Martin's Press.

Pekkarinen, Jukka. 1989. "Keynesianism and the Scandinavian Models of Economic Policy." In Hall 1989, pp. 311–45.

Petersson, Olof. 1987. *Democracy—ideal and reality.* Uppsala: Maktutredningen.

———. 1994. *The Government and Politics of the Nordic Countries.* Stockholm: Fritzes.

———. 1998. *Democracy across Borders: Report from the Democratic Audit of Sweden 1997.* Stockholm: SNS Förlag.

Pierson, Paul, editor. 2001. *The New Politics of the Welfare State.* Oxford: Oxford University Press.

Piven, Frances Fox, and Richard A. Cloward. 1971. *Regulating the Poor: The Functions of Public Welfare.* New York: Vintage Books.

Ploug, Niels, and Jon Kvist. 1995. "The Rise and Development of the Welfare States: Lessons from Northern Europe." In *Welfare, Development, and Security: Three Danish essays*, edited by the Danish National Institute of Social Research, Centre for Development Research, and Danish Commission on Security and Disarmament, pp. 7–34. Copenhagen: Ministry of Foreign Affairs.

Pontusson, Jonas. 1991. "Labor, Corporatism, and Industrial Policy: The Swedish Case in Comparative Perspective." *Comparative Politics* 23: 163–79.

———. 1992. *The Limits of Social Democracy: Investment Politics in Sweden*. Ithaca: Cornell University Press.

Powell, G. Bingham, Jr. 1982. *Contemporary Democracies: Participation, Stability, and Violence*. Cambridge, MA: Harvard University Press.

Rawls, John. 1971. *A Theory of Justice*. Cambridge, MA: Harvard University Press.

Reegård, Stein. 2001. "The American Model and the Nordic Labour Market," unpublished paper, Seminar: "The Nordic Alternative." Stockholm, March.

Rehn, Gösta. 1985. "Swedish Active Labor Market Policy: Retrospect and Prospect." *Industrial Relations* 24(1): 62–89.

Rokkan, Stein. 1966. "Norway: Numerical Democracy and Corporate Pluralism." In *Political Oppositions in Western Democracies*, edited by Robert A. Dahl, pp. 70–115. New Haven, CT: Yale University Press.

Rothstein, Bo. 1996. *The Social Democratic State: The Swedish Model and the Bureaucratic Problem of Social Reforms*. Pittsburgh: University of Pittsburgh Press.

———. 1998. "Breakdown of Trust and the Fall of the Swedish Model." Paper delivered at the annual meeting of the American Political Science Association.

Ruin, Olof. 1974. "Participatory Democracy and Corporativism: The Case of Sweden." *Scandinavian Political Studies* 9: 171–84.

———. 1982. "Sweden in the 1970s: Policy-Making Becomes More Difficult." In *Policy Styles in Western Europe*, edited by Jeremy Richardson, pp. 141–67. London: George Allen & Unwin.

Rustow, Dankwart A. 1955. *The Politics of Compromise: A Study of Parties and Cabinet Government in Sweden*. Princeton, NJ: Princeton University Press.

Ruth, Arne. 1984. "The Second New Nation: The Mythology of Modern Sweden." *Dædalus* 113(2): 53–96.

Samuelsson, Kurt. 1968. *From Great Power to Welfare State*. London: George Allen & Unwin.

Sartori, Giovanni. 1968. "Democracy." In *International Encyclopedia of the Social Sciences*, vol. 4, edited by D. L. Shills, pp. 112–21. New York: Macmillan.

Sassen, Saskia. 1996. *Losing Control? Sovereignty in an Age of Globalization*. New York: Columbia University Press.

Schiller, Bernt. 1974. *LO, paragraf 32 och företagsdemokratin*. Stockholm: Prisma. (Originally published in Landsorganisationen. *Tvärsnitt. Sju forskingsrapporter utgivna till LO:s 75-årsjubileum 1973*. Stockholm: Prisma, 1973)

Schmitter, Philippe C. 1974. "Still the Century of Corporatism?" *Review of Politics* 36: 75–131.

Schumpeter, J. 1950. *Capitalism, Socialism and Democracy*, 3rd ed. New York: Harper Torchbooks.

Schwerin, Don S. 1980. "The Limits of Organization as a Response to Wage-Price Problems." In *Challenge to Governance*, edited by Richard Rose, pp. 71–106. London: Sage.

———. 1982. "Corporate Incomes Policy: Norway's Second-Best Institutions." *Polity* 14: 464–80.

Scott, Franklin D. 1975. *Scandinavia*. Cambridge, MA: Harvard University Press.

———. 1977. *Sweden: The Nation's History*. Minneapolis: University of Minnesota Press.

Singleton, Fred. 1998. *A Short History of Finland.*, 2nd ed., revised and updated by A. F. Upton. Cambridge: Cambridge University Press.

Snidal, Don N., and Arne O. Brundtland. 1993. *Nordic-Baltic Security.* Washington, D.C.: Center for Strategic and International Studies.

Söderpalm, Sven Anders. 1975. "The Crisis Agreement and the Social Democratic Road to Power." In *Sweden's Development from Poverty to Affluence, 1750–1970*, edited by Steven Koblik, pp. 258–78. Minneapolis: University of Minnesota Press.

Steincke, K. K. 1920. *Fremtidens Forsørgelsesvæsen: Oversigt over og Kritik af den Samlede Forsørgelseslovgivning samt Betænkning og Motiverede Forslag til en Systematisk Nyordning.* Copenhagen: Schultz.

Steinmo, Sven. 1993. *Taxation and Democracy: Swedish, British and American Approaches to Financing the Modern State.* New Haven, CT: Yale University Press.

Storing, James A. 1963. *Norwegian Democracy.* Oslo: Universitetsforlaget.

Strand, Henning. 1999. "Some Issues Related to the Equity-Efficiency Trade-Offs in The Swedish Tax and Transfer System." Paris: OECD Economics Dept. Working Papers no. 225.

Stråth, Bo. 1978. *Nordic Industry and Nordic Economic Cooperation.* Stockholm: Almqvist & Wiksell.

Strode, Hudson. 1949. *Sweden: Model for a World.* New York: Harcourt, Brace.

Sundbo, Jon, Annemarie Knigge, Susanne Dalsgaard Nielsen, and David Bunnage. 1982. *Arbejdsfravær.* Copenhagen: Socialforskningsinstituttet.

Sundelius, Bengt. 1992. "Scandinavia." In *Foreign Policy in World Politics*, edited by Roy Macridis, pp. 303–29. Englewood Cliffs, NJ: Prentice-Hall.

Sweden. 1980. Statistika Centralbyrån. *Allmänna valen, 1979*, vol. 1. Stockholm: Statistika Centralbyrån.

Swedish Employers' Confederation. 1975. *Job Reform in Sweden: Conclusions from 500 Shop Floor Projects.* Stockholm: SAF.

Swedish Institute. 2000. *Financial Circumstances of Swedish Households.* Stockholm: Swedish Institute.

Swedish Institute. 1996. *Fact Sheets on Sweden: Labour Relations in Sweden.* Stockholm: Swedish Institute.

Swedish Social Democratic Party. 1975. *Programme of the Swedish Social Democratic Party.* Stockholm: SAP.

Sysiharju, Anna-Liisa. 1981. "Primary Education and Secondary Schools." In *Nordic Democracy*, edited by Erik Allardt et al., pp. 419–43. Copenhagen: Det Danske Selskab.

Tawney, R. H. 1920. *The Acquisitive Society.* New York: Harcourt, Brace and Howe.

Tilton, Tim. 1987. "Why Don't the Swedish Social Democrats Nationalize Industry?" *Scandinavian Studies* 59(2): 142–66.

———. 1990. *The Political Theory of Swedish Social Democracy: Through the Welfare State to Socialism.* Oxford: Oxford University Press.

Time (European edition). 1976. "Sweden's Surrealistic Socialism: Cries and Whimpers in Socialism's Showcase," June 7, 6–11.

Tingsten, Herbert. 1941. *Den svenska socialdemokratins idéutveckling.* Stockholm: Aldus. Reprinted in 1967. (Translated in 1973 as *The Swedish Social Democrats: Their Ideological Development.* Totowa, NJ: Bedminster)

———. 1955. "Stability and Vitality in Swedish Democracy." *Political Quarterly* 26: 140–51.

———. 1966. *Från ideer till idyll: Den lyckliga demokratien.* Stockholm: Norstedts.

Tomasson, Richard F. 1970. *Sweden: Prototype of Modern Society.* New York: Random House.

Uhrskov, Anders. 1982. Interview with Ritt Bjerregaard. *Tidens Stemme* 38(4): 41–43.

United States. Census Bureau. 2001. *Statistical Abstract of the United States, 2001.* Washington, D.C.: GPO.

United States. Central Intelligence Agency. 2002. *Factbook 2002.* http://www.odci.gov/cia/publications/factbook. Accessed March 28, 2003.

United States. Social Security Administration. 1999. *Social Security Programs throughout the World.* Washington, D.C.: Government Printing Office.

Valentin, F. 1980. *Fordeling af påvirkningsmuligheder,* Arbejdsnotat 14. Copenhagen: Lavindkomstkommissionen.

van den Noord, Paul, and Christopher Heady. 2001. "Surveillance of Tax Policies: A Synthesis of Findings in Economic Surveys." Paris: OECD Economic Department *Working Papers,* no. 303.

Vartiainen, Juhana. 2001. "Understanding Swedish Social Democracy: Victims of Success?" In *Social Democracy in Neoliberal Times: The Left and Economic Policy since 1980,* edited by Andrew Glyn, pp. 21–52. Oxford: Oxford University Press.

Viklund, Birger. 1977. "Education for Industrial Democracy." *Working Life in Sweden.* (May). New York: Swedish Information Service.

Vinde, Pierre, and Gunnar Petri. 1978. *Swedish Government Administration,* 2nd rev. ed. Stockholm: Prisma.

von Eyben, W. E. 1981. "Democracy and the Administration of Justice." In *Nordic Democracy,* edited by Erik Allardt et al., pp. 223–38. Copenhagen: Det Danske Selskab.

Waddington, Jeremy, and Reiner Hoffman. 2000. *Trade Unions in Europe: Facing Challenges and Searching for Solutions.* Brussels: ETUI.

Wallace, Helen, and William Wallace, editors. 2001. *Policy-making in the European Union,* 4th edition. New York: Oxford University Press.

Waltz, Kenneth. 1959. *Man, the State and War.* New York: Columbia University Press.

Wechselmann, Ilja. 1975. *Klassekamp kontrol.* Roskilde: Roskilde Universitetsforlag.

Wendt, Frantz. 1981. "Nordic Cooperation." In *Nordic Democracy,* edited by Erik Allardt et al., pp. 653–76. Copenhagen: Det Danske Selskab.

Wheeler, Christopher. 1975. *White-Collar Power: Changing Patterns of Interest Group Behavior in Sweden.* Urbana, IL: University of Illinois Press.

Wilson, Frank L. 1983. "Interest Groups and Politics in Western Europe: The Neo-Corporatist Approach." *Comparative Politics* 16: 105–23.

Wyden, Peter. 1959. "Sweden: Paradise with Problems." *Saturday Evening Post* (December 19): 22–23, 64, 67.

Yergin, Daniel, and Joseph Stanislaw. 1998. *The Commanding Heights: The Battle between Government and the Marketplace that Is Remaking the Modern World.* New York, NY: Simon and Schuster.

Zetterberg, Hans L. 1981. "Hur värderingarna förändras i välfärdsstaten." In *Väl-*

färd—och sedan? Teorier och experiment för ett alternativt samhälle, edited by
Nordal Åkerman, pp. 106–22. Stockholm: Rabén & Sjögren.

SERIALS CITED

Denmark. Danmarks Statistik. *Statistisk Tiårsoversigt.*
———. *Statistiske Efterretninger.*
Financial Times.
New York Times.
Nordic Council. *Yearbook of Nordic Statistics / Nordic Statistical Yearbook.*
Norway. Statistisk Sentralbyrå. *Stortingsvalget.*

Index

About the Authors

ERIC S. EINHORN is Professor and formerly Chairman in the Department of Political Science at the University of Massachusetts at Amherst.

JOHN LOGUE is Professor in the Department of Political Science and Director of the Ohio Employee Ownership Center at Kent State University, Kent, Ohio.